edexcel
advancing learning, changing lives

INFORMATION TECHNOLOGY LEVEL 2

BTEC First

Alan Jarvis | K Mary Reid | Karen Anderson
Richard McGill | Jenny Lawson | David Beaumont | David Gray

A PEARSON COMPANY

Published by Pearson Education Limited, a company incorporated in England and Wales, having its registered office at Edinburgh Gate, Harlow, Essex, CM20 2JE. Registered company number: 872828

www.pearsonschoolsandfecolleges.co.uk

Edexcel is a registered trademark of Edexcel Limited

Text © Alan Jarvis, K Mary Reid, Karen Anderson, Richard McGill, Jenny Lawson, David Beaumont and Dave Gray 2010

First published 2010

13 12 11 10
10 9 8 7 6 5 4 3 2 1

British Library Cataloguing in Publication Data
A catalogue record for this book is available from the British Library.

ISBN 978 1 846909 16 0

Edited by Melanie Birdsall and Caroline Low
Designed by Wooden Ark
Typeset by Tek-Art
Original illustrations © Pearson Education Limited 2010
Cover design by Visual Philosophy, created by eMC design
Picture research by Maria Joannou
Cover photo/illustration © Shutterstock/Yuri Arcurs
Back cover photos © Shutterstock/Macs Peter tc; Vartanov Anatoly tr; www.imagesource.com c
Printed in the UK by Scotprint

Websites and Hotlinks
There are links to relevant websites in this book. In order to ensure that the links are up to date, that the links work, and that the sites are not inadvertently linked to sites that could be considered offensive, we have made the links available on the Pearson website at www.pearsonschoolsandfecolleges.co.uk/hotlinks. When you access the site, search for either the express code is 9160V, the title BTEC First Information Technology Student Book or ISBN 978 1 846909 16 0.

Disclaimer
This material has been published on behalf of Edexcel and offers high-quality support for the delivery of Edexcel qualifications.

This does not mean that the material is essential to achieve any Edexcel qualification, nor does it mean that it is the only suitable material available to support any Edexcel qualification. Edexcel material will not be used verbatim in setting any Edexcel examination or assessment. Any resource lists produced by Edexcel shall include this and other appropriate resources.

Copies of official specifications for all Edexcel qualifications may be found on the Edexcel website: www.edexcel.com

Contents

About your **BTEC Level 2 First Information Technology Student Book** v

Unit	Credit value	Title	Page
1	5	Communicating in the IT industry	1
2	5	Working in the IT industry	29
3	10	Computer systems	51
4	10	Business IT skills	101
9	10	Customising software	135
10	10	Setting up an IT network	175
16	10	Database systems	209
17	10	Website development	267
23	10	Computer graphics	319
26	10	Developing computer games	359

	Page
Glossary	391
Index	395

The following optional and optional specialist units are available on the Pearson Education website at www.pearsonschoolsandfecolleges.co.uk/btecfirstit

Unit	Credit value	Title
7	10	Installing computer hardware
18	10	Software design
27	10	Spreadsheet modelling
28	10	Multimedia design
29	10	Presenting information using IT
30	10	Animation techniques

Credits

The authors and publishers would like to thank the following individuals and organisations for permission to reproduce photographs in the book:

Alamy Images/WoodyStock p. **1**; Pearson Education Ltd/Jules Selmes p. **3**; Robert Harding/Bananastock p. **6**; Shutterstock/Andresr p. **27**; Alamy Images/Neal Fisher p. **29**; Image Source Ltd p. **31**; Pearson Education Ltd/David Sanderson p. **42**; Pearson Education Ltd/Mind Studio p. **43**; Shutterstock/Stephen Coburn p. **44**; Shutterstock/Izabela Zaremba p. **45**; Shutterstock/Monkey Business Images p. **46**; Shutterstock/Yuri Arcurs p. **49**; Shutterstock/Wutthichal p. **51**; Image Source Ltd p. **53**; Alamy Images/Krys Bailey p. **55**; Shutterstock/Elena Schweitzer p. **55**; Shutterstock/bbostjan p. **58**; Shutterstock/Dmitry Melnikov p. **62**; Getty Images/PhotoDisc p. **62**; Shutterstock/Ajay Bhaskar p. **99**; Shutterstock/Yuri Arcurs p. **101**; Shutterstock/Roger Jegg p. **103**; Pearson Education Ltd/Gareth Boden p. **133**; Shutterstock/Dmitriy Shironosov p. **135**; Shutterstock/ansar80 p. **137**; Shutterstock/photobank.ch p. **173**; Shutterstock/Macs Peter p. **175**; Pearson Education Ltd/Gareth Boden p. **177**; Pearson Education Ltd/Peter Morris p. **194**; Shutterstock/AVAVA p. **207**; Shutterstock/Kasia p. **209**; Pearson Education Ltd/Clark Wiseman, Studio 8 p. **211**; Pearson Education Ltd/Mind Studio p. **213**; Shutterstock/Yuri Arcurs p. **265**; Plainpicture/Johner/Jonas Ingerstedt p. **267**; Pearson Education Ltd/Jules Selmes p. **269**; Shutterstock/Liv Friis-Larsen p. **317**; Alamy Images/I. Glory p. **319**; iStockPhoto/Ashwin Kharidehal Abhirama p. **321**; Shutterstock/JinYoung Lee p. **324**; Thinkstock/Hemera p. **327**; Shutterstock/Steve McWilliam p. **328**; Shutterstock/JinYoung Lee p. **335**; Shutterstock/JinYoung Lee p. **336**; Shutterstock/Konstantin Sutyagin p. **343**; Shutterstock/EcoPrint p. **346**; Shutterstock/Denis Babenko p. **347**; Shutterstock/Yuri Arcurs p. **357**; Science Photo Library/Paul Rapson p. **359**; Pearson Education Ltd/Gareth Boden p. **361**; Alamy Images/Robert Dant p. **366**; Shutterstock/ZTS p. **366**; Shutterstock/Thorsten Schuh p. **366**; Thinkstock/Jupiterimages p. **369**; Thinkstock/Polka Dot Images p. **370**; Shutterstock/Bruce Rolff p. **377**; Pearson Education Ltd/Mind Studio p. **389**.

The authors and publishers would like to thank the following individuals and organisations for permission to reproduce photographs in the web units which can be found on the Pearson Education website at www.pearsonschoolsandfecolleges.co.uk/btecfirstit:

Unit 7 Corbis/Science Photo Library/AB Still Ltd p. **1**; Shutterstock/Pedro Vidal p. **3**; Pearson Education Ltd/Gareth Boden p. **11**; Photographers Direct/Graham Hare p. **11**; Andrew "bunnie" Huang (http://bunniestudios.com) p. **13**; Photographers Direct/Peter Garwood p. **14**; Pearson Education Ltd/Gareth Boden p. **33**; **Unit 18** Alamy Images/Ross Pierson p. **1**; Shutterstock/Ajay Bhaskar p. **3**; Shutterstock/Aleksandr Kurganov p. **4**; Pearson Education Ltd/Gareth Boden p. **37**; **Unit 27** Shutterstock/Belle Media p. **1**; Shutterstock/ansar80 p. **3**; Pearson Education Ltd/Jules Selmes p. **43**; **Unit 28** Alamy Images/Roger Davies p. **1**; iStockPhoto/Jesper Elgaard p. **3**; Alamy Images/Bernhard Classen p. **8**; Shutterstock/TebNad p. **9**; Shutterstock/PHOTOCREO Michal Bodnarek p. **14**; Shutterstock/Stephen Coburn p. **35**; **Unit 30** The Kobal Collection/Walt Disney Pictures p. **1**; Shutterstock/Tracy Whiteside p. **3**; Moviestore Collection/Warner Independent Pictures p. **5**; Shutterstock/Phase4Photography p. **32**.

Acknowledgements:
Unit 1 Twitter home page p. **18**; **Unit 7** Student voice written by Ryan Kearney with assistance from author Richard McGill p. **3**; **Unit 7** Linksys, Cisco Systems Inc.; p. **23**; **Unit 7** Techguys; p. **24**; **Unit 17** ASOS.com p. **276**; **Unit 17** NHS p. **288**; **Unit 23** Student voice written by Sagaal Abokor with assistance from author Richard McGill p. **321**; **Unit 23** Vizual Impact logo is the Trademark and Copyright of Vizual Impact Ltd. p. **331**; **Unit 28** Comparethemeerkat.com p. **8**.

Adobe product screenshot(s) reprinted with permission from Adobe Systems Incorporated.

Microsoft product screenshot(s) reprinted with permission from Microsoft Corporation.

About your BTEC Level 2 First Information Technology

Choosing to study for a BTEC Level 2 First Information Technology qualification is a great decision to make for lots of reasons. This qualification is the first step in a career in the IT industry. The IT industry is an exciting and constantly changing one with a wide range of opportunities – from working in computer games development to working with robotic systems or supporting scientists in combating global warming. The opportunities are endless.

Your BTEC Level 2 First in Information Technology is a **vocational** or **work-related** qualification. This doesn't mean that it will give you *all* the skills you need to do a job, but it does mean that you'll have the opportunity to gain specific knowledge, understanding and skills that are relevant to your future career.

What will you be doing?

The qualification is structured into **mandatory units** (ones you must do) and **optional units** (ones you can choose to do). This book contains 10 units (with a further 6 optional units on the Pearson Education Website – www.pearsonschoolsandfecolleges.co.uk/btecfirstit) – giving you a broad choice no matter what size your qualification.

- BTEC Level 2 First **Certificate** in Information Technology: 1 mandatory unit and optional units that provide a combined total of 15 credits.

- BTEC Level 2 First **Extended Certificate** in Information Technology: 2 mandatory units and optional units (no more than 10 optional specialist credits) that provide a combined total of 30 credits.

- BTEC Level 2 First **Diploma** in Information Technology: 3 mandatory units and optional units (no more than 20 optional specialist credits) that provide a combined total of 60 credits.

Unit number	Credit value	Unit name	Cert	Ex. Cert	Diploma
1	5	Communicating in the IT industry*	M	M	M
2	5	Working in the IT industry	O	M	M
3	10	Computer systems	O	O	M
4	10	Business IT skills*	O	O	O
9	10	Customising software	O	O	O
10	10	Setting up an IT network	O	O	O
16	10	Database systems*	O	O	O
17	10	Website development	O	O	O
23	10	Computer graphics	O	O	O
26	10	Developing computer Games	O	O	O

The following optional and optional specialist units are available on the Pearson Education website at www.pearsonschoolsandfecolleges.co.uk/btecfirstit

7	10	Installing computer hardware	O	O	O
18	10	Software design	O	O	O
27	10	Spreadsheet modelling	-	OS	OS
28	10	Multimedia design	-	OS	OS
29	10	Presenting information using IT	-	OS	OS
30	10	Animation techniques	-	OS	OS

* Units 1, 4, 6, 16 and 19 are a part of the Key Stage 4 Programme of Study for IT.

M = Mandatory
O = Optional
OS = Optional Specialist

How to use this book

This book is designed to help you through your BTEC Level 2 First Information Technology course. This book contains many features that will help you use your skills and knowledge in work-related situations and assist you in getting the most from your course.

Credit value: 5

1 Communicating in the IT industry

This unit is about the communication skills which are needed by people who work in the IT industry. Some of these skills are specific to the IT industry, such as the use of specialist methods of communication, for example the use of video conferencing. But other skills, such as being able to give clear verbal explanations, are relevant to working in any industry. Communication is central to almost every aspect of business and private life, so being able to communicate clearly and effectively, by speaking, writing and other methods, is a very useful skill to develop.

This unit also looks at the impact IT has had on the society we live in. Over the last 40 years or so IT has had a tremendous impact on the way we do many things. It has brought many advantages, such as new ways to communicate and stay in touch, including email and mobile phones. But not all of the changes have been beneficial, and you will also be looking at some of the negative effects too. For example, IT has provided new ways for criminals to break the law.

Learning outcomes

After completing this unit you should:

1. be able to communicate information to suit audience, purpose and content
2. be able to use IT tools to communicate and exchange information
3. understand the impact of IT on individuals, communities and society.

Introduction

These introductions give you a snapshot of what to expect from each unit – and what you should be aiming for by the time you finish it!

Assessment and grading criteria

This table explains what you must do in order to achieve the assessment criteria for each unit. For each assessment criterion, shown by the grade button **P1**, there is an assessment activity.

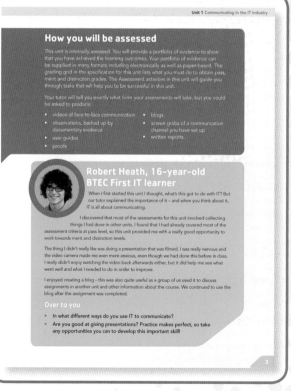

Assessment

Your tutor will set **assignments** throughout your course for you to complete. These may take a variety of forms, from reports and presentations to posters and podcasts. The important thing is that you evidence your skills and knowledge to date.

Stuck for ideas? Daunted by your first assignment? These students have all been through it before…

Activities

There are different types of activities for you to do: **assessment activities** are suggestions for tasks that you might do as part of your assignment and will help you develop your knowledge, skills and understanding. Each one of these has **grading tips** that clearly explain what you need to do in order to achieve a pass, merit or distinction grade.

BTEC Assessment activity 1.1 P1 P2 P3 P4

You work as an IT technician within a small company.

1. You have been asked to prepare a training program on using email for IT users within the company. Prepare written training materials in two different versions: one for non-technical users and the other for users with good technical knowledge of IT. P2 P3

2. Working in pairs, email copies of your guides to each other and proofread each other's work to check for spelling, grammar and formatting errors. P4

3. Prepare and give a presentation on using email which is designed for non-technical users of IT within the company. Following your presentation, have a discussion with your tutors or classmates about your presentation style and the content of the presentation. P1

Notes:

You may be required to prepare or give a presentation for another unit, so you may not need to prepare a separate presentation to cover P1 for this unit. As long as the presentation is IT-related, this will also cover P1.

The discussion you have can be about any topic. However, if you have a discussion about the sort of personal characteristics which are valued by employers in the IT industry, then this will cover P1 for Unit 2 as well.

Grading tips

To cover P1 you need to demonstrate effective interpersonal skills in face-to-face communication on at least three different occasions.

For P2 and P3, you need to show that you understand the different requirements of technical and non-technical users. The email guide for non-technical users must explain how to carry out all the basic tasks required (read email, send email, add attachments, etc.) in detail and should avoid technical jargon. The guide for technical users only needs to cover these basic tasks briefly, and should have more detail on advanced features such as creating mailing lists, out of office replies, etc.

For P4 you will need to show before and after copies of the documents with the changes you have made highlighted. You will also need to provide evidence, for example screenshots, that you have emailed the materials, checked the attachments you received for viruses and made corrections to the work you received.

Your tutor will need to either video or audio record your presentations and discussions or complete a checklist.

There are also suggestions for activities that will give you a broader grasp of the world of IT and a deeper understanding of key topics.

Activity: Video a presentation

It's difficult to know how you come across to others when giving a presentation. Although it can be daunting, video recording a presentation is a very useful training technique, as you can watch yourself and see how others see you. This will help you develop better presentation techniques.

Prepare a 10-minute presentation titled 'My plans for the future'. Give the presentation and have it filmed, then watch the video back and see how you did. Discuss with your tutor and classmates how you could improve your presentation style.

How to... activities

These activities run through the steps involved in software and hardware processes that you will need to carry out successfully to complete the assessment activities in this book and in your career in IT.

How to... Check the performance of the system

- Click on **Start** then **Control Panel** then **Administrative Tools** then **Performance**.
- Allow the tool to run for a few minutes and a real-time graph will be drawn. The colour codes are given below the graph.
- If the average disk queue time is high then the data transfer from memory to the hard disk is not as fast as it could be.

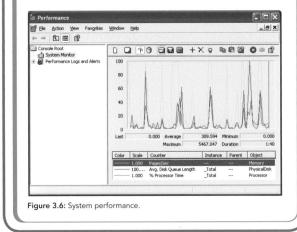

Figure 3.6: System performance.

Personal, learning and thinking skills

Throughout your BTEC Level 2 First Information Technology course, there are lots of opportunities to develop your personal, learning and thinking skills. Look out for these as you progress.

PLTS

By communicating IT-related information to both technical and non-technical audiences, you will show that you are a **reflective learner**.

By using IT tools to provide constructive support and feedback to others' draft documents, you will show that you are a **team worker**.

Functional skills

It's important that you have good English, Mathematics and ICT skills – you never know when you'll need them, and employers will be looking for evidence that you've got these skills too.

Functional skills

Completing this assessment activity will provide evidence for your functional **English** skills in **speaking and listening** and in **writing**.

Key terms

Technical words and phrases are easy to spot, and definitions are included. The terms and definitions are also in the glossary at the back of the book.

Key term

Body language – non-verbal communication which includes gestures, facial expressions and body posture. You may not always be conscious that your body language is communicating your feelings, but it is often very easy to see from someone's body language that they are bored, happy or angry, etc.

WorkSpace

Case studies provide snapshots of real workplace issues, and show how the skills and knowledge you develop during your course can help you in your career.

WorkSpace Simon Evans
IT Manager at a large NHS hospital in North London

We have about 1,200 staff, doctors, nurses and admin staff who use the 900 PCs in the hospital. In the IT support department we run a 24-hour telephone helpdesk with at least four staff on duty answering helpdesk calls during the day and two at night. Although answering calls is a junior job in the IT department, it's a very important one because this is the main contact the users have with the IT staff.

For support department positions we don't look for people who have the best technical knowledge, because we can always provide staff with training.

Skills

The most important skill helpdesk staff need is good interpersonal communication. They need to be able to deal with problems that may seem very simple and trivial to them but are big issues for our users. They must be able to listen carefully to what the users say and give appropriate technical explanation and instructions in a way that is simple to understand.

Users can also email problems and questions to us, so the helpdesk staff need to respond to those too. This means they must be able to write clear explanations. Too many young people come for an interview for a job as a junior IT Technician and can't explain themselves clearly or write an email that makes sense.

Think about it!

1. Why does Simon say technical skills are not that important for the helpdesk staff?
2. Which skills does he say are most important?
3. What other skills do you think are important for a helpdesk technician?
4. Which of these skills do you think you already have and which do you need to develop further?

27

Just checking

When you see this sort of activity, take stock! These quick activities and questions are there to check your knowledge. You can use them to see how much progress you've made.

Edexcel's assignment tips

At the end of each chapter, you'll find hints and tips to help you get the best mark you can, such as the best websites to go to, checklists to help you remember processes and really useful facts and figures.

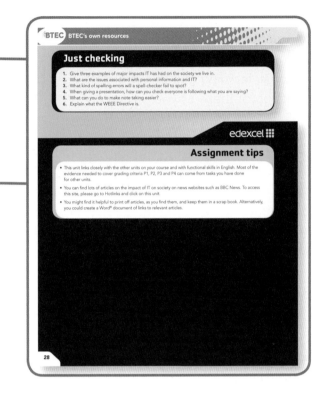

Don't miss out on these resources to help you!

Have you read your **BTEC Level 2 First Study Skills Guide**? It's full of advice on study skills, putting your assignments together and making the most of being a BTEC Information Technology learner.

Your book is just part of the exciting resources from Edexcel to help you succeed in your BTEC course. Visit www.edexcel.com/BTEC or www.pearsonfe.co.uk/BTEC 2010 for more details.

1 Communicating in the IT industry

This unit is about the communication skills which are needed by people who work in the IT industry. Some of these skills are specific to the IT industry, such as the use of specialist methods of communication, for example the use of video conferencing. But other skills, such as being able to give clear verbal explanations, are relevant to working in any industry. Communication is central to almost every aspect of business and private life, so being able to communicate clearly and effectively, by speaking, writing and other methods, is a very useful skill to develop.

This unit also looks at the impact IT has had on the society we live in. Over the last 40 years or so IT has had a tremendous impact on the way we do many things. It has brought many advantages, such as new ways to communicate and stay in touch, including email and mobile phones. But not all of the changes have been beneficial, and you will also be looking at some of the negative effects too. For example, IT has provided new ways for criminals to break the law.

Learning outcomes

After completing this unit you should:

1. be able to communicate information to suit audience, purpose and content
2. be able to use IT tools to communicate and exchange information
3. understand the impact of IT on individuals, communities and society.

Assessment and grading criteria

This table shows you what you must do in order to achieve a pass, merit or distinction grade, and where you can find activities in this book to help you.

To achieve a **pass** grade the evidence must show that you are able to:	To achieve a **merit** grade the evidence must show that, in addition to the pass criteria, you are able to:	To achieve a **distinction** grade the evidence must show that, in addition to the pass and merit criteria, you are able to:
P1 demonstrate effective interpersonal skills in face-to-face communication **See Assessment activity 1.1 on page 13**		
P2 communicate IT-related information to a technical audience **See Assessment activity 1.1 on page 13**		
P3 communicate IT-related information to a non-technical audience **See Assessment activity 1.1 on page 13**		
P4 use IT tools safely to effectively communicate and exchange information **See Assessment activity 1.1 on page 13**		
P5 select, set up and use a specialist communication channel to communicate and exchange information **See Assessment activity 1.2 on page 26**	**M1** justify why a specialist communication channel is effective for a given purpose **See Assessment activity 1.2 on page 26**	**D1** explain how to ensure safe and secure use of a specialist communication channel **See Assessment activity 1.2 on page 26**
P6 explain the social impacts of the use of IT **See Assessment activity 1.2 on page 26**	**M2** discuss the potential threats which the use of IT has introduced **See Assessment activity 1.2 on page 26**	

How you will be assessed

This unit is internally assessed. You will provide a portfolio of evidence to show that you have achieved the learning outcomes. Your portfolio of evidence can be supplied in many formats including electronically as well as paper-based. The grading grid in the specification for this unit lists what you must do to obtain pass, merit and distinction grades. The Assessment activities in this unit will guide you through tasks that will help you to be successful in this unit.

Your tutor will tell you exactly what form your assessments will take, but you could be asked to produce:

- videos of face-to-face communication
- observations, backed up by documentary evidence
- user guides
- proofs
- blogs
- screen grabs of a communcation channel you have set up
- written reports.

Robert Heath, 16–year-old BTEC First IT learner

When I first started this unit I thought, what's this got to do with IT? But our tutor explained the importance of it – and when you think about it, IT is all about communicating.

I discovered that most of the assessments for this unit involved collecting things I had done in other units. I found that I had already covered most of the assessment criteria at pass level, so this unit provided me with a really good opportunity to work towards merit and distinction levels.

The thing I didn't really like was doing a presentation that was filmed. I was really nervous and the video camera made me even more anxious, even though we had done this before in class. I really didn't enjoy watching the video back afterwards either, but it did help me see what went well and what I needed to do in order to improve.

I enjoyed creating a blog – this was also quite useful as a group of us used it to discuss assignments in another unit and other information about the course. We continued to use the blog after the assignment was completed.

Over to you

- In what different ways do you use IT to communicate?
- Are you good at giving presentations? Practice makes perfect, so take any opportunities you can to develop this important skill!

1. Be able to communicate information to suit audience, purpose and content

Start up

Ways to communicate

Think of all the different ways of communicating with people, including at college or school, at home and at work. For example, you probably use instant messaging software, such as MSN® Messenger, to communicate with your friends.

For each different method that you think of, list:

- the features that make it easy to communicate using that method
- the difficulties associated with that method of communication.

In the IT industry, communication can have special challenges because of the technical nature of the sector. IT is also widely used at home and in business by non-technical people, who can find the use of terminology very confusing. As IT professionals you need to learn to communicate as effectively as possible with the IT users you work with and support.

1.1 General communication skills

There are a number of factors you need to consider when communicating with an individual or group. The first consideration is your audience. Who are they? Is it one person or a group of people?

- **In person, one-to-one.** This is probably easiest because you can see the person and judge whether they are following what you say. If you are explaining how to do something, you can usually show the person as well as tell them.
- **In person to an audience.** When you are giving a presentation or training session to a group of people, you have to consider the needs of many people. For example, some people may be following what you say while others may not understand you.
- **Over the telephone.** This can be more difficult because you don't have the visual cues which tell you whether the person you are talking to understands you. You also won't be able to show that person what to do, and verbal explanations can be complicated and difficult to follow.

Adapting content and style to audience

You will need to consider how you can modify your language, use of terminology and the speed with which you talk to best suit your audience. Clearly you will talk in a different way to another IT professional than to someone who knows very little about IT.

Varying your voice

Talking in a boring, monotone voice is not going to help your audience concentrate on what you are saying. Varying your intonation, pausing briefly and asking questions are all effective techniques to maintain your audience's interest.

Terminology

You must use language and terminology that your audience will understand. If your audience is non-technical, avoid using non-essential technical terms and make sure you clearly explain any that you do use.

Format

Using different formats to present information can make it more interesting for your audience. For example, you could make a lengthy explanation more interesting by including pictures or diagrams in a written document and videos or music in a presentation.

Providing accurate information

As an IT professional, people will expect you to provide them with correct information about IT issues. Of course, you can't know everything – so if people ask questions you can't answer, don't be afraid to say, 'I don't know, I'll find out'. Giving false or inaccurate information is very frustrating for people, and it's very damaging for your own reputation.

You should also take care when expressing opinions, because there is a big difference between facts and opinions. In your personal life it's fine to express opinions about your likes and dislikes. However, you need to be more careful in your professional life, because people will see you as the IT expert and will take things you say about technical matters as facts. For example, if you say 'ABC laptops are unreliable', this opinion might be based on one of their laptops you previously owned. However, if you have read in a magazine article that ABC laptops were proved in tests to be unreliable, then that is a fact you can tell people about.

Techniques for engaging audience interest

Using technology

When giving a presentation, consider using technology to help maintain your audience's interest in what you are saying. For example, Microsoft® PowerPoint® is widely used to prepare slides to support presentations. However, if your slides only contain text and you simply read the text off the slides, this is unlikely to engage your audience. Consider adding diagrams and multimedia elements such as animations, sound clips (for example, a short interview) or short videos to your slides, to make your presentation more appealing for your audience.

When using PowerPoint®, bear in mind the following points:

- Your slides should only support your presentation – giving the presentation is your job. Be prepared to speak in a confident, interesting and knowledgeable way.

- Never read the text on your slides out! This is very boring, and what's the point of you being there?

- Don't make your slides too complex – it is best to keep each slide to around five lines of text. The text should simply summarise the main points of what you are saying.

- Keep diagrams or charts simple, as your audience will find very detailed charts hard to read.

- Choose a slide template and stick to the colours and fonts provided by the template. This way your slides will be consistent. Bright, striking colours work best for projection onto a screen.

- Make sure the text size and colour combinations will be legible for your audience. Have a trial run in the room where you will give the presentation to find out how large the slides will be when projected and how far the audience will be sitting from the projected slides.

- Be aware that some colour combinations are difficult for people with visual defects, such as colour blindness, to read. For example, red and green will appear almost identical to someone with colour blindness.

Remember that practice makes perfect. The more presentations you give, the more confident you will become.

Activity: Video a presentation

It's difficult to know how you come across to others when giving a presentation. Although it can be daunting, video recording a presentation is a very useful training technique, as you can watch yourself and see how others see you. This will help you develop better presentation techniques.

Prepare a 10-minute presentation titled 'My plans for the future'. Give the presentation and have it filmed, then watch the video back and see how you did. Discuss with your tutor and classmates how you could improve your presentation style.

Ensuring the message gets across

Watch the people you are talking to carefully. Are they nodding in agreement or are they looking confused or bored, maybe even falling asleep? If your audience doesn't seem to be following what you are saying, it's a good idea to stop, ask some questions and check they have understood you.

1.2 Interpersonal skills

We communicate with others not just by what we say but also by the way in which we say it. Although speaking and writing are the most obvious ways in which we communicate, there are other specialist ways that can be used. For example, techniques such as lip reading and signing can be used with people who have hearing impairments.

Methods for communicating interpersonally

Verbal exchanges

Speaking to each other, either in person or over the telephone, is the most common method of communicating interpersonally. In addition to what we say, and the language and terminology we use, we can communicate a great deal through our tone of voice and body language.

Signing and lip reading

People with a hearing impairment use communication techniques, such as lip reading and signing.

- Lip reading is used to understand speech by watching the movement of the lips, face and tongue.
- Sign language is a method of communicating using hand movements and facial expressions to convey meaning.

There are many different sign languages used in different parts of the world, just as there are different verbal languages.

Techniques and cues

Body language

Understanding and using **body language** is an important skill in interpersonal communication. Most of us can tell fairly quickly whether another person is bored or confused simply by looking at their facial expression or the way they are sitting. A good communicator will respond to these signs. When you are speaking yourself, use positive body language to show interest and enthusiasm, rather than a bored, irritated or disinterested attitude.

Paying attention and active engagement

It is important to use body language to give the people you are communicating with a positive feeling. This includes showing with your body language that you are listening carefully when they are speaking or asking questions. Nodding in agreement is one way of doing this.

When answering a question, it is often useful to paraphrase the question – to state a brief version of the question in your own words before answering it. This will enable you to check that you have understood the question correctly.

Key term

Body language – non-verbal communication which includes gestures, facial expressions and body posture. You may not always be conscious that your body language is communicating your feelings, but it is often very easy to see from someone's body language that they are bored, happy or angry, etc.

Another useful technique, especially when giving a long and complex explanation, is to give a summary at the end to remind the listener of the key points. This is called summarising.

Positive and negative language

In addition to body language, the words you use and your tone of voice will communicate a lot to the listener about your attitude and how you are feeling. For example, if you shout people will assume you are angry.

When communicating interpersonally in a professional context, you need to take care to use positive language. For example, when providing support to an IT user, you need to use supportive, encouraging language.

Activity: Positive language

Look at these two telephone conversations between an IT technician and a user who has a problem with her computer.

Conversation 1		Conversation 2	
Technician 1	Hello, what's your problem?	Technician 2	IT Help desk – how can I help you?
Caller	Hi, it's Sally in accounts.	Caller	Hi, it's Sally in accounts.
Technician 1	Oh yeah, you've called several times before. What's the problem now?	Technician 2	Hi Sally, what can we do for you today?
Caller	I keep sending stuff to the printer but nothing comes out.	Caller	I keep sending stuff to the printer but nothing comes out.
Technician 1	Oh, didn't you do the basic IT training? Printing is covered on that.	Technician 2	OK ... Is other people's work printing OK or do they have the same problem?
Caller	Well, I did but I'm not sure we covered this. I feel like an idiot ...	Caller	Yeah, they can print OK. I feel like an idiot not being able to fix this.
Technician 1	Yes, well, have you checked which printer you have selected?	Technician 2	Oh don't worry, that's what we are here for. Let's get you printing as well. Can you go to the File menu and choose Print for me?
Caller	No, I'm not sure how to do that ...	Caller	Yes, I've done that.
Technician 1	Check your notes from the basic IT training. I'm very busy with lots of calls here. If that doesn't help, call me back later.	Technician 2	So tell me the name of the printer shown at the top where it says 'name'.
			(Continued...)

Which conversation shows the use of positive language by the technician? Explain why you think the language is positive.

1.3 Communicate in writing

The ability to communicate in writing is a different skill from communicating verbally, although some of the same issues apply. You need to consider the people who will be reading your communication and adapt the content accordingly. This is particularly important when writing about technical subjects for a non-technical audience, for example a user guide or an email to an IT user about a support issue.

Following guidelines and procedures

You should always take care with written documents because they are a permanent record of what you have said. Many organisations have guidelines and procedures for sending information by email or in other written formats. This is to protect both the reputation of the company and keep information confidential. Organisations may also require their employees to use certain templates for documents, to ensure they comply with company standards.

Identifying and conveying key messages in writing

When writing any kind of document it is important that you get the message across in a clear and unambiguous way. Before you start writing, make sure that you are clear about the key messages that you are trying to communicate. You will then be able to lay out the document in a logical fashion. For example, in a report for an assignment you need to be clear about what the report should cover. You should structure your report with an introduction, sections which cover the assignment tasks in a sensible order (usually the order they are listed in the assignment brief) and a conclusion.

Different types of written documents have different styles and purposes. For example, formal letters have a defined structure (with address, **salutation** and complementary **close**). Emails are less formal and have no fixed salutation or close.

Whatever type of document you are producing, you need to ensure the following:

- **Your document is clear and gets the message across.** Technical explanations can be difficult to put in writing, so bullet points are often better than a long, complex explanation. You can also use subheadings to help your readers find information quickly on the page.
- **The spelling and grammar are correct.** Poor spelling and grammar in business emails and letters look very unprofessional. Even in informal communications like personal emails, it is good practice to check and correct your spelling and grammar.

Key terms

Salutation – how you start a letter. This is usually 'Dear Sir' or 'Dear Madam', or if you know the person 'Dear Miss Jones', for example.

Close – how you finish a letter. In formal letters, you should write 'Yours sincerely' if you know the name of the person to whom you are writing, or 'Yours faithfully' if you do not.

Key term

Emoticons – icons or combinations of characters which express a feeling. For example, writing 'Such a lovely day ☺' shows that you are happy. There are many other emoticons in common use, such as :s, which means 'confused'.

- **Your communication is professional.** When sending emails in a business context, the standards are not the same as when sending personal communications. Use of **emoticons** is not appropriate. Neither is text in capitals, such as 'DO YOU UNDERSTAND?', which looks as if you are shouting.

Reviewing and proofreading own written work

Always make sure your written communications are correct and professional by reviewing and proofreading your work before submitting or sending it. Spelling and grammar checkers will only find some errors; the rest you must check for yourself. For instance, if you use a word that is correctly spelled but appears in the wrong context, the spell-checker will not highlight it. For example, you could easily type 'What country are you form?' and the spell-checker would not pick up this error, because it recognises 'form' as a correct spelling.

Many people find it easier to proofread printed documents than text appearing on a computer screen. Proofreading needs care and attention – it's all too easy to read what you meant to write rather than what you actually wrote.

Reviewing and editing documents created by others

Another excellent way to check your work is to ask someone else to read it through. It's much easier to spot mistakes in other people's work than in your own, so before you hand in an assignment, swap it with a friend to check for errors in each other's work.

Microsoft® Word® provides some useful tools for reviewing documents. You can add comments to a document using the Review tab on the Ribbon. You can also turn on the Track Changes feature, which allows you to see all the edits made to a document: new text is shown underlined and deleted text remains visible but is struck through; a black bar in the margin shows where changes have been made. An example of work that has been edited using Track Changes is shown in Figure 1.1.

Once you have edited the document with Track Changes switched on, you or someone else can review each editing change and accept or reject it. Books and magazine articles are often written in this way – the author's work is edited by someone else who makes alterations using Track Changes and adds comments that the author then reviews.

Note taking

Note taking is an extremely useful skill to develop, for the purposes of both your education and your later working life. It's very difficult to remember what is said during lectures, lessons, meetings and training sessions, so notes can really be helpful.

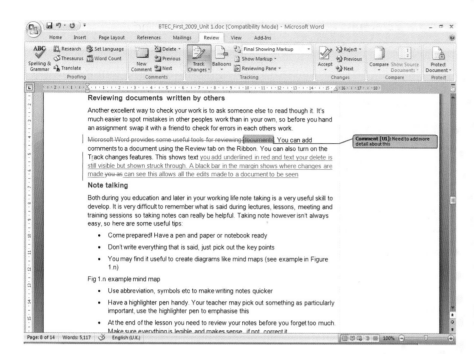

Figure 1.1: Word® Comments and Track Changes.

Taking notes isn't always easy, so here are some useful tips:

- Come prepared! Have a pen and paper or notebook ready.

- Don't write everything that is said – just pick out the key points.

- You may find it useful to create diagrams like mind maps (see the example in Figure 1.2).

- Use abbreviations and symbols to make writing notes quicker.

- Have a highlighter pen handy. When your tutor says that something is particularly important, use the highlighter pen to emphasise it.

- After the lesson, review your notes before you forget too much. Make sure everything is legible and makes sense; if not, correct it.

- File your notes carefully in chronological order, along with earlier notes for each unit. Lost notes are no use.

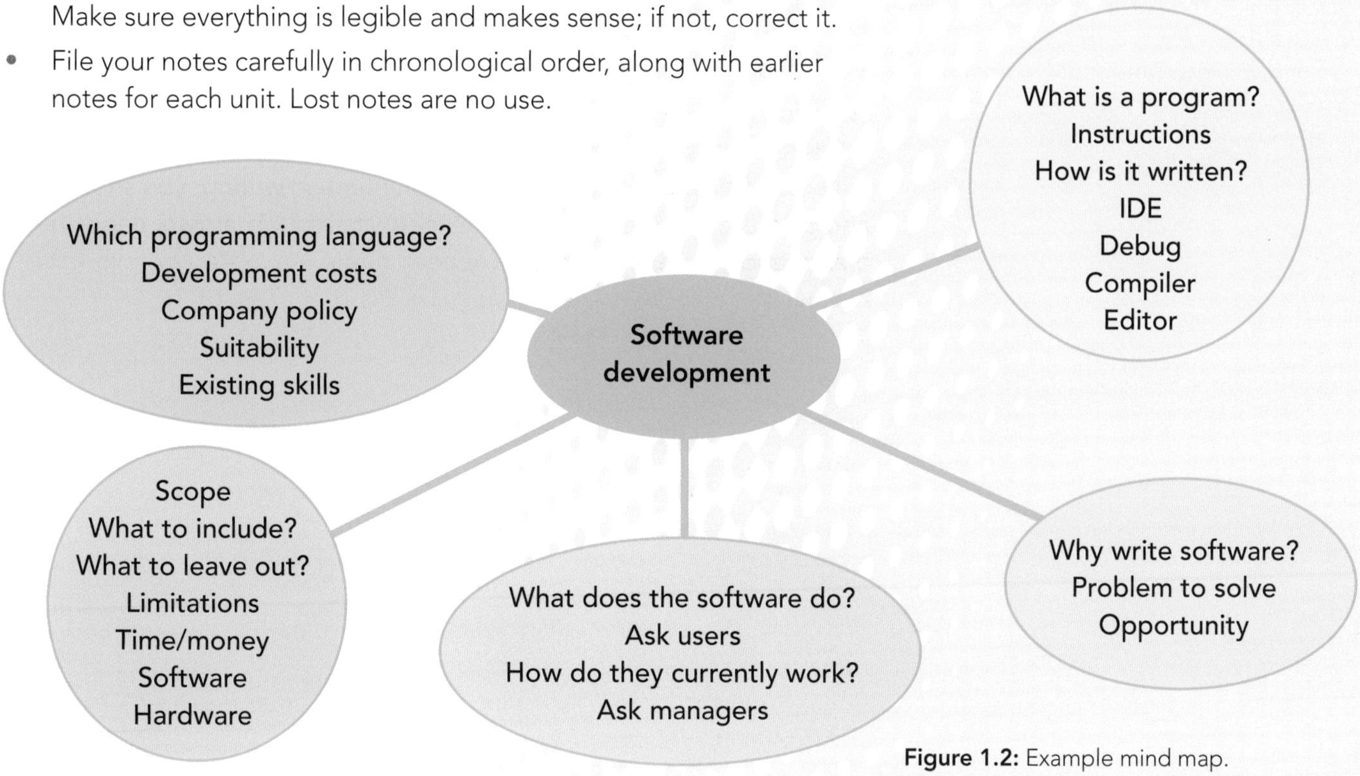

What is a program?
Instructions
How is it written?
IDE
Debug
Compiler
Editor

Which programming language?
Development costs
Company policy
Suitability
Existing skills

Software development

Scope
What to include?
What to leave out?
Limitations
Time/money
Software
Hardware

What does the software do?
Ask users
How do they currently work?
Ask managers

Why write software?
Problem to solve
Opportunity

Figure 1.2: Example mind map.

1.4 Audience

As mentioned on pages 4 and 5, one of the most important things to consider is your audience. You need to adapt the style and content of what you say or write so that your communication is effective. For example, you may need to consider the following different aspects in relation to your audience.

- **Age.** The way you speak and the language you use will probably not be the same when talking to an adult as when talking to a friend of the same age or to a child. With young children you would need to keep your language very simple, while when talking with your friends you might use slang that an older adult would not understand.

- **IT knowledge.** The terminology you use and the amount of detail you give in a technical explanation will need to change depending on the IT knowledge of the person you are speaking to.

- **Culture or country.** People who speak English as an additional language may need you to speak in simpler English, for example with less jargon and technical terms than you might normally use.

- **Disability.** When communicating with someone with a hearing disability, for example, you may need to make sure that you speak clearly and that your face is visible to the person all the time so they can lip read what you say.

In IT there is a large amount of technical terminology. **Acronyms** are also widely used, such as UPS (uninterruptable power supply) and DHCP (Dynamic Host Configuration Protocol). When speaking to technical people, you need to make sure they understand the specific terminology and acronyms you are using.

When speaking to non-technical audiences, try and avoid technical terms and acronyms if possible. If you must use them, explain them fully. When using an acronym for the first time in writing, you should also give the full name in brackets, for example, UTP (Unshielded Twisted Pair).

Key term

Acronym – a term which is referred to by its initial letters, such as GMT for Greenwich Mean Time or BBC for British Broadcasting Corporation.

BTEC Assessment activity 1.1 (P1) (P2) (P3) (P4)

You work as an IT technician within a small company.

1. You have been asked to prepare a training program on using email for IT users within the company. Prepare written training materials in two different versions: one for non-technical users and the other for users with good technical knowledge of IT. (P2) (P3)

2. Working in pairs, email copies of your guides to each other and proofread each other's work to check for spelling, grammar and formatting errors. (P4)

3. Prepare and give a presentation on using email which is designed for non-technical users of IT within the company. Following your presentation, have a discussion with your tutors or classmates about your presentation style and the content of the presentation. (P1)

Notes:

You may be required to prepare or give a presentation for another unit, so you may not need to prepare a separate presentation to cover (P1) for this unit. As long as the presentation is IT-related, this will also cover (P2).

The discussion you have can be about any topic. However, if you have a discussion about the sort of personal characteristics which are valued by employers in the IT industry, then this will cover (P1) for Unit 2 as well.

Grading tips

To cover (P1) you need to demonstrate effective interpersonal skills in face-to-face communication on at least three different occasions.

For (P2) and (P3), you need to show that you understand the different requirements of technical and non-technical users. The email guide for non-technical users must explain how to carry out all the basic tasks required (read email, send email, add attachments, etc.) in detail and should avoid technical jargon. The guide for technical users only needs to cover these basic tasks briefly, and should have more detail on advanced features such as creating mailing lists, out of office replies, etc.

For (P4) you will need to show before and after copies of the documents with the changes you have made highlighted. You will also need to provide evidence, for example screenshots, that you have emailed the materials, checked the attachments you received for viruses and made corrections to the work you received.

Your tutor will need to either video or audio record your presentations and discussions or complete a checklist.

PLTS

By communicating IT-related information to both technical and non-technical audiences, you will show that you are a **reflective learner**.

By using IT tools to provide constructive support and feedback to others' draft documents, you will show that you are a **team worker**.

Functional skills

Completing this assessment activity will provide evidence for your functional **English** skills in speaking and listening and in writing.

Just checking

1. List three things you need to consider about your audience when talking to them.
2. List three things you can do to improve PowerPoint® presentation slides.
3. Explain, with an example, the difference between facts and opinions.
4. Give an example of how you can show you are listening when someone is talking to you.
5. Before sending a business email, what methods can you use to check it is correct and makes sense?

2. Be able to use IT tools to communicate and exchange information

2.1 Communicating and exchanging information

There are many IT-based methods of communicating and exchanging information. These include documents, presentations, web pages and email.

Documents

Documents, such as letters and reports can be word processed. More sophisticated documents like leaflets, brochures and newsletters can also be word processed or may use desktop publishing software. Today, virtually every printed document, from a simple letter to a book like this one, is prepared using IT.

Presentations

Software such as Microsoft® PowerPoint® is designed to:

- create slides to support a presentation you are giving to an audience
- allow you to prepare a standalone presentation which can be left running, for example a presentation advertising a product at an exhibition or in a shop
- be sent to people to view as they wish.

Presentation slides can include text, graphics, animations and video.

Web pages

There are literally millions of web pages on the Internet, communicating every imaginable type of information. Interactive websites, such as Facebook®, Twitter™ and MySpace™ also allow users to exchange information. Although these social networking sites are mainly for personal use, some businesses advertise their services and communicate to their customers using these types of services.

Many traditional and new retailers sell goods and services over the Internet. Indeed, the World Wide Web has become the primary source of information for almost everything, including government services, maps and travel information.

Email

Email has become the primary method of business communication. As well as allowing you to send messages, you can also attach files, such as word-processed reports and spreadsheets.

2.2 IT tools

IT tools, such as word processors and presentation software have many features to help users create documents that communicate effectively.

Software

You can enhance many documents by including images, such as photographs, screenshots, diagrams and charts. Word processing, presentation and desktop publishing software all provide facilities that make it relatively easy to include these items. In many technical documents, such as user guides, annotated screenshots communicate far more effectively than long written explanations.

Specialist software for the visually impaired
Windows® comes with a number of built-in tools to help people who are visually impaired, including:

- magnifier (see Figure 1.3)
- narrator
- mouse pointer.

Activity: Tools for the visually impaired

Find out how to access each of the Windows® tools mentioned above. Then find out what each tool does and how it can help people with a visual impairment.

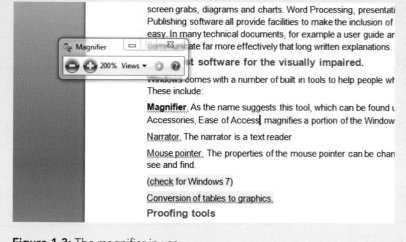

Figure 1.3: The magnifier in use.

Conversion of tabular information to graphics

Communicating information contained in tables of numbers is best done using a chart or graph. Trends in data are difficult to spot when the data is presented as numbers, but are much easier to understand when the data is shown as a graph. Applications, such as Microsoft® Excel®, have tools to convert numerical data to charts. (See *Unit 27 Spreadsheet modelling*, pages 36–37.)

Proofing tools

Spell-checker

Office® software, such as Microsoft® Office® 2007, comes with proofing tools including spelling and grammar checkers. Words which are not in the spelling dictionary are underlined in red and words or sentences which are considered grammatically incorrect are underlined in green. With grammar errors you right click on the word and either choose the corrected version or the **Grammar** option to see a more detailed explanation of the problem, as shown in Figure 1.4.

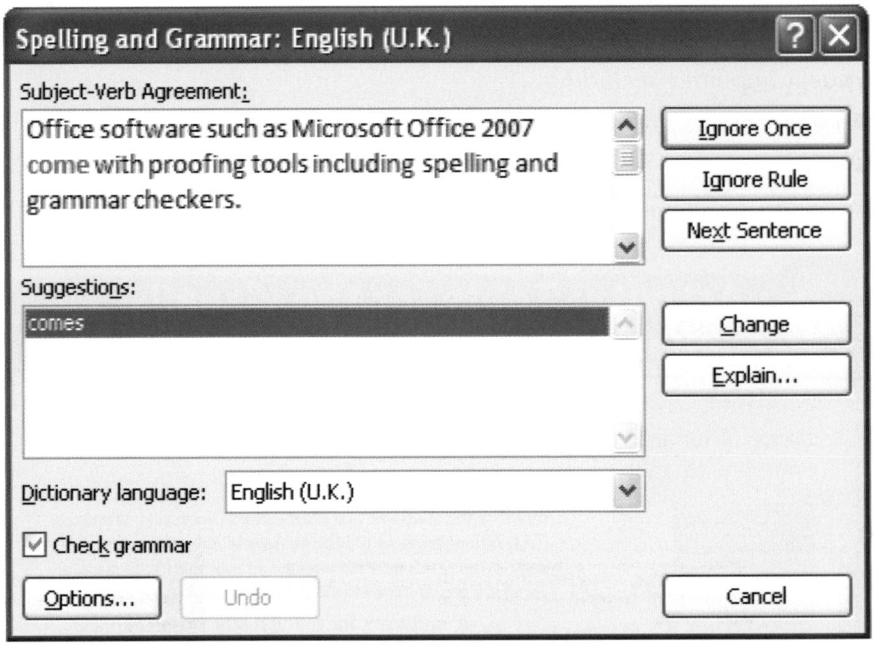

Figure 1.4: Grammar checker.

By clicking on the **Explain** button you can see an explanation of the grammar rule that is being applied, as shown in Figure 1.5.

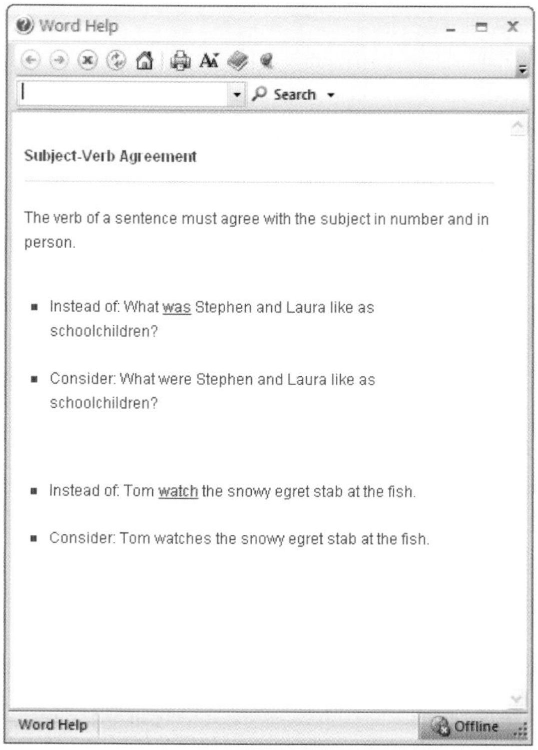

Figure 1.5: Grammar explanation.

Thesaurus

Another tool you may find useful is the Thesaurus provided with Office®
2007. If you are writing a report or letter and find yourself using the
same word again and again, the Thesaurus can help you find a different
word with the same meaning. It will also list antonyms (words which
have the opposite meaning).

For example, imagine you are writing a report on providing help to IT
users and you are using the word 'help' too much. The Thesaurus in
Word® will list other words with a similar meaning, such as 'assist' and
'facilitate' (see Figure 1.6).

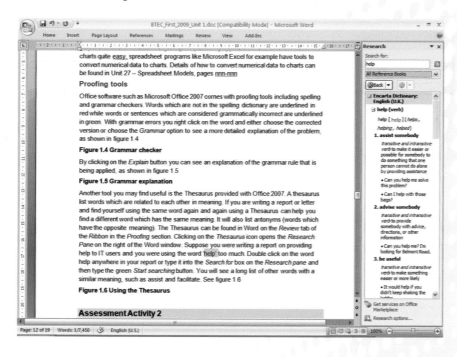

Figure 1.6: Using the Thesaurus.

2.3 Specialist communication channels

In addition to widely used tools such as word processors, IT also provides a number of specialist methods of communication using the Internet.

Blogs

Blogs have become a popular way to communicate using the Internet. A typical blog includes text, photos and in some cases video (a **vlog**). Twitter™ is a popular **microblogging** and social networking site. Twitter™ users can create entries (known as Tweets) up to 140 characters in length and share them with their 'followers' (people who have subscribed to a particular person's Twitter™ page). An example of a Twitter™ page is shown in Figure 1.7. To access Twitter's home page, please go to Hotlinks and click on this unit.

Did you know?

Twitter™ has been used in many unusual ways.

- Astronauts on both the Space Shuttle and the International Space Station have sent 'tweets' from space on their progress.

- During natural disasters like forest fires, sites such as Twitter™ have been used to pass information between people.

Figure 1.7: Twitter™ page.

Blogging is often used for social chatting about thoughts and feelings and people's day-to-day activities. However, it can also be used for other purposes including political campaigning, education (allowing learners to share information and discuss issues), advertising, fundraising and to communicate with others during emergencies.

Wikis

A wiki is a collaborative website which allows a group of users to work together to create and edit a series of linked web pages without having to know very much about web development. Wikis have a number of uses, such as supporting research and education, as they make it easy for groups of users to share information.

Did you know?

Wiki is a Hawaiian word for 'fast'.

Podcasts

Podcasts are downloadable audio media files. They are usually related to some theme or ongoing story and can be downloaded by anyone from a website. Once downloaded, you can listen to a podcast at any time on a computer or portable media player.

Video conferencing

Video conferencing (also known as web conferencing) allows groups of people who are physically remote to communicate using video and audio links. This can save a lot of time and money on travel. Video conferencing has been around for a long time and pre-dates the Internet. However, it has only become widely used since the development of efficient video compression techniques and broadband Internet.

2.4 Safety

Personal information

Electronic communications are quick and easy, but they also involve real dangers. Unlike paper-based records, electronic personal records can easily be transferred, stolen and misused. You need to remember to be careful with your personal information, as not everyone is who they say they are on the Internet. Paedophiles and other criminals trawl social networking sites and IM (instant messenger) services looking for gullible people to take advantage of. Criminals have been known to use social networking sites to collect information about passwords. For example, many people use their mother's maiden name or their pet's name as a password, and this information can sometimes be found on an individual's pages on a social networking site.

Although you may think you are well aware of the dangers, you should always be on guard. Think carefully before giving someone your phone number or address or, worse still, agreeing to meet them in person.

Uploading and viewing digital content

When you upload digital content (like photos and videos) to the Internet, remember that these often become available to everyone on the Internet, not just your friends and family. This material may therefore be used in ways that you did not originally intend. For example, employers might check the Facebook pages of people applying for jobs to check their character.

Respect towards others

It is important to respect the people that you communicate with on social networking sites. Negative or offensive comments can be seen by a much wider audience than you might imagine.

(i) Did you know?

The term 'podcast' is derived from the name of the Apple Media Player iPod® and the word 'broadcasting'.

(i) Did you know?

Some of the communication channels we have looked at, such as wikis and blogs, are open by their nature (for example, the idea of a wiki is that different people can contribute to it). Unfortunately, this makes them vulnerable to abuse. For example, the online collaborative encyclopaedia Wikipedia regularly suffers vandalism to some of its articles for political or other reasons.

Data protection regulations

Data Protection Act (1998)

In the UK personal information about living individuals is protected by the Data Protection Act (1998). This law requires any company that keeps personal information about people on its computers, to register with the Data Protection Registrar and to keep the eight Data Protection Principles. These principles are:

- data may only be used for the purposes for which it was collected
- data must not be passed on to other people without the consent of the person whom it is about
- people have a right of access to the information held about them
- personal information may be kept for no longer than is necessary and must be kept up to date
- personal information may not be sent outside Europe unless the person whom it is about has agreed
- all organisations that process personal information must register with the Information Commissioner's Office
- organisations that keep personal information are required to have adequate security measures in place
- people have the right to have incorrect information about them corrected.

Securing data

There are a number of ways that data can be secured. Some examples are described below.

Encryption

This is a method of encoding data so that only the intended recipient can decode it. For example, you can encrypt data on the hard drive of your computer so that if it is stolen the data cannot be read.

You can also use encryption when connecting to the Internet over a wireless link. This is very important if you are sending private or confidential information (for example, Internet banking passwords and security information), as it is possible for other people to intercept wireless communications and misuse any information they collect.

Firewalls

A firewall is a piece of software (or sometimes a dedicated hardware device) that examines all data arriving on your computer or network from the Internet and rejects any that break the firewall rules. This can prevent computers from becoming infected by certain types of viruses. Firewalls also help prevent hackers from gaining unauthorised access to systems.

(i) Did you know?

You can tell if a web page is secure in Microsoft® Internet Explorer® 8 by looking in the address bar. The web address should start with 'https' and there should be a padlock icon.

Backups

No method can guarantee to prevent data being lost or corrupted, so making regular backups is essential to keep important data safe.

Secure sites

When sending sensitive data over the Internet (for example, entering passwords or credit card details on a web page), it is important that the page you are using is secure. Secure web pages encrypt the data you send so that if anyone else intercepts it they cannot view it.

Just checking

1. List two Windows® tools that people with visual impairments might find useful.
2. When a word in Word® 2007 is underlined in green, what does this mean? How can you deal with this problem?
3. Explain the difference between a blog and a wiki.
4. List the eight Data Protection Principles.
5. What methods can you use to secure data sent over a wireless network link?

3. Understand the impact of IT on individuals, communities and society

It is hard to believe the impact IT has had on our society over the last 40 to 50 years. Many of the things we take for granted in our everyday lives now rely on IT systems.

3.1 Impacts

IT has changed and continues to change how we do things, from shopping to working to listening to music. Let's look at a few examples.

Social impacts

How we spend our free time

During the 1980s and 1990s children and young people spent a lot of their free time watching television. Today, although television remains a popular pastime, many young people spend more time on the Internet, using social networking sites, instant messenger applications and playing computer games.

 Did you know?

The first ever email was sent in 1971 using the Arpanet, which went on to become the Internet. Today around nine billion emails are sent each year.

The first text message was sent in 1992. Today over one billion text messages are sent every week in the UK alone.

Effects on local communities

With so much information and goods and services available online, some traditional facilities, such as village shops, have experienced a reduction in customers to the extent that their continued presence in the community is no longer necessary or economically viable. This can have a negative effect on local communities, in that there is a less diverse range of shops for local people to enjoy.

Economic impacts

Employment structure and working practices

IT has changed the nature of work in many professions. Examples of jobs which have been revolutionised by IT include administrators who used to keep paper-based records and typists who typed letters on a typewriter.

IT has also created many new jobs and IT skills are now required by almost every job. With Internet access widely available, people can communicate and work away from the office, so home working is now a popular option for many employees.

Sustainability

Computers use electricity and, with so many in use in homes and businesses, they make a significant contribution to energy consumption and related issues, such as climate change.

Furthermore, with computer hardware developing rapidly, there is the problem of how to deal with older computer equipment that is no longer required. The disposal of unwanted electrical equipment (not just computers) is covered by the Waste Electrical and Electronic Equipment Directive (WEEE Directive, 2007). Under these regulations, manufacturers of electrical equipment are required to provide users who purchase a new piece of electrical equipment with a method of disposing of the equipment that their purchase is replacing.

Legal impacts

Ownership, copyright and plagiarism

Copyright law protects people who produce their own original work (e.g. books, songs and films). With music and films available to be downloaded over the Internet, it has become very easy to steal material in copyright. Many file sharing web services have been set up which allow users to share copyrighted material, particularly films, making it freely available. (For more on copyright, see *Unit 4 Business IT skills*, page 115.)

The Internet makes it very easy to copy and paste materials from a web page into a document. **Plagiarism** is a common problem in assignment work submitted by learners in schools, colleges and universities. Quoting other people's work is fine as long as you acknowledge the source of the information, but passing off other people's work as your own is not allowed.

Key term

Plagiarism – copying someone else's material and claiming that it is your own original piece of work.

Ethical impacts

Privacy of information

With so much personal information kept on computers, personal privacy has become an issue. Almost every aspect of your life is recorded on a computer, including your medical records, what you buy at the supermarket, who you call on your mobile and what you search for on search engines, such as Google. Personal information relating to living individuals held on computers is covered by the Data Protection Act (1998) (see page 20).

Activity: Life before computers

Do you have relatives, such as uncles, aunts or grandparents, over the age of 50? Ask them about life without computers, the Internet and mobile phones.

- How did they do things like communicate and spend their free time?

- How does their life when they were young compare with yours?

Chat to them about whether technology has really made things easier or better.

3.2 Unequal access

The many benefits of Internet access are clear. But what happens to people who can't get high-speed access to the Internet?

Local and national implications

In the UK many people who live in rural areas cannot get broadband Internet access because they live too far from a telephone exchange and it's too expensive for the telephone or cable companies to lay cables for a small number of subscribers.

Activity: Broadband access

What is being done for people in the UK who cannot get broadband Internet access? Investigate the latest developments, such as WiMAX.

There is also an age issue, with some older people finding it difficult to come to terms with new technology. As services, such as banking and utilities (for example, water, gas and electricity supplies) become increasingly Internet-based, older people may struggle to access these facilities. They may also be placed at an economic disadvantage as

Internet goods and service are often cheaper that their traditional alternatives. For example, many gas and electricity suppliers offer a cheap rate for people who manage their account online.

It is also worth remembering that Internet access is not free. Some less affluent families may not be able to afford Internet charges, placing them at a disadvantage when compared with wealthier families.

Global implications

People who live in less economically developed countries may also struggle to get Internet access. Many aspects of society, particularly education and economic development, rely on the Internet and computer technology. People who don't have easy access to these are in danger of being left further behind. The division between people who have easy access to computer technologies and those who do not is sometimes called the **digital divide**. A number of projects, such as One Laptop Per Child and 50x15, have been set up to help tackle this problem by developing low-cost computing solutions.

Activity: Access to the Internet

- Discuss in small groups the disadvantages of not having access to the Internet. What could be done to help resolve the problem?

- Find out what One Laptop Per Child, 50x15 and similar projects are doing to help bridge the digital divide.

3.3 Abuse of IT

As with so many things in life, good things have a downside. This is certainly the case with the IT revolution and with the Internet in particular. There is a whole range of threats and annoyances that IT users need to be aware of and protected against.

Threats

Cyber bullying

Cyber bullying can be a worrying problem for young people. There are a range of different methods that can be used, including social networking sites like Facebook, emails and chatrooms. Cyber bullies often encourage their friends to join in the bullying.

Key terms

Digital divide – the gap that exists between people who have easy access to the Internet and other technology and those who do not.

Cyber bullying – when a person or group try to threaten, tease or embarrass someone using a mobile phone or the Internet.

Activity: Cyber bullying

Read more about cyber bullying by going to the Hotlinks site and clicking on this unit then search for cyber bullying on the website link provided.

Then discuss the following questions in small groups.

- Have you ever been a victim of cyber bullying?
- Why do people do this?
- How can it be discouraged or prevented?
- Is it only children who suffer cyber bullying?

Spam

Spam is unwanted email advertising. Anyone with an email account will tend to get unsolicited emails, most of which are annoying rather than dangerous. But email users should take particular care with emails that have attachments, as these may contain viruses.

Phishing

Phishing is a method used by criminals trying to trick people into providing their online banking password and security details. The scam works by criminals sending people an email which looks as though it comes from their bank. The email tells them to click a link within the email which then directs them to a web page that looks like the log-on screen to their online bank account. However, the web page is under the criminals' control and allows them to discover the victim's username, password and other security details. The criminals then use these details to steal money from the victim's bank account.

Activity: Phishing filter

- Microsoft® Internet Explorer® includes a 'phishing filter'. How does this work?
- What other email-based scams can try to trick you out of money?

Denial of service attacks

This is a method of preventing a web server from providing a service by overwhelming it with so many requests that it is unable to cope. There are several reasons why these types of attack might be made. For example, a criminal might attempt to blackmail an online retail company by threatening to attack the site unless given a large sum of money. Sometimes political sites are attacked in this way by people who don't agree with the political views expressed on the sites.

PLTS

By explaining the social impacts and potential threats of the use of IT, you will show that you are an **effective participator**.

Functional skills

Producing the materials about the social impacts of IT will provide evidence for your functional **English** skills in writing.

Assessment activity 1.2

BTEC · P5 · P6 · M1 · M2 · D1

1. Following on from the training materials you developed in Assessment activity 1.1, you have now been asked to prepare some materials that explain the social impacts of IT and discuss the potential threats which the use of IT has introduced. Your boss wants you to try out a new method of delivering the material and has asked you to choose and use a specialist communication channel. **P5 P6 M2**

2. Your boss has asked you to justify your choice of the method of delivery for question 1 and to explain why it was effective. **M1**

3. Your boss now wants you to produce a set of guidelines for other employees that explain how to stay safe and secure while using the specialist communication channel that you chose. **D1**

Grading tips

- For question 1, you will need to choose one of the specialist communication channels listed in section *2.3 Specialist communication channels* on pages 18–19, and use it to present the material on the social impacts of IT.

- To achieve **M2** you will need to cover the potential threats introduced by IT. Some of these are listed in section *3.3 Abuse of IT* on pages 24–25.

- For **M1** you will need to explain your reasons for your choice of specialist channel. For example, the channel you chose might be better suited to the type of material you have produced (you will need to say why it is better suited) or it may be more convenient for the users to access (again, you will need to say why it is more convenient).

Just checking

1. Give two examples of jobs that have been changed by IT.
2. How has IT made copyright difficult to enforce in some circumstances?
3. Why are some people in the UK unable to connect to broadband Internet?
4. Describe three ways in which IT systems can be abused.

Simon Evans

IT Manager at a large NHS hospital in North London

We have about 1,200 staff, doctors, nurses and admin staff who use the 900 PCs in the hospital. In the IT support department we run a 24-hour telephone helpdesk with at least four staff on duty answering helpdesk calls during the day and two at night. Although answering calls is a junior job in the IT department, it's a very important one because this is the main contact the users have with the IT staff.

For support department positions we don't look for people who have the best technical knowledge, because we can always provide staff with training.

Skills

The most important skill helpdesk staff need is good interpersonal communication. They need to be able to deal with problems that may seem very simple and trivial to them but are big issues for our users. They must be able to listen carefully to what the users say and give appropriate technical explanation and instructions in a way that is simple to understand.

Users can also email problems and questions to us, so the helpdesk staff need to respond to those too. This means they must be able to write clear explanations. Too many young people come for an interview for a job as a junior IT Technician and can't explain themselves clearly or write an email that makes sense.

Think about it!

1. Why does Simon say technical skills are not that important for the helpdesk staff?
2. Which skills does he say are most important?
3. What other skills do you think are important for a helpdesk technician?
4. Which of these skills do you think you already have and which do you need to develop further?

Just checking

1. Give three examples of major impacts IT has had on the society we live in.
2. What are the issues associated with personal information and IT?
3. What kind of spelling errors will a spell-checker fail to spot?
4. When giving a presentation, how can you check everyone is following what you are saying?
5. What can you do to make note taking easier?
6. Explain what the WEEE Directive is.

edexcel

Assignment tips

- This unit links closely with the other units on your course and with functional skills in English. Most of the evidence needed to cover grading criteria P1, P2, P3 and P4 can come from tasks you have done for other units.

- You can find lots of articles on the impact of IT on society on news websites such as BBC News. To access this site, please go to Hotlinks and click on this unit.

- You might find it helpful to print off articles, as you find them, and keep them in a scrap book. Alternatively, you could create a Word® document of links to relevant articles.

2 Working in the IT industry

The main reason for studying IT is usually because you want to follow a career as an IT professional. You might not yet have a very clear idea of exactly what you want to do within the IT industry, but the good news is that it's an exciting sector which is always changing and developing, so you're likely to have plenty of choice. It's hard to imagine another career with such wide-ranging possibilities that has such an important influence on almost every area of life.

In the future you could be working with robotic systems, developing technology to deliver 3D HD (High Definition) TV to people's homes, or supporting scientists combating global warming. The list of possibilities is almost endless.

In this unit you will look at some of the typical IT job roles. You will also consider the skills and attitudes employers look for in their employees.

Learning outcomes

After completing this unit you should:

1. know the characteristics that are valued by employers in the IT industry

2. know the common job roles undertaken by people working in the IT industry.

Assessment and grading criteria

This table shows you what you must do in order to achieve a pass, merit or distinction grade, and where you can find activities in this book to help you.

To achieve a **pass** grade the evidence must show that you are able to:	To achieve a **merit** grade the evidence must show that, in addition to the pass criteria, you are able to:	To achieve a **distinction** grade the evidence must show that, in addition to the pass and merit criteria, you are able to:
P1 describe the characteristics valued by employers in the IT industry **See Assessment activity 2.1 on page 40**		
P2 describe common IT industry job roles **See Assessment activity 2.2 on page 48**		
P3 explain the characteristics required for a specific job role in the IT industry **See Assessment activity 2.2 on page 48**	**M1** explain why certain characteristics are important for a specific job role **See Assessment activity 2.2 on page 48**	**D1** justify a choice of an appropriate job role for a given set of employee characteristics **See Assessment activity 2.1 on page 40**

How you will be assessed

This unit is internally assessed. You will provide a portfolio of evidence to show that you have achieved the learning outcomes. Your portfolio of evidence can be supplied in many formats including electronically as well as paper-based. The grading grid in the specification for this unit lists what you must do to obtain pass, merit and distinction grades. The Assessment activities in this unit will guide you through tasks that will help you to be successful in this unit.

Your tutor will tell you exactly what form your assessments will take, but you could be asked to produce:

- an article
- an advertisement

These could be paper or web-based.

Alice Wang, a 17-year-old studying BTEC First IT

This was an interesting unit for me, as although I enjoy IT I didn't really understand the different jobs that you can do with an IT qualification. I was surprised that there are so many different sorts of IT-related jobs. This unit has given me a lot to think about, as I really need to decide which area I want to specialise in.

The visiting speakers we had were interesting. They gave us a really helpful insight into what it means to work in IT on a day-to-day basis and the sort of tasks that are involved. It was also quite scary too, as the level of technical knowledge they have is very high.

All the things we learned about the kinds of skills employers look for were also very useful. I know how difficult it is to find a good job, so it certainly made me think about how to develop those sorts of skills and how to demonstrate them to employers.

Over to you

- How can you make the most of visiting speakers?
- Do you know what career you would like to follow? Do you have a plan of how to get there?

1. Know the characteristics that are valued by employers in the IT industry

Start up

Career plans

Discuss with a friend:

1. what sort of job do you want to do?
2. what day-to-day tasks would you enjoy doing at work?

Perhaps you already have some ideas about which IT tasks you enjoy and don't enjoy doing. This course will help you to decide. It's important to think about these things, as otherwise you may end up in a job you don't enjoy. Also, planning ahead for your future career means you can choose the courses or units to study that will help you progress towards your goal.

As you progress towards a career in IT, it is well worth preparing yourself for employment. Employers in IT and in many others sectors tend to be quite demanding, and the best and most interesting jobs will go to the candidates who are well prepared. You might imagine that for a job in IT, technical skills are the most important. In reality, although technical skills are of course important, many other skills and attitudes are equally (and in some cases more) valued.

You will need many of the skills listed in this unit to do well on your course, so now is a good time to develop them. Then, when it comes to job interviews, you will be able to tell prospective employers how you have developed and demonstrated the skills they are looking for.

1.1 General skills

There are a number of general skills, not specifically related to IT, that employers in the IT and many other industries are looking for in a prospective employee.

Interpersonal skills

Communication or interpersonal skills are highly valued by many employers. In the IT industry it is likely that your job will involve working closely with other people. These are likely to be both IT professionals and IT users whose knowledge of the technical aspects of IT may be very limited.

Planning skills

Even in your first IT job you will probably be expected to deal with several issues at the same time and to keep to tight deadlines. You will, therefore, need to be able to plan in order to get the tasks you have

Did you know?

You will study interpersonal skills in more detail in Unit 1: Communicating in the IT industry (pages 7–8).

been set completed on time and to organise all the information and resources you will need.

There are a number of ways you can plan tasks you have to complete. These can be as simple as writing a 'to do' list or making a note on a diary or calendar of when you need to complete various tasks by. There is also sophisticated planning software available, such as Microsoft® Project. As well as making a plan for your tasks and deadlines, you will need to monitor your progress against the plan and adjust the plan if things change.

Organisational skills

You will have to be able to carry out work tasks efficiently. For example, you need to make sure you have the equipment and information you require to do the job. This might be as simple as having a pen and paper with you and knowing the address and telephone number of a business you are visiting.

In business, people don't like excuses such as 'I'm sorry, I forgot to bring it' or 'I would have let you know but I didn't have your number'. Of course, occasionally we all make mistakes, but well-organised professionals don't have to make excuses like these very often.

Activity: Organising your work

Being well organised can save you a lot of time and effort in the long run. Do you have a course folder for all your notes, handouts and assignments, etc.? If not, get yourself a folder and take it to school or college every day. Use card dividers to split the folder up into units and keep all the information for each unit together.

Time management

Time management is related to planning and organisational skills. It involves making the most of your time and making sure you keep your appointments and deadlines. Being organised and making sure you have the right equipment with you for the job will help you avoid wasting time.

Because life is very busy and there are so many things to remember, many people find it essential to keep a diary of their meetings, appointments and deadlines. Paper diaries can be useful but many people prefer using an electronic diary. There are different diary systems available, for example, Microsoft® Outlook® and Google Mail™ webmail service both provide calendars linked with their email systems. The Google Calendar™ is shown in Figure 2.1.

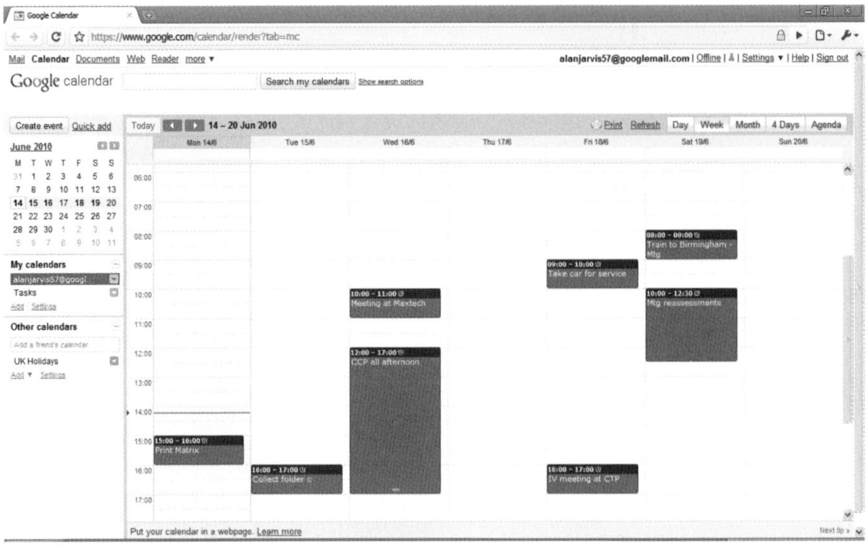

Figure 2.1: The Google Calendar™.

Activity: Time planner

Many people find a weekly planner an extremely useful way of making sure they have enough time to do all the things they need to do.

If you don't already have one, make your own weekly planner.

- Make a table with the days of the week across the top and hourly time periods down the side.

- Add all of your lessons to your planner.

- Now add periods of private study. (These can be at home or in the school/college resource centre, but they should be time you are allocating to do research or work on homework and assignments, etc.)

- Now add any other regular weekly commitments you have, for example a part-time job or sports practice.

If you prefer, you can create a weekly planner using an electronic calendar like Google Calendar™. This will allow you to set up repeating appointments for your lessons and study periods.

Many professionals also find it useful to write down important information, such as meeting notes, names and addresses and 'to do' lists, in a notebook. This is much better than trying to keep all this information in your head or on various scattered bits of paper – a notebook helps you to be more organised and efficient.

Team working

In your first job in IT you probably won't be working on your own. You are much more likely to be working as part of a team, and you will probably be the most junior member of the team. A team normally has a leader who will allocate tasks and monitor progress.

For a team to work well you must:

- Understand what your role is within the team and what you are expected to do. If this isn't clear you must speak to the team leader.

- Understand what the roles of other team members are and what information or support you need to provide for them.

- Deal with problems with another team member in a positive way. For example, if someone in your team isn't providing you with the information you need to do your task, speak to them politely first to try to resolve the problem. If that doesn't work then speak to the team leader.

- Remember that working in a team involves give and take, and you must be able to cooperate with the other team members. In addition, you will have to do your best to get on with people who you might not choose as your friends.

- Support the team leader by following their instructions carefully and keeping them up to date with your progress.

Teams are very effective when they work well together. Team members can contribute different skills and strengths that complement each other, and the team spirit can encourage everyone to do their best.

Activity: Team work exercise

1. Work in a small team of three or four people to plan a charity fundraising event.

   Discuss and agree on a team leader then decide what kind of event you will organise. Carry out research into various aspects of the event, for example, which charity to support; when and where the event will take place; how to advertise it; who will be responsible for what, etc.

2. Once you have planned the event in detail, discuss with your group how you found working as a team.

   - Was it easier or harder to complete the task working in a team rather than doing it on your own?

   - Did you work well together as a team?

   - How difficult was it to choose a team leader?

   - Did the leader do a good job?

Numeric skills

The level of numeric skills you need in your work will partly depend on the type of job you do. However, almost every job (not just IT jobs) requires basic numeracy skills, including the ability to carry out arithmetic and day-to-day mathematical calculations, such as working out percentages. Some IT careers such as programming may require a higher level of mathematical ability.

Creativity

As with numeracy, how creative you will need to be partly depends on the type of job you will do. Some jobs such as web page design or desktop publishing require a lot of creativity. But creativity doesn't just mean artistic creativity. Many employers value people who have creative, innovative ideas for new products or for improving existing products or services.

Problem solving

You don't have to work in IT for very long to realise that IT systems often suffer from problems of one sort or another. Problem-solving skills are partly to do with experience and partly to do with the approach you take to problems.

The more experience you have with IT equipment, the better you are likely to get at problem solving. However, good problem solvers also use the right approach. This includes collecting information on the problem before jumping to any conclusion, and testing any theories you have about the problem carefully and methodically.

1.2 Industry-specific skills

Technical knowledge

Obviously, technical knowledge is important in IT. As well as general IT knowledge, many employers need specific skills in a certain technical area. At the start of your career in IT you are unlikely to have all the relevant knowledge, but you will be expected to learn fast and pick up the skills quickly.

It is important that during your education you keep in touch with the important IT issues and developments that affect business. At the moment security is a big issue and it is likely to remain so, but developments are happening all the time. Employers will expect you to be knowledgeable and well informed on these important topics. They won't necessarily expect you to be a technical expert, but you should know something about the issues.

If there is a particular area you are interested in working in (for example, web development), you must do as much research as you can and develop your skills as much as possible in that area. Simply completing the unit for that subject won't really impress employers – you need to show that you have done more than the minimum requirement and have a real interest in that area.

Working procedures

Employers will also be keen for you to have some knowledge of typical **working practices** in the IT industry. Some of the information about working practices will be covered in the units you will be studying. Furthermore, any work experience or industry visits you do, or speakers you listen to, will also help you in this area.

You should have good understanding of the legislation that applies to IT in particular, including data protection and copyright laws. Every employer is keen to make sure they do not break the law, so they need their employees to be aware of their responsibilities in these areas.

Health and safety knowledge

Health and safety is another important area employers will want you to have some knowledge of. They will expect you to be aware of your responsibilities under the Health and Safety at Work Act 1974 and to know how to stay safe in the workplace.

Table 2.1: Health and safety risks for users of IT.

Health and safety risk	Potential consequences to user	How to minimise risk of injury
Bad posture	Sitting incorrectly at the computer can cause a wide range of problems ranging from muscle aches and pains to more serious injuries like repetitive strain injury (RSI). RSI involves pain in the shoulder, neck, arm, wrist or hand. It can result from repeatedly doing small actions, such as using a keyboard or manipulating a mouse.	To avoid these problems users should sit correctly at the computer, using an adjustable chair and a footrest if necessary, and take regular breaks.
Eyestrain	Looking at a computer monitor for long periods can give the user sore eyes and headaches.	The monitor should be correctly adjusted (top of the monitor at eye level) and positioned to avoid reflections and glare. Computer users should have a regular eye test (at least every two years).

Key term

Working practices – rules that determine how you carry out your work. They will often be specific to the industry you are working in.

Did you know?

For more on data protection and copyright, see *Unit 1: Communicating in the IT industry*, pages 20 and 22.

Did you know?

In 2008–09 nearly a quarter of a million people were injured through accidents in the workplace. Also in that period, over 1,500 people or businesses were prosecuted due to health and safety at work issues.

Table 2.2: Health and safety risks an IT Technician needs to be aware of.

Health and safety risk	Potential consequences to user	How to minimise risk of injury
Electrical hazards	Computer equipment is electrically powered, so all computer users are at some risk. • Electric shock can stop the heart beating properly or prevent a person from breathing. A shock can also cause burns inside the body or can make the muscles go into spasm. • Thermal burns can occur if faulty electrical equipment overheats. • Electrical faults may cause fires.	• Keep liquids away from any electrical equipment. • If you need to remove the lid from a computer case, ensure the power is off and the power cable is removed from its socket. • Check mains cables or plugs are not damaged in any way before using.
Trip hazards	There is a risk of injury from falling over. There is also the potential to damage equipment and hurt other people during a fall.	• Be careful of trailing cables when working around computers. • When installing a computer, make sure no cables could trip up anyone.
Manual handling	If you are involved in setting up computer systems, you may have to move heavy boxes and equipment. • You may damage your back by lifting objects incorrectly. • You may injure other parts of your body by dropping objects.	• Always lift items in the correct way, bending at your knees not your back. • Never lift an item which weighs more than 20 kg on your own.
Use of tools	Even simple tools like a screwdriver can be dangerous if misused.	• Always use the correct tool for the job (e.g. never try to use a flat blade screwdriver on a cross head screw). • Do not force tools – they may slip and give you a nasty cut. • Power tools need to be handled with care. • You must wear the correct protective clothing, including gloves and goggles.
Working at height	IT technicians may occasionally need to use ladders, for example, to install network cables in a roof space. Care needs to be taken, as falling from a ladder can cause serious injury or even death.	Use the ladder according to the manufacturer's instructions and erect it properly so that it is stable.

(i) Did you know?

You can find lots of detailed information about these, and many other, health and safety issues on the Health and Safety Executive website. To access this site, go to Hotlinks and click on this unit.

1.3 Attitude

Every employer will tell you that they are looking for people with the right attitude. Employees who demonstrate the right attitude are more likely to succeed in their chosen career, with a greater chance of promotion, better pay and more interesting work.

Some of the most common attitudes that employers say they are looking for in an employee are shown in Table 2.3.

Table 2.3: Attitudes preferred by employers.

Attitude	Why employers are looking for it
Determination	Work can sometimes be difficult and there may be problems to overcome, so determination to succeed and solve problems is important. People who give up easily and lack the determination to see a difficult problem through won't impress their employers.
Independence	In your first job in IT you probably won't be working on your own, but employers will expect you to develop the ability to work unsupervised and to use your own initiative rather than always waiting for instructions.
Integrity	Being honest and truthful in the workplace is vital, because employers want people they can trust. For example, they will expect you to work just as hard when your supervisor is not around as when he or she is. You may also be trusted with expensive equipment which you will be required to look after.
Tolerance	In life we need to be tolerant of other people's differences, whether differences of attitude, culture or personality. As mentioned on page 35, when working in a team you need to do your best to get on with all team members. This might mean tolerating other team members' ways of working. As an IT expert, you will probably have to deal with people who know very little about IT. This can be frustrating and requires patience.
Dependability	Employers rely on their employees to run their business efficiently and effectively. Workers who turn up late every day, who take too much time off sick or who don't complete the tasks they are set won't last long in most jobs. To get on in your career you will need to show that you are reliable. This means turning up for work when you are supposed to and doing the tasks you have been asked to do. If for some reason you are unable to meet a commitment, you need to let your supervisor know, giving them as much notice as you can, so they can make alternative arrangements.
Leadership	While you are unlikely to be in a leadership position in your first job, your employer will be looking for leadership qualities in you. Someone who is a good leader works well with others and inspires and encourages them. They are good at planning and organising and can take the initiative. In fact, leadership skills are a combination of all the other skills we have mentioned.
Confidence	This skill has both positive and negative aspects. • An over-confident and arrogant person will not fit in well in the workplace. Their arrogance is likely to upset other people, and over-confidence in technical matters may lead to mistakes. • However, well-placed confidence in your knowledge and ability is a positive attribute, especially in situations where you are supporting non-technical users. Such users would not feel confident if the person providing them with advice and support did not seem sure about what they were doing or the information they gave.
Self-motivation	Work can sometimes be difficult and may become repetitive. People who lack self-motivation may not do a difficult or repetitive job properly or may give up all together, leaving other people to pick up the pieces.

You might think it's impossible to show an employer that you have the skills described in Table 2.3. In fact, you will already be developing many of these skills in order to complete your BTEC course, and you can demonstrate this to a future employer. For example, you could tell an employer at interview that you have good time management skills as you managed to cope with all the different assignments you had to do and you handed them in on time. You could mention that, to make sure you met all your deadlines, you used a weekly planner or electronic calendar to manage your time effectively.

Activity: Skills audit

Creating a skills audit or development plan can be a very useful exercise as you plan for your future career.

- Make a list of all the attributes, general skills and industry-specific skills listed in this unit.

- For each attribute or skill, rate yourself on a scale of 1 to 4, where 1 is you have this skill fully developed and 4 is you completely lack this skill.

- Swap your list with a peer to review and discuss your ratings and modify them if necessary. Remember this should be done in a positive, supportive manner!

- Once you have agreed your ratings with a peer, for every skill or attribute rated 2 or higher make a list of the ways in which you may be able to develop this skill. For example, if one of the skills you need to develop is time management, then maybe you could develop this skill by using diary software to plan your time better.

PLTS

By describing the characteristics valued by employers and justifying the job roles you choose for different employees, you will show that you are an **independent enquirer**.

Functional skills

Writing the article could provide evidence for your functional **English** skills in writing.

BTEC Assessment activity 2.1

You have got a new job working for 'Jobs in IT', an IT recruitment agency. The company finds suitable candidates for jobs in the IT industry. You got the job because of the course you did and the knowledge you showed about job roles in the IT industry at the interview. Now the company wants to use your knowledge to encourage more people to apply for IT jobs.

1. Your boss has asked you to write an article to be published in a computing magazine describing the characteristics which employers in the IT industry value. **P1**

2. Continue your article by adding a description of an imaginary job candidate who has strong technical knowledge, particularly in using and configuring Windows® and dealing with technical problems. They also have excellent team working and interpersonal skills. Suggest a suitable role for this candidate and explain why their characteristics make them suitable for that particular job role. **D1**

Grading tips

For **P1**, you can probably find some examples of this sort of article on the Internet – they will be relevant to all sorts of jobs, not just IT ones. Remember to cover both the general and the industry-specific characteristics as listed in the unit content of the specification.

For **D1**, the key thing is to justify why the characteristics of your imaginary canidate make them suitable for the job role you have chosen for them. Give examples of how the characteristics would benefit them in the job role.

Just checking

1. List three interpersonal skills which employers value.
2. What sort of numeric skills will most employers expect you to have?
3. Give an example of how you might need to demonstrate tolerance in the workplace.
4. What laws do you need to be aware of in the workplace?

2. Know the common job roles undertaken by people working in the IT industry

There is a wide range of IT-based jobs which cover many different tasks. Because IT is used in so many industry sectors, the type of work done will vary depending on the sector that you work in. For example, a programmer's job is writing programs, but if the programmer works in the defence sector, the type of programs they write will be very different from those written by a programmer working in finance and banking.

2.1 General IT roles

General IT roles can very broadly be divided into the following categories:

- IT service
- network management
- hardware-related
- software development
- technical writing
- data and information.

Let's look at some of the roles in each category.

IT service management and delivery

Many young people start their IT careers working in IT service delivery (sometimes called IT support). This involves supporting IT users with software issues that occur in their everyday work. Many medium and large companies have an IT support department with technicians on hand to answer user queries. This is sometimes called the IT help desk, and support can be provided by telephone, email or in person.

What skills and characteristics are needed?

Interpersonal skills are very important in software support roles, because a support technician spends a lot of time talking to users and explaining how to do things and fix problems. You need to be patient, polite and a good listener. Sound written communication skills are also important, as is a strong understanding of software issues and common user problems, such as network and printer issues.

> **(i) Did you know?**
>
> There are over a million people employed in computer-related jobs in the UK, with over half of these in software and computer services. There are over 100,000 specialist software companies in the UK and more new companies that create software than anywhere else in Europe. (Source: UK Technology Marketing Toolkit)

Case study: Khalid, IT Support Technician

I studied BTEC First and National and then I studied Computing at university. I'm now working in my first job as an IT Technician in a large NHS hospital.

We have a rota of tasks each day which is set by our supervisor. Most days I have to spend some time answering calls on the IT helpdesk. Calls can be about all sorts of problems, from simple things like forgotten passwords to complex issues, such as intermittent system crashes that we have to do research on and maybe pass up to the senior technicians. To be honest this part of the job can be quite hard because people can sometimes be frustrated and quite angry when their computer is not working properly.

We also spend some time going around the hospital doing hardware and software installations and repairs. This is more interesting than manning the helpdesk. We deal with many different types of installations, from network cabling to printers.

We also spend some time in the workshop setting up and testing new computer systems before they are installed in the hospital. I'm learning new things all the time, which is great because to progress in this industry you need a lot of practical technical knowledge.

1. **What non-technical skills do you think Khalid will need to do his job?**

2. **What is the best way to deal with angry and frustrated IT users?**

Network management

As the name suggests, a network manager supervises and maintains a large network of computers, servers, printers and other equipment in an organisation. Large organisations which have many offices and computers will typically employ network managers to run their network. Companies like ISPs (Internet Service Providers) will also have people who do this job.

Network management involves:

- monitoring the network to check whether it is providing a good level of performance
- configuring network hardware such as routers to provide the required network facilities
- dealing with problems and faults
- designing and implementing changes and additions to the network.

What skills and characteristics are needed?

First-rate, detailed technical knowledge of network software and hardware is essential for this job. Sound problem-solving skills are also required.

Hardware-related roles

There is a limited number of jobs available in building and manufacturing hardware, as most of this work is done outside the UK. There are some roles, however, in selling, installing and configuring hardware, including that used on PCs, servers, network equipment and printers. There are also some roles in repairing computer equipment. However, as computer hardware becomes more common and less expensive, these roles will eventually mostly disappear. This is because, apart from very high end server equipment, PC equipment is becoming 'throw away' as it is too cheap to make repairs economic.

There are virtually no hardware-only jobs, as every hardware job has aspects of software in it. For example, a job that involves installing hardware will also include installing and configuring the related software.

What skills and characteristics are needed?

Working in hardware repair or installation requires excellent practical skills. Troubleshooting and fault-finding skills are also vital. You will need a sound understanding of computer systems and related hardware. Health and safety knowledge is critical, including the precautions you need to take when working with electricity, lifting heavy objects, using ladders (for example, to install cables in a ceiling space) and operating tools, including power tools like drills. (For more information, see pages 37–38.)

Case study: Calvin, System Builder

I work for a small computer manufacturer in North London that specialises in high end systems for gamers. I completed my BTEC First and National and got the job after doing my work experience in the company.

I spend a lot of time in the workshop assembling PCs from various components. We build the systems to customer order, so each one is slightly different. As well as installing and testing the hardware, we install various software packages depending on what the customer wants.

This work can get a bit routine after a while, but we also do sessions with technical support helping customers who have problems with the computers they have bought. We also spend time doing repairs to systems that have been returned.

Occasionally we go to trade shows or gaming conventions where we set up the systems on the stand – these are really fun and interesting.

For this job I need an eye for detail – the computers must be assembled correctly or faults can occur and customers will complain. I have to build the systems quite quickly too, so it is important to have good practical skills.

1. **How does Calvin show integrity in his work? Why do you think this is an important attribute for his employer?**

2. **Some of the work Calvin does is quite repetitive. What attributes does he need to deal with this aspect of his job?**

Software development

This is a very broad area covering many different types of roles. The job of a programmer can vary depending on the type of programming done:

- web development – for example, designing and creating web pages and writing web server software, perhaps to create an online shop
- applications programming – for example, writing programs for end users, such as a game or a business application
- system programming – for example, writing device drivers for new hardware, updating operating system components or dealing with security issues that have been identified with an operating system
- communication programming – for example, writing software for network devices such as a mobile Internet modem or a WiFi router.

There are also a number of different terms for people who work in software development, such as solutions development and implementation, and applications programmers.

What skills and characteristics are needed?

To be a programmer you need the sort of mind that can deal with complex and abstract problems, such as algorithms. You will probably also need excellent mathematical skills.

Case study: Alice, Junior Programmer

I work as a Junior Programmer at a small software company that specialises in software for the motor trade (garages and car dealers). I got the job after I completed my degree. I'd studied BTEC First and National before that.

I'm currently working as part of a small team developing the new version of one of the company's software products, which allows car dealers to keep track of all the cars they have for sale. I'm responsible for updating just a small part of the software which prints reports.

I spend most of my time working out how the software currently works (this can be quite tricky as I did not write it) and then making the changes as described in the specification provided by the designers. I need to be patient and have an analytical mind. I'm the sort of person who enjoys solving puzzles, so I quite enjoy this work. I feel a real sense of achievement when I manage to get things working the way they should.

1. **What non-technical skills do you think Alice needs in her job?**

2. **How do you think Alice goes about finding out how the software works? What information does she need to find out about it to do her job?**

Technical writers

Technical writers write documentation for hardware and software products. Towards the end of the software or hardware development process, a technical writer will start work on the manuals and help files for the system.

What skills and characteristics are needed?

Excellent written English is an important skill, along with the ability to explain complex procedures in a clear and understandable way. A good understanding of technical systems is also important, as the technical writer must fully understand the system to be able to write clear manuals and other documentation.

Case study: Anita, Technical Writer

I work as a Technical Writer for a large software company that creates software systems mostly for military and aviation applications.

I'm working on a couple of projects at the moment:

- writing a manual for airline crew who operate an on-board entertainment system we make for passenger planes
- writing help pages for a military communications system.

I spend quite a lot of time getting to understand the software and meeting with the programmers to discuss how it works and how it will be used. I also have meetings with the users or clients to discuss what type of documentation they want and how they would like it presented.

I then need to spend time writing the documentation. I usually work as part of a small team, and I have to write the documentation following quite strict guidelines. Once I have written my part of the documentation it gets reviewed and edited by other people. I then have to respond to their comments and makes changes to my work as required.

I usually have to work to quite tight deadlines because we have to wait until the systems are nearly complete before we can write the documentation. Our clients are always keen that the documentation doesn't delay completion of the project. Sometimes there are last-minute changes to the systems and we have to update the documentation in a very short timescale, which means I occasionally need to work late.

In this job I need very good written English and an eye for detail. I need to be able to understand quite complex technical applications in a short time and recognise how non-technical people would use these applications.

1. **What non-technical skills does Anita need to do her job well?**

2. **Anita has to follow strict guidelines in her work. What sort of things do you think these guidelines might cover?**

Data and information

There are a variety of roles involved with data and information. Many businesses rely heavily on databases to store information on customers, stock, orders, etc.

Data administrators set up and maintain databases and ensure the data in them is correct. They develop and maintain queries and reports which extract information from the data. Information security is also very important to many organisations, and so they employ people who check the security and validity of their data.

Security of personal data is a big issue. There have been a number of high profile cases recently where laptops or CDs containing the personal data, for example bank account details, of large numbers of people have been lost. The job of a data administrator can include securing data by making sure passwords are up to date and using techniques like encryption. It may also involve training users about how to keep their data secure.

What skills and characteristics are needed?

A good understanding of database technology is important, as well as a sound knowledge of current security issues and the Data Protection Act 1998.

Case study: Paul, Data Analyst

I'm a data analyst working for my local police authority. The police authority enters an enormous amount of data into their database, including details of incidents and crimes, as well as information about the time police officers spend doing various tasks and the resources used.

I spend most of my time creating reports from this data. I create some of these reports regularly, like the monthly crime statistics. Others I only do when they are requested.

For example, the Chief Constable might want to know how many hours each police officer spent on the beat last month. I might also need to create a report to help in the process of solving a serious crime. Recently I had to create a database query which searched through all the statements that the Police had taken about a crime and identified every time a certain person's name was mentioned. I used the query to create a printed report which provided all the information the detective in charge of the case needed.

I also have to check that the data entered is correct, and deal with enquiries from police officers about how to use the system to both enter and extract data.

1. **What legislation would be particularly relevant to Paul's job?**

2. **What skills do you think Paul needs to do well in his job?**

2.2 Investigation and design

Software development is a very broad area which includes many different job roles. When developing a new software system there are a number of stages involved and these are reflected in the different job roles that exist at each stage.

The investigation and design stage of software development is completed at the beginning of the process.

Systems Analyst

In a commercial software development project, a Systems Analyst is someone who uses their knowledge of software development and the application area involved to identify what the software will need to do. They will also investigate how the current system works and what benefits the new system is likely to bring. They may also investigate what the hardware requirements are.

What skills and characteristics are needed?

This is often quite a complex job and systems analysts will often have had many years' experience of software development before taking on this role. They also need a good understanding of the business area the software is being developed for. For example, if the software is being developed for a banking system, the systems analyst must have a sound understanding of banking.

System Designer/Architect

Once the systems analyst has discovered what the software will need to do, the System Designer or Architect creates a design which defines how the software will work.

What skills and characteristics are needed?

As with the systems analyst role, a System Designer will probably have many years' experience as a programmer. They also need an excellent understanding of software design techniques.

Project Manager

There will be many staff working on a large software development project, so a Project Manager will be appointed to run the overall project, making sure everyone knows what they are doing, that deadlines are kept to and that the project runs smoothly.

What skills and characteristics are needed?

A Project Manager needs to have experience of working on a project, and a good understanding of the tasks involved in an IT project and how long they are likely to take. They need to be good at dealing with people and be well organised and efficient.

Activity: What jobs are available

Carry out some research on job websites (you can access some examples by going to Hotlinks and clicking on this unit). Find three or four jobs which appeal to you. Try to find ones that match the qualifications and experience you will have in two to three years' time (there is no point looking at highly paid jobs which require technical expertise).

- What sorts of tasks does the advert say the job involves?
- Do you think you have the skills for this job?
- What further skills will you need to develop?

PLTS

By explaining why certain skills and characteristics are particularly relevant for certain job roles, you will show that you are an **independent enquirer**.

Functional skills

Writing the advert will provide evidence for your Functional **English** skills in writing.

Assessment activity 2.2 (P2) (P3) (M1)

A number of IT jobs have become available in your local area, including all the different job roles listed in this unit.

1. The IT recruitment agency you work for has asked you to write a brief guide for job hunters which describes common IT roles. **P2**

2. Write a job advert for one of the roles described in your guide. The advert should describe and explain the characteristics which are required for the role. **P3**

3. Add to the advert an explanation of why certain characteristics you have described are important for that job role. **M1**

Grading tips

- The layout and formatting of your guide and advert are not so important. But you must make sure your guide covers all the different common IT roles listed in the unit content in the specification. For each role you need to write a description of what it typically involves. **P2 P3**

- For **M1**, you need to explain why certain skills or personal characteristics are particularly relevant for the job you have created the advert for. For example, someone who works as an IT help desk technician will need excellent communications skills as they need to explain how to do things to non-technical IT users.

Just checking

1. Give two examples of the sorts of skills a network manager needs.
2. What sort of job might suit you if you have an analytical mind and like solving puzzles?
3. What sorts of skills would you need to work on an IT helpdesk?

WorkSpace **Oliver Lloyd**
Web Developer

I completed my BTEC Level 2 and Level 3 courses and then went on to study at university before getting a job as a Web Developer.

I found my job a bit of a culture shock to start with. Although the work atmosphere was quite relaxed and friendly, there was a lot of pressure to get work done quickly and to a very high standard. I was expected to use quite a few software technologies I had only really touched on before. The other project team members gave me some help, but they were too busy to spend a lot of time explaining things to me, so I had to find things out for myself and learn fast. This meant some long nights getting things working to meet deadlines.

I joined the company with another trainee but he didn't pass his probationary six months and they let him go. I was a bit shocked by this as he was very good technically, although he was often late for work and sometimes didn't come in at all. I spoke to my manager about it and he explained that in a small company they can't afford to carry employees who don't make the grade.

Why I like the job

Although I have found some aspects of working here hard, I have enjoyed the challenge. It is a great feeling when things come together and the website you've been working on is completed, the customer is happy with it and it goes online for everyone to use. There's a real sense of achievement in that.

Think about it!

1. Why do you think Oliver found his first job a bit of a 'culture shock'?
2. What things do you think you might find hard when you start your first full-time job in IT?
3. What attributes do you think Oliver's employer values most?
4. What technical skills do you think a web developer should have?

Just checking

1. List three general skills that employers value.

2. What skills do you need to be a good team worker?

3. List three aspects of health and safety relevant to a computer technician.

4. Explain why dependability is an important attitude and give some examples of how you might demonstrate it.

5. Working as a network manager, what sorts of tasks would you expect to be carrying out?

6. What skills would you need to work as a technical writer?

7. Explain what a systems analyst does.

edexcel

Assignment tips

- There is lots of information on the Internet about the skills and characteristics that employers look for and the different IT job roles and what they involve. You can try a couple of recruitment sites by going to Hotlinks and clicking on this unit, but there are many more you could try.

- You can discover a lot about IT job and employer requirements by speaking to other people. Visiting speakers, work experience supervisors, friends and relatives are all valuable sources of information. Make sure you take the opportunity to ask questions about what they do and what is expected of them at work.

- If you have a part-time job, even if it is not IT-related, you may be able to speak to your boss about the general attributes they look for in prospective employees.

- To understand why certain characteristics are particularly relevant for a job role, you need to think about the tasks that are involved in that job role. For example, working on an IT helpdesk means you will have to deal with people who may be angry or frustrated because their computer is not working. To deal with angry people, you need skills such as good spoken communication and patience. These skills are not often required by a programmer, but a programmer needs other skills, such as the ability to deal with complex abstract problems.

Credit value: 10

3 Computer systems

This unit introduces you to the basic concepts of computing. Many of the topics are dealt with in more depth in other units.

If you have taken courses in IT before, you may find that you already know some of the theory. You are still advised to study this unit carefully, as it does require you to apply your knowledge in practical contexts.

As you work through the unit, you should be asking some questions about the computer systems in use at your centre, and a discussion with the technical staff will be very beneficial. If you own a computer yourself then you will probably want to experiment with some of its facilities.

You may have thought about working eventually as a computer technician, systems administrator or computer engineer. This unit helps you to take the first step along the path to those careers. Or maybe you want to work as a programmer, database manager or web designer? For all those roles you need to have a good understanding of how computer systems work.

Whatever job you end up doing, as an IT practitioner you will be expected to carry out basic tasks, such as installing a new computer system or repairing faults. This unit introduces you to these very useful skills.

Learning outcomes

After completing this unit you should:

1. know the common components of computer systems
2. know the different uses of computer systems
3. be able to connect computer hardware
4. be able to configure computer software.

Assessment and grading criteria

This table shows you what you must do in order to achieve a pass, merit or distinction grade, and where you can find activities in this book to help you.

To achieve a **pass** grade the evidence must show that you are able to:	To achieve a **merit** grade the evidence must show that, in addition to the pass criteria, you are able to:	To achieve a **distinction** grade the evidence must show that, in addition to the pass and merit criteria, you are able to:
P1 identify the common components of a computer system **See Assessment activity 3.1 on page 70**	**M1** describe different ways to connect to a computer network **See Assessment activity 3.1 on page 70**	
P2 describe the purpose of different types of computer systems **See Assessment activity 3.1 on page 70**		
P3 represent how data flows around a computer system **See Assessment activity 3.1 on page 70**		
P4 specify suitable components to meet user requirements **See Assessment activity 3.2 on page 76**	**M2** give reasons for the choice of components to meet a given need **See Assessment activity 3.2 on page 76**	**D1** suggest alternative setups based on user feedback **See Assessment activity 3.2 on page 76**
P5 connect hardware safely to a computer system, testing for functionality **See Assessment activity 3.3 on page 81**	**M3** explain working practices and health and safety procedures when connecting hardware devices **See Assessment activity 3.3 on page 81**	
P6 configure software for a given user requirement **See Assessment activity 3.4 on page 98**		**D2** discuss how the configuration of software will help a given user perform their tasks **See Assessment activity 3.4 on page 98**
P7 identify potential security risks **See Assessment activity 3.4 on page 98**		

How you will be assessed

This unit is internally assessed. You will provide a portfolio of evidence to show that you have achieved the learning outcomes. Your portfolio of evidence can be supplied in many formats including electronically as well as paper-based. The grading grid in the specification for this unit lists what you must do to obtain pass, merit and distinction grades. The Assessment activities in this unit will guide you through tasks that will help you to be successful in this unit.

Your tutor will tell you exactly what form your assessments will take, but you could be asked to produce:

- information leaflets
- web pages
- diagrams
- presentations with supporting handouts
- practical work with observation records or witness statements
- screenshots
- written reports
- user guides or memos.

Gemma Tsang, Trainee Systems Administrator

I was always interested in computers, but I mainly used them for keeping up to date with my friends and doing coursework. When I started studying computer systems I found that I really wanted to know much more about how they worked. In fact, I made up my mind to work with computers and train to be an IT professional. So this unit was the starting point for my career in IT.

There's so much to learn. Nobody can know everything there is to know about computer systems, so you tend to get to know one system very well to begin with. I like helping the users at my company when they have problems with their own laptops, with the printers or with the network. Later I hope to move to a bigger organisation where I can expand my knowledge and learn about other types of system as well.

Over to you

- Do you use computers for anything beyond your studies and social life?
- At this point, what aspect of IT would you most like to learn about?

1. Know the common components of computer systems

What type of computers have you used?

Think back to when you were younger and try to list all the different computers that you have used. Include games consoles and smart phones, as well as laptops and desktop computers.

Discuss in a small group:

- How have computers changed over the years?
- What new devices can you buy now that were unavailable some years ago?
- What will computers be like in the future?

1.1 Computer systems

There are many different types of computer system, but each one generally falls into one of three categories:

- **Personal computers** – designed for one person to use at a time, including desktops, laptops, netbooks, PDAs, mobile phones, games consoles and tablets.
- **Servers** – control networks and other devices.
- **Embedded systems** – hidden inside other machines, such as televisions.

Desktop computer

The familiar desktop personal computer is built around a base unit, which may be designed as a tower or desktop unit. The base unit houses all the internal parts of the computer system, such as the processor, RAM and disk drives, and also has external ports which allow it to be connected to other devices.

A number of **peripheral devices**, such as a mouse, screen, keyboard and printer, are connected to the base unit. In an office, a desktop will normally be linked into a local network and, through that, to the Internet. In a home a desktop will usually be connected to a broadband Internet connection and may be linked into a home **Wi-Fi** system.

A mouse is the most common pointing device in a desktop system.

Laptop

The components that sit in the base unit of a desktop are hidden away in the slim body of a laptop. It usually does not have as many facilities and ports as a desktop, but additional devices can be plugged in.

Key terms

Personal computer – computer designed for a single user.

Peripheral device, or peripheral – any hardware component in a computer system other than the processor or main memory.

Wi-Fi – a wireless method of data transmission that uses radio signals in local area networks and for Internet access.

Most laptops provide a touchpad as a pointing device, as an alternative to a mouse.

Laptops can be plugged into a docking station on a desk. This has a full range of ports so that the laptop can be used with a full-size screen and keyboard, a mouse, a local network and a broadband Internet connection.

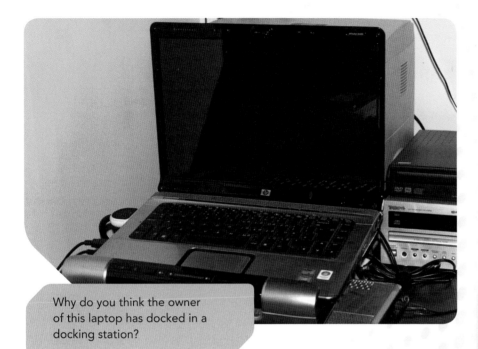

Why do you think the owner of this laptop has docked in a docking station?

Notebook and netbook

Notebooks and netbooks are small laptops. They are usually less powerful than standard laptops, but are cheaper and easier to carry around. All notebooks and netbooks have Wi-Fi interfaces and are designed to be used for web browsing and email.

Personal digital assistant (PDA)

A personal digital assistant (PDA) is a very small handheld device, also known as a palmtop computer. The small screen size limits its capabilities to some extent. Many use touchscreens for input.

Most PDAs provide Wi-Fi access for web and email use. Some are now combined with a mobile phone, and can use **3G** networks to access the Internet.

Most users link PDAs to a personal computer on a daily basis, so that they can **synchronise** data, such as emails and the entries in a calendar.

Key terms

3G – a fast wireless method of data transmission that uses radio signals and is commonly used for mobile phone networks.

Synchronise – update data held on two different systems so that they match each other.

What if you lost a Personal Digital Assistant (PDA) like this? Could you recover the information stored on it?

Smart phone

Smart phones are mobile phones that have many of the functions of a PDA. In addition they normally have a digital camera and the facility to play audio files.

Although most smart phones have a numerical keypad, some offer a full keyboard. Others use touchscreens which can function as keyboards when required.

Games console

Small handheld games consoles have a built-in screen and input buttons. Many have touchscreens.

Larger games consoles usually link to a television to provide a screen. Joysticks and other game controllers are built into the console. Additional devices with remote sensors can also be connected. These consoles usually offer Internet access so that videos can be downloaded and played as well as games.

Tablet

A tablet computer is a type of laptop with a large touchscreen, which replaces the keyboard. Some tablets are specifically designed for reading e-books, while others can be used for a wide range of purposes, such as inputting data and signatures into a form or drawing design sketches for a customer. An example of a tablet is shown on page 327 of *Unit 23: Computer graphics*.

Server

Any personal computer can be connected into a network. A small network of two or three computers in an office or home does not require any additional computers. But the task of managing a large network requires a powerful computer known as a **server.**

A server has several storage devices (hard disk drives) and a means of connection to all the computers in the network.

Embedded device

Computer systems are also hidden away inside many other kinds of machine. They all need a processor, plus some form of input and output, but these don't need to take the form of keyboard, mouse and screen. These hidden computer systems are known as embedded systems, and they can be found in music systems, cars, games consoles, phones and domestic appliances, such as DVD players and washing machines.

Key term

Server – a networked computer used to manage software and/or hardware resources for all users (clients).

1.2 Hardware components

You will probably be familiar with the main components that make up a personal computer system, as shown in Table 3.1.

Table 3.1: Components of a personal computer system.

Component	Description
Processor or CPU (central processing unit)	This carries out the instructions in a program and controls all the other components. The processor is normally stored on one chip.
Main memory	This holds all the data that is being used by a computer system while it is active. Main memory requires power to work, so it is emptied when the computer is switched off. Main memory is normally provided on one or more RAM (random access memory) semiconductor chips.
Storage devices	Unlike the main memory, these do not lose the data when they are switched off. All storage devices keep data on **storage media**, such as disks and tapes.
Storage media	These are the actual disks or chips that are used to store digital data. Storage media are placed in a disk drive, which then reads or writes data. Storage media include hard disks, CDs, DVDs and flash memory chips.
Input devices	These transfer data to the CPU. Examples include keyboard, mouse, touchscreen and microphone, as well as a variety of specialised devices like barcode readers and scanners.
Output devices	These receive data that is transferred to them from the CPU. Examples include screen, speakers and printer.
Network connection	This is a combination of software and hardware that enables a computer to be linked to a network or to the Internet.

Did you know?

'Media' is the plural for 'medium'.

The input, output and storage devices are often known as peripheral devices, or just peripherals.

The processor controls the whole computer system. None of the other components can do anything unless they are in communication with the processor. Any device that has to pass data to or from the processor can only do so under the control of the processor.

These devices all work at different speeds, and the processor has to ensure that they all receive signals at the right time and in the right order.

Processors

Most desktop and laptop computers have very similar processors installed. The market is dominated by Intel and AMD, who each produce several series of processors for different types of computer.

The speed of a processor is measured in hertz (Hz), where 1 hertz = 1 cycle per second. The cycle is the fetch–execute cycle, which is the process of copying one program instruction from main memory to the processor then carrying out the instruction. Today's processors can carry out many thousands of millions of cycles per second, so the processor speed is measured in gigahertz (GHz).

The speed of the processor is not the only measure of a processor's performance. Some processors with slower cycle times are constructed to handle instructions more efficiently, so may actually work through programs faster than processors with higher speeds.

Memory

RAM

Main memory is made up of **RAM** semiconductor chips, as shown below. RAM means 'random access memory', which indicates that all data stored in memory can be accessed equally quickly.

It is difficult to see what a RAM chip does just by looking at its casing. Can you guess how much data this one holds?

Key terms

RAM (random access memory) – electronic memory (a type of semiconductor chip) inside a computer. As it has no moving parts, it is very fast, working at the speed of electricity. RAM is used to hold programs and data when a computer is running, usually copying them from the hard disk. Anything in RAM is lost when the power goes, so data needs to be saved to hard disk or other storage before the computer is switched off.

Capacity – the amount of data that can be stored. Capacity is measured in bytes, kilobytes (KB), megabytes (MB) or gigabytes (GB). (See page 73.)

RAM chips require power to hold on to their data. When a computer is switched of, the data in RAM is erased.

The main property of RAM is its **capacity**, which is measured in megabytes (MB) or gigabytes (GB). This is the number of bytes that can be stored in memory while the computer system is switched on.

For a program to run, it must first be copied from storage to main memory. As it runs, it creates additional data files. For example, when you load word-processing software into memory, you create a document that contains further data. Documents and other data also have to be stored in main memory.

Several programs and their data files can be held in different parts of main memory at the same time. So the capacity of main memory determines how many programs can be loaded and how many documents you can create.

If you try to load too many programs, or work on too many documents at the same time, you will get a system message telling you that the system is running out of resources. If this happens frequently, you can add extra RAM to a system or replace existing RAM chips with larger ones.

Activity: Capacity of main memory

You can find out the capacity of the main memory in your system in Windows®. Go to the **Start** menu, select **Control Panel** then select **System**. The amount of RAM will be displayed in the **General** tab.

Cache

Cache is a small and very fast memory that is closely attached to the processor. It holds recently used data, so that if the processor needs to use that data again it can read it from the cache instead of having to read it from main memory.

Storage media

Data is held on storage media, such as disks and tapes. Main memory only holds the programs and other files that the computer is actually using, and only for as long as it needs them. So all programs and data files need to be stored on a medium so that they can be loaded into memory when needed.

Storage media might be:

- **Read-only memory (ROM)** – data is stored permanently and cannot be erased, and no new data can be added. The most common type is CD-ROMs.
- **Recordable (R)** – data is stored permanently and cannot be erased. But new data can be added until the media is full up.
- **Read and write (RW), or rewritable** – data can be erased and new data can be added.

The main types of storage media are shown in Table 3.2.

Table 3.2: Types of storage media.

Storage media	Characteristics	Technology used
Hard disk – magnetic read and write media	These can have a high capacity and are used as the main backing store for virtually all computer systems.	**Magnetic** – tiny spots on the surface are set up as individual magnets to represent the data.
CD-ROM – read-only optical disks	These can hold up to 700 MB.	**Optical** – tiny pits on the surface represent the data and these are detected by the light from a laser.
DVD (Digital Versatile Disks)	These are high-capacity CDs that can be used for a wide range of digital data, including video. They come in several formats: • plain DVD (i.e. ROM) • DVD-R • a number of competing rewritable formats (DVD-RW, DVD+RW, DVD-RAM).	
Flash memory	This is used in memory cards and USB flash drives (also known as memory sticks). These are rewritable.	**Flash** – this uses a memory chip, but it does not need power to hold on to the data.

Key term

Drive – another term for a storage device.

 Did you know?

Sometimes hard drives are referred to as internal drives because they are placed inside the base unit or main casing.

Storage devices

Storage devices are used to read data from and write data to storage media, such as disks. They are normally known as **drives**. Some drives are designed so that the storage media cannot be removed, while others are removable.

Most drives work with removable media, such as CDs, DVDs of all types and flash memory, which can be used to transfer data from one computer system to another. New software is often presented on a removable medium, so that users can install it on their own system.

DVD drives can read CD-ROMs as well as DVDs, so CD drives are uncommon today.

The disks used in hard disk drives (HDDs) are fixed media and cannot usually be removed, though removable ones are available that can be locked away for security.

Activity: Finding out the capacity of storage media

You can discover the capacity of the storage media on a computer system by going to the **Start** menu and opening **My Computer**. You will see a list of all the drives. Right-click on each in turn and select **Properties**. In Figure 3.1 the hard disk in Drive C has a capacity of 162 GB, and 47.7 GB of this has been used.

Input devices

There are many input devices that can be used with a personal computer, as shown in Table 3.3.

Table 3.3: Input devices used with a personal computer.

Input device	Description
Mouse	Pointing device that controls a pointer on the screen. The standard mouse has two buttons, which send instructions to the operating system. A further button or fingertip wheel is sometimes added to carry out extra actions.
Keyboard	The standard keyboard uses the QWERTY key layout and includes a numeric keypad, some control keys (such as Insert, Page Up and the arrow keys) and programmable function keys (F1, F2, etc.). Most mobile phones use a numerical keyboard with characters assigned to each key.
Touchscreen	Tablets, PDAs and some mobile phones have screens that react to touch by a stylus or finger. These can be used to perform tasks that would otherwise be done by the mouse or keyboard.
Touchpad	Most laptops provide a touchpad as a pointing device.
Graphics tablet	This is a flat surface that you can 'draw' on with a stylus. It can be used to interact with the operating system, or in applications to draw images.
Microphone	A microphone linked to a personal computer can capture sounds for Internet voice conversations or for recording purposes.
Webcam	A web camera can be linked to a personal computer to record videos or to send live images during Internet conversations.
Scanner	A scanner 'reads' paper documents and turns them into electronic files, usually saved as images. It can also scan in text and then optical character recognition (OCR) software recognises the letters and turns the text into a word-processed document.
Game controller	Most games consoles provide a game pad with several buttons and a control stick. Other controllers include motion sensors, such as the Nintendo® Wii Remote™, steering wheels for driving games, light guns for shooting games, balance boards and floor pads.

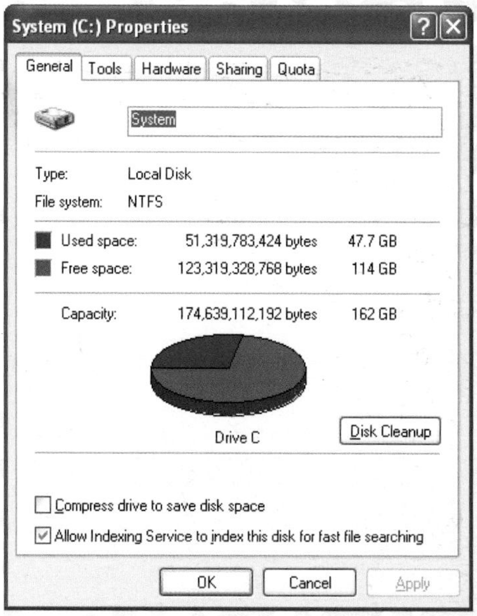

Figure 3.1: Capacity of a hard disk.

Output devices

Printers

The most common types of printer used today are inkjet and laser printers.

- **Inkjet printers** — squeeze tiny bubbles of ink onto the paper to form the characters and images. The quality of the output is measured in dots per inch – the more dots per inch the better the picture quality, although they take longer to print.

- **Laser printers** — use the same technology as photocopiers. The laser places an electrostatic charge on a drum to match the image. Toner powder is attracted to the charged areas on the drum, and the image is printed when the paper is pressed against the drum and briefly heated.

Laser printers produce high-quality output but cost more than inkjet printers. Colour laser printers are considerably more expensive than black laser printers. Laser printers are generally faster than inkjet printers.

Monitors

The main output device for a computer system is the monitor, or screen. Monitors are measured in two ways:

- **size** – the diagonal length of the display area
- **resolution** – the number of pixels (colour dots) that it can display horizontally and vertically.

Generally speaking, larger screens give higher resolution and cost more.

There are two main types of screen (shown below):

- **CRT (Cathode Ray Tube) monitor** – the traditional type of monitor that is still found on older desktop systems
- **LCD (Liquid Crystal Display) screen** – this gives a completely flat screen and is now commonly used for desktops, as well as laptops and handheld systems.

LCD screens use far less power than CRT screen, but they do need back lighting. The display cannot be easily seen from an angle.

Why do you think LCD screens (left) have largely replaced CRT monitors (right)?

Speakers

Almost all personal computer systems have a small speaker. The sound quality is not high, so it is usually possible to attach a pair of separate speakers or a headset.

Network connectivity

We are dependent on computer networks for most of our communications. Personal computers may be linked into **local area networks**. Mobile phones depend on good connections to mobile phone networks. The Internet itself is a vast network of networks.

Networks use a number of different methods to send data from one computer or device to another. For example, if you send an email to someone living on the other side of the world, your message may be transmitted by computer cables, telephone cables, microwave signals and radio signals before reaching its destination.

These methods of sending data fall into two groups: those that use wires and those that do not.

- **Wired connections** — are used for local area networks, where the computers are physically linked to each other. A network interface card (NIC) must be fitted to a personal computer before it can be connected through wires to a local area network. The most common type of NIC is an Ethernet card.
- **Wireless connections** — transfer data without the use of cables or wires. Generally, wireless connections are not as fast or as reliable as cables but they can be very convenient. They are an increasingly popular technology for small networks because the computers, especially laptops, can be moved around while remaining connected to the network.

(For more on Network connections see *Unit 10: Setting up an IT network*, pages 175–205).

Wireless networks normally use radio transmissions:

- **Wi-Fi** – a wireless radio technology that can be used to send data between devices and computers. You can build a small network in an office or at home using Wi-Fi instead of cables. Some mobile phones can use Wi-Fi technology to access the Internet.
- **Bluetooth** – a radio technology that is similar to Wi-Fi but only works over short distances and is slower. It is mainly used to send data between two devices such as a mobile phone and headset, or between a digital camera and laptop.
- **3G** (3rd Generation) – another radio technology that is used by mobile phone networks. It can carry more data than the older mobile phone systems.

Key terms

Local area network – computers and other devices linked together into a network within a building.

Bluetooth – a wireless method of data transmission that uses radio signals to send data between devices over short distances.

Activity: Finding out about current network connections

Network connections are being improved all the time – indeed, new methods may be available by the time you read this.

Find out whether other types of network connection are now being used in addition to the ones listed above.

If you have a laptop you can sometimes link into a Wi-Fi network while you are out and about. Many Wi-Fi networks are private and can be protected by passwords. But there are also public Wi-Fi networks which may be provided by a commercial organisation like a hotel or coffee shop, or by the government.

Costs

The costs of complete personal computers and of individual peripherals tend to come down over time, but these devices are then replaced by new ones with higher specifications. Try to keep in touch with the current prices by reading magazines, visiting computer shops or searching on the Internet. Remember to consider the price of media, both for storage (for example disks) and for printing (paper). When comparing the prices of printers, it is important to remember the cost of the ink cartridges or toners and to calculate how often these will have to be replaced.

Activity: Current costs

Use computer magazines and the Internet to find out the current costs of a range of devices that you might want to add to the personal computer that you use.

1.3 Software components

Software is a general term used for programs. Hardware refers to the physical components of a computer system, but on its own it can do nothing. Software is needed to control the hardware and to turn it into a useful machine.

Software falls into two categories.

- **Systems software** — controls a computer system
- **Applications software** — carries out specific tasks for an organisation or for an individual user.

Systems software must be in place on a computer system before applications software can be used.

Key term

Systems software – software that controls the computer system.

Systems software

Systems software includes the **operating system**, together with add-on programs known as **software utilities**. A user working with applications software, such as a spreadsheet, is not usually aware of the systems software. However, the IT professionals in an organisation, such as systems administrators, spend most of their time working directly with the systems software.

The processor controls how the computer system uses resources such as memory, input devices, output devices and storage devices. These can be controlled only through the instructions in the systems software.

Systems software often works in the background while a user is working with applications software. For example, when you are word processing a document and you send it to the printer, you are not aware of all the processes that the systems software has to go through to make it happen. The applications software works directly with the systems software, so that the user does not have to worry about it.

Activity: Check out your operating system

If you are running Windows® on your desktop computer at home, you can look at the **Windows directory** on the **C: drive**. In it you will find a very large number of programs, which together control the computer system.

Key terms

Operating system – the essential core of the systems software that controls the processor and its communications with memory and with input, output and storage devices.

Software utilities – extra systems software programs that work with the operating system.

Tools – small useful programs or modules.

Software utilities

A number of programs support the operating system and these are known as software utilities or system **tools**.

Some of the software utilities on your system can be found in Windows® by going to the **Start** menu, selecting **All Programs** then **Accessories** then **System Tools** (see Figure 3.2). You will meet some of these tools later in this unit.

Figure 3.2: Software utilities in the Systems Tools folder.

Applications software

A computer system can do nothing at all without systems software. But it must also have applications software, for example a hospital patient records system, a desktop publishing package, an arcade game or an Internet browser.

Applications software can be used for many purposes. Here are a few general categories that might be used in an organisation:

- carry out business **transactions**
- create business documents such as letters and reports
- handle communications such as access to the Internet and internal email
- manage finances
- present information to an audience, either in printed or electronic form
- create and manipulate images
- manage projects
- design products.

Applications software is also used outside the business environment for many purposes, such as for playing games, recording music, researching your family tree and a host of other leisure pursuits.

Bespoke software

Sometimes an organisation will have applications software developed specifically to meet its own needs. This is known as bespoke software. For example, the system used by air traffic controllers is a special, one-off bespoke system.

In many cases an organisation will find that one of the standard office applications software meets their needs perfectly well. For example, virtually everyone uses one of the standard word-processing packages, so it would be very surprising if an organisation developed its own word-processing software.

1.4 Security

As a user you need to be aware of a number of threats that could damage your computer system or put you at risk in some way.

Malware

The term 'malware' is short for malicious software. This is a computer program that finds its way into a personal computer and causes damage. Creating and releasing malware is treated as a criminal activity in many countries. Malware includes computer viruses, spyware, worms and Trojan horses.

> ## Key term
>
> **Transaction** – a single action such as placing an order, making a phone call, making a booking or withdrawing cash.

Viruses

Computer **viruses** can cause a lot of damage to software by deleting and altering programs and data. They can be spread from one computer to another through a network system, or on portable media such as flash drives.

Most viruses are carried on email attachments. These can then infect the computer system by deleting or altering files. Many viruses can also automatically send out new emails with the virus attached, to any addresses in the email address book. Since the process is automatic, viruses can spread around the world very rapidly.

Spyware

Spyware is another kind of program that is installed on a computer without the user being aware of it. This can happen when free software is downloaded from a website. Spyware monitors the way in which the computer is being used and scans files for passwords and other confidential data. This information is then transmitted back to the person who created the spyware.

As well as the security dangers, spyware can take up memory and can slow down a computer.

Worms and Trojan horses

A worm is a malicious program that has a similar effect to a virus, but it does not spread through emails and attachments. Instead it works its way round a computer network.

A Trojan horse is a computer program that the user installs because it looks useful. But once in place it allows a hacker to gain unauthorised access to the computer. This means that significant information, such as credit card details or company data, can be stolen.

Phishing

'Phishing' is a type of fraud. You may have received an official-looking email that asks you to click on a link to a bank website to confirm your details. If it is the name of the bank where you have an account, you may be tempted to log in with your user name and password. But the email and website will be a fake. If you enter your login details the criminals behind it will be able to log in to your real account and take money from it.

Spam

Spam is the general term for unwanted online messages, including emails, comments on blogs or instant messaging, or text messages. Spam emails are often referred to as junk emails.

Many spam messages promote websites, some of which are very dubious. It is thought that around 80 per cent of all emails in the world are spam, which wastes much of the capacity of the Internet communications channels. They also increase the time to download emails and take up space on a personal computer.

Key term

Virus – a small computer program that can cause damage to a computer system. Viruses are usually spread by being attached to programs or documents, which are then distributed on storage media or by email.

(i) Did you know?

Spyware should not be confused with cookies, which are very small data files. Cookies are usually harmless and they actually speed up access to websites as they can remember passwords and preferences.

(i) Did you know?

Banks never send emails asking you to log in via a link in an email, so treat any such emails with suspicion.

1.5 Data flow

Block diagrams

A computer system can be illustrated by a simple diagram, as shown in Figure 3.3.

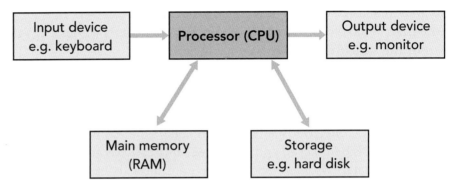

Figure 3.3: A block diagram of a computer system.

This diagram shows that the processor is at the centre of all the data flows in a computer system.

- Programs and other files are stored on the hard disk storage.
- The processor loads up a software application by copying it from the hard disk into main memory.
- New data is entered into the processor via input devices.
- The processor stores the data in main memory.
- The processor sends data to output devices.
- The processor saves data to the hard disk storage when instructed to do so.

Flow diagrams

Although a block diagram is a good way to understand how data moves around the system, we will look a little more closely at how the processor manages all those data flows.

In old computers, each peripheral device would be connected separately to the processor. Today, data moves through all the parts of a computer system along connections known as buses.

A bus carries data between lots of different devices at the same time. It is best to think of a bus as a motorway which many vehicles can drive along simultaneously – it is not one of the vehicles!

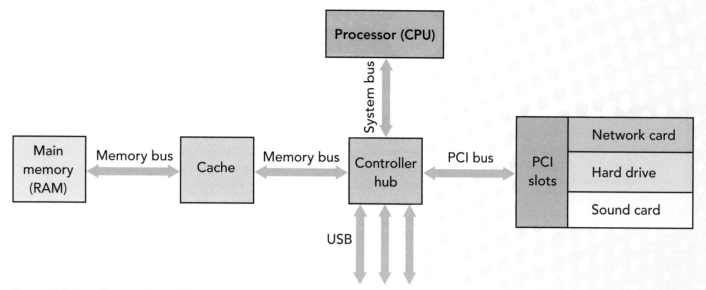

Figure 3.4: Data flowing through buses.

A bus carries data from input devices as well as output devices, and also from storage drives which act as both input and output devices. Figure 3.4 is a flow diagram that shows how the buses work with the processor.

The CPU is connected directly to a controller hub through the **system bus**. You can think of the controller hub as a big motorway interchange, where the data transfers from one bus to another. Other buses are then connected into the system through the hub.

- **Memory bus** – carries data to and from RAM and cache memory.
- **PCI (Peripheral Component Interconnect) bus** – a standard way of connecting peripherals to a computer. It carries data to and from some PCI slots. Various devices, such as a network card, can be slotted into the PCI slots.
- **USB (Universal Serial Bus)** – a newer standard which allows many types of peripherals to be 'daisy-chained' together on one bus – up to 127 devices can be linked on one bus. Many devices that were previously connected through the PCI bus now use USB connections.
- **Other buses** can be added to the hub. For example, later in this unit (page 80) you will learn about Firewire, and a Firewire bus can also be connected to the hub.

Icons

You will sometimes see diagrams similar to Figures 3.3 and 3.4 in which the simple rectangles are replaced with little drawings (icons) of devices. This helps to make the diagrams more understandable.

BTEC **Assessment activity 3.1** **P1 P2 P3 M1**

You have started work as a trainee ICT support technician for TLA Technical Support. You and a colleague will be visiting local businesses and organisations to advise them about ICT and fix any problems they have.

One of the businesses that you will be working with is a small garden design company called Garden of Dreams. Siân is the garden designer. She uses specialist software to create 3D drawings of her designs so that she can see what they look like from all angles. She also prints these off to give to her customers.

Although Siân is very familiar with the garden design software, she thinks she could be using computers better for other aspects of the business, such as keeping accounts, planning her jobs and producing invoices for her customers. Siân admits that she does not know much about computers and she would like you to explain the basic facts to her. She has asked you these questions:

1. Please tell me about all the different types of computer that are available, and what they are used for. **P2**

2. What are the main components that make up computer systems? **P1**

3. How do these components work together? Please show me in a diagram. **P3**

4. How can computers be linked into a network? **M1**

Grading tips

- For question 1, don't forget that mobile phones and PDAs are also computers.

- For question 2, give examples of the kinds of devices used in different types of computer system.

- For question 3, use a diagram to show how data flows around a computer system. Make sure you describe what is going on in the diagram.

- For question 4, describe the different types of network connections that are available and explain when each might be used.

Just checking

1. What are the differences between a personal computer and a server?
2. What is an embedded system? Give examples.
3. What are storage devices and storage media?
4. What are RAM chips used for?
5. Explain the differences between ROM, R and RW media.
6. Why are some storage disks fixed and others removable?
7. What is the difference between the size and resolution when referring to monitors?
8. Why might you need to install a network interface card?
9. What kind of damage can be done by malware?

2. Know the different uses of computer systems

2.1 Components

A computer system is a combination of hardware components, systems software and applications software, and there are many thousands of possible combinations. This is what makes a computer system so different from any other machine. By putting together your choice of components, you can create a machine for carrying out a specific task, such as playing a particular game or posting a video.

In this section we will be examining a few of the very many ways in which components can be put together to suit the needs of users and the jobs they want to do.

2.2 Users

Computer users fall into two broad categories:

1. **home or business users** — utilise computers and data communications as tools within their normal work

2. **ICT professionals** — include administrators who work with operating systems and developers who create software.

In this section we will be concentrating on the needs of home and business users. They can use ICT successfully only because of the many ICT professionals who have developed the hardware and software, who manage the data and networks and who help them to use it.

2.3 User requirements

You need to know how to select a combination of hardware and software to meet the particular needs of an individual user. Before you begin you should ask these questions about your user.

- What tasks will the user be doing on the computer system?
- Will the user be doing these tasks at home or at work?
- What level of ICT skills does the user already have?
- Which software is the user familiar with?
- Does the user have any particular needs or requirements, for example disabilities?
- What is the maximum cost?

The answers to these questions should allow you to identify the minimum specification for a computer system.

In practice it's always a good idea to go beyond the minimum specification, because as new software and hardware come on to the market, users don't want to find that they cannot use them. Also, once users have started using a system they normally discover its capabilities and want to do new tasks with it.

Business needs

Whenever an employee uses applications software, they are working as a user. Today we do not expect users to have any technical skills in managing their computer systems. Instead they should be able to concentrate on their business tasks, using a computer as a tool.

Business users work with applications software in order to carry out the business of the organisation. These tasks could include communicating with others through the Internet, creating documents, spreadsheets and presentations, creating and editing images, interacting with a database and working with specialist software related to their work.

All business users need to have basic ICT skills. But most business users have some training in specific software applications and can become very proficient in using them.

Many business functions can be carried out using standard office applications software, such as a word processor, spreadsheet, database management system, Internet browser, email client and calendar management.

Specialist business software could include:

*   accounting software, to manage accounts and budgets
*   graphical design software, to design images and manipulate photos for business documents
*   desktop publishing software, to design and print leaflets, advertisements and notices, etc.

Home use

Personal computers in the home are used for many purposes, for example learning, entertainment, communication, managing voluntary organisations, etc. Most provide basic office applications software, such as a word processor, spreadsheet and Internet browser. In addition, many home users play computer games, watch videos, download music and use social networking sites through their computers. Fast Internet connectivity is essential for many of these activities.

Games consoles are essentially computers for playing games, but they increasingly offer Internet access, allowing the user to use the Web and webmail.

Other needs

The IT needs of business users and home users largely depend on what they want to use their computers for. But there are a few other things to consider:

*   Many home and business users prefer portable systems, so they can take their computers with them to meetings and events and while travelling. A laptop, notebook or netbook may suit them best.
*   Many people who use PDAs and mobile phones also have a laptop or desktop system. These users will want to synchronise the two systems at regular intervals so they carry the same data.

- Costs are an important consideration, especially for home users. Manufacturers try to produce systems particularly for home use at a lower price. These tend to be less powerful than business systems, and often have more limited applications software.

Users with special needs

Some users have special needs which can be met through adaptations to software plus specialist hardware devices. A couple of examples are given below.

- **Voice control** – users who cannot manipulate a mouse because of visual impairment or other disabilities can use voice commands to control the system. Voice-controlled systems may become used more widely in the future for embedded systems, so that you could, for example, talk to your washing machine!

- **Alternative input devices** – these can be used according to the type of disability. For example, an enlarged keyboard and mouse, graphics tablet, large touchpad or joystick could help someone with poor hand control. A foot-operated mouse is available for someone with no hand control. Mouth-controlled input devices can be built for people with severe physical impairment.

Systems software and standard applications software also offer accessibility features which can make it easier for people to use them, depending on their disability.

Activity: Accessibility features

Windows® offers a number of tools to make it easier for users with special needs.

- From the **Start** menu, select **All Programs** then **Accessories** then **Accessibility**. Find out what each tool does.

- Check the browsers on desktop computers and portable devices and find out how to zoom in and out, and whether you can change font size and colours.

- Finally, which applications that you use offer to correct or predict spellings?

2.4 Performance requirements

Performance is a way of describing how well a device in a computer system does its job. This often relates to its capacity or the speed at which it works.

Storage capacity

The capacity of memory is measured in bytes (B), kilobytes (KB), megabytes (MB) or gigabytes (GB). 1 KB is approximately one thousand bytes, 1 MB is approximately one million bytes, and 1 GB is approximately one thousand million bytes. Generally speaking, one byte can store a single keyboard character.

Table 3.4 shows the standard ways of measuring metric units.

Table 3.4: Metric units.

Metric units		Name	Abbreviation
	1,000	kilo	k
	1,000,000	mega	M
	1,000,000,000	giga	G
	1,000,000,000,000	tera	T

Standard metric units are measured in thousands, for example:
1000 m = 1 km and 1000 watts = 1 kilowatt. But when it comes to digital data, bytes are never counted in thousands. They are always counted in groups of 1024 bytes. This is because of the way they are physically stored and accessed. Powers of 2 feature very heavily in computer storage and $1024 = 2^{10}$.

1024 is close to 1000, so the accepted convention is 1024 bits = 1 kilobyte (abbreviated to 1 KB or 1 KByte).

Table 3.5: Digital units.

Metric unit		Name	Abbreviation	Digital unit
	1,000	kilo	k (metric) K (digital)	1,024
	1,000,000	mega	M	1,048,576 = 1,024 × 1,024
	1,000,000,000	giga	G	1,073,741,824 = 1,024 × 1,024 × 1,024
	1,000,000,000,000	tera	T	1,099,511,627,776 = 1,024 × 1,024 × 1,024 × 1,024

For everyday purposes you can think of 1 MB as 1 million bytes, and 1 GB as 1 thousand million bytes.

Data transmission speed

Another performance factor is the speed at which data can be transferred from a drive to the processor.

It is useful to compare the speeds of different types of drive, but this is not as easy as it sounds because of the different technologies used. The first DVD drives that were produced read the data at 1.35 MB per second. Today the speed is given as a multiple of the original speed. So, for example, a DVD drive with a speed of 16x reads data 16 times faster than 1.35 MB per second, i.e. at 21.6 MB per second. (This speed refers to reading data from the DVD. Writing to a DVD is a slower process.)

The data transmission speeds for flash drives are also measured in MB per second. Again, this speed refers to reading data from the flash drive, rather than writing data, which takes longer.

Processor speed and type

As we saw on pages 73–74, the speed of a processor is measured in hertz (Hz), where 1 hertz = 1 cycle per second. This is usually given in GHz, where 1 GHz is a thousand million cycles.

Battery life

When using a portable system away from a power supply, the user is dependent on the battery. Most users want to be able to use the battery for as long as possible before having to recharge it.

The life of a battery is measured in watt hours (WHr). If a battery has a life of 24 WHr, and a portable device uses 1 watt per hour, then it will last for 24 hours before needing to be recharged.

A netbook typically uses 30 watts per hour, so a 24 WHr battery will last for less than an hour.

Technical specifications

A **technical specification** is a document that gives the performance of a device, such as capacity and speed. When you purchase a complete computer system, the technical specification will list the performance characteristics of each of the components.

Table 3.6 shows the typical technical specifications for computer systems at the time of writing (2010).

Table 3.6: Technical specifications for computers and memory.

Device	Capacity	Other factors
Processor		Processor speed = 2 to 4 GHz
RAM	2 GB to 96 GB	
Cache	1 MB to 12 MB	
Hard disk drive	160 GB to 2 TB	
DVD/CD drive	4.7 GB to 17 GB	Data transfer speed = 16x to 24x, equivalent to 21.6 to 32.4 MB/sec
USB flash drive	1 GB to 256 GB	Data transfer speed = 15 to 30 MB/sec
Battery		Battery life = 24 to 90 WHr

Did you know?

Over time, the period between recharging gets less, and most users should consider purchasing a new battery after 18 to 24 months.

Key term

Technical specification – the list of the properties of a device in a computer system. It usually refers to the capacity and performance of the device.

Activity: Current specifications

Use computer magazines and the websites of computer retailers to find out the current capacity and speed of the devices listed in Table 3.6.

Activity: Upgrading a computer

If you want a bit of a challenge, have a look at the computer owned by a friend. Find out what they want to use the computer for and whether their current system meets their needs. Produce a short report for them in which you recommend some upgrades that would improve the performance of the system at the lowest cost.

PLTS

By specifying suitable components to meet user requirements and explaining your choices, you will show that you are an **independent enquirer**.

By inviting feedback from users and dealing positively with praise, setbacks and criticism, you will show that you are a **reflective learner**.

Functional skills

Presenting your proposals and obtaining feedback could provide evidence for your functional **English** skills in speaking and listening.

BTEC Assessment activity 3.2

For this activity you can either work on a real case study given to you by your tutor or you can continue to work on the Garden of Dreams scenario from Assessment activity 3.1 (page 70).

1. You are going to design a new computer system for the user.
2. Give a list of suitable hardware and software that would meet the user's needs. **P4**
3. Explain your choice of components, stating how they would be right for the user. **M2**
4. Present your proposals and ask for some feedback. Suggest alternative set-ups based on the feedback you receive. **D1**

(If you are working on the Garden of Dreams scenario, then you will have to ask your tutor or someone else to play the role of Siân for you and give you feedback.)

Grading tips

- For question 1, the hardware should include the basic computer system plus any additional peripherals that you think would be valuable for the user. The software should cover both systems and applications software plus any relevant utilities.

- For question 2, justify your choice for each item you listed in question 1. You might like to present the answers to questions 1 and 2 together in one table.

- For question 3, it is essential that you get some feedback from a potential user. It would be helpful if this was written feedback, but if not then you should record the user's comments carefully. Take on board the feedback you have received and think of an alternative set up that would meet the user's needs even better.

Just checking

1. Explain why business computer users may have different requirements from home users.
2. Give two reasons why a portable computer system could be useful to someone at work.
3. Describe two devices that might be used by a visually impaired computer user.
4. List three changes that could be made to a computer system to improve its performance.

3. Be able to connect computer hardware

3.1 Health and safety

If you are going to set up a computer system for a user, you need to be able to do this safely. Health and safety policies will have been adopted for employees at your centre. Many of these are designed to reduce the risk of injury. Although strictly speaking they do not apply to learners, nevertheless you should always adopt good health and safety measures when carrying out practical activities as part of your studies.

For information about electrical hazards, manual handling and other health and safety risks involving IT equipment, see *Unit 2: Working in the IT industry*, pages 37–38.

Health and safety for users

If users cannot reach the computer equipment easily, or are uncomfortable, they will not be as productive as they could be. When you set up a computer system for a user you should be aware of their safety needs.

- Work surfaces should be large enough for the tasks to be done, clear of obstructions, and have a matt surface. It should be possible to raise or lower the work surface to suit the user. There should be enough space for a mouse mat.

- Screens should have brightness controls and be capable of tilt and swivel. They should be positioned at 90 degrees to a window to avoid glare and reflections. A document holder can be attached to a screen to hold documents at eye level.

- For desktop computers, keyboards should be movable and the angle of the slope should be adjustable. A wrist support should be built into the keyboard or provided separately. The pressure required to depress the keys should be checked – too much pressure will make the user's hands ache, but too little pressure will make their fingers slip off the keys.

- Cabling should be ducted or fixed in place so that it cannot cause an accident.

Using computers for a long time can cause a number of problems including repetitive strain injury (RSI), eyestrain and general aches and pains. (See also *Unit 2: Working in the IT industry*, page 38).

3.2 Working practices

Working procedures

There are a few simple procedures that you should follow when working on computer hardware.

- As a learner or trainee you should always be supervised when carrying out practical tasks. As a trained employee you may be left unsupervised for periods of time, but you should only do what you have been instructed to do.

- Carefully follow the instructions given by your supervisor or tutor. This is to protect you. If anything goes wrong with the task, but you have followed instructions, then you will not be held to blame.

- Wear suitable clothing. Make sure that you do not have any trailing fabric or jewellery that could become tangled in the equipment.

- Make sure that you have been shown how to use any tools you are given. If in doubt, ask for advice.

- Static electricity can cause serious damage to electronic components, even if you do not feel a static shock while handling them. The only safe way to avoid the problem is to switch off and disconnect all devices that you are working on. (For more information on how to protect against electrostatic discharge, see *Unit 7: Installing computer hardware*, page 11.)

- Thoroughly test the system before handing it over to another user.

Assess and minimise risks

All organisations should identify someone with responsibility for health and safety. It is the duty of all employers to assess the risks to their employees and to minimise those risks.

A risk assessment includes the following steps:

- identify the hazards
- decide who might be harmed and how
- evaluate the risks arising from the hazards and decide whether the existing precautions are sufficient or whether more needs to be done
- record the findings
- review your assessment from time to time.

After the risks have been assessed the employer should take steps to minimise risks – that is, to make the chance of an accident occurring as low as possible. It is usually impossible to remove risks entirely.

When you carry out a task with equipment, whether as a learner or an employee, you too should assess any risks before you start and try to minimise them. To do this you should collect all the components and tools that you need then ask yourself:

- Could I accidentally damage the hardware? If so, how can I prevent damage occurring?
- Could I accidentally hurt myself? If so, what should I do to keep myself safe?

Communicating progress and outcomes

All employees have to keep logsheets of any tasks that they undertake, and you should do the same when learning new skills. Normally an employee would be given a standard logsheet to complete for every job that they do. You may not have such a form but you should keep a record of the date, time started, time finished, the serial number of the computer, the tasks you carried out and any testing you did. Finally you should note whether the equipment now functions as intended.

Activity: Health and safety policies

Find out if there are any health and safety policies at your place of study that apply to you as a learner. If you have a job, find out who the Health and Safety Officer is.

3.3 Hardware connections

Connecting peripheral devices

The various devices that make up a personal computer system have to be connected to each other. Computers themselves can then be connected into networks.

These connections use various types of data transfer. Whatever the method, each consists of the following:

- **a method of transferring the electronic data** – this could be through a cable made of copper or optical fibres. Alternatively the method could use radio, infrared or microwave signals.

- **an interface** – this consists of a **port**, which is a socket where cables can be plugged in or signals picked up, plus built-in software that controls it.

There are a number of types of connection, including:

- **serial connections** — use cables that transfer binary patterns in a steady stream from one component to another.

- **parallel connections** — transfer many bits at the same time along a set of parallel wires. In the past, a parallel connection was often used to connect a printer to the CPU.

Several years ago, each device in a computer system had its own direct connection to the processor. Today it is more common for several devices to be linked together in a 'daisy chain', sharing a single port. Examples include:

- **USB** (Universal Serial Bus) — is a widely used interface that can be used with most peripherals, especially the slower ones. USB cables also carry a power supply, which means that small peripherals, such as speakers, do not need a separate power cable.

- **Firewire** (also known as IEEE 1394) is an interface that uses serial connections. It was originally developed for Apple computers but can now be used on others as well.

Appropriate connections

There is a growing use of wireless connections using the Wi-Fi or Bluetooth protocols (see page 63) to link devices, such as a mouse and keyboard, to a personal computer. Many small devices have been developed that take advantage of easy USB connectivity. These include gadgets such as fans, paper shredders, lights and staplers.

Ethernet connections are used to create local area networks of computers. They commonly use a type of serial cable referred to as Cat5 or Cat 5e. Each of the devices in the network is fitted with a Network Interface Card (NIC). Some peripheral devices, such as printers, can be linked directly into the network through an Ethernet connection.

A list of devices with common connections is shown in Table 3.7.

Table 3.7: Typical computer connections.

Device	Type of connection
Printer	USB, Firewire or Wi-Fi Some old printers still use parallel connections. Printers in a local network may use an Ethernet connection.
Speakers	Standard audio ports
Digital camera	USB or Firewire
Scanner	USB or Firewire
Web cam	USB or Firewire
Bar code reader	USB, Firewire, Bluetooth or serial RS232
Graphics tablet	USB, Firewire, Bluetooth or serial RS232
USB devices	USB

3.4 Testing

When you have connected a device to a personal computer you normally have to run some software to initiate it, for example to install a printer driver on the system and check that the communications are working satisfactorily. At this stage you should test the peripheral thoroughly to make sure that it is functioning correctly.

When you test something you should:

- Check that it works correctly under normal circumstances. For example, send a document to a printer that you have just connected.
- Check that it works correctly under abnormal circumstances. For example, find out what happens if several users try to send documents to the printer at the same time.
- Try to find a situation in which it will not work correctly. For example, you know that a printer will not work if the power supply fails while it is part-way through printing a document, but you could test to see what happens when the power is returned.

BTEC Assessment activity 3.3 **P5** **M3**

This is a practical activity. You will be connecting peripherals to meet the needs of a user. This could be based on the Garden of Dreams case study, or on a scenario provided by your tutor.

1. Connect at least two peripherals to a personal computer. Test the peripherals to make sure that they work properly once connected. You should provide evidence of your work in logsheets, observation records and/or videos. **P5**

2. Write a report explaining the good working practices and the health and safety procedures that you should follow when connecting hardware devices. Show that you carried out your tasks safely. **M3**

Grading tips

- For task 1, follow the safety instructions given by your tutor. You should be supervised at all times.
- For task 2, you need to show that you have followed health and safety procedures and have not taken any shortcuts.

PLTS

By following instructions and working safely, you will show that you are a **team worker**.

Functional skills

Writing a report explaining the good working practices and the health and safety procedures could provide evidence for your functional **English** skills in writing.

Just checking

1. Describe three hazards that could cause injury to someone working with computers.
2. What is USB and what is it used for?
3. Describe one way in which a digital camera can be connected to a personal computer system.
4. Why should you test any connections that you set up?

4. Be able to configure computer software

4.1 Requirements

As we saw on pages 71–73, the needs of users vary depending on the tasks they want to carry out on the computer. You need to choose hardware and software to meet those needs. Once the hardware and software have been installed, there are still some changes that you can make to ensure the systems are right for the users.

Most software can be **configured** to suit an individual user, for example by changing the appearance of the user interface or the way in which it operates. Configuration allows users to personalise the software so that it matches their own way of working. The configuration choices the user makes are often known as preferences.

Both systems software and applications software can be configured. In Windows®, the information about the user's preferences is stored in the registry, which is a database accessed by the operating system.

Key term

Configure – to make changes to a software application to suit a particular user or task.

Tasks

Most users at home and in the office want to use standard office applications, such as word processing. Many also want to use some non-standard applications, such as:

- uploading and managing photos
- photo editing for resizing, cropping and manipulating photos
- video editing for selecting sections of a video and adding sound and captions
- media playback for listening to sound files (especially music) and watching videos.

4.2 Systems software

Operating systems

The core of the systems software is the operating system. You will probably be familiar with a version of Microsoft® Windows®, which is widely used on desktop computers.

Another operating system that you may also have heard of is the Mac OS series. More complex operating systems are used for network systems, such as Windows® Server™, Mac OS Server, Unix® and Linux.

The operating system is actually a collection of programs, each of which carries out a specific task. Extra programs can often be added to the main operating system. For example, when a new printer is added to a system, the relevant printer driver has to be installed to enable the operating system to communicate with the device.

The operating system carries out these tasks as needed:

- allows the user to select and launch programs
- launches some programs automatically
- allocates space in memory to programs
- loads programs by transferring them from storage into main memory
- runs programs by transferring instructions one at a time from memory to the processor then executing them
- manages the backing store by creating, opening, moving, deleting and renaming files
- manages input and output devices by controlling the data that flows between them and the processor
- allows the user to configure the system – that is, to make changes to the way in which the operating system works.

The operating system is designed to make the computer system as efficient as possible.

Systems software tools

Systems software tools allow the system administrator to watch what the operating system is doing and make changes to the way it works. A user who is not a systems administrator is also able to make certain changes to the way the operating system functions.

To make changes to the system, go to the **Start** menu and select **Control Panel** (see Figure 3.5). You will not be able to change the core functions of the operating system. However, you can modify aspects of the display, add or remove fonts, manage folders, install new software, install new hardware drivers and change how the mouse responds, etc.

From the Control Panel you can also carry out the following tasks, and many more:

- add or remove programs
- install printers
- check the performance of the system
- set up network connections (this is covered in the next section)
- drive formatting.

The operating systems for mobile phones and PDAs can often be configured by the user as well.

Drive formatting

Drive formatting can only be carried out by an administrator. Your system will normally have a C drive (that is, hard disk) where all the programs, data and your documents are stored. If your system has more than one drive, then probably one hard disk has been partitioned into two virtual drives. (Partitions behave like separate drives but are physically on the same hard disk.)

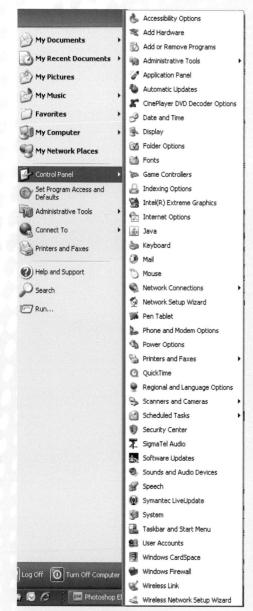

Figure 3.5: The Control Panel on Microsoft® Windows®.

You can change the size of the partitions and you can also format a partition. But be warned: when you format a partition or drive you destroy all the data on it. Formatting should only be done in very specific circumstances where the data has been fully backed up. You are warned not to do it experimentally.

Diagnostic tools

There are a number of system software tools that allow you to check the performance of the system and identify any problems. You will find some of these under **Administrative Tools** in the **Control Panel**. The most important one is **Performance**, which shows you how fast data is being transferred between the processor and main memory, and between the processor and hard disks.

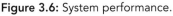

How to... Check the performance of the system

- Click on **Start** then **Control Panel** then **Administrative Tools** then **Performance**.

- Allow the tool to run for a few minutes and a real-time graph will be drawn. The colour codes are given below the graph.

- If the average disk queue time is high then the data transfer from memory to the hard disk is not as fast as it could be.

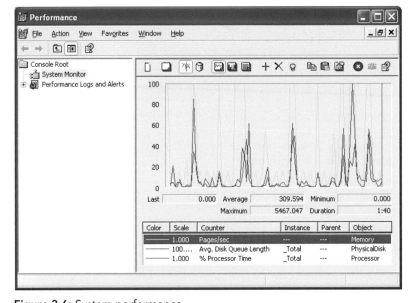

Figure 3.6: System performance.

Network connections

You will want to set up or configure a number of network connections for a variety of purposes.

- Files can be shared with other users on a network. They need to be located in a suitable folder before they can be shared.

- A workgroup is a set of computers in a network that are used by people who need to share documents and other data. They may also want to share access to a printer.
- Internet access can be shared between several computers on a network.
- You can connect to a Wi-Fi network anywhere.

You can use the system software tools in the **Control Panel** to configure network connections. Suitable hardware must be installed before the software can be configured. Most of these tasks can only be carried out by an administrator.

You can also access a Wi-Fi network if your system is set up for Wi-Fi. Most Wi-Fi networks are security enabled wireless networks and you will be required to give a password before you can use them. Others may be unsecured, which means that anyone can use them. However, you would be in an open network and there is the possibility that other users could monitor your actions.

How to... Share a folder with other users on a network

- In **My Documents**, find a folder that you want to share with others.
- Right click on the folder and select **Sharing and Security**.
- Under **Network Sharing and Security**, tick **Share this folder on the network**.

St Paul's School Properties

General | Sharing | Customize

Local sharing and security
To share this folder with other users of this computer only, drag it to the Shared Documents folder.

To make this folder and its subfolders private so that only you have access, select the following check box.

☐ Make this folder private

Network sharing and security
To share this folder with both network users and other users of this computer, select the first check box below and type a share name.

☑ Share this folder on the network

Share name: College

☐ Allow network users to change my files

Learn more about sharing and security.

ⓘ Windows Firewall is configured to allow this folder to be shared with other computers on the network.

View your Windows Firewall settings

[OK] [Cancel] [Apply]

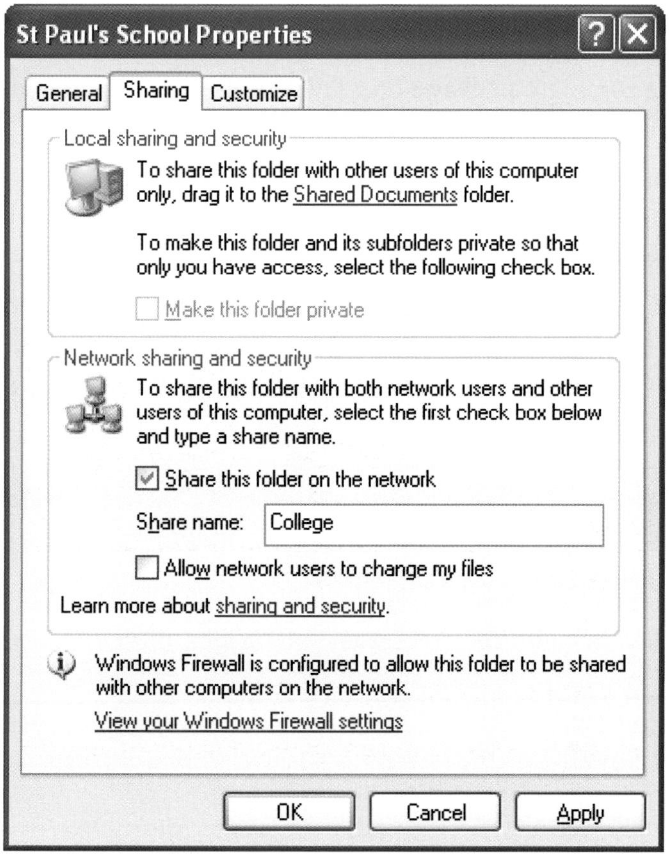

Figure 3.7: Sharing a folder.

> ### 🖥 How to... Use the Network Setup Wizard
>
> - You can use the Network Setup Wizard to share an Internet connection, printers, files and folders. Before you do so, please check that you have permission to carry out these tasks.
> - Click on **Start** then **Control Panel** then **Network Setup wizard**.
> - Follow the instructions in the wizard.

> ### 🖥 How to... Connect to a Wi–Fi network
>
> - Click on **Start** then **Connect To**. Then select **Wireless Network Connection**.
> - You will be presented with a list of Wi-Fi networks that are within range. Select the one that you wish to connect to. Enter a password if requested.

4.3 Applications software

Office applications software

Office applications software is software that can be used for many different tasks in business and at home. It is ready-made and is designed to meet the needs of a wide range of users. It is normally sold as a complete **package** on a DVD or downloaded from the Internet, and can be installed and used immediately.

The end user is able to choose which components of the package to install. Users also receive full documentation, which may be in the form of a printed manual but is more likely to be provided in electronic form.

Office software packages are available for word processing, spreadsheets, database management, graphics (drawing and painting) and presentation graphics, as shown below in Table 3.8.

Key term

Package – an application or software package is an extensive collection of programs which form one application. This description applies to most applications software these days.

Table 3.8: Examples of office software packages.

Package	Purpose	Examples	Uses and features
Word processing	Preparing documents	• Corel® WordPerfect® • Lotus Word-Pro • Microsoft® Word®	Used to produce letters, reports, invoices, leaflets, newsletters, etc. Includes additional features for creating email messages, web pages, mailing labels, and mail merge letters.
Spreadsheet	Storing data in a table of cells, carrying out calculations, and creating graphs and charts	• Lotus 1-2-3 • Microsoft® Excel®	Used for accounts, budgets, scientific calculations, statistical analysis, simple databases and form designs. Can carry out 'what if' queries.

Package	Purpose	Examples	Uses and features
Database management system	Structuring and organising the data used in a database	• Lotus Approach • Microsoft® Access®	Used to store business data such as: • stock in a shop or factory • orders from customers • orders sent to suppliers • case notes for doctors, social workers, etc. • personnel (employees') mailing lists or log sheets.
Graphics software	Creating or manipulating images, including photos that have been scanned in or imported from a digital camera, or images created using graphics software	• Microsoft® Paint® • Adobe® Photoshop	Used to create or edit images for use in standard stationery (as logos), publicity materials (leaflets, brochures, posters) or web pages.
Presentation software	Creating the illustrations for talks and lectures	• Microsoft® PowerPoint® • Lotus Freelance Graphics	Used to create a slideshow that can be projected directly from the computer on to a screen, and to print notes for the speaker and the audience.
Games software	Entertainment		Widely enjoyed in the home. Can also be used in an educational context, where children can learn and explore ideas through the medium of games. The competitive nature of games can make them addictive, and the high quality of the graphics and animation add to the enjoyment.
Web browser	Viewing pages on the Web	• Microsoft® Internet Explorer® • Mozilla Firefox®	Used to download and interpret the HTML code of a web page to create the page on-screen.
Email software	Creating, sending, receiving and storing emails	**Webmail**: • Microsoft® Hotmail® • Google Mail™ • Yahoo!® Mail **Email client**: • Microsoft® Outlook®	Webmail is a user's private space on a public website that is used to send and receive emails from any computer in the world that is online. An email client is used to manage emails on a user's own computer.

Activity: Office application packages

Make a list of all the office applications packages that you have access to at your centre. Are there others that you would like to use?

4.4 Utilities

Software utilities are useful add-on programs that work with the operating system. These include the file manager, diagnostic tools, disk utilities, backup, synchronisation and clean-up tools.

In Windows®, many utilities can be accessed by clicking on the **Start** menu then **All Programs** then **Accessories** then **System Tools**.

File managers

A file manager lets you organise your files and folders. In Windows® the file manager is called **Windows Explorer** (see Figure 3.8). Whenever you click on **My Computer** or **My Documents** you are using the file manager.

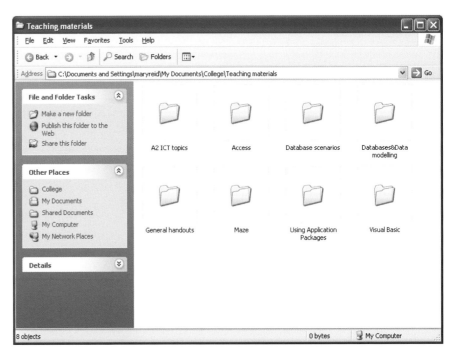

Figure 3.8: Windows Explorer.

How to... Use Windows Explorer to move files

Go directly to **Windows Explorer** by clicking on **Start** then **All Programs** then **Accessories**.

The left-hand pane is called the Explorer Bar and offers you some tasks that can be carried out with the files and folders on display (see Figure 3.8).

Click on the **Folders** icon in the main toolbar.

You can now easily move files from one folder to another by dragging the file from the right pane to the folder on the left.

Backup

In business, every single file on a computer system should be copied and the copy kept safely. This copy is known as a **backup**, and it can be used if the original is damaged. At home, you would be wise to keep backups as well, especially of important documents.

On a network, all the files will be backed up regularly. This is an automatic process during which all the files on the system are copied on to a removable disk or digital tape. In most organisations this will happen in the middle of the night when no one is at work on the system. A network administrator will then remove the disk or tape in the morning and lock it in a fire-proof safe. For larger systems the backup is copied automatically to a storage medium in a completely different building.

How to... Create a backup

- Click on **Start** then **All Programs** then **Accessories** then **System Tools**.
- Select **Backup**.
- The Backup Wizard asks whether you want to back-up or restore data. Select **Backup files and settings**. Click **Next**.
- You are then asked what you want to back up. You would normally select **My documents and settings**. Note that you can select the bottom option and select the files you want backed up. Click **Next**.
- Browse to the location where you want to store your backup, for example a flash drive that you have plugged in. You must make sure that the location has enough space for all the data that you are backing up.
- Choose a name for the backup and click **Next**. When you click **Next** on the final window, the backing up process will begin. This can take some time if there is a large amount of data to be backed up.

How to... Restore data

If you have accidentally deleted a file, or want to revert to a previous version, you can restore the file using the Backup Wizard.

Synchronisation

A user may store important data, such as a calendar, in more than one place. A calendar lists appointments and meetings. On a business network, a shared calendar may be available to several people, but each person may want a copy on their own laptop or PDA. The calendars on all devices need to match each other, and synchronisation is the process of updating all calendars so that they match.

Windows® offers a utility for synchronising data across a network. It can be found in Accessories.

If a user owns a PDA or mobile phone with calendar facilities, they will want to synchronise the data with the calendar on their main system. PDAs and mobile phones provide synchronisation software for that purpose.

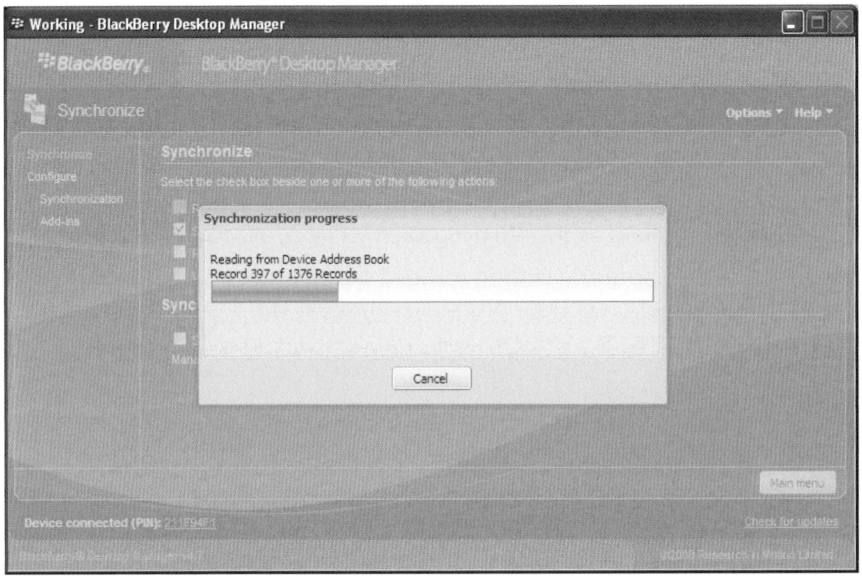

Figure 3.9: Synchronisation utility.

Disk utilities

There are several utilities that help you to improve the performance of the hard disks in your system.

You may notice that your operating system has become quite slow, especially when it is saving or loading files. There are two options in the **System Tools** that you can try:

- **Disk Cleanup** – this checks through all the data on the hard disk. Over time old programs and data can clog up a disk, so the cleanup tool finds these and deletes them. Some applications software stores temporary files, such as cookies, so one of the options within Disk Cleanup is to remove these. It will also compress any data that hasn't been used for a long time. This frees up space so that more software and data can be stored on the hard disk.

- **Disk Defragmenter** – this rearranges all the files on a hard disk so that they make the best use of the space. It only really improves performance if the disk is more than 75 per cent full.

How to... Use Disk Cleanup

- Click on **Start** then **All Programs** then **Accessories** then **System Tools**. Select **Disk Cleanup**.

- Select the drive you want to work on then click **OK**.

- After a few minutes a window will appear which will give you some options. Do not remove files that are important or that you are not sure about. You can safely remove cookies and temporary files.

How to... Defragment a disk

- You can find the Disk Defragmenter in **Accessories** under **System Tools**. Click on **Analyze** first to see whether your disks do need to be defragmented.

- If you then go ahead, be warned that it can take a long time to defragment a disk.

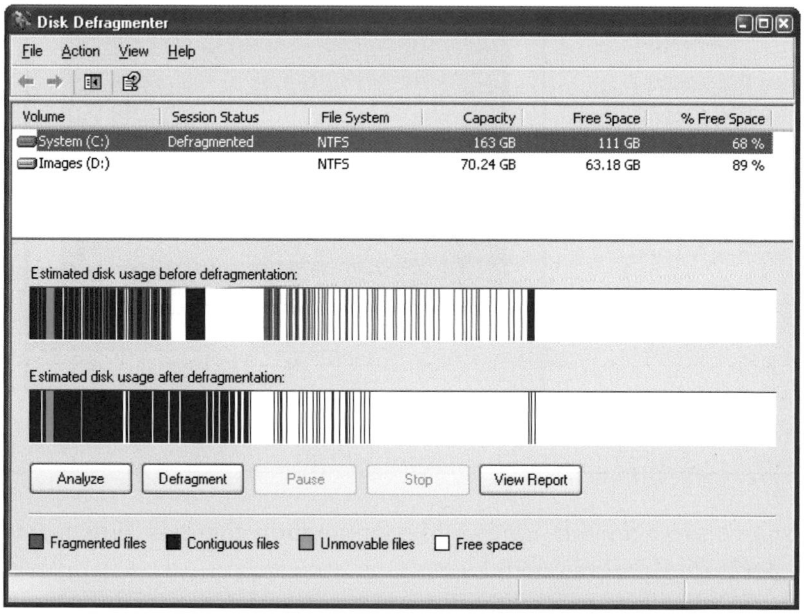

Figure 3.10: The Disk Defragmenter.

4.5 Configure software

Users can make many changes to the configuration of their own personal computer system. But when a desktop computer is linked into a network, the network administrator may limit the changes that users can make. In this section we will assume that you have full access to all the configuration options on a computer.

All the examples refer to Windows®, but you should find similar options available to you if you use another operating system. Different versions of Windows® vary in the way they present options to users, so the illustrations may not exactly match what you can see on your computer system.

Editing the desktop

There are a number of system software tools in the **Control Panel** that can be used to change the appearance of the desktop and of many applications as well.

How to... Configure the display

- Click on the **Start** menu then select **Control Panel**.

- Select **Display** (see Figure 3.11). This allows you to do the following:

  – Select a theme for your desktop. Each theme is a set of colours, sounds and icons that work together. Alternatively, you can configure each element separately under the **Appearance** tab.

  – Select one of the preset backgrounds for the desktop (known as a wallpaper) or find an image of your own.

  – Select and configure a screen saver from the ones available.

  – Choose colours, fonts and icons to be used in each window.

  – Place a web page on the desktop instead of wallpaper.

  – Select the screen resolution (usually 1024 x 768 or 1280 x 1024; smaller screens may be set at 800 x 600).

Figure 3.11: Display properties in Windows®.

You can make a limited number of configuration changes directly from the desktop. Here are some ideas:

- move the icons around on the desktop

- go directly from the desktop to many of the **Control Panel** options – for example, if you double-click on the time (in the bottom right corner) the **Date/Time** properties box will open

- frag the Taskbar (at the bottom of the screen) and any of the toolbars to the top or sides of the desktop. (If it will not move, right click on the **Taskbar** and check that it is not locked.)

Shortcuts

You can create a **shortcut** to a program, a document or a folder. If you click on a shortcut, it will carry out the most appropriate action, for example launch the software, open the document or display the contents of the folder.

You will find a number of shortcuts on the desktop. A large icon for a shortcut, like the one in Figure 3.12, displays a small bent arrow to indicate that it is a shortcut.

When you select **All Programs** in the **Start** menu, what you actually see are shortcuts to the programs, like the **Calculator** icon, for example. Using either dragging or copying and pasting, you can place a shortcut:

- in any folder

- on the desktop (e.g. you can copy a program shortcut from the **All Programs** menu to the desktop).

Key terms

Shortcut – an icon that allows you to go directly to a file without having to search through all the folders in **My Computer** to find it.

Google Earth

Figure 3.12: A shortcut icon.

How to... Work with shortcuts

You can create a new shortcut to an important document.

- Open the **My Documents** folder and locate the document.

- Right-click on the document icon and select **Create Shortcut**.

- The shortcut icon will appear in the folder. You can now drag this to wherever you would like it to be, including the desktop.

- To delete a shortcut, right click on it and select **Delete**. This will not delete the actual software or document, but only remove the shortcut.

- To copy and paste a shortcut, right-click on it and select **Copy**. Go to wherever you want to place the shortcut, right-click and select **Paste**.

- To add a shortcut to the **Start** menu, find the program in the **All Programs** menu, right-click on it and select **Pin to Start menu**. For example, Windows Explorer is very useful so you may want to pin it to the **Start** menu, to make it readily available.

Creating startup options

You may want certain frequently used applications to launch automatically when the system is started up. Shortcuts to these applications have to be stored in the **Startup** folder, which you can find under **All Programs**.

How to... Set the system startup options

- In **All Programs**, find the shortcut that you want to be launched on startup.

- Drag it into the **Startup** folder.

Most software packages also offer you a startup option, usually by selecting **Preferences** or **Options**. For example, the **Internet Options** in Internet Explorer® (found in the **Tools** menu) lets you select your home page (see Figure 3.13). This is the page that is opened when the browser is launched. The home page can be any page on the Internet or a web page that you have created and stored on the hard disk.

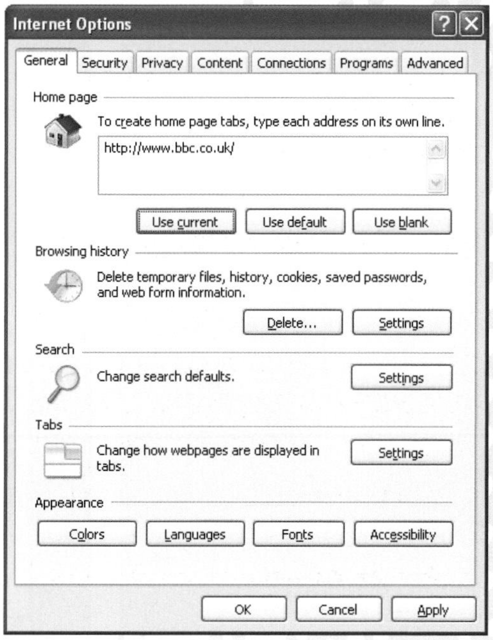

Figure 3.13: The Options box in Internet Explorer®.

In Microsoft® Office® software, you can change the default file location. This is the folder where the application will initially look for files and save files. You can change this location to another folder.

How to... Change the default file location

- Launch Excel®, and click on the **Office** button. At the bottom of the drop-down menu, click on **Excel options**.

- Click on **Save**. Under **Default File Location** enter the full path to the folder that you want as the default. Be careful!

- You can also specify the standard font to be used on spreadsheets, and how many sheets will be provided in a new workbook.

You can make similar changes in the other Microsoft® Office® programs.

Creating and reconfiguring application toolbars

Many business applications software packages are built to the Windows® standard. They include Microsoft® software as well as software produced by other companies. This means that many of the configuration options that you select in Windows® will also affect these applications. For example, the choice of colours that you make in **Display** will also be active in these applications.

Some applications (for example most games, as well as some specialist software) are not built to the Windows® standards. These may or may not allow you to change how they appear.

Most applications display a set of icons which represent options that the user can choose from. These bands of options are known as **toolbars**. Toolbars that 'float' anywhere on-screen are known as **toolboxes**.

Key terms

Toolbar – a set of icons, displayed in a row, that represent user options.

Toolbox – a floating toolbar.

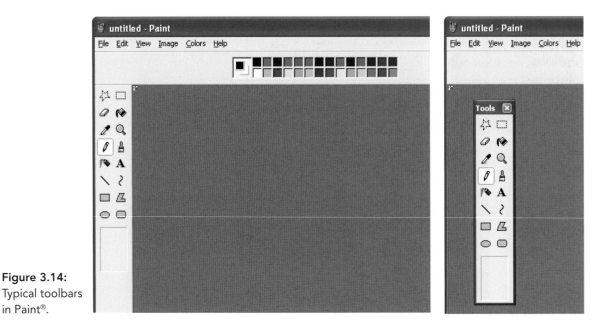

Figure 3.14:
Typical toolbars in Paint®.

Figure 3.15:
The formatting toolbar is now a floating toolbox.

Microsoft® Office® 2007 changed the way in which toolbars were presented. Several toolbars are presented across the top of the screen in a wide ribbon. The individual toolbars are known as groups. There are tabs above the ribbon, and when one of these is clicked a different ribbon is displayed.

Figure 3.16: The Page Layout ribbon in Microsoft® Word®.

You cannot configure the ribbons. However, at the top of the window lies the **Quick Access** toolbar. You can place the most commonly used icons here.

How to... Configure the Quick Access toolbar

- In a Microsoft® Office® application, click on the small arrow to the right of the **Quick Access** toolbar.
- Select the required options.
- Click on **More Commands** to find other options.

Figure 3.17: The Quick Access toolbar.

Folder management

Files are stored in computer systems in directories, also known as folders. Any user can set up their own folders, and this is a sensible way of organising a lot of personal documents and other files.

The appearance of the folders and files can be configured to suit the user. To switch between different views of the folder, click on the **Views** icon in the toolbar. For serious use of the file manager you would be advised to use the **Details View**.

You can change some of the properties of each file. For example, you might want to make some files 'read only', in which case no one would be able to make any changes to them. Or you might want to hide a file from the user's view.

How to... Change the properties of a file

- In Windows Explorer, right click on a file. Select **Properties**.
- Under **Attributes**, tick one or other of the tick boxes labelled **Read only** and **Hidden**.

User feedback

If you configure software for a particular user, it is very important that you let them try it out and give you feedback. In fact, if you can show them what the possibilities are and how to configure it for themselves, they will be able to continue to experiment until they find a configuration that suits them perfectly.

4.6 Security

ICT systems have to be protected from a number of threats. Someone may access a system illegally in order to read sensitive information and, even though they may not cause any damage to the system, they may create all kinds of problems to the organisation. Worse still, they may actually change data or even delete it.

On pages 66–67 you learned about a number of security risks when using the Internet. We are now going to see how to prevent some of these happening.

The main aims of security are:

* to maintain the system as intended
* to protect the system from unauthorised changes being made to the software or data
* to protect the system from both accidental and deliberate illegal access
* to detect successful and unsuccessful attempts at illegal access
* to provide a means of recovery if things go wrong, by the use of backups.

Virus protection

The best way to prevent virus damage is to install virus protection software on networks or on personal computer systems.

Virus protection software works with a virus data file, which contains information about all known viruses. The software uses the data file to check whether programs or data have been infected. It can be configured to check every new file that is placed on the system, including all emails, and it will also spot any unexpected changes to the system.

A full virus check can be run periodically to check that nothing has slipped through. Since new viruses are being released all the time, it is very important to regularly update the virus data files that enable the software to detect and identify the viruses.

Firewall

A firewall is a piece of systems software that protects the system from unauthorised access. Firewalls are commonly used to check all the communications between a system and the Internet. If it detects any unexpected attempts to access the system via the Internet, it will block them and report them immediately to the user.

Password protection

A computer in a network can access files that are stored on the hard disk of the file server. But that does not mean that you can access just any file you like when you use the network.

If you have a network system at your school, you probably have to key in two pieces of information when you log in:

- your username (sometimes called your User ID)
- your password.

Network administrators have the job of sorting out the **file permissions** for users. They will have given you your own username, which is not confidential.

You will also have been given a password, and you should keep it secret. You will probably be allowed to change your password whenever you like, and you should remember it without writing it down anywhere.

Never allow anyone else to log on using your username and password, as they could alter your files or even delete them. Even if they mean no harm they could change your work accidentally.

When someone logs on to the network with their username and password, the network software makes sure that they can only use the files for which they have permission.

Physical security

All ICT systems have to be protected from loss and damage. This applies to the hardware (the components of the computer system and the network cabling) as well as to the software and data held on the system.

An ICT system can be damaged by:

- catastrophic events, such as fire, flood or major damage to the building
- environmental problems, such as high temperatures or damp
- electrical and magnetic interference
- minor faults, such as damaged cables or broken components
- lost disks, keys or components.

The majority of these problems are caused by accidents. But someone who wants to harm an organisation could inflict damage deliberately. Any damage to the hardware puts the software and data at risk as well.

In addition, unauthorised access to ICT systems can happen as a result of:

- people gaining entry to buildings and rooms
- theft of hardware, disks and documents
- tapping into networks.

Unauthorised access is normally deliberate. But if the security in a building is inadequate, then someone may innocently wander into a forbidden area.

Key term

File permissions – the rules that are set up by the network administrator for each user, identifying which files they can access or change.

(i) Did you know?

Usernames and passwords are used on some websites. This is done for two reasons:

- to identify people who are using the website, especially if they want to buy something, receive information or join an online community
- to restrict access to private websites.

By exploring how the configuration of software will help a given user perform their tasks, you will show that you are a **creative thinker.**

By identifying potential security risks to the system, you will show that you are an **independent enquirer**.

Functional skills

Explaining how the configurations to the software you have implemented will help the user to carry out their tasks could provide evidence for your functional **English** skills in speaking and listening.

Rooms containing ICT systems can be protected by:

* locks and burglar alarm systems
* keeping all removable media in locked boxes and drawers
* placing computer systems in a part of the building that cannot be reached easily from outside
* keeping the room at an even temperature.

Activity: Security measures by retailers

Investigate the security measures used by an online retailer.

* How do they protect their data and the data given to them by customers?
* How do they stay within the law?

You will be able to find out some of the answers by making a purchase (you can drop out at the last minute if you do not want to buy). The company will not let you into most of their security secrets, but you could make a good guess about the procedures they follow and the software they use.

BTEC Assessment activity 3.4

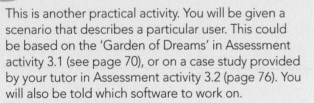

This is another practical activity. You will be given a scenario that describes a particular user. This could be based on the 'Garden of Dreams' in Assessment activity 3.1 (see page 70), or on a case study provided by your tutor in Assessment activity 3.2 (page 76). You will also be told which software to work on.

1. Configure the software to meet the needs of the user. **P6**
2. Explain how the configurations to the software you have done will help the user carry out their tasks on the computer. **D2**
3. Identify the possible security risks in the computer system you have set up. **P7**

Grading tips

* For task 1, read the description of the user very carefully. You should configure the software especially for them, not as you might like it.
* For task 2, you should discuss the advantages and disadvantages of the configuration changes that you have made.
* For task 3, concentrate on the system you have set up but also think about potential security risks in general.

Just checking

1. List five things that can be changed using the Control Panel in Windows®.
2. What is meant by synchronisation?
3. What does the Defragmenter utility do?
4. What can you clean up with Disk Cleanup?
5. How can you protect a computer from viruses?
6. Why should you backup data?

WorkSpace Asad Khan
Computer Service Technician

When I left college I started work as a trainee Computer Service Technician. My company sorts out computer problems and installs new systems for companies and individuals.

For the first month my employer sent me on an intensive course at a training centre. There was a lot to learn, but I had to pass before I was allowed to start work. After that I was allowed to install new equipment for clients, but always under supervision. My work was appraised after three months and from then on I could work on my own.

I still get sent on courses from time to time, to keep me up to date on the latest kit.

Typical day

Most weeks I work normal office hours, but I am also on call for one weekend a month.

On a typical day I report into the office and am given two or three job sheets. I then travel to the first client's workplace. The client may want us to install a new printer, set up a couple of laptops or repair a faulty Wi-Fi network. When the job is finished I make sure that the client is happy with the work. I may have to spend some time with users to show them how to use new equipment.

Some of the computers are seven years old or more, but if the client wants to keep them going I have to know about old systems, as well as new ones.

I complete a logsheet for each job that I do and I hand the logsheets in at the beginning of the next day. On the logsheet I write down the name and address of the client, the date and time that I started the job and the time I finished. I also describe the problem and what I did to solve it. The client then has to sign my form so I can't cheat! In fact, my employer has a number of ways of checking up on my work, from phoning clients to noting the mileage on my company van.

The best thing about the job

I love working with computers so this is my dream job. But I'm not one of those boring people who can talk about nothing else. I'm sociable and enjoy finding out about other people's lives. This job gives me the chance to meet lots of different people and travel to new places.

The pay is quite good and I get overtime for any weekends that I work. My training is free and keeps me up to date, so I will be able to apply for more senior posts in a couple of years.

Think about it!

1. What have you learned in this unit that provides you with the background knowledge and skills used by a computer service technician?
2. What other skills would you need to do the job?

Just checking

1. What is Wi-Fi and what is it used for?
2. The processor is the heart of a computer system, but what does it do?
3. Explain what is meant by the capacity of storage media. Give some examples of typical capacities.
4. Describe the differences between inkjet and laser printers.
5. What is the difference between systems software and applications software? Give two examples of each.
6. Why are phishing and spam emails unwelcome?
7. How can you work out how long a laptop battery will last between one recharge and the next?
8. Why should trainees always be supervised when carrying out practical tasks?
9. What information should you supply on a logsheet for a practical task?
10. What are the main functions of an operating system?

edexcel

Assignment tips

To work towards a distinction in this unit you will need to achieve all the pass, merit and distinction criteria in the unit and have evidence to show that you have achieved each one.

How do I prepare for the assignment activities?

• To learn and practise the skills that you will be assessed on, you should carry out all the activities in this unit yourself. You will also be given a chance in class to practise many of the techniques described in Sections 3 and 4.

• You will find it helpful to make notes of all the steps you take when connecting hardware and configuring software. You can then use the notes to create your own 'How to...' manual, which you can refer to at any time.

• You will probably know some of these techniques already, but others may be new to you. No one can know everything in IT, so never be afraid to ask if you do not understand what to do or if you are not sure about the reason for doing anything.

• You should keep yourself and your equipment safe at all times. Do not carry out any of the connection or configuration tasks unless you are supervised. You will not pass P5 unless you carry out the tasks in a safe and sensible way.

How do I provide assessment evidence?

• All your evidence should be presented in one folder, which should have a front cover and a contents page. You should divide the evidence into four sections corresponding to the four tasks.

• Evidence can be in the form of a written report supported by any combination of observation records, logsheets, checklists, screenshots, photos, videos, presentations, leaflets and other documents that you have prepared.

• For P6 you should include evidence of the state of the system both before and after you configured it.

4 Business IT skills

Businesses face many problems, from effectively launching new products to updating office computer systems. They often want to think about alternative solutions to problems before they choose one that is most suitable.

Spreadsheets are a useful tool to help businesses make choices. This unit explores how finding appropriate information and using this in a spreadsheet can help businesses to make decisions that solve their problems.

You will find out the type of problems faced by businesses. You will also find out the information that they use to make decisions and where this information can be found. Always remember that choosing reliable and accurate data is important to any decision.

You will then need to understand how to set up and manipulate a spreadsheet to find solutions to business problems and provide answers to 'What if?' questions. Presenting the solutions in a suitable format is vital if they are to be clearly understood by the people viewing them.

You will have to evaluate your solutions and your use of ICT to make sure that they are effective. If solutions do not solve the problems, you will need to suggest improvements.

Learning outcomes

After completing this unit you should:

1. understand the requirements for solving business problems
2. know how to find information to support business solutions
3. be able to use spreadsheet models to support business solutions
4. be able to present business solutions
5. be able to evaluate business solutions.

Assessment and grading criteria

This table shows you what you must do in order to achieve a pass, merit or distinction grade, and where you can find activities in this book to help you.

To achieve a **pass** grade the evidence must show that you are able to:	To achieve a **merit** grade the evidence must show that, in addition to the pass criteria, you are able to:	To achieve a **distinction** grade the evidence must show that, in addition to the pass and merit criteria, you are able to:
P1 explain information requirements for solving a business problem **See Assessment activity 4.1 on page 112**		
P2 prepare a business plan **See Assessment activity 4.1 on page 112**	**M1** justify choices made in the business plan **See Assessment activity 4.1 on page 112**	
P3 identify and select data from appropriate sources to solve a business problem **See Assessment activity 4.2 on page 116**	**M2** validate sources and acknowledge copyright **See Assessment activity 4.2 on page 116**	**D1** evaluate sources for accuracy, currency, completeness and reliability **Assessment activity 4.2 on page 116**
P4 set up and test a spreadsheet model including automated features to solve a business problem **See Assessment activity 4.3 on page 127**	**M3** explore possibilities by answering 'What if?' questions **See Assessment activity 4.3 on page 127**	
P5 develop the model based on user feedback **See Assessment activity 4.3 on page 127**		
P6 present a business solution using a range of software tools to suit the audience **See Assessment activity 4.4 on page 132**	**M4** justify the use of software tools **See Assessment activity 4.4 on page 132**	
P7 carry out an evaluation of a business solution **See Assessment activity 4.4 on page 132**		

How you will be assessed

This unit is internally assessed. You will provide a portfolio of evidence to show that you have achieved the learning outcomes. Your portfolio of evidence can be supplied in many formats including electronically as well as paper-based. The grading grid in the specification for this unit lists what you must do to obtain pass, merit and distinction grades. The Assessment activities in this unit will guide you through tasks that will help you to be successful in this unit.

Your teacher will tell you exactly what form your assessments will take, but you could be asked to produce:

- a requirements report
- a business plan
- a sources list
- spreadsheets with data
- screenshots and printouts
- test plans and results
- user feedback
- presentations
- a written report or web page
- an evaluation of your work.

Lee Campbell, 16–year-old ICT student

This unit helped me to understand the problems that businesses face and how spreadsheets can help them to solve these problems. I use a spreadsheet at home on my computer, but it was interesting to see how businesses can use them as well.

I didn't realise quite how much information businesses need to collect before they make a decision and how important it is that the information is accurate. If the information put into a spreadsheet is incorrect, then any decision based on that information is also likely to be incorrect.

Looking for information on the Internet was fairly easy, but time-consuming. I found out that you can find some information in other places, like business catalogues or by talking to people in business.

The most interesting part of this unit was setting up the spreadsheet and considering how changes to the information can help to solve problems. Now I have learned how to do all this, I hope it might be helpful to me in any job I get in future where I need to use computers.

Over to you

- Lee uses a spreadsheet at home. How might you use a spreadsheet to help you solve your own problems at home?
- Lee noticed that information can be found in many places. Why might you need to find information from more than one place?
- What jobs might Lee do in future that could require him to use a spreadsheet?

1. Understand the requirements for solving business problems

What to sell? How to sell it?

Designz is a business based in Leeds that designs stationery, business cards and leaflets for businesses like cafés, estate agents and hairdressers.

The company has recently taken on a new designer with experience in designing catalogues and books. Designz is thinking of offering this service to local customers, but wonders if there are enough in the local area.

The company is considering launching its own website to show its new services to customers in a wider area. It is aware that the website must be clear and also attractive to customers. It has three reps that visit businesses.

The reps have told the owner, Jagannath, that they will need mobile phones with Internet access, so they can show clients the website. Jagannath is not sure what phone model to buy.

- Working with a partner, discuss what problems this business might face.
- Make a list of these problems.

1.1 Business problems

Understanding the problem

Businesses face problems in their day-to-day operations. Many of these are important issues that affect the costs and operation of the business, so they need to plan solutions carefully. A business must make sure that it fully understands the nature of the problem before planning a solution. Typical problems that a business might face include:

- networking an office
- setting up a company website
- launching a new product or service
- upgrading an IT system.

Networking an office
This means linking all the computers together, so that people can share information. The business must decide how to do this and make choices about the following.

- **Hardware:** How many computers will be linked together? How will they be linked? What printers and other peripherals will be part of the network?
- **Software:** Which software will we use to run the system? What licences are needed?

- **Staff:** How many staff are needed to manage the system? What training will they need?
- **Data and security:** Where will information be stored? What access rights will different members of staff have to the information on the network?
- **Budget:** How much should we spend?

Setting up a company website

A business may want to set up a website to communicate with its customers. It will need to make decisions about the following.

- **Design:** Will we design the site ourselves or use a specialist website designer?
- **Features:** Will the site provide information (like a solicitor's website)? Can you make bookings using the site (like a theatre or hotel website)? Can you buy products (like on Amazon)?
- **Hosting:** Will we host and run our own site or use a specialist business to do this?
- **Search engines:** Will we pay to get our company name on the first page of search engines?

These decisions will affect the size and cost of the website. The business will also need to consider its budget.

Launching a new product or service

Launching a new product (such as a new low-calorie drink) or service (such as an aqua aerobics class at a gym) can be a major problem. If the launch is not successful the business can lose money, and in some cases it may even be forced out of business.

A business will need to think about the following.

- **The product:** What do people want to buy? How much will the product cost to make or buy in? What materials will be used to make the product?
- **Staff:** How many people do we need to make the product or provide the service? How many people do we need to sell it?
- **Budget:** How much should the budget be for making the product or providing the service? How much should we spend on marketing, to attract customers to buy the product or use the service?

Upgrading an IT system

Old IT systems can cause problems for businesses. Outdated computers and software may mean that a business does not work effectively. It may cost more to maintain an older system and there is the risk of disruption to the business if it breaks down.

When a business needs to upgrade its computer system, it needs to make decisions about the following.

- **Computer models and software:** Which should we choose from the alternatives available?
- **Budget:** How much should we spend on the new IT system?
- **Installation:** Should we install the new system ourselves or pay a specialist to do this?

Key term

Budget – an amount of money allocated for a particular purpose.

- **Support:** Do we need to employ a specialist to give support, in case the system has problems?
- **Training:** What training will staff need to use and manage the new system?

Spreadsheet modelling

A **spreadsheet model** is a useful tool for helping a business to plan and solve problems such as these. The spreadsheet can:

- include information about the costs of different solutions to the problems (e.g. the costs of upgrading an IT system)
- include the budget available for the solution
- add up costs and compare the total costs of different solutions
- be used to find out how making changes to costs or budgets will affect the returns on a new product.

There are many other problems where a spreadsheet might be useful to a business, including building an extension to an office, organising a car park, developing an advertising campaign or relocating to new premises.

How to develop spreadsheet models is covered in detail in *Unit 27: Spreadsheet modelling*.

Key terms

Spreadsheet – a computer program that allows the user to enter numbers and text into a table with rows and columns, and then manipulate those numbers.

Model – something that mimics real life. With a model you can make predictions or plans and try to answer questions.

Activity: Business problems

With the help of your teacher, invite a speaker to your school. It could a family member or a friend who runs or manages a business, or someone from a business where the school has contacts.

Ask the speaker to talk about the problems that the business has faced and how they solved the problems. Then think about how IT could be useful to help solve these problems. You could use the table below to help you. Add a new row for each problem you identify.

Problem	Solution	How IT helped

1.2 Information requirements

The first stage in a solution to a problem is to find out information that will help to make a decision on the best solution. A business can find information in different ways.

It can talk to users of products

For example, if a business wants to upgrade the mobile phones used by its managers, it might ask other businesses about the phones that they are using. This will provide information about how useful the different features of each phone are and the monthly cost of calls. A business that wants to launch a new low fat brand of ice-cream might ask a **tasting panel** to comment on different flavours and how much they would be willing to pay for a low-fat product.

It can observe activities

A business that wants to launch a new product might observe how customers react. For example, film companies often test movies on an audience before they are launched. If people do not like the ending of a film, the film company might decide to use a different ending instead.

It can check existing documents

For example, if a business wants to buy new computers it might check the price lists of suppliers for costs. If a business thinks that its software may need upgrading, it could look at records, such as time sheets to see how long jobs are taking using the existing software.

Key term

Tasting panel – a group of people who agree to taste products and provide feedback. They are often used by a business to help with its product development.

Activity: Consumer panel

A consumer panel is a group of people that might potentially buy a product. The company making the product invites the consumer panel to try the product out before it is launched and provide feedback.

Set up a group of your friends as a consumer panel to find out what they want in a new computer game.

Design a questionnaire that will help you collect data that you can collate and analyse to make decisions about the game you will make.

Then use the questionnaire to make decisions about:

- the type of game your consumer panel would want
- the main features of the game
- the price of the game
- the platform for the game (e.g. console, PC).

Activity: Finding advertising costs

Imagine you run a small flower shop. You want to advertise that you are now offering a wedding service, providing all the flowers for the guests and the tables.

Investigate the cost of placing different advertisements in local newspapers and magazines.

You may be able to find out the costs by:

- contacting the publishers of the newspapers/magazines
- looking in the newspapers/magazines – some print their advertising costs
- looking on the Internet.

Show your results in a table.

Outcomes of investigation

Once a business has investigated the possible solutions, it will want to analyse and present the information it has gathered in a way that will help it make the best decisions. Some of the tools used by businesses are management reports, charts, graphs and simulations. For example, a business that has the views of people from a tasting panel might produce a report, including charts and graphs, to show that one type of ice-cream is likely to be more popular than the others.

Management reports

A management report could be a written document or a presentation including text or tables. It is produced to help managers make their decision about the best solution. For example, the report could show the main features that people want to see in a new breakfast cereal or the costs involved in training staff to use a new IT system.

Charts and graphs

It can sometimes be easier to show what is happening in a chart or graph than in text. For example, a business might want to know whether a new product would be bought by more males or more females. A pie chart could show the percentages more clearly than a paragraph of text. An example is shown in Figure 4.1. The breakdown of the costs of two alternative computer systems might be easier to see on a bar chart than in a table.

Simulations

A business might use the information it has gathered to create a **simulation** of the solution it would like to use. For example, a business that wants information on a new product could make a sample of the product and ask a group of potential customers to try it out. A business wanting to introduce a new website might trial a design before creating the actual site. A large business could test a new IT system in just one office before introducing it to every office in the business.

Benefits

Collecting the right information before considering solutions to business problems is important because the information can help managers to make decisions about the most cost-effective solutions.

Inform management decisions

Managers need information in order to investigate the different possible solutions and then make a choice of the best solution. It's important for managers to get all the information that might affect their decision.

For example, the manager of a take away restaurant is trying to decide whether to launch a website to promote her business. She will need information about how much the website will cost to develop, how many people might view the website and whether a leaflet might get the information about her business to more potential customers. Finding out that customers are more likely to find out about the business from a leaflet will help her to make the right decision.

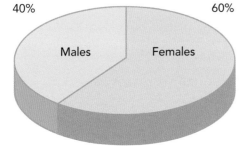

40%   60%

Figure 4.1 A pie chart showing the percentages of males and females that might buy a new product.

Key term

simulation – an imitation of the real thing.

Create cost-effective solutions

Information helps managers to choose solutions that are **cost-effective**. There is likely to be a budget for any solution, such as the cost of networking an office. Keeping costs down will leave the business with more money to spend in other areas of the business.

But cost information must be accurate. For example, a business might not make the right decision about which computer system to install if the full costs are not included (e.g. if the cost of monitors is missing).

Cost information must also be up to date. For example, if the prices of computers have gone up, managers need to know about this in order to make the right decision.

A business must take into account the **total cost of ownership** (TCO). For example, buying a cheap printer that has expensive cartridges may mean that the total costs are higher than buying a more expensive printer with cheaper cartridges.

Constraints

The solution that businesses choose to problems they face can be affected by many **constraints**, including:

- budget
- existing systems
- resources
- business preferences
- supplier contracts.

Constraints like these will limit the options open to businesses and will make them more likely to choose one option than another.

Budget

A business is likely to set a budget for any solution to a problem. If the budget is large, this may mean that there are many alternative solutions to choose from. Smaller businesses may have a more limited budget and fewer solutions available. For example, a dress designer may not be able use the same quality material in his new clothes range as a fashion designer who designs for catwalk shows. A small garage may only be able to update the software that runs its database every three years rather than every year.

Existing systems

The system already used by a business may affect its solutions. Some equipment only works with other equipment and extra equipment may be needed. For example, a printer with a serial connector won't link to a laptop with a USB port without an adaptor.

Resources

The resources available may affect the choice of solution. For example, if a restaurant does not have a chef that can cook Thai food well, then it may not be able to offer this type of food. A UK cycle maker might want to use certain parts for its bikes. But if it finds out that these parts are only available from abroad, at great cost, it may not be able to use them and may have to find cheaper alternatives.

Key terms

Cost-effective – economical in terms of what is gained for the money spent.

Total cost of ownership (TCO) – the total cost of purchasing and running a system.

Constraint – a factor that limits or restricts a decision.

Business preferences

Owners and managers may have their own preferences when it comes to choosing a solution to a problem. For example, a manager may insist that a computer network must be available to all employees of the business rather than to just certain departments. Managers might like to use a particular **brand name** of computer in the business because they have used this brand before and it has performed well.

Supplier contracts

Businesses often have **suppliers** that provide them with materials to make products or offer services. For example, printers have paper suppliers and food shops get their supplies from farms and factories. If a business wants to update its IT system, but has a long-term contract agreed with a supplier, it may not be possible for the business to change to another supplier who is offering better or cheaper products.

Case study: YourCard

Karen Jenkins runs a small business, YourCard, which makes hand-made greetings cards. She always makes all the cards herself, either from her own designs or from designs given to her by customers.

Karen wants to offer a new service delivering cards directly to her customers' friends. But she knows that this will increase her postage costs.

She likes to buy all her materials from businesses that promise to use recycled paper, although she knows this can cost more.

She has always used a particular well-known brand of computer to plan her designs. Karen's friend Rahila designs computers for a large business and

has offered to build a computer for Karen, but Karen insists she wants to carry on using what she is used to.

1. **Copy the table below and use it to write down the constraints that might affect Karen's business. Add a new row for each constraint.**

2. **Explain how each constraint might affect her business.**

Constraint	How it affects the business

Key terms

Brand name – the name of a product that identifies it and differentiates it from other products to customers.

Supplier – provider of goods or services.

Business plan – a document that shows how a business is going to achieve its objectives.

Inputs – in a simple business plan, the data about resources required to solve a business problem.

1.3 Business plan

In order to provide the best solution to its problems, it's very important for a business to draw up a **business plan**. A simple plan to solve a business problem will include:

- inputs
- outputs
- processes.

Inputs

The **inputs** into a business plan are data about the resources required to solve business problems. For example, for a business launching a new vegetarian dish to be sold in supermarkets, the inputs might be data on the different types of ingredients that are available for use in the dish and the cost of these ingredients. For a business networking its office, the inputs might be data about the models and costs of computers, printers, scanners, servers and the type of network.

Outputs

The **outputs** of a business plan are the information produced from the data that will be used by a business to solve its problems. Outputs might be in the form of reports for managers on alternative website designs or graphs and charts showing how costs change as features are added to websites.

Processes

The **processes** in a business plan are the actions that lead to changes or that convert data into information. They include:

- calculations, such as adding up all the costs of launching a new computer game
- logical operations, such as IF, AND and OR (for example, to compare the total cost of a new product to the budget)
- macros, such as adding the same header to many different graphs and tables.

Using a spreadsheet model

The inputs, outputs and processes in the business plan are related. Businesses use spreadsheet models to carry out the processes that convert inputs to outputs. (Using spreadsheets is covered in detail in *Unit 27: Spreadsheet modelling* and later in this unit.)

For example, a business launching a new vegetarian dish may find data that includes:

- the nutritional values of different ingredients
- the amounts of each ingredient in the dish
- the costs of the ingredients.

These inputs can then be processed using a spreadsheet. For example, the total cost of ingredients for each dish could be calculated or the total nutritional values of the dish could be totalled. The outputs could be a chart showing the total nutritional values of the dish and the total costs of the dish.

Timelines

Timelines are important in business plans. Any solution to a problem must be achieved in time, so deadlines must be built into a plan. If a business experiences delays in launching a new Christmas-related product and doesn't release it until February the following year, the product is unlikely to sell as many as predicted at launch.

Research

Research is also important. Data about inputs must be accurate. Otherwise the outputs and solutions could be incorrect. See the section on Checking information on pages 115–116.

Key terms

Outputs – in a simple business plan, the information produced from data, such as reports, graphs and charts.

Processes – in a simple business plan, the actions that lead to changes or that convert data into information, including calculations, logical operations and macros.

Case study: T–Print

T-Print is a business that buys in T-shirts and then prints designs onto the shirts. It creates designs for customers on its computer or uses the customer's own designs. The company has developed a new product aimed at sports clubs. It will give supporters a package of T-shirt, cap and scarf, all with the club logo, and presented in a cloth bag. It is aiming to advertise this product in the local paper and have a stall at two local summer fairs.

1. **In a group, discuss the inputs and outputs the business would have when launching the new product.**

2. **Produce a table showing the inputs and outputs.**

Assessment activity 4.1

You are an IT consultant. An estate agent, Price&Move, has asked you to make recommendations for creating a local area network. You need to make recommendations on the:

- hardware
- software
- network type.

Price&Move has the following staff: one administration assistant, two sales staff and two valuations staff.

The budget that Price&Move has set for the project is £6,000. The business receives £2,000 for each house sold.

The network will be used to:

- keep a database of customers and properties
- keep a photographic record of properties
- produce letters and leaflets
- communicate with customers and others in the office
- keep records of property sales.

1. As part of your recommendation you will need to produce a requirements report. This should explain the hardware and software that will be used to solve this problem. **P1**

2. Prepare a business plan with details of the inputs, outputs and processes that are needed for the solution you are recommending. **P2**

3. Explain and justify why you have chosen the inputs and process in your business plan and why you have rejected other alternatives. **M1**

Grading tips

- Make sure that you include all the information that will be needed to solve this problem, where it will be researched and what the outcomes will be. **P1**

- Consider how you will show the links between inputs, processes and outputs. You could use a diagram for example to support your explanation. **P2**

- In your justification, make sure you take into account the constraints on the decision and how they have affected your choice of solution. **M1**

PLTS

By preparing a business plan and justifying the choices you made in the business plan, you will show that you are an **independent enquirer**.

Functional skills

Preparing a business plan could provide evidence for your functional **English** skills in writing.

Just checking

1. Name four business problems that a business may face where a spreadsheet could be helpful in finding a solution.
2. Where might a business find information on the prices of suppliers?
3. What is a simulation?
4. 'A benefit of looking for information is that it can lead to cost-effective solutions.' Explain what this means.
5. Why is the budget a business has a constraint on any solution to a problem?

2. Know how to find information to support business solutions

2.1 Data requirements

Businesses need data to help them make decisions about the solutions to their problems. They need to carry out research to find this data. Research could involve asking customers or other businesses, observation, looking on the Internet or using data in reports.

Businesses may need data about the following.

- **Products:** What products are available to help solve the problem? For example, a business that wants to network its office needs to know what products it will need to do this, such as the computers, printers, scanners and servers and the features of each.

- **Technologies**: Have any new technologies been developed which might help solve the problem? For example, a business upgrading its IT system will want to know if a new operating system has been developed that has better features than the one it uses in the existing system.

- **Manufacturers**: Which companies make the products we need to help solve the problem? For example, a business that wants to network its office needs to know the different manufacturers of the computers, printers and scanners that it needs.

- **Suppliers:** Which suppliers can provide products or services to help solve the problem? For example, a business launching a new product needs to know who could supply parts or ingredients. A business that wants to launch its website needs to know what suppliers could help it design or run the site.

Making decisions

Businesses have to make important decisions from the information they have collected.

Considering alternatives

They need to consider the alternatives they have found. For example, a business that wants to network its office will need to decide whether to link all its equipment with cables or whether to operate a wireless environment. A business that wants to invest in new cars will need to consider the features it needs the cars to have, such as size or miles per gallon.

Investigating costs

A business also needs to investigate the costs of its alternative solutions. These will include:

- the set up costs (the costs the business will need to pay at the start)

- the ongoing costs that it will need to pay

- the costs of paying any new staff it will need or training staff.

> **(i) Did you know?**
>
> In 2010 Dyson launched a new vacuum cleaner in the UK. The City DC26 was designed for people living in small spaces in cities. Over 90% of people in the UK live in cities and 2.3 million homes are smaller than 50 square metres. James Dyson developed the product over 5 years after he challenged his engineers to create a cylinder vacuum cleaner small enough to sit on an A4 piece of paper.

For example, a business with offices in different locations in the UK and abroad wants to link its offices with video conferencing. It will need to consider the costs of different systems and having them installed, the cost of maintaining the system if faults occur and the cost of training staff to use the system.

2.2 Sources of data

Where can businesses find the data they need to find effective business solutions? There are a variety of different sources that they might consider.

Internet

The Internet is probably the first method that many businesses use to find data about products, technologies, manufacturers, suppliers and prices. They can investigate vast amounts of information fairly easily and quickly using a search engine.

It's important to check that any data you find on the Internet is accurate and reliable (see page 115 for the importance of accurate information). Using trustworthy sources of data, such as the price list of a reputable business or information on a government website, will help. Cross-checking against other sites will also help confirm that the information is accurate. Be careful when using sites that give opinions, such as blogs, or sites where data is entered by many people, such as Wikipedia.

Other sources of data

The Internet is not the only source of information that businesses can use. Sometimes other sources can be more suitable to their needs.

Trade magazines

Trade magazines are aimed at businesses in a particular industry or profession, such as *Advanced Photoshop* for 3D designers, *World Textile Publications* for the textile, dyeing and printing industry and *Behind the Chair* for owners of beauty salons. Trade magazines regularly include articles on new technologies and reviews of new products. Suppliers may advertise their prices in these publications, knowing that businesses likely to buy their products will read them.

Brochures

Brochures are sent out by suppliers and manufactures to businesses they think might buy their products. They usually include a list of the products or services provided and the latest prices.

Retail outlets

A business may visit shops to see what products they have for sale and the prices that are being charged.

Advertisements

Adverts for suppliers and manufacturers can be found in a variety of locations, including on television, radio or in the cinema, in magazines or newspapers, and on billboards or posters. Advertising is often designed to persuade customers to buy and may contain limited data, but have a great impact. For example, clothes advertisements try to create an image, but say little in words about the actual product.

Activity: Finding information

1. Imagine you run a disco for functions, such as parties and weddings. You play music from playlists on your computer through speakers. You want to upgrade your computer.

   Make a list of the possible sources that you might use to find the information.

   Then make a list of the different things that you might consider when making your decision, including:

   - products
   - technologies
   - manufacturers
   - suppliers.

2. Funtime is an entertainment company. After many requests from customers, Funtime would like to provide a new service offering entertainment for children at weddings. The company has asked you to create a list of entertainers who might provide this service.

   Use the Internet to investigate suppliers in the local area who might be suitable for this new service.

   How else might you have found this information?

Copyright

When using data that belongs to other people you must be careful to acknowledge the **copyright** of the author. In the UK the Copyright, Designs and Patents Act 1988 gives the creators of written work, music and films, for example, rights to control the ways in which their material may be used.

If businesses are using information (e.g. photographs, articles or financial data) from another source in a report, they must obtain permission to use the information from the copyright holders. If permission is given, they must acknowledge the holders of the copyright material, by stating the name of the copyright holder, the title and date of the original publication and any other relevant information.

They must also check that they have given the name of the correct copyright holder.

Checking information

When using data that you have found through research, it's also important that you validate the information (check it is correct). You must check it for:

Key term

Copyright – the exclusive right of authors of original work to produce, publish and sell their work. It protects them from other people copying their work and gives them the right to control how other people use their material.

- **accuracy** – are the prices advertised by a supplier the actual prices being charged?
- **currency** – are the features of a new product the most up to date?
- **reliability** – does the data come from a source that you can trust?
- **completeness** – have you included all the alternative products or suppliers that you could choose for your solution?

Activity: Creating a database

An insurance company has decided to change the mobile phones of all its sales representatives to smart phones, so they have Internet connection and touch screen facilities.

- Create a database of the alternatives that you might consider, the features of each and the costs. Then choose one alternative.
- Ask a small number of people to comment on your selection of alternatives and on your final choice. Did they agree or not? If not, think about why and consider if there was a problem with the information you collected.

PLTS

You will show yourself to be an **independent enquirer** by:

- identifying and selecting data from appropriate sources to solve a business problem
- evaluating sources for accuracy, currency, completeness and reliability.

Functional skills

Finding data and evaluating its validity could provide evidence for your functional **ICT** skills in finding and selecting information.

BTEC Assessment activity 4.2 (P3) (M2) (D1)

Price&Move is happy with your recommendations for the local area network. It would now like you to choose appropriate hardware, software and type of network. You must research the data you need to help you make your choices.

1. Identify and select data from appropriate sources to help you choose the hardware and software for the local area network. **P3**
2. Validate your sources and acknowledge copyright. **M2**
3. Evaluate the sources you have chosen for your information. Interrogate your database and check carefully for accuracy, currency, completeness and reliability. **D1**

Grading tips

- You will need to consider a variety of sources to help you find the information and produce a list of your sources. Place the data you collect into a database. **P3**
- Make sure that you check that the sources given are correct and that you have given correct acknowledgment for any data you have used. State the name of the copyright holder, the title of the information, the date of publication, and any other information that the copyright holder has asked you to state. **M2**
- Use your evaluation to consider if other sources are required and if further research is needed. **D1**

Just checking

1. What might a business buying new computers need to know from manufacturers?
2. 'The Internet is not the only source of data.' Name four other sources of data.
3. Name two ways in which you can check Internet data for accuracy.
4. What is copyright?
5. A business wants to use information from another business. How does copyright affect how they use the information?

3. Be able to use spreadsheet models to support business solutions

3.1 Spreadsheet models

Spreadsheet software is designed to allow data to be stored and manipulated. Modelling a situation in a spreadsheet and then creating different models by changing the **variables**, **formulas** and data can help a business find a solution to its problems.

How to create and use of spreadsheets is covered in *Unit 27: Spreadsheet Modelling*. This rest of this unit considers the purpose of spreadsheets and how they might be used by businesses to solve problems.

Key terms

Variable – a storage area in a program for data. This data might come from user input or from a calculation done within the program.

Formula – used to carry out calculations in a spreadsheet. A formula must begin with an equals sign and can use either actual values (numbers) or references to cell addresses.

Purposes of spreadsheet models

Estimating costs

A business can use a spreadsheet to add up the costs of a possible solution. For example, a hospital wants to install a television, video and music system in a waiting room to keep people entertained while they wait. The spreadsheet allows calculations of costs to be made and the total cost to be calculated. Figure 4.2 shows the costs of this solution and Figure 4.3 shows how these costs have been calculated.

	A	B	C	D	E	F	G
1	Cost of installing a television, video and sound system						
2							
3		Number	Length (metres)	Hours worked	Cost	Total cost	
4	Large television	1			£ 1,000.00	£ 1,000.00	
5	Smaller televisions	2			£ 300.00	£ 600.00	
6	Cable		80		£ 0.50	£ 40.00	
7	Speakers	4			£ 150.00	£ 600.00	
8	Amplifier	1			£ 350.00	£ 350.00	
9	MP3 player	1			£ 150.00	£ 150.00	
10	Video	1			£ 200.00	£ 200.00	
11	Installation			6	£ 60.00	£ 360.00	
12	Repair and repainting of room			8	£ 30.00	£ 240.00	
13							
14	Total					£ 3,540.00	
15							

Figure 4.2 The total costs of installing the system.

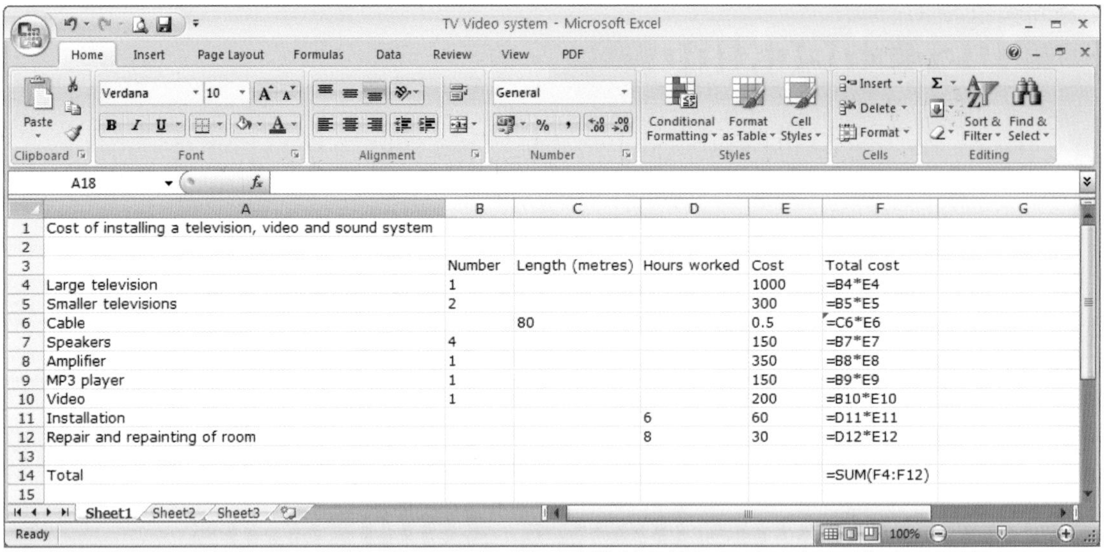

Figure 4.3 Total cost calculations showing the formulae.

Comparing alternatives

A business can use a spreadsheet to compare the costs of alternative solutions to problems. They can choose the least expensive or most cost-effective solution if it wants.

For example, a hotel wants to provide new uniforms and work clothes for all its restaurant staff. The spreadsheet in Figure 4.4 shows the costs of four alternative companies that could supply the uniforms. All these companies would provide designs for the uniforms and make them. The business can work out the cheapest alternative, which is supplier D.

The hotel has a budget of £10,000. The spreadsheet has also been designed to show whether the costs of buying the uniforms from each company are within budget or not. Of course, supplier D may not provide the uniforms in the fabric that the business wants. If this is the case, the business may choose supplier A, which does use the fabric it wants and is within budget. This is the best quality alternative it can afford.

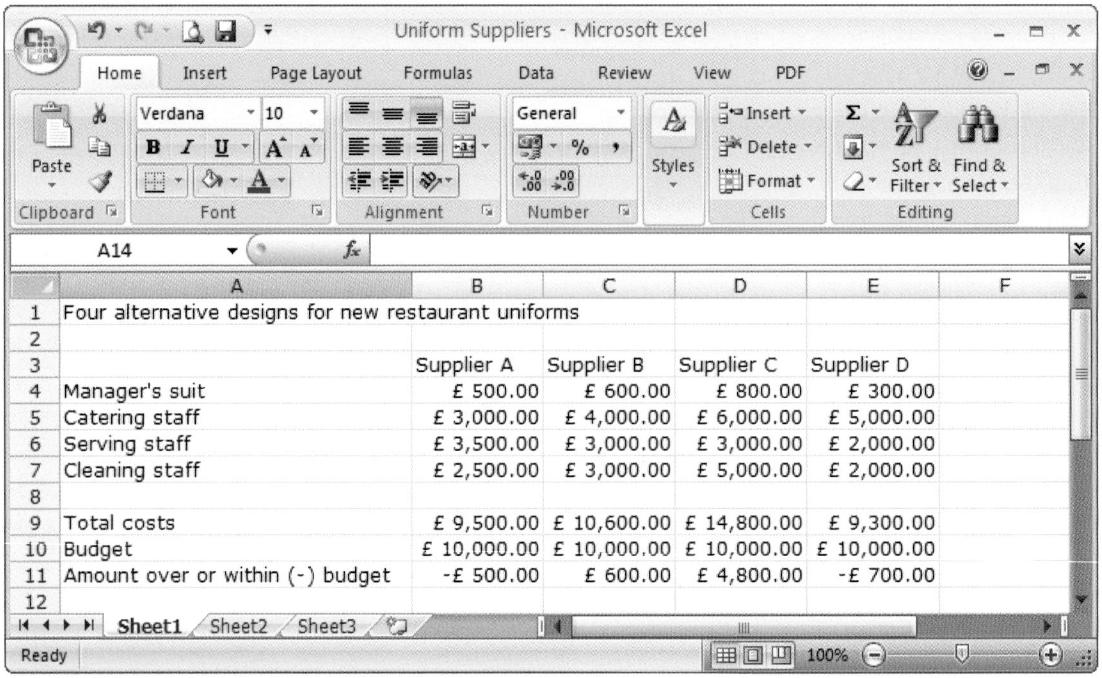

Figure 4.4 The total costs of four new uniform designs.

Calculating returns

The returns are the payments made to a business by its customers. A spreadsheet can be used to calculate the returns that a business might receive. For example, a restaurant in Manchester has recently lost customers. It has decided to open earlier, at 6.00pm instead of 7.30pm, and to attract customers with an 'early bird' menu. Figure 4.5 shows the possible returns for the business over a number of months. It also shows the profit or loss the business might make.

	A	B	C	D	E	F	G	H	I
1	Extra returns from opening earlier								
2									
3		Nov	Dec	Jan	Feb	March	April	Total	
4	Week 1	£ 650.00	£ 950.00	£ 300.00	£ 300.00	£ 400.00	£ 400.00	£ 3,000.00	
5	Week 2	£ 650.00	£ 950.00	£ 300.00	£ 300.00	£ 400.00	£ 400.00	£ 3,000.00	
6	Week 3	£ 450.00	£ 500.00	£ 200.00	£ 200.00	£ 350.00	£ 350.00	£ 2,050.00	
7	Week 4	£ 450.00	£ 500.00	£ 200.00	£ 200.00	£ 350.00	£ 350.00	£ 2,050.00	
8	Total returns	£ 2,200.00	£ 2,900.00	£ 1,000.00	£ 1,000.00	£ 1,500.00	£ 1,500.00	£ 10,100.00	
9									
10	Monthly extra costs	£ 1,800.00	£ 2,100.00	£ 1,400.00	£ 1,400.00	£ 1,500.00	£ 1,500.00	£ 9,700.00	
11									
12	Extra profit	£ 400.00	£ 800.00	-£ 400.00	-£ 400.00	£ 0.00	£ 0.00	£ 400.00	

Figure 4.5 The returns, costs, profits and losses for the restaurant of opening earlier.

Considering business impact

A spreadsheet can also be used to calculate the effect of business problems on a business. For example, a small grocery store has just had to change its supplier as its existing supplier has gone out of business. Figure 4.6 shows the change will affect the cost of the grocery store's supplies.

	A	B	C	D	E
1	The effect on a business of changing supplier				
2					
3	Product	Old supplier	New supplier	Change	
4					
5	Lettuce	£ 300.00	£ 310.00	£ 10.00	
6	Carrots	£ 500.00	£ 520.00	£ 20.00	
7	Brocolli	£ 420.00	£ 410.00	-£ 10.00	
8	Cabbage	£ 400.00	£ 420.00	£ 20.00	
9	Turnips	£ 90.00	£ 100.00	£ 10.00	
10	Sprouts	£ 320.00	£ 300.00	-£ 20.00	
11	Tomatoes	£ 600.00	£ 660.00	£ 60.00	
12	Potoatoes	£ 750.00	£ 760.00	£ 10.00	
13	Cougettes	£ 200.00	£ 220.00	£ 20.00	
14	Pears	£ 300.00	£ 320.00	£ 20.00	
15	Apples	£ 670.00	£ 620.00	-£ 50.00	
16	Oranges	£ 660.00	£ 640.00	-£ 20.00	
17	Bananas	£ 600.00	£ 630.00	£ 30.00	
18	Kiwi Fruit	£ 200.00	£ 200.00	£ 0.00	
19	Tangarines	£ 300.00	£ 310.00	£ 10.00	
20	Clemetines	£ 110.00	£ 110.00	£ 0.00	
21	Mixed nuts	£ 200.00	£ 180.00	-£ 20.00	
22	Grapes	£ 180.00	£ 200.00	£ 20.00	
23					
24	Total	£ 6,800.00	£ 6,910.00	£ 110.00	
25					

Figure 4.6 The impact on the business of the new supplier.

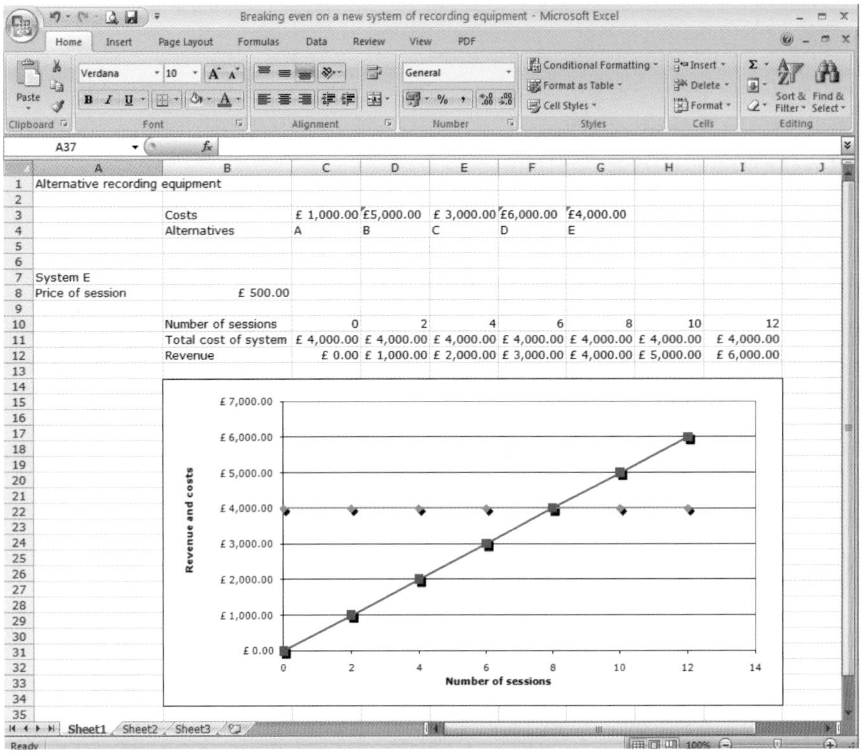

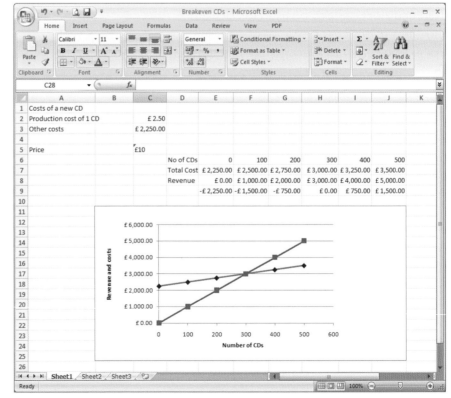

Figure 4.7 Breaking even on a new system of recording equipment.

Calculating the break even point

Example 1: A recording studio wants to upgrade its recording equipment. The cost of the system it has chosen is £4,000. It sells recording sessions for £500.

A recording studio has costed out a number of alternative systems of recording equipment and has chosen system E. The **break even point** is calculated where the total revenue from sales equals the total costs. It will break even at 8 sessions. Its revenue of £4,000 (8 x £500) will equal its costs of £4,000. With a budget of £4,000, it could afford this system.

You may also come across other situations where the term break even is used.

Key term

Break even point – where total revenue (the amount of money) is equal to total costs.

Did you know?

In 2009 Virgin Galactic (the first business offering to launch commercial space flight) said that it would break even within two years of its commercial launch. The business, controlled by Sir Richard Branson, was investing US$300 million in the project.

Example 2: A band wants to sell a new CD. The cost of producing the CDs is £2,250, plus £2.50 for each CD. The price is £10.

If the CD has the costs given above and is sold for £10, then it will break even at 300 CDs. Its revenue of £3,000 (£10 x 3) will equal its costs of £3,000 (£2,250 + [300 x £2.50]). This is shown in Figure 4.8.

Figure 4.8 Breaking even on the launch of a new CD.

Automated features of spreadsheets

Spreadsheets can be saved as screenshots to use in a presentation or printed out to use as part of a report. They also have automated features. You can draw graphs from information in a spreadsheet, like the graph in Figure 4.7. Other features that might be used from the spreadsheet include macros, script and user interface.

Macros

Macros allow users to carry out a task that would otherwise require a number of keystrokes or menus by making a single mouse click (see *Unit 9: Customising software* pages 164–165). Macros can be used to automate repetitive tasks that are done many times, making the task easier. They can be used to apply formatting to the content of cells, for example making text bold, changing the font size to 12 and changing the colour to blue.

Script

A script is a small program that runs within an application to automate it. A script can be used to add data to a spreadsheet cell, format a range of cells, or copy information from a database. For example, a business can use a script to copy records from a database with data about sales into a spreadsheet so that the data can be analysed further, such as producing graphs and charts. Examples of scripts can be found on the Internet.

User interface

A user interface is a way of making life easier for users of spreadsheets. Instead of having to look through a complex spreadsheet to type in data and look at the results, all of the inputs and results can be shown on one sheet. The rest of the spreadsheet will be hidden from view.

The data input can be controlled by using list boxes, combo boxes and option buttons, for example. When data is input into the spreadsheet the output is automatically updated on the same form. This means that the user doesn't need to scroll through the spreadsheet to find the area they want.

Figure 4.9 on the next page shows a user interface which includes data about the sporting preferences of five consumer groups. For example, two people like rugby in group 5. The number of the group and the sporting preferences are chosen from drop down lists (in the lists sheet), the data is sorted automatically in the analysis sheet and the graph is shown automatically on the Data Input sheet. All the spreadsheet cells except the cells used to input the data can be protected and hidden to stop users changing them.

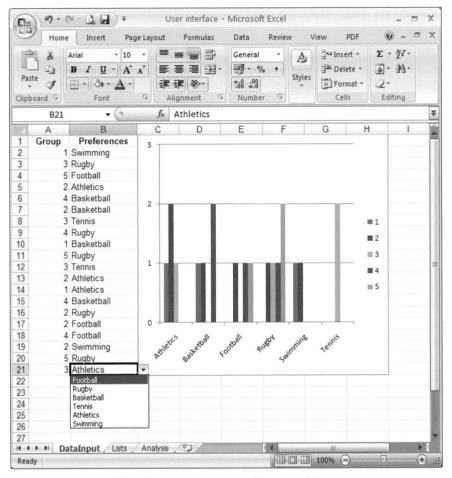

Figure 4.9 User interface showing sporting preferences of five consumer groups.

Activity: Redecorating a gym

A gym wants to use one of its rooms as a place for people to meet for a coffee after exercising. It will need to redecorate the room and has been given decorating costs by five different decorators (see Table 4.1). It also has to consider the costs of the other items it wants to buy:

- 12 chairs costing £100 each
- a carpet costing £500
- a coffee machine costing £200
- a television costing £500.

The gym has a budget of £6,650.

1. Use a spreadsheet to find out:

a) the least expensive of these options for the gym

b) which decorators are within budget.

2. The business sells annual membership for £665 a year. Using the costs for decorator 5, draw a break even graph.

Table 4.1: Decorating costs from five different decorators.

	Decorator 1	Decorator 2	Decorator 3	Decorator 4	Decorator 5
Stripping wallpaper	£ 1,000.00	£ 800.00	£ 800.00	£ 1,500.00	£ 1,000.00
Replastering	£ 800.00	£ 700.00	£ 1,000.00	£ 1,000.00	£ 1,000.00
Painting walls	£ 1,500.00	£ 1,400.00	£ 1,200.00	£ 1,000.00	£ 1,200.00
Painting wood	£ 1,000.00	£ 900.00	£ 600.00	£ 900.00	£ 1,250.00

What if? questions

A spreadsheet can be used to examine **What if? questions**. These questions consider what might happen to the alternative solutions to the problems a business faces if variables are changed. For example, a business that is upgrading its computer system might need to consider 'What if the supplier we have chosen goes out of business?' or 'What if the products we have chosen are no longer produced?' A business setting up its website might need to consider 'What if the designer increases the price?' or 'What if a competitor brings out a website with new features?'

Spreadsheets can be used to consider different What if? questions. Look again at Figure 4.7 on page 120. The business had a budget of £4,000 so it could afford system E, the system it chose in Figure 4.7. It could also afford systems A and C. It could not afford systems B and D.

What if the budget increased to £5,000? This is higher than the cost of system E. It could now also afford system B, which costs £5,000, if it wanted this. This is shown in Figure 4.10.

The business may also consider quality. What if system D was the best quality? In this case the business would need to increase its budget to £6,000.

Budgets are not the only variables that can change in spreadsheets. Businesses need to consider What if? questions about changes in:

- costs – the costs of designing a business website may rise or fall; if costs rise a business may not be able to afford to buy resources with its existing budget.

- quantities – the number of computers in a network may increase or decrease; if more are needed a business may not have enough in the existing budget.

Key term

What if? questions – this type of question is used to consider the possible outcomes if variables are changed. Spreadsheets are very useful for exploring What if? questions.

 Did you know?

When the new Wembley stadium was originally planned in 2000, the cost for building the stadium was calculated at £326.5m by the Australian contractor, Multiplex. By the time the company had signed to build the stadium the cost had risen to £445m. When it was completed and ready for the 2007 FA Cup final, the final figure was £798m. The increase was blamed on rising costs of materials and delays in construction.

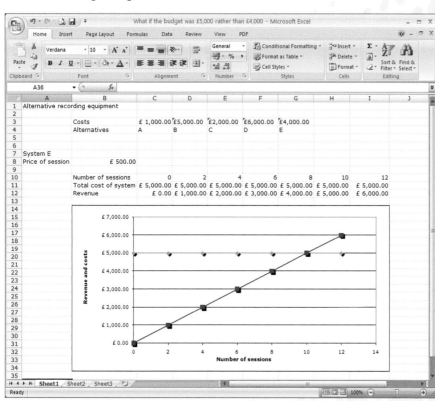

Figure 4.10 What if the budget was £5,000 rather than £4,000?

Activity: What if? questions

(a) Look at your spreadsheet for the answers to the activity on page 122. What if the budget rises to £6,800?

(b) In groups, use spreadsheets to consider the following What if? questions that the gym redecorating a room might consider. In each case decide which decorator it might choose. For each question use the values from the original spreadsheet for the activity on page 122. Use the original budget of £6,650.

1. What if decorator 3 goes out of business and decorator 5 lowers the cost of painting wood to £1,000?

2. What if decorator 2 agrees to paint the walls for the same price as the wood?

3. What if the gym buys only eight chairs?

4. What if all the decorators charge £1,500 for stripping the wallpaper?

5. What if:
- decorator 1 reduces the cost of stripping wallpaper by £300
- decorator 2 increases the cost of replastering by £50
- decorator 3 increases the cost of stripping wallpaper by £400
- decorator 4 reduces the cost of stripping wallpaper by £500
- decorator 5 reduces the cost of replastering by £300?

3.2 Developing the model

A business needs to consider how the model can be developed, so that it can work better to achieve a solution to the business's problem. A business will make its decision based on the feedback collected from users and also from people looking a screenshots and printouts, both before and after changes are made. The business must also decide if the spreadsheet is fit for the purpose it was intended for.

A business must then decide if it wants to create a new spreadsheet or make improvements. If it wants to make improvements to the existing spreadsheet, what will they be? The business might decide to:

- include more information
- change the formulae to make different calculations
- make the spreadsheet easier to use
- make the information easier to understand
- change the function of the spreadsheet
- add a user interface.

For example, a business might decide that it needs to see the costs of a new project in more detail. This might help it to decide where it can cut costs if it needs to do this. Figure 4.11 shows the cost of system C in Figure 4.7 (see page 120) in more detail.

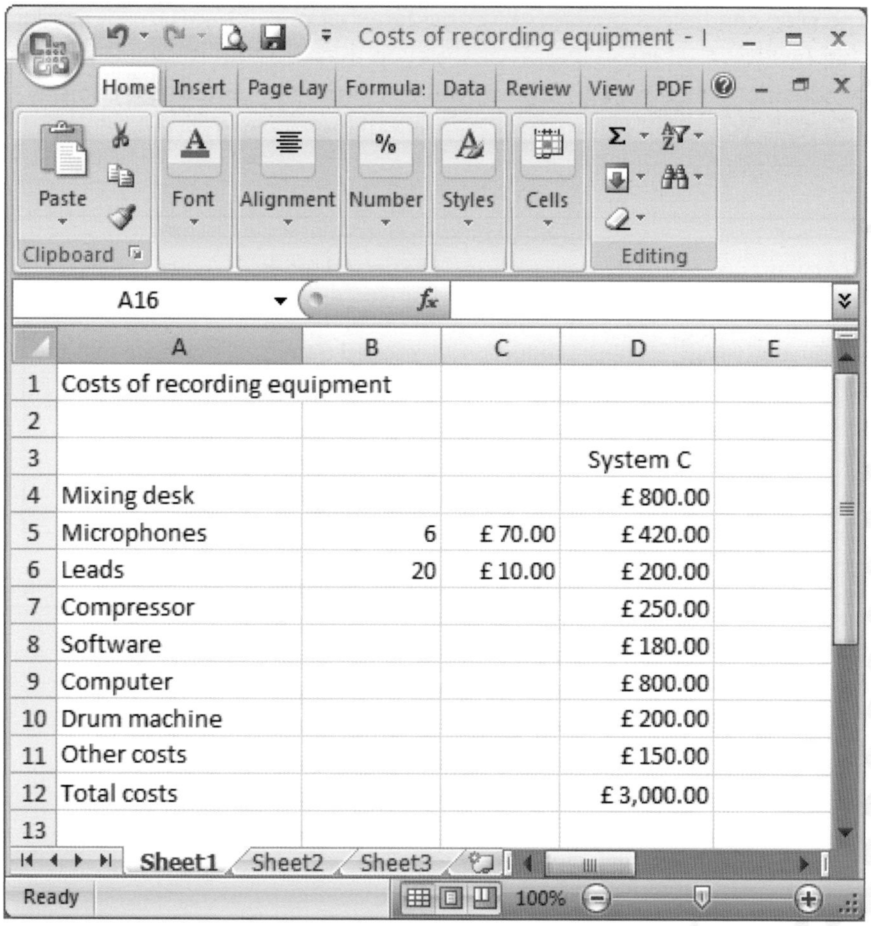

	A	B	C	D	E
1	Costs of recording equipment				
2					
3				System C	
4	Mixing desk			£ 800.00	
5	Microphones	6	£ 70.00	£ 420.00	
6	Leads	20	£ 10.00	£ 200.00	
7	Compressor			£ 250.00	
8	Software			£ 180.00	
9	Computer			£ 800.00	
10	Drum machine			£ 200.00	
11	Other costs			£ 150.00	
12	Total costs			£ 3,000.00	
13					

Figure 4.11 The costs of a system of recording equipment.

3.3 Testing

It is important for a business to test any spreadsheet model that it produces. If the spreadsheet doesn't work correctly, or in the way that the business wants, then the business might not find the best solution to its problem. A business could test the spreadsheet in a number of ways:

- using a **test plan**
- carrying out a user test
- assessing fitness for purpose.

Using a test plan

You should use a test plan to make sure that you carry out all the tests that need to be done. A test plan document will include information such as what is being tested, why it is being tested (the purpose of the test), how the test will be carried out, what the expected results are and what the actual results are.

Look back at Figure 4.4 (page 118). What if the budget was reduced to £8,000 from £10,000? In this case the business would not be able to afford any of the suppliers, as all costs are higher than this. Figure 4.12 shows a test plan for this What if? question.

Key term

Test plan – a document that specifies how a system, such as a spreadsheet, will be tested.

The plan can help a business to consider what might happen if it made changes to variables in its spreadsheet. In this case the business wants to consider if a change in the budget will affect the uniforms it can buy. The plan allows the business to compare the expected results of any action with the actual results.

Action	Reason	Expected results	Actual results
A what if? situation which involves changing the budget of a business that is buying uniforms for its restaurant.	I want to find out how a reduction in the budget will affect the uniforms that can be bought	If the budget is reduced from £10,000 to £8,000 it will not be able to afford any of the alternatives as they will all be over budget.	A smaller budget did mean that the business could not afford any of the alternatives.

Figure 4.12 Test plan for a change in the budget for uniforms.

Carrying out a user test

The business could ask people to do a **user test** of the spreadsheet. This is where a group of end users actually try using the spreadsheet. The business can check the functionality of the spreadsheet. It can check that the spreadsheet is working correctly and in the way that it wants.

The business can then ask the users for feedback on the spreadsheet using a **questionnaire**. The questionnaire could include the following questions.

- How easy was the spreadsheet to use?
- Did it work correctly?
- What improvements could be made to the spreadsheet?

When designing a questionnaire, you can use **closed questions**, with definite answers. This type of question will provide you with numerical data which you can then analyse. You can also use **open questions**.

Assessing fitness for purpose

Another important test is to find out if the spreadsheet is suitable for its intended purpose. To do this you need to ask the following questions:

- What was the objective of the spreadsheet?
- What was it designed to do?
- Did it do this?

For example, if a spreadsheet has been designed to find the cheapest designer of a new website, you will need to make sure that all the costs have been included. If it does not include all the relevant costs, then it will not be fit for its purpose.

Key terms

User test – where a group of end users try using the spreadsheet to test that it is working in the way a business wants.

Questionnaire – a list of questions designed to find out the views of respondents.

Closed question – a question with a set of answers that respondents must choose from. For example: "Did you have any problems with the spreadsheet? Yes or no?" or "Did you find the spreadsheet (a) easy or (b) difficult to use?"

Open questions – questions where the respondent can give any type of answer. For example: "Why did you choose this computer?"

Activity: Test plans

1. Write out a test plan to check that alternatives will change as expected when the budget is increased, as shown in Figure 4.10 on page 123.

2. Write out a test plan to check that your spreadsheet gives the expected results for question (a) in the activity on page 124.

BTEC Assessment activity 4.3 P4 M3 P5

1. Price&Move has asked you to produce, test and develop a spreadsheet model to consider alternative costs for setting up their local area network. The spreadsheet model should contain some automated features. **P4**

2. You will then need to develop this model based on user feedback. You will need to produce screen shots and printouts of your spreadsheet, test plans and the results of tests and user feedback. **P5**

3. Show the effects on costs if variables change by considering some What if? questions. These should include changes in budgets and costs. You will also need to generate a break even graph and consider how these changes will affect the graph. **M3**

Grading tips

- Test the spreadsheet yourself first to make sure the spreadsheet works as you expected. **P4**

- Then test the spreadsheet with different users, such as your teacher, other staff or you friends to get a variety of different views. Make sure that any developments you make are based on their comments. **P5**

- Remember that you have a budget of £6,000 for the network. Each house sold earns the business £2,000 in revenue. You will need to draw the total revenue line and then experiment with changes in the budget and costs to examine the effects on your proposal for a network. Consider how both increases and decreases in the budget and costs affect your suggestions. **M3**

PLTS

You will show yourself to be a **creative thinker** by:

- setting up and testing a spreadsheet model to solve a business problem

- exploring possibilities by asking What if? questions.

Functional skills

Setting up and developing a spreadsheet model could provide evidence for your functional **Mathematics** skills in representing and analysing.

Just checking

1. Explain how a spreadsheet can be used to:
   (a) calculate costs of a new piece of equipment
   (b) consider alternative suppliers
   (c) consider returns.
2. What is meant by breaking even?
3. How might a user interface be used when creating spreadsheets?
4. What is a 'What if?' question?
5. How can you use a questionnaire as part of a user test?
6. What is meant by fitness for purpose?
7. Name four ways in which a spreadsheet model can be developed.

4. Be able to present business solutions

Once a business has decided on a solution to its problem, it must consider how to present the solution to the different audiences who will be interested in the solution. The audience might be managers or other staff within the business, or it might be customers or suppliers.

You can present the solution in a number of ways, making use of software tools that are available. *Unit 29: Presenting information using IT* covers presenting information using software such as word processing, desk top publishing, PowerPoint and graphics packages.

4.1 Presenting the business solution

Word processing

You can write up the solution in the form of a report using word processing software, such as Microsoft Word®. The report should explain the problem and how the business plans to solve it.

Spreadsheets

You can use the spreadsheet you have created as part of your presentation of the business solution to show how the costs have been calculated. It is useful to include screenshots or printouts of your spreadsheet to illustrate the points that you want to make. For example, spreadsheets can be used to show solutions to numerical problems. They can show how costs have been calculated.

Graphics

Graphs or charts can be drawn from data in the spreadsheet to illustrate a solution. You can use a line graph such as the graphs in Figures 4.7 and 4.8 (see page 120). Charts could be bar charts or pie charts of different costs. Figure 4.13 shows a bar chart drawn using the data from Figure 4.5 (see page 119). It shows that even though the business has costs that are greater than returns in some months, it is worth opening earlier as total returns over the period are greater than total costs. Drawing graphs from spreadsheets is covered in *Unit 27: Spreadsheet modelling.*

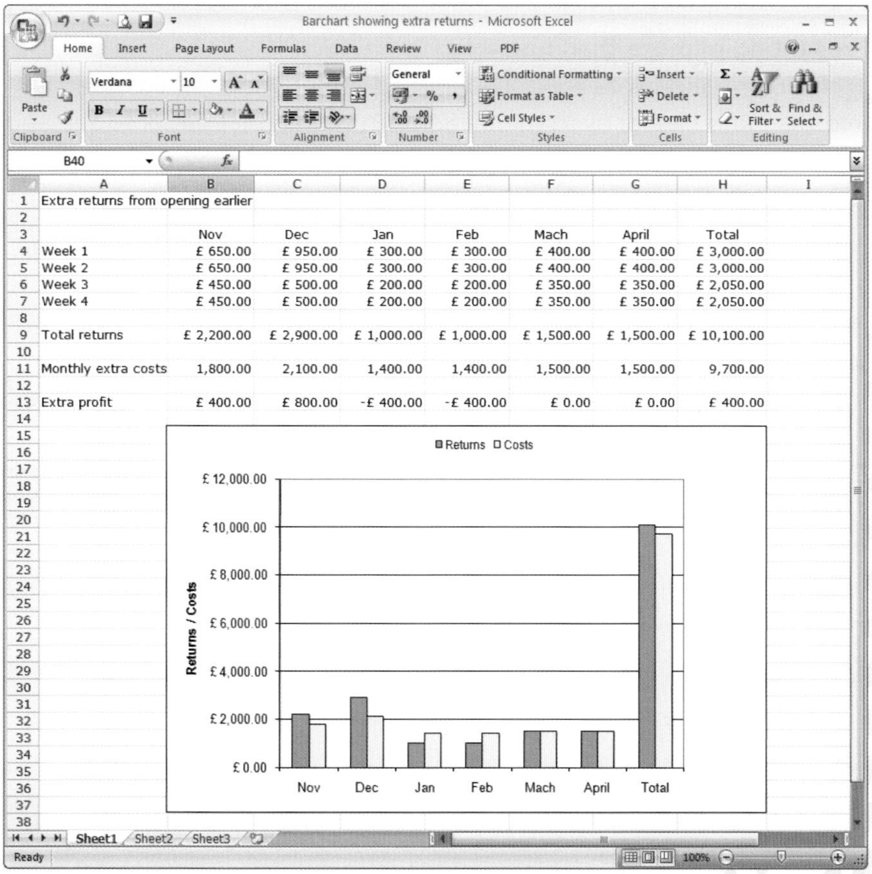

Figure 4.13 Bar chart showing the returns from a restaurant opening earlier.

Presentation

You can create a presentation as a set of PowerPoint® slides or web pages. These can make use of screenshots that you have created from your spreadsheet. You could also create a user guide to show the user of a spreadsheet how to make changes to the spreadsheet.

Presenting to different audiences

When presenting information it is important to consider the needs of the viewer. Different people might prefer the solution to be presented in different ways.

- A manager of a business launching a new website might want to see that it falls within budget. You could show this using graphs produced from a spreadsheet.
- The user of a spreadsheet might want to see how they can make changes to the spreadsheet. You could show this using screen shots of the spreadsheet.
- A designer might want to see what tasks are involved in running a new website. You could show this using a spreadsheet.
- A customer might want to see the different features of products shown on charts.

In addition, different people have different preferences for how information is presented: some people find it easier to understand if they see pictures, while others prefer to read. Some prefer to actually see an activity being carried out or to practise it themselves.

Presenting in more than one way

Some information is easier to understand if it is written, while other information is clearer as a picture. Some information is easier to see as figures in a spreadsheet; other information is better as a graph.

In addition, the audience may need to see the same information presented in more than one way. For example, a manager needs to see a breakdown of the costs for different network options. A graph will give him an instant picture of which networks fall within budget. But he may also need to see all the figures so he can make a detailed analysis of which costs can be cut.

4.2 Recommendations and justification

When you present your solution to a business problem, you will need to make a recommendation on the best solution.

A business also has to justify its decision. It needs to give reasons, supported by the spreadsheet. Some examples are shown in Table 4.2.

Table 4.2 Some examples of business recommendations and justifications.

Problem	Recommendation	Justification
A retail business is setting up a new website to promote its goods.	The business should choose a website designer in Manchester rather than London.	The designer in Manchester is cheaper than the designer in London, and can produce a design more quickly.
A travel agency is upgrading the computer system in its offices.	The business should choose the ABC brand of computers rather than the XYZ brand.	This brand has all the features the business wants for its budget.
A clothing company wants to launch a new range of sports clothing.	The business should launch a new range of sports clothing aimed at teenagers rather than another consumer group.	Teenagers buy more sports clothing than any other consumer group.

Activity: Redecorating a gym

Use the spreadsheet that you created for the activity on page 122 to illustrate the solution to the problem of choosing a decorator.

Create suitable graphs and charts to illustrate the solution that you have chosen.

5. Be able to evaluate business solutions

A business must **evaluate** the solution it has chosen to its problem. Evaluation involves making a judgement about how effective the solution is. This can be done in a number of ways:

- evaluating the solution against the original requirement
- evaluating the use of IT tools
- the development of the model
- suggesting improvements.

Evaluating the solution against the original requirement

A business needs to consider what it was trying to achieve and whether its solution did this. For example, a business has a machine that is ten years old that constantly breaks down. It has £10,000 to buy a new machine but wants it to be up to date. If it buys a machine for £9,000 with the latest technology it might judge that it has achieved its objectives, as it has bought up-to-date equipment, within its budget.

Evaluating the use of IT tools

A business must judge how well it used software to find its solution. Did it set up the spreadsheet correctly? Did the spreadsheet work as expected? Did it use a database to store and search for information?

The development of the model

Did the development of the model help the business to find the best solution? Did it gather enough information from users about the model? Did it make changes that were recommended or not?

Suggesting improvements

Did any changes that the business made to the model improve it?

If a business judges that its solution is not what it wanted, does not solve its problem or is not the best solution to its problem, it may suggest other improvements. These could be:

- finding out more information or gathering more accurate information
- changing how the spreadsheet works
- getting more feedback or increasing any testing
- changing what it wants to achieve
- finding alternatives that it had not previously considered.

> ## Key term
>
> **Evaluation** – making a judgement about how successful the solution is, often against criteria such as the original objectives. The evaluation may also involve giving reasons for the choice.

BTEC Assessment activity 4.4   (P6) (P7) (M4)

Price&Move now wants you to present a business solution for setting up the local area network to all staff in the business.

1. Present your solution using a range of software tools. You could present your solution using PowerPoint, written report or web page. Make sure that you present your solution in a way that takes into account the needs of the audience. **P6**

2. Justify your use of software tools. This means giving reasons why you have used the spreadsheet in particular ways, why you have chosen a certain test plan, the software you have chosen and why you have developed the model. **M4**

3. Carry out an evaluation of your solution. You must judge whether you have achieved the objectives you set out to achieve. Evaluate to what extent the use of IT and whether any changes you made to your spreadsheet model helped you to achieve your objectives. **P7**

Grading tips

- Choose a presentation method that is appropriate to your client, Price&Move, which is an estate agent. You need to take into account whether the presentation will be to one person or to a number of people and who the people in the audience will be. **P6**

- In your justification of choice of software, take into account the jobs that the software has to do and the requirements of the business. Give reasons why you have developed the spreadsheet in the way that you have (e.g. to make it easier for the user group or to show solutions to problems more clearly). **M4**

- Evaluation means making a judgement. You are judging against criteria – not whether you liked it, enjoyed it or found it easy. Make sure you evaluate your solutions to the business problem against the criteria you have set. Make sure you state the reasons for your judgement. **P7**

Just checking

1. A photographic business has the costs for a new dark room from three suppliers. State two types of graph that it could use to illustrate these costs.
2. How might a business present a report?
3. Why might a graph be used to present information rather than a paragraph of text?
4. What is a recommendation?
5. Name three ways that a business might evaluate its solution to a problem.

Cara Janes
Estimator for a printing company

The business I work for

I work for Printerz. The business prints a variety of products including leaflets, business cards, advertising posters and small magazines. Our customers are people or businesses who want jobs printing quickly. Some jobs are fairly small, such as 100 business cards. But they can be larger, such as 10,000 advertising leaflets.

My job

My job is to estimate the costs of printing a job. I can then decide what price to charge so that we can make a profit.

We keep information about past customers and the prices we have charged them on a database. Sometimes I can just quote the same price. But for new customers I have to calculate all the costs of the printing using a spreadsheet. I then work out the price we need to charge to make a profit.

The challenges that I face

It's very important that the quotes I give are competitive. If they aren't, then we'll lose customers. They'll just go to other printers. I must make sure that our prices are similar to or better than those of our competitors.

But we also need to make a profit. So we must keep our costs as low as possible. I must check that the prices of materials we are buying from suppliers are the best I can get. Our other printing costs must be kept as low as possible.

Think about it!

1. How might Cara find out about (a) the cost of materials from suppliers and (b) the prices charged by competitors?
2. What information might be contained in (a) the database and (b) the spreadsheet that Cara uses?
3. What might happen to the business if the costs of materials go up?

Just checking

1. Name the three parts to a business plan.

2. What is a user test?

3. What is a test plan?

4. 'The suppliers' data was not up to date.' Explain why this might be a problem for a business.

5. Explain briefly how a business could use a spreadsheet to compare the costs of two different new alarm systems for its offices.

6. State two examples of 'What if?' questions that can be considered using a spreadsheet.

7. 'A business has to justify its choice of solution to a problem.' Explain this statement.

8. Why might a PowerPoint® presentation be better for presenting a solution to a business problem than a written report?

edexcel :::

Assignment tips

- Make sure you clearly understand the nature of the problem that you are solving for the business in your assessment, for example creating a local area network for a business.

- Be aware of how long you have to complete the project. You will need to break down the overall time period into sections and plan how long you will have to carry out research, make choices, write your spreadsheet and test it, make improvements and carry out an overall evaluation.

- Check back to the grading criteria that you have covered all parts of the assessment. Check that you have covered all the criteria that are given for the grade you hope to achieve.

- Annotate screen print outs to make explanations clearer.

- Make sure that you have included everything in your portfolio. If it is not included you will not gain any marks for it.

- Make sure your assessment is well organised and follows a logical pattern. Use a contents page to show how the assessment is planned.

- Keep evidence of all your research. This is important to show that you are using evidence to justify the judgements that you are making.

- Gather research information from a variety of sources to ensure that your data is accurate. Test your suggestions on a variety of users so you get a range of views about its effectiveness.

- Use information from other units to support your decision and judgments, In particular, information from *Unit 27* on spreadsheets, *Unit 29* on presenting information and *Unit 10* on networking will be useful.

- Ask someone to check through your portfolio before you submit it to suggest improvements or to identify anything they feel is unclear.

9 Customising software

This unit is about making additions and changes to common Microsoft® Office® System applications, such as word processing programs and spreadsheets, to make them easier to use. These additions and changes, or customisations as they are known, include altering the default settings, modifying the menus and toolbars, creating templates and forms, and creating macros and shortcuts.

Microsoft® Office® System applications such as Word® and Excel® have lots of features, but some users may find the more advanced features difficult to use. In addition, there may be some tasks that users have to repeat time and time again. When working as an IT technician, you may get asked to make things easier or less repetitive for users. There may also be occasions when you simply get asked to modify the way a user's Windows® desktop looks.

These are all examples of when you need to know how to customise software.

Before you attempt this unit you should complete *Unit 27: Spreadsheet modelling*, so that you fully understand how spreadsheets work before you start looking at how to customise them.

Learning outcomes

After completing this unit you should:

1. understand why application software is customised
2. be able to customise application software
3. be able to create templates in application software
4. be able to create macros and shortcuts in application software.

Assessment and grading criteria

This table shows you what you must do in order to achieve a pass, merit or distinction grade, and where you can find activities in this book to help you.

To achieve a **pass** grade the evidence must show that you are able to:	To achieve a **merit** grade the evidence must show that, in addition to the pass criteria, you are able to:	To achieve a **distinction** grade the evidence must show that, in addition to the pass and merit criteria, you are able to:
P1 explain why software may be customised to meet user requirements **See Assessment activity 9.1 on page 154**		**D1** evaluate the benefits and drawbacks of customisation **See Assessment activity 9.1 on page 154**
P2 customise application software to meet user requirements **See Assessment activity 9.1 on page 154**		
P3 test customised software to ensure it meets user requirements **See Assessment activity 9.1 on page 154**		
P4 create templates to meet user requirements in different application packages **See Assessment activity 9.2 on page 163**	**M1** evaluate how effectively the templates meet user requirements **See Assessment activity 9.2 on page 163**	
P5 record and test a macro to meet a given requirement **See Assessment activity 9.3 on page 172**	**M2** explain the benefits of using macros **See Assessment activity 9.3 on page 172**	
P6 assign and test shortcuts **See Assessment activity 9.3 on page 172**		

How you will be assessed

This unit is internally assessed. You will provide a portfolio of evidence to show that you have achieved the learning outcomes. Your portfolio of evidence can be supplied in many formats including electronically as well as paper-based. The grading grid in the specification for this unit lists what you must do to obtain pass, merit and distinction grades. The Assessment activities in this unit will guide you through tasks that will help you to be successful in this unit.

Your tutor will tell you exactly what form your assessments will take, but you could be asked to produce:

- practical tasks
- a written report with screenshots.

Rashad Abdel, 16–year-old learner

I'm studying BTEC Level 2 IT at school. I didn't think I would learn that much in this unit. I thought I already knew a lot about applications like Word® and Excel®. I didn't realise there was so much you could do to customise these applications. I knew about templates, but I didn't know you could create forms with them. I found creating macros interesting. It's quite difficult as it's tricky to get them right. There's a lot more to learn about macros and I'm looking forward to that at Level 3.

When it came to the assessment for this unit, I found the pass criteria were quite straightforward – they were mostly practical tasks, which is what I enjoy. The merit and distinction criteria were much harder because I had to think carefully about how the macros and templates would be used and what their benefits were. My first draft for D1 was quite brief – I talked about how macros and templates make things quick and easy for the user. But my tutor said this wasn't enough for a distinction grade, so I had to think of some actual examples. I spoke to my mum's friend, who works as an administration assistant in a solicitor's office. She uses lots of Word® templates and gave me some great examples of how the templates save her a lot of time. They make it easy for junior members of staff to create complex documents as they don't have to know how to create the documents from scratch. I used this example in my re-drafted work for D1 and that really helped.

Over to you

- Do you already know a lot about how to use Word®, Excel® and other Microsoft® Office® System applications?
- Do you know what a template and macros are? Do you know how people use them in the workplace?
- Do you have friends or relatives who use Microsoft® Office® System applications at work? You could talk to them about the features they use and the things they find difficult.

1. Understand why software is customised

Would customisation help?

Most computer users make use of applications like Microsoft® Word® and Excel® a lot, especially at work. However, there may be many things that they find difficult to do or repetitive tasks which could be automated.

1. In a group, choose Word® or Excel®. Then write down:
   a. five things you find difficult in this application
   b. five tasks you do repeatedly.
2. Discuss whether you could use the customisation features in these applications to simplify these tasks.

1.1 Why is software customised?

There are lots of different types of software.

- **System software** — is part of the operating system of the computer. It provides a user interface and various tools to control and protect your computer.

- **Utility software** — is used to control and configure your computer. These are sometimes part of the operating system, but you can also purchase add-on utilities like anti-virus software.

- **Application software** — is used to carry out work tasks, such as writing a letter or creating a presentation. The most common types of application software are word processors and spreadsheets. Application software is the focus of this unit.

Most software can be customised to suit the requirements of the user. There are a number of reasons why we might want to customise software:

- to make a particular feature easier to use, perhaps to meet the needs of a novice user

- to help a user complete a complex task quickly and easily, with the minimum of user input

- to improve the accuracy of data entered, by adding validation to help ensure data is correct.

As a future IT technician, you may be asked to customise Microsoft® Office® System software to meet particular user needs. Throughout this unit, we will be using Microsoft® Office® 2007 and the Windows® 7 operating system for all the examples. What you see on your screen may differ slightly, depending on your operating system or the way your system is set up.

1.2 Types of customisation

There are a number of different ways that Microsoft® Office® System applications can be customised:

- **Changing default settings.** The **default** settings control the way an application works and are set when it is installed. However, these settings may not be the best for all users and changing them may make the application easier to use.

- **Modifying menus and toolbars.** The layout of the **toolbars** and menus is also set at installation. Depending on the application features that are used most often, it may be more convenient to change this arrangement. For example, a user might prefer to have different toolbars displayed when the application starts.

- **Creating templates and forms.** Templates save time when creating standard documents like business letters and forms. They are also used to make sure that all the employees in a company produce consistent documents, for example all memos and letters have the same layout. Forms created in a Word® document or Excel® spreadsheet provide an easy way for users to enter data.

- **Macros.** These allow regularly used functions to be automated. A task that might take several keystrokes or menu selections can be simplified by creating a **macro** that carries out the task with a single mouse click.

- **Creating shortcuts.** Shortcuts provide a quick way of doing something. For example, **keyboard shortcuts** allow you to select a command or run a macro by pressing a combination of keys instead of having to use the mouse. Other types of shortcuts include hyperlinks and drive mappings.

Key terms

Defaults – the settings that have been set by the application maker. They are the settings that are used, unless the application user changes them.

Toolbars – groups of icons used to control the functions of the program. All Microsoft® Office® System software has them. The default setting for toolbars places them at the top of the program window under the menu bar. However, toolbars are 'floating' and can be dragged into any position in the program window. Different toolbars can be displayed if required, using the Toolbars option under the View menu.

Macro – a method of automating a series of functions within a Microsoft® Office® System application.

Keyboard shortcut – a key combination that runs a certain command. For example, the built-in shortcut **Ctrl+S** will save a document in most Microsoft® Office® System applications.

Activity: Using forms

- Find out if your centre of learning or place of work uses any Word® forms. If so, what are they used for and why are they used? Do the people who use them find they are easier or more difficult to use than a standard Word® document?

- Have you filled in any forms recently? Would these forms be easier to complete by hand or on the computer?

1.3 Benefits of customising application software

There are a number of potential advantages to customising applications:

- **Ease of use.** This is one of the main benefits. Customisation can make complex procedures easier for novice users.

- **Speed.** Customisation can make features in an application quicker to use by reducing the number of keystrokes or mouse selections required. This is particularly important when a commonly used task requires quite a complex series of user inputs.
- **Accuracy.** Where applications such as Excel® or Access® are used to enter data, it is important that the data entered is accurate. You can reduce the chance of incorrect data being entered by adding customised data entry facilities to validate the input data.
- **Consistency of style.** Many organisations like to maintain a corporate image. For example, they want their logo and contact details to be used in a **consistent** way on all their documents – for example, always in the same position and using the same font and point size. This can be done by using standard templates throughout the company for documents such as business letters.
- **Improved productivity.** Because customised applications can be quicker and easier to use than the standard versions, they can make people more productive. Instead of spending time doing repetitive tasks or struggling with complex procedures, people have more time to do more productive tasks, such as dealing with customers.

Key term

Consistency – the same style and layout is used on all documents so you can easily recognise that they come from the same organisation.

1.4 Drawbacks of customising software

There are, of course, disadvantages to customising software, including:

- **Training.** Users require training on customisations that are added to the standard applications. This costs time and money.
- **Support.** The customisations produced need support. Since the customisation is unique, commonly used sources of support, such as the Microsoft® website, are not of any help. Support probably needs to be provided by the person or team that wrote the customisation. Since people may leave the company or move to other jobs, it is important that they provide sufficient documentation to allow other people to support the customisation.
- **Increased complexity.** The more complex an application becomes, the more likely it is that something will go wrong and the more difficult it can be to fix. Customising existing applications may cause technical problems and may make the application more unreliable.

Despite the disadvantages, customisations are often made to Microsoft® Office® System software to make things easier for users. This is particularly the case with people who use applications such as Word® and Excel® a lot. The Word® document I am typing into right now for this book uses a template that provides all the styles for the headings and features, such as the 'Key terms' and 'Knowledge check' boxes. This template was developed by Pearson Education Limited for all the authors writing for this book. It helps ensure consistency between the authors and helps us get an idea of how the book will look when it is complete.

Just checking

1. List two reasons why you might want to customise software.
2. Describe four basic types of customisation that can be applied to software.
3. List three advantages of customising application software.
4. List three disadvantages of customising application software.

2. Be able to customise application software

We now need to look at how to make simple changes, such as modifying default settings, changing the user interface and altering how certain tools and functions work.

2.1 Resources

Imagine you want to make a change to the way your computer works or how the user interface looks, but you're not sure if it is possible or how you can do it. Where would you go for help? There are a number of resources you can use.

Help facilities

Windows® 7 and almost all applications have a help facility built in which may provide instructions on how to carry out the customisation you are interested in. Pressing the **F1** key on the top left of your keyboard will bring up the help menu in the application you are running. You can also go to the **Help** menu or icon in most applications or click on the **Windows Start** menu and choose **Help and Support**.

Manuals and books

With the growth of the Internet, manuals and books are not as popular as they used to be. However, manuals for your application software may be available on the installation CD in the form of an Adobe® Acrobat® file. You can also buy books which describe how to use the features of the most popular application programs; some of these books focus on customisation.

Websites

Websites are probably the most popular resource for finding out how to do something with your computer. Search engines allow you to find a wide range of resources, including:

Key terms

Margins – the gaps between the edge of a piece of paper and where the text starts.

Page orientation – this sets how print will be displayed on the paper. The long side at the top is called *landscape* orientation; the short side at the top (the normal setting for letters, etc.) is called *portrait*.

- information provided by the software maker
- FAQ (Frequently Asked Questions) pages with answers to common problems
- technical forums with advice and guidance from users.

Microsoft® provides a searchable support website for Microsoft® Office® System products (such as Word® and Excel®), known as Microsoft® Office Online®. You can also access this site from the Help menu in Microsoft® Office® System applications, or by going to Hotlinks and clicking on this unit.

2.2 Default settings

Most applications have a wide range of settings to suit different user requirements. Some of them depend on the country where you live. The default settings are the settings that are used unless you select something different.

Printer settings

The default printer is the one your printouts will go to unless you select a different printer. The default paper size for word processing documents needs to be set to A4 for people who live in Europe. But in the USA, the standard size paper is known as 'letter', which is slightly smaller than A4.

How to... Set the paper size and default printer

Paper size is set in Word® on the **Page layout** tab of the Ribbon. This also allows you to set other characteristics for printing, such as **margins** and **page orientation** (portrait or landscape).

Many Microsoft® Office® System users have access to more than one printer, such as a networked laser printer and a local colour inkjet. The default printer is the one that documents are printed on if you choose **Quick Print** from the **Office** menu. It is also the first one listed in the **Print** dialog box. You can change the default printer, to be used by all applications, by going to **Start** then **Devices and Printers**. This will open the **Devices and Printers** window, as shown in Figure 9.1.

The default printer is the one with the tick next to it. To change the default, right-click on the printer and choose **Set as default** from the menu that pops up.

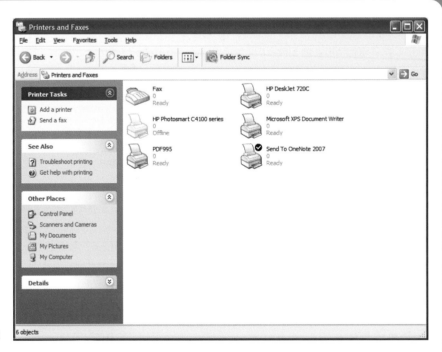

Figure 9.1: Devices and printers window.

Text settings

You can also change default settings for the text font and size used in Word®. This is usually set to 11 point Calibri when you install Word®, but you might prefer another size and font. Instead of changing it every time you type a new document, you can set a different default.

How to... Change the default text font and size used in Word®

Go to the **Home** tab in the Ribbon, click the **Font Dialog Box Launcher** (bottom right of the Font group). This will display the **Font** dialog box on your screen as shown in Figure 9.2.

Choose the default font you would like all new documents to start off in, then click the **Default** button. You will then see a warning message reminding you that you are changing a default setting that will affect all new documents. The default settings for every new Word® document are held in a template called **Normal**. We will look at templates in more detail later (see pages 155–162).

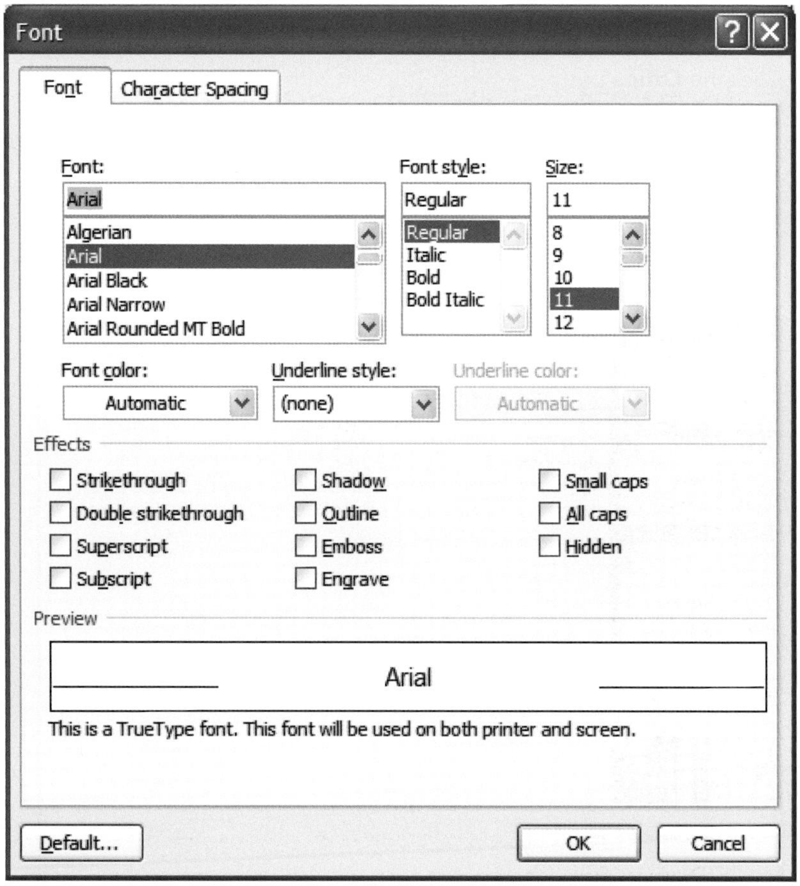

Figure 9.2: The Font dialog box.

Page layout settings

You can also set the default for a number of page layout options.

How to... Set the default for page layout options

Select the **Page Layout** tab then click the **Page Setup dialog box launcher** (bottom right of the Page Setup group). This displays the **Page Setup** dialog box. In the **Margins** tab, you can set the page margins and page orientation for the current document by selecting the options you want and clicking **OK**. If you click the **Default** button instead of **OK**, the changes will apply to all new documents.

File locations

You can also change the default folder (also known as a directory) where files are saved in Microsoft® Office® System programs. Normally when you save a new document, the default folder, shown in the **Save As** dialog box, is **My Documents**. But you can change this so files are saved in some other location.

How to... Change default file locations

Click the **Office** button in Word® (top left with the Microsoft® Office® logo), then select the **Word Options** button on the bottom right. Click **Save** on the left of the dialog box and you can then change how files are saved, as shown in Figure 9.3.

To change the default location, click the **Browse** button next to the **Default file location** box and choose a new folder.

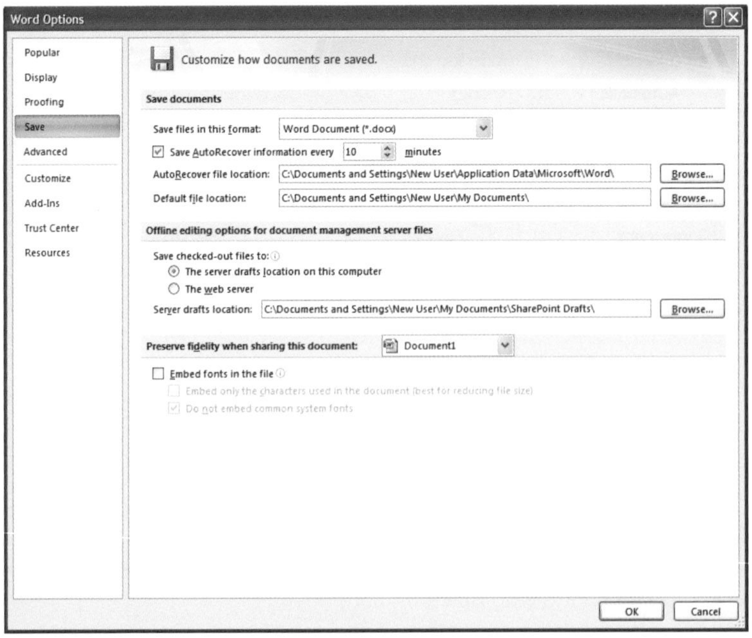

Figure 9.3: Word® Save options.

2.3 Interfaces

The 'human interface' is what users see on-screen when they interact with the computer. It has many aspects: windows, menus, dialog boxes and so on. Some of these can be customised to suit a user's particular needs.

The desktop

You probably already know that you can customise the Windows® desktop to your tastes. Let's look at some examples.

> **(i) Did you know?**
>
> You can find out about the wide range of other desktop settings you can customise using the help system. Click **Start**, then **Help and Support**. Then search for 'customize desktop'.

How to... Customise your desktop

Right-click on the desktop and choose **Properties**. This will bring up the **Personalization** dialog box, as shown in Figure 9.4.

From here you can change the way your desktop looks in a number of ways.

- **Themes.** This allows you control the overall look of the Windows® display. Choosing a different theme changes your desktop background, window colour, sounds and screen saver all at once.

You can also change individual aspects of your interface.

- **Desktop background.** Here you can change the desktop background (previously known as wallpaper).

- **Window colour.** This allows you to change the colour scheme of your windows.

- **Sounds.** You can choose different sounds to signify various Windows® events.

- **Screen saver.** You can choose the type of screen saver and related settings.

- **Icon type and arrangement.** If you click the **Desktop** tab, then **Customize** desktop button, you can change what icons are displayed and the icon pictures. Right-clicking anywhere on the desktop background will display a menu that allows you to use different size icons and order them in different ways (for example, by type or name).

Figure 9.4: The Properties dialog box.

Generally these settings are purely a matter of user preference, although people with eyesight problems may find that changing the size or colour of the window items is beneficial.

Toolbars

Many applications provide toolbars with icons that represent the different functions available to the user. Office 2007®, for example, has the Quick Access Toolbar, located to the right of the Microsoft® Office® button. The commands that appear on this toolbar can be customised to suit the user's preferences.

How to... Modify the Quick Access toolbar

In Word 2007® click the **Customize** icon to the right of the **Quick Access** toolbar and the **Customize** menu drops down, as shown in Figure 9.5.

You can add new commands to the Quick Access toolbar by choosing them from the menu. You can also have the Quick Access toolbar displayed below the Ribbon by selecting that option from the menu.

If the command you want to add to the Quick Access toolbar is not shown, you can click on **More Commands** to see a full list of the commands you can add.

If you prefer the Ribbon to disappear when you are not using it, you can select the option **Minimize the Ribbon**. This will leave the tabs of the Ribbon showing but not the Ribbon itself. Click the tab you require and the whole Ribbon will reappear.

You can also add many of the items on the Ribbon to the Quick Access Toolbar by right-clicking on them and choosing **Add to Quick Access Toolbar**.

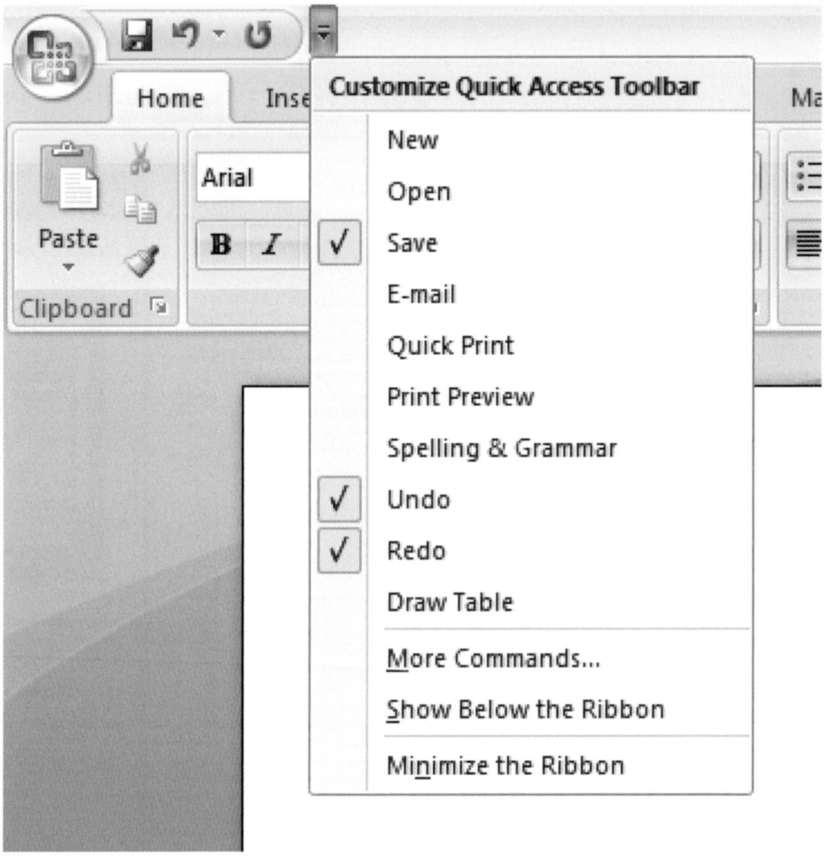

Figure 9.5: The Quick Access toolbar Customize menu.

Customising the Quick Access toolbar

Carry out a small survey among your fellow learners to find out which commands they regularly use in Word® and Excel®. Based on the results of your survey, customise the Quick Access toolbar so it contains the most commonly used commands.

Menus

Many application programs have menus and some allow you to customise the way these menus work. One menu every Windows® user is familiar with is the Start menu at the bottom left of the screen. This is the main menu you use to run different applications, find disks, folders and files and to adjust Windows® settings. You can customise the way the Start menu looks.

How to... Customise the Start menu

Open the Control Panel, click the **Appearance and themes** link and then click the Task Bar and Start Menu at the bottom. This will display the **Taskbar and Start Menu Properties** dialog box – see Figure 9.6.

clicking the **Customize** button. This takes you to the **Customize Start Menu** dialog box, as shown in Figure 9.7.

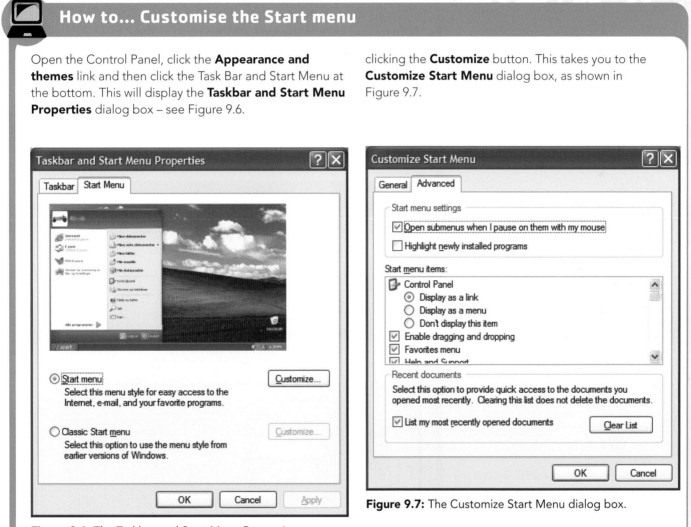

Figure 9.6: The Taskbar and Start Menu Properties dialog box.

This dialog box allows you to control how the Taskbar behaves and the style of the Start Menu. You can further customise the items that are listed in the Start menu by

Figure 9.7: The Customize Start Menu dialog box.

This dialog box allows you to control which items appear on the Start menu and how they look. For example, you can choose to have the Control Panel displayed as a link or a menu or not at all. The easiest way to see the difference between a link and a menu is to try these options out.

Mouse settings

Further examples of how you can change the user interface are the mouse and keyboard settings. The mouse and the keyboard are as much a part of the user interface as the information that appears on the screen.

How to... Change mouse settings

Open the **Control Panel** by choosing **Start, Control Panel**. Choose the **Printers and other hardware** link then click the **Mouse** link. This will display the **Mouse Properties** dialog box, as shown in Figure 9.8.

This tabbed dialog box allows you to customise a number of aspects of how the mouse works. For example, if you find double-clicking quickly a bit tricky, you can reduce how fast you need to double-click for the computer to recognise it. You can also adjust the look and behaviour of the mouse pointer using the **Pointer Options** tab.

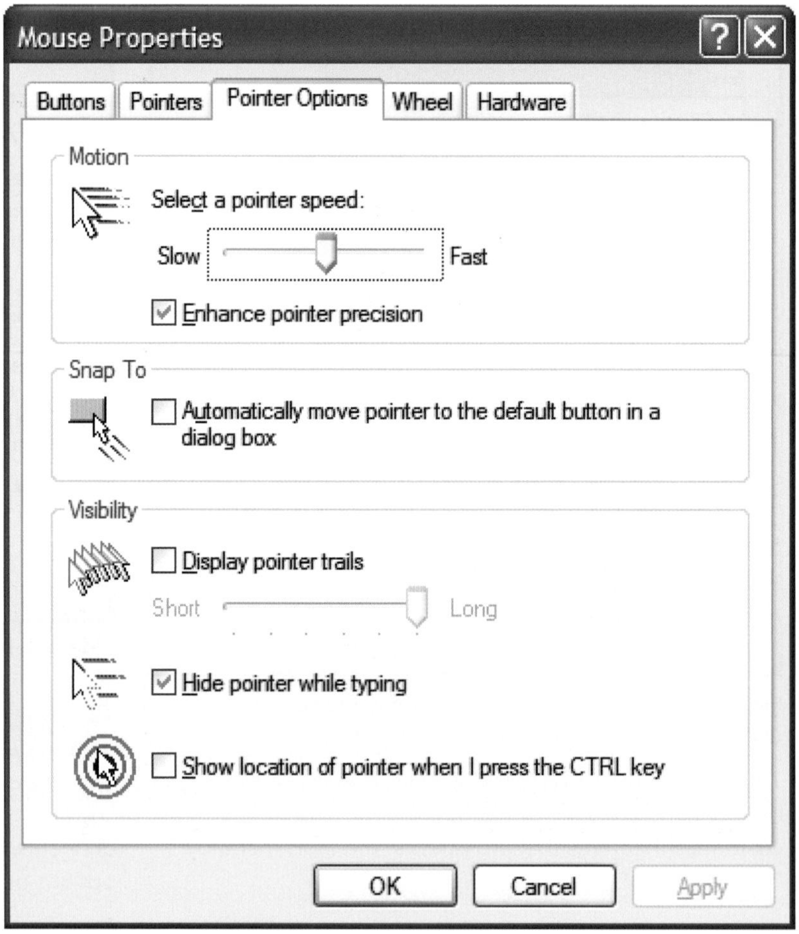

Figure 9.8: The Mouse Properties dialog box.

2.4 Specific tools

Modern software, such as Microsoft® Office®, comes with many sophisticated features designed to make the user's life easy. To get the most out of these features, you can customise the settings that control how they work. Let's look at some examples in Word®.

Spelling and grammar options – custom dictionary

Word® offers facilities that check your spelling and grammar when you write a document. You can customise how this works. For example, if you don't want Word® to highlight spelling and grammar errors as you type, you can switch off this feature.

 How to... Set spelling and grammar options

Click the **Office** button (top left with the Microsoft® Office® logo), then select the **Word Options** button on the bottom right and click on **Proofing** on the left of the dialog box (see Figure 9.9). This dialog box lets you control the way the spelling and grammar checkers work. For example, you can control how the spell-checker deals with words in upper case and words that include numbers, such as post codes.

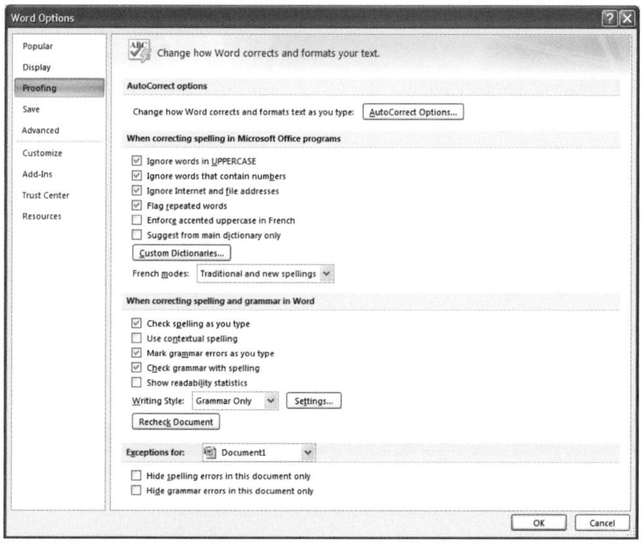

Figure 9.9: The spell and grammar check options dialog.

Word® contains several dictionaries which it uses to check spellings, for example it has different dictionaries for checking American and UK spellings of the same words. To make sure that you are using the correct dictionary, click on the **Popular** link at the top of the **Word Options** dialog box and then click the **Language Settings** button.

This will display the **Microsoft Office Language Settings** dialog box, as shown in Figure 9.10. This controls the dictionary that is used for all Microsoft® Office® System 2007 applications. Check you have English (United Kingdom) set as the primary editing language.

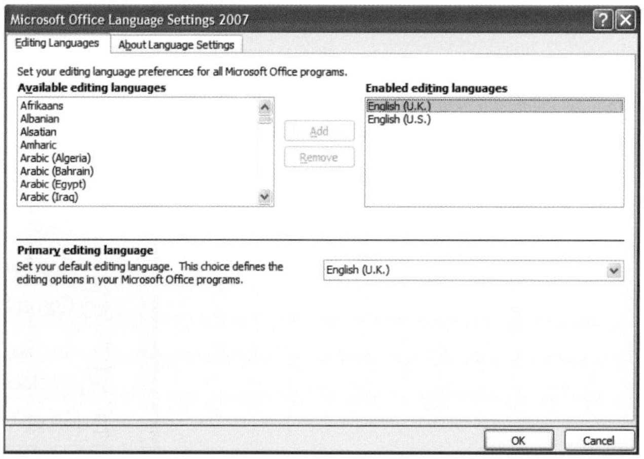

Figure 9.10: Microsoft® Office® Language Settings dialog box.

The spell checking facility can only accept the spelling of words that are in the dictionary you have selected. Words that aren't in the dictionary, such as people's names or the names of companies, will be highlighted as errors. However, you can add them to the custom dictionary. For example, if you have typed the name Hasmita, it will be shown as a spelling error as it is not in the dictionary. But if you right-click on the name and choose **Add to dictionary**, the name will be added and no longer shown as an error.

Activity: Spelling and grammar settings

1. There are a number of other spelling and grammar settings that you can change in the **Proofing** section of the **Word Options** dialog box. Find out what these settings do and consider why you might want to use them.

2. Here's a real challenge! Find out why entries that you add to your spelling dictionary are not added to the main dictionary, but instead are added to your custom dictionary.

3. There are a number of things you can do with custom dictionaries. Find out more about them and how to modify your custom dictionary. Then find out how and why you might want to add new custom dictionaries. Start by clicking the **Custom Dictionary** button on the **Spelling and Grammar Option** dialog box. Use the help system to assist you.

Autocorrect

The Autocorrect feature in Word 2007® can automatically correct certain types of spelling errors as you type. For example, if you often type 'clikc' instead of 'click', you can add this to the AutoCorrect entries, as shown in Figure 9.11. To display the **AutoCorrect** dialog box, choose the **Proofing** link on the **Word Options** dialog box.

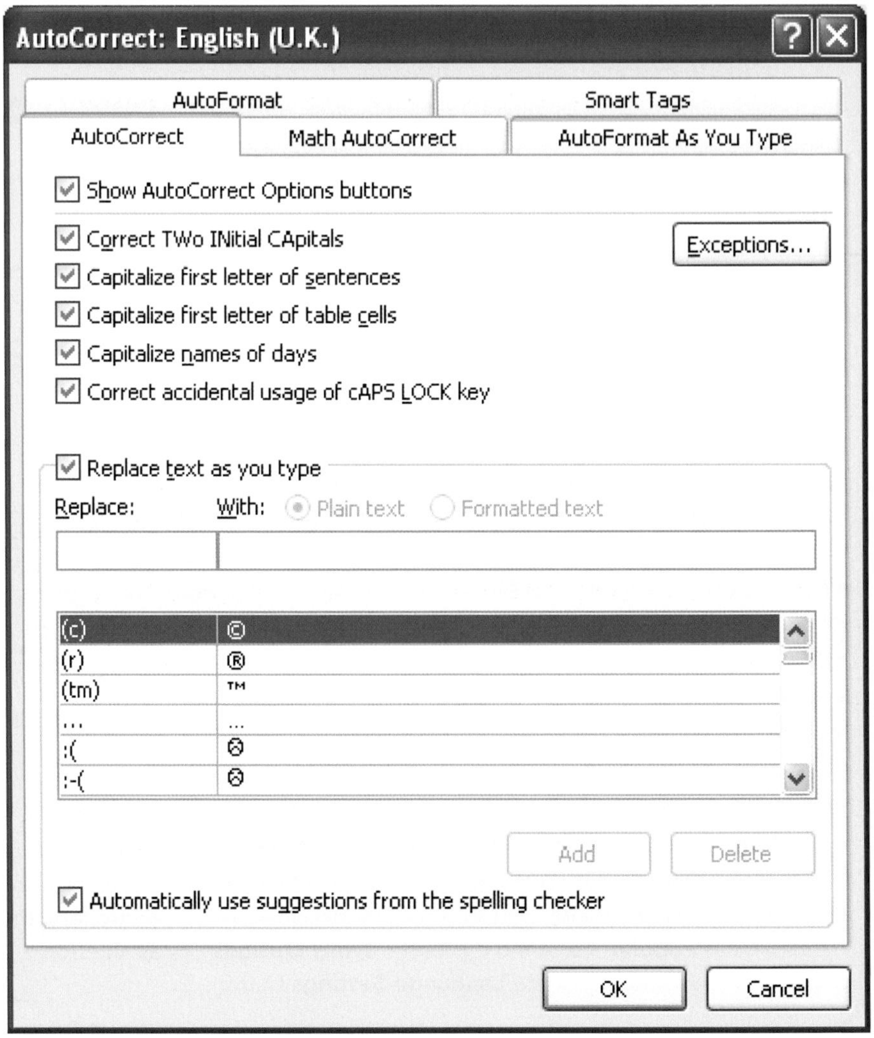

Figure 9.11: Adding AutoCorrect entries.

You must be careful when adding AutoCorrect entries – the word you enter to be corrected must *not* be a real word. Otherwise you would never be able to type that word – Word® would keep changing it to the 'correct' spelling. So, for example, you could not use AutoCorrect if you often type 'form' rather than 'from', since 'form' is a real word.

You can also use AutoCorrect to insert commonly used phrases. For example, if you often need to type the name of the school or college you attend, you can use AutoCorrect. Imagine you go to Northgate Technology College – you can make an autoCorrect entry to change a shortened version of the name, like 'ntc', to 'Northgate Technology College'.

AutoCorrect also carries out a number of formatting corrections, such as capitalising the names of days of the week or changing two capital letters at the beginning of a word to just one.

Activity: Using AutoCorrect

- Think about the mistakes you often make when typing, such as 'clikc' instead of 'click'.
- Make a list of your most common mistakes then carefully check that each incorrect word you type is not a real word (for example, 'form' instead of 'from').
- If it is not a real word, create an AutoCorrect entry to correct each error.
- Test that AutoCorrect works properly by typing the incorrect spellings and see whether they are corrected.

Did you know?

Although the spell-checker is very useful there are some types of error it cannot spot, for example if you use a word which is correctly spelt but is not the correct word to use, such as 'too' instead of 'to'. So you must still proofread your work carefully to check for errors.

AutoRecover

By default, Word® saves AutoRecover information (called AutoSave in previous versions) every 10 minutes. This information allows you to recover edits to your document that you have not saved if Word® or your computer crashes. With this setting, the most you will lose is your last 10 minutes of editing. You can increase or decrease how often AutoRecover information is saved by clicking the **Office** button, choosing **Word Options** at the bottom and then selecting the **Save** section of the **Options** dialog box.

Formatting

How to... Apply styles and themes to your documents

You can apply the built-in styles available in Word® from the **Home** tab of the Ribbon. Figure 9.12 shows a document with Title and Subtitle styles applied.

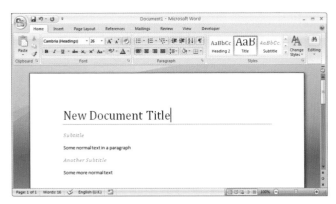

Figure 9.12: Applying styles to a document.

If you have used styles to format your document, you can then try different themes. You select themes from the **Page Layout** tab of the Ribbon. If you click the **Themes** button on the left, a list of available themes pops up. Move your mouse over the different themes to preview each theme applied to your current document, as shown in Figure 9.13. Remember you must have used styles to format your document – if you apply individual formats to your text, themes will not work.

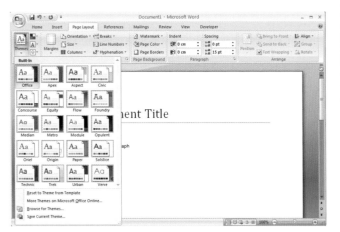

Figure 9.13: Applying themes to a document.

You can also customise your chosen theme if you don't like some aspect of it, for example you might not like one of the colours it uses for text. To do this, apply the theme first then click on the **Colors, Fonts or Effects** button in the themes section – the appropriate list will then pop up. The **Theme Colors** list is shown in Figure 9.14.

Figure 9.14: Theme colours.

This list shows you colours that will be applied for each of the different themes. If you want to change one of the colours in your currently selected theme, click the **Create New Theme Colors** link at the bottom of the Theme Colors list. This will display the **Create New Theme Colors** dialog box – see Figure 9.15.

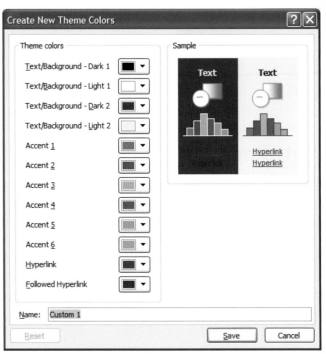

Figure 9.15 Create New Theme Colors.

Find the aspect of the Theme you want to change and choose the colour using the drop-down boxes. Your customised theme will be saved as a new theme – enter a name for it in the **Name** box at the bottom of the dialog box.

There are a number of ways you can customise the formatting of text. New in Microsoft® Office® 2007 is the way you can format Word® documents (and Excel® spreadsheets and PowerPoint® presentations) using **themes**.

To understand how themes work you need to understand the concept of **styles**. Once you have created a style, you can apply all the format settings to your text in one go, instead of having to apply them one at a time. Styles also make it easier to keep your document formatting consistent, as you apply the same formats each time you use the style.

Word includes a lot of predefined styles you can use in your documents.

2.5 Testing

Imagine you are working as an IT technician for a company. The marketing director asks you to customise a Microsoft® Office® System theme to be used on all the documents the company produces. Before you give the theme to everyone to use, you will need to check two things:

- your theme must meet the marketing director's requirements
- your theme must work correctly with all the different types of documents it will be used for. Remember that themes can be used in PowerPoint® presentations and Excel® spreadsheets as well as Word® documents.

You will need to carry out these checks for any customisation you develop that will be used by others. If you don't do these checks, you might discover too late that your customisation does not meet the needs of the people who will use it, or that it does not work correctly.

Checking that what you have developed meets the requirements is usually quite simple. All you normally need to do is show what you have produced to whoever set the requirements in the first place.

Testing that your customisation works properly can be a little trickier. With a simple customisation, you might just need to try it out on two or three different users' computers. With something more complex like a theme, it can be very difficult to predict all the different ways that the theme might be used in various types of documents, spreadsheets and presentations. To be reasonably sure your customisation works correctly, you need to try it out in as many different ways as you can think of.

Key terms

Theme – in Microsoft® Office® 2007 a Theme is a set of formatting choices that include the theme colours, fonts (including heading and body text fonts) and effects (including lines and fill effects). You can quickly and easily format an entire document to give it a professional and modern look using a theme. The same themes are available across all the Microsoft® Office® System applications.

Style – a predefined set of text formatting options (such as font, font size, text colour and indentation).

BTEC Assessment Activity 9.1 P1 P2 P3 D1

The SuperSim Games Company is developing a standard computer set-up which will be used on all the computers in the company. You have been asked to configure a computer with the set-up in place. The company users can then trial the set-up to see whether they are happy with it before it is installed across the whole company.

The set-up must include:

- a default printer
- the user interface should include a desktop background with an appropriate image for a computer games company
- the Control Panel and Run items should be removed from the Start menu
- the Office 2007® AutoCorrect tool should be set to correct 'SGC' to 'SuperSim Games Company'
- the name 'SuperSim' should be added to the custom spelling dictionary, so it is not shown as an error
- the Word® AutoSave option should be set to save AutoRecover information every five minutes
- there should be a customised Office 2007® theme for the company, called 'SGC', based on an existing theme but with modified colours. P1 P2

You must thoroughly test each of these customisations to ensure they work properly (for example, you should test the Office® customisations work in all Microsoft® Office® System applications) and provide evidence that you have done so. P3

The IT manager at SuperSim has also asked you to produce a report which explains why software may be customised, including a discussion on the benefits and drawbacks of customisation. D1

Grading tip

To achieve the distinction criterion you need to discuss the benefits and drawbacks of a wide range of customisations, not just those you have completed for this task. You need to explain in detail what the benefits and drawbacks are, giving specific examples.

PLTS

By developing tests to ensure your customisation works correctly and explaining the benefits and drawbacks of customisations, you will show you are an **independent enquirer**.

Functional skills

Completing the customisation will give you evidence for your functional **ICT** skills in use ICT systems.

Writing the report on the customisations will provide evidence for your functional **English** skills in writing.

Just checking

1. Give two examples of default printer settings that you might need to change.
2. Where would you go to change the settings that affect how the mouse works? What settings can you change?
3. When you type your name (or a friend's name) in Word®, it might be highlighted as a spelling error. How can you prevent this happening?
4. What must you check (and why) before adding an AutoCorrect entry?

3. Be able to create templates in application software

3.1 Application packages

Templates are a useful way of customising applications. They help ensure documents within an organisation are consistent, and they also save time because people don't need to type the same text and set the same formatting over and over again. Templates are mostly created in Word® and Excel®, but they can be created for other applications too. For example, PowerPoint® has lots of presentation slide templates with colourful and professional-looking graphics and colour schemes.

Word® templates

Word® comes with a number of built-in templates. It's worth having a look at how to use these, before finding out how to create your own.

How to... Use Word® templates

Click the **Office** button then choose **New** and the **New Document** dialog box will appear. Click the **Installed Templates** link on the left to see a scrolling list of all the different templates available. (These are the templates installed locally, not the ones you can access online.) Click on a template to see a preview of it on the right – as shown in Figure 9.16.

When you've chosen the template you want, click the **Create** button at the bottom of the dialog box and Word® creates a new unnamed document with the text and formatting from the template. With the more sophisticated templates, you also get fields which you can type into. The example shown in Figure 9.17 is one of the Resume templates. (Resume is the American word for a CV.)

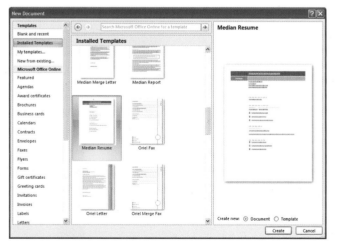

Figure 9.16: The New Document dialog box.

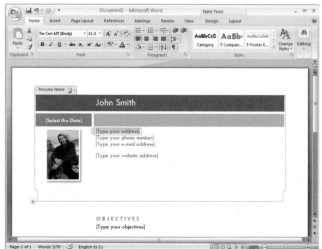

Figure 9.17: The Resume template in use.

Creating your own templates is quite easy. A template is simply a Word® document that is saved as a template rather than a standard document. So the first step in creating a template is to create the text and formatting you want. But before you start creating the template, you need to consider its design.

3.2 Templates

User needs

The first stage in designing a template is to find out what the user requires. In the future you may become an IT technician, and most of your work will be to support the users of the IT system in your place of work. You must, therefore, learn ways to identify user needs and design solutions that meet them.

Identifying user needs may sound like a fairly easy task: you just go and ask the users what they want! But it is usually more complex than that. There may be many different users to consider, and you may have to take into account issues such as company standards for document layout and formatting. You need to find out some basic details:

- what type of document is required (for example, is it needed for data entry)
- design:
  - what logos and other graphics are required on the document
  - what is the layout of any existing documents that the template will replace?

Once you have collected this information, use it to produce a draft version of the template. You need to show your draft template to the users to see whether it meets their needs.

How to... Create a simple template

To create a template you just need to type the text you require. Remember to leave out anything that will change each time the template is used, although you might include an instruction like 'Type sender's name here'. An example of a memo template is shown in Figure 9.18.

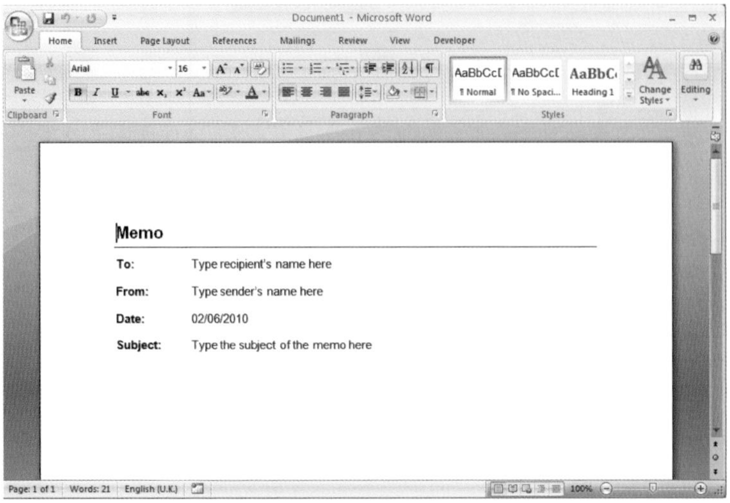

Figure 9.18: A memo template.

Don't type the date into the template. Instead, insert an updating date field: go to the **Insert** tab on the Ribbon and choose **Date and Time** from the **Text** group. This will display the dialog box shown in Figure 9.19. Choose the date format you want then click the check box labelled **Update automatically**, and then click **OK**. This date will automatically update to the current date whenever the template is used.

When you have entered the text for your template, you need to save it as a template instead of a normal document. To do this, click the **Office** button and choose **Save As**, then select **Word Template** in the menu that pops up.

You must save your template in a special folder for it to appear in your list of templates. If you are using Windows® 7 or Windows Vista® this folder is: *C:\Users\ [user name]\AppData\Roaming\ Microsoft\Templates*. (Note: *[user name]* is the name of the current logged-on user.)

Once you have saved the template in the correct folder, it is ready to use. To do this click the **Office** button and choose **New** then click the **My Templates** link on the left and you will see the **My Templates** dialog box, as shown in Figure 9.20.

Click on the **Memo** template you have just created then click **OK**. You will now get a new document based on your template. Remember this isn't the original template – it's a copy of it.

When saving your template, as with any file, make sure you give it a meaningful name, such as *Memo*.

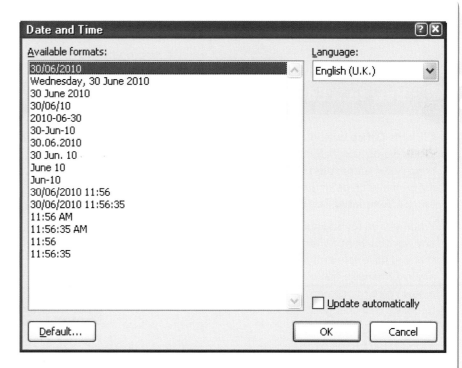

Figure 9.19: Automatic updating of the date.

Figure 9.20: My Templates dialog box.

Whenever you use a template to create a new document, you get a copy of the template, not the original. So how can you edit and modify the original?

How to... Edit and modify a template

Click the **Office** button and choose **Open** to display the **Open** dialog box. Select **All Word Templates** in the drop-down list next to the **File name** box. In the folder list on the left side of the dialog box, scroll to the top and choose **Templates** (see Figure 9.21).

When you've found your template, you can modify it in any way you want. When you save your changes, check that you have selected the file type **Document Template** again. Otherwise you may find that you have just saved a new Word® document called *Memo.doc* and your template is unchanged!

Figure 9.21: Open dialog box.

Other features

Form fields

The templates we have looked at so far have really just been normal documents saved in a special location. When a user opens a template, they just get a copy of the original document. One disadvantage of this is that the user can edit all parts of the document. This can be a problem with some types of document, such as complex forms. The user might mess up the format or layout of the document, especially if they are inexperienced at using Word®. To avoid these problems, the **Forms** tools can be used to create a locked form – this only allows the user to enter data in certain fields.

Creating a form

Forms, such as questionnaires or surveys can be quite complex, so you may need to sketch out a hand-drawn version before attempting to create the form in Word®. Forms can have text fields, check boxes and drop-down fields – you need to consider which of these form **input controls** is most suitable for each entry.

- **Text fields** — are best where it is difficult to predict what input the user will make (such as a name).
- **Check boxes** — are used for responses where only 'yes' or 'no' is allowed.
- **List boxes** — are used where the response can be selected from a limited list of options, for example: title: Mr, Miss, Ms or Mrs.

When you have decided on the basic layout of your form, you can start work on the actual document.

Key term

Input controls – Windows® features which allow you to input data to an application. Typical examples include text boxes for inputting text and list boxes which allow you to select an input value from a list.

How to... Create a form in Word®

In order to create a form, you need to display the Developer tab in the Ribbon. Click the **Office** button and choose **Word Options** and then check you have the **Popular** section displayed. Click the **Show Developer tab in the Ribbon** check box. The **Controls** section of the Developer tab allows you to insert text fields, check boxes and drop-down fields into your document. The **Protect** section of the Developer tab allows you to protect the document, so the user can only type into the fields you have created and cannot edit the rest of the document. The Developer tab is shown in Figure 9.22.

Figure 9.22: The Developer tab.

To show how forms are created we'll start work on a simple form for a survey. Type the text shown in Figure 9.23. With your cursor next to the text *Family Name*, click on the **Rich Text Field** button and a text box will be inserted into your document, as shown in Figure 9.23.

Next we'll insert a drop-down box (combo box) to allow the user to choose their title (Mr, Mrs, Miss, etc.).

Enter the text *Title* under the **Family name** box. With your cursor next to this text, click the **Combo** box button on the **Controls** section of the **Developer** tab. This will insert a combo box control. Then click the **Properties** button in the **Controls** section to display the **Content Control Properties** dialog box as shown in Figure 9.24.

To enter the titles that will display in the drop-down box, click the **Add** button then enter the title in the dialog that appears and click **OK**. Do the same for the next title and so on. Some of the titles have already been entered in Figure 9.24. To remove an item from the list, click on it and then click **Remove**. The **Move** buttons can be used to move items up or down the list.

Figure 9.23: Inserting a text box.

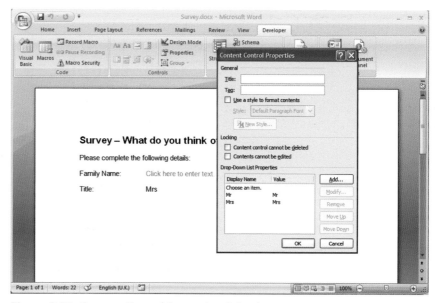

Figure 9.24: Content Control Properties dialog box.

Once you have completed the form, you need to protect it so the users can only fill in the form and not edit any other part of the document. Then you need to test that the form works as you expect and save it as a template.

How to... Protect, test and save a form in Word®

To protect the document, click the **Protect Document** button in the **Developer** tab, then choose **Restrict Formatting and Editing** from the drop-down menu that appears. This will display the **Protect document** task pane.

Under **Editing restrictions**, select the **Allow only this type of editing in the document** check box. In the list of editing restrictions, select **Filling in forms** (see Figure 9.25). Then click the **Yes, Start Enforcing Protection** button and a dialog will pop up asking you for a password (don't enter one at this stage). Click **OK** and the document will be protected so you can only type in the **Family name** text box and choose a title from the drop-down box.

Having locked the document you should try out all the input controls to check they work as you expect. You should not be able to type anywhere except in the fields you have created.

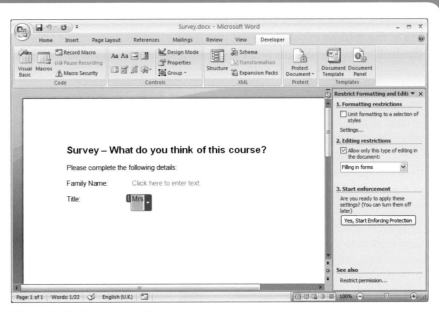

Figure 9.25: Protecting a form.

Once you are happy with the form you can save it. First delete any entries you have made so you save a blank form. **Save** it while it is protected so that, when a user opens the document, the form will be ready to use. You can save it as a template so that each time it is opened a new copy is created.

Excel® templates

Like Word®, Excel® comes with a number of built-in templates, and you can create your own in a similar way.

One of the benefits of using templates in Excel® is that you can build formulae into them. This means that the templates can be used by people who don't know how to create formulae – all they need to do is enter the numbers and the formulae will automatically do the calculations. This can also avoid errors caused by users entering formulae incorrectly. However, you must check carefully that the formulae you put in the template are correct.

We'll look at an example of how to create a template for an **invoice**.

Key term

Invoice – a document requesting payment for goods or services.

Activity: Creating an Excel® template

The spreadsheet shown in Figure 9.26 is an example of how an invoice template could be designed. Formulae have been entered to calculate:

- the total for each item sold (quantity x unit price)
- the net total (total before VAT)
- the amount of VAT
- the grand total.

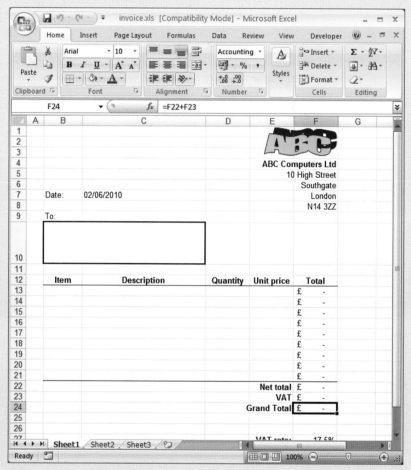

Figure 9.26: Invoice template.

Once you have entered the formulae and completed formatting the invoice template spreadsheet, you need to save the sheet as a template. You do this in a similar way to a Word® template. Click the **Office** button, choose **Save as** then click **Other formats** to display the **Save as** dialog box. Choose **Excel Template** from the **Save as type** drop-down box.

Testing an Excel® template

To test the template properly, you need to think of some test invoices. First, you need to work out the total price, net total, VAT, etc. for these test invoices. This is known as test data. For example, you could type the details into a Word® table then do the calculation by hand or with a calculator. You must check the results carefully to make sure they are correct. You should come up with a minimum of six different invoices, some with a small number of items and quantities, others with larger amounts. See Figure 9.27 for an example.

Test data for Invoice template

Invoice 1

Item	Description	Quantity	Unit Price	Total
1	ABC1 motherboard	2	£97.50	£195.00
2	AMD CPU	2	£85.50	£171.00
3	200GB hard disk	3	£125.00	£375.00
4	DVD Writer	1	£45.75	£45.75
5	CD Writer	1	£28.50	£28.50
			Net Total	£815.25
			VAT (17.5%)	£138.25
			Grand Total	**£953.50**

Invoice 2

Item	Description	Quantity	Unit Price	Total
1	XYZ motherboard	5	£155.00	£775.00
2	Intel P4 CPU	5	£125.75	£628.75
3	300Gb Hard disk	10	£175.50	£1755.00
4	Super Power graphics card	7	£95.20	£666.40
5	Tower case	8	£34.90	£279.20
6	LCD 17inch monitor	5	£135.00	£675.00
7	DVD Writer	8	£45.75	£366.00
			Net Total	£5145.35
			VAT (17.5%)	£900.44
			Grand Total	**£6045.79**

Figure 9.27: Example test data.

Once you have completed the test data, you should use the template to create invoices with the same items, quantities and prices as your test data. As you complete each invoice using the template, compare the results with the calculations you did manually on the test data. If you find there are differences in the results, then there must be an error. If every invoice is wrong, the error must be in the formulae you used in the template. If just one or two invoices are wrong, the error must be in the calculations you did manually. You need to identify the error and correct it. If necessary, edit and save your template again. (Excel® templates are saved in the same folder as Word® templates.)

BTEC Assessment activity 9.2 (P4) (M1)

Create two templates for the SuperSim Games Company – one for Excel® and one for Word®, as described below. **P4**

Excel® template
Create a 'paper-saving' Excel® template. This template should have narrow margins (about 0.7 cm along the top, bottom, left and right) and the page orientation set to landscape. Add a **footer** to the template with the company name, company logo (choose a suitable piece of clip art for this) and page number.

Word® template
Create a questionnaire template using a Word® form. The questionnaire is to gather users' opinions on the games the company makes. The questionnaire will be placed on the company website so users can download it, complete it and email it back to the company. The questionnaire should record basic information, such as the user's name, gender and age. Example questions should include:

- Which game did you buy from the three produced by SuperSim: 'Cave Raiders', 'The Last Stand' or 'Ghost Hunters'?
- What platform was the game for (e.g. PC, Xbox®, PS2®, Wii™)?
- Do you think this is an interesting game?
- Was it easy to install and play?

For some of the questions you can use a numerical scale from 1 to 5, where 1 is 'Very much agree' and 5 is 'Completely disagree'. Use check boxes or drop-down lists to allow the person filling in the questionnaire to make their selection for each question.

Final report
When you have produced these templates, write a report evaluating how effectively the templates meet the user's requirements. **M1**

Grading tips

To work towards a merit you should evaluate the way templates meet the user requirements. Using the Word® questionnaire you have created, consider the benefits of completing this on the computer rather than printing it out. Also, are there better ways of providing a questionnaire to users? What if the users don't have Word® installed on their computer?

PLTS

By evaluating the effectiveness of your templates, you can show you are a **reflective learner**.

Functional skills

By creating a questionnaire in Word®, you will provide evidence for your functional **ICT** skills in develop, present and communicate information.

Writing the report on the templates will provide evidence for your functional **English** skills in writing.

Key term

Footer – text that prints at the bottom of every page. It is often used for things like page numbers.

Just checking

1. What kind of input control would be best to allow a user to enter their title (Mr, Mrs, Miss, etc.) on a Word® form?
2. How can you include a date in a template so that it is always correct whenever the template is used?
3. What must you do to make a document a template rather than just a standard document?
4. What is the difference between a locked and an unlocked form document?

4. Be able to create macros and shortcuts in application software

Did you know?

- Macros can be used as a method of cheating in multi-player online role-play games. By automating key stokes the player can repeat simple actions in the game time and time again, and therefore earn a large amount of the games currency. For this reason the use of keystroke macros are forbidden in most of these games.

- You can't have a space in a macro name.

Remember

It's a good idea to practise the steps you plan to record in the macro before you switch the recorder on. That way you have a better chance of recording the macro correctly first time.

4.1 Macros

Templates are a simple and effective way to customise an application, but **macros** are much more powerful.

Once a macro has been created, you can also create a shortcut that allows the user to run the macro. We will cover shortcuts later in this section (see pages 169–170).

You can create macros in most of the Microsoft® Office® System applications, but we will look only at Excel®.

There are two ways you can create a macro:

- use the macro recorder facility
- write program code.

The simplest way is to use the macro recorder facility to record the tasks you wish to automate. You can then replay your recorded macro whenever you want to do that particular sequence of tasks.

The other method is to write the program code using the Visual Basic Editor. The first method might seem the simpler of the two, but there are various restrictions on what you can record in a macro. However, editing the Visual Basic macro code is not required for this unit.

Recording macros

Let's look at recording a simple macro. Imagine you'd like to record a macro to add a **header** to an Excel® worksheet. Instead of having to set up a header each time you use a new worksheet, the macro will automatically do it for you.

You can't really test out your macro on the current worksheet, since it now has a header. You need to move to a new worksheet by using the worksheet tabs at the bottom of the Excel® window. Then press the **Ctrl+h** shortcut key combination that you set for the new macro. You won't see very much on the screen (it will flash a few times as the macro changes in and out of Page Layout view). But if you now go to the **View** menu and choose **Page Layout**, you will see that this sheet now has a header, set by the macro.

How to... Record a macro

To record the macro you have to switch on the macro recorder and then carry out the steps required to set up the header. First, open Excel® and use either a new worksheet or one that does not already have a header set up.

Before you can record a macro you need to have the **Developer** tab showing in the Ribbon. If it is not displayed, go to the **Excel Options** dialog box and check the option to turn it on. This is similar to how it is done in Word®.

Then go to the **Code** section of the **Developer** tab and click **Record Macro** to see the dialog box shown in Figure 9.28.

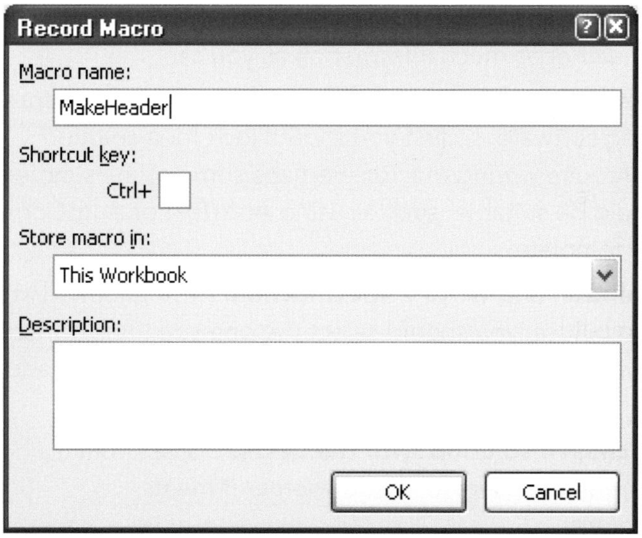

Figure 9.28: The Record Macro dialog box.

There are a number of things you must enter in this dialog box:

- **Macro name.** Each macro must have a name, and Excel® will insert a default name – *Macro1* if this is the first macro you have recorded. You should change the name to something more meaningful, like *MakeHeader*, as shown in Figure 9.28.

- **Shortcut key.** You can assign a shortcut key to the macro. This will enable you to run it by pressing the **CTRL** key along with another key of your choice. In this example the 'h' key has been chosen (for 'header').

- **Store macro in.** The default setting in this drop-down box is the current workbook – this means the macro will only be available in this workbook. If you want to be able to use this macro in any workbook, the drop-down box should be set to **Personal Macro Workbook**.

- **Description.** You can add information here which describes the macro.

Once you have made the required entries in the dialog box, click **OK** – but be careful because, once you do this, the macro recorder is on and everything you do will be recorded in the macro. Also remember that, at the end, you must stop the macro recorder by clicking the **Stop recording** button on the **Developer** tab.

Once the macro recorder is switched on, start creating the header macro. First go to the **Insert** tab then click **Header and Footer** in the text section. This will change your view of the spreadsheet into **Page Layout** view. Then position your cursor in the header box – see Figure 9.29. Add a header as shown, including your name and the page number. To add an automatic page number, click the **Page Number** button in the **Header and Footer Elements** section of the **Design** tab.

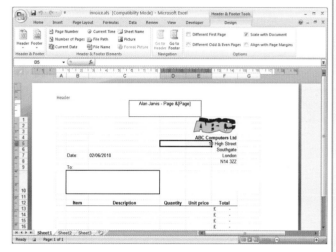

Figure 9.29: Adding a header.

Now click in one of the spreadsheet cells to close the **Design** tab. To return the spreadsheet to Normal view rather than Page Layout view, click the **View** tab in the Ribbon, then click the **Normal** button on the left of the tab. This will return the spreadsheet to the view you had when you started to record the macro. The final but very important step is to stop the macro recorder. Click the **Developer** tab then click the **Stop recording** button in the **Code** section, as shown in Figure 9.30.

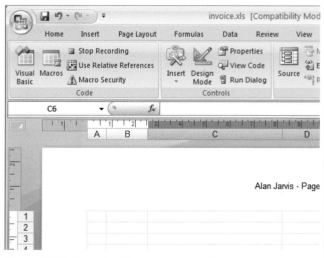

Figure 9.30: Stopping the macro recording.

Define user need

As an IT professional you may be asked to create a macro for a particular user or group of users. The term macro may not be used – you might just be asked to help users with a particular problem they have, or with something they find difficult or time consuming to do. After investigation you may decide that a macro would provide a good solution, but you will need to carry out a number of steps first:

- **Thoroughly investigate what the problem is.** Sometimes technicians are tempted to jump very quickly to a solution without fully understanding the users' problem. This can lead to a solution that does not fully meet the need. You must talk to the users, get them to show you what they are having difficulties with and ask questions to gather as much information as you can.

- **Look for alternative solutions.** Remember there are disadvantages to customising software, so first you should look for a solution that doesn't require writing macros. Perhaps some of the simpler solutions would be suitable, such as using AutoText or AutoCorrect, or creating a template.

- **Choose a solution and write a specification.** Having looked at the different possibilities, you should select the one you think is most suitable and write a specification that describes the problem and how your solution will deal with it.

- **Check your chosen solution with the users.** Discuss your specification with the users to check whether it meets their requirements.

As a learner, it isn't really possible to carry out these tasks for real. However, your fellow learners, family and friends might be able to act as your 'users' and provide you with a problem that some kind of customisation might solve.

Activity: Creating a template or macro

1. Discuss with your fellow learners, family and friends what tasks they regularly carry out using Word® or Excel®. Find out as much detail as you can about the tasks.

2. Select one task that could be carried out more easily using a template or macro.

3. Using the steps described on page 165, create a template or macro to meet the requirements they have described to you.

Assign a macro

You've already seen how a macro can easily be assigned to a shortcut key, but you might want to assign the macro to the Quick Access Toolbar. This is the small toolbar that appears to the right of the Microsoft® Office® button.

 How to... Assign a macro to the Quick Access Toolbar

Click the **Customize Quick Access Toolbar** button, to the left of the Quick Access toolbar, then choose **More Commands**. This will display the **Excel Options** dialog box, with the **Customize** section selected, as shown in Figure 9.31. Then choose **Macros** from the **Choose Command from** drop-down box, as illustrated.

You should then see the **MakeHeader** macro you recorded earlier. Click on that macro then click **Add** to add it to the list of commands on the toolbar on the right. Then click **OK**. You should now see an additional icon on the Quick Access Toolbar which you can use to run your macro.

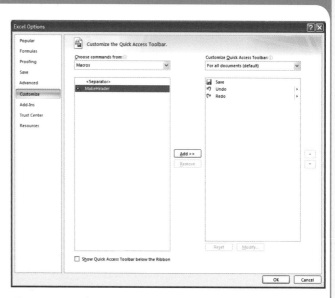

Figure 9.31: The Customize section of the Excel options dialog box.

 Activity: Assigning a macro to the Quick Access Toolbar

Using a macro you have previously created, assign it to a Quick Access Toolbar icon.

Storage

When you create a macro you need to choose where it will be stored. There are a number of options.

Storing a macro in the document or spreadsheet
Storing the macro you create in the particular document or spreadsheet workbook means that you can only use the macro in that document or spreadsheet. This is the best option if the macro is designed to work with that particular document.

Storing a macro in a template
If you are creating a template you can store the macro in the template. When you use the template the macro is available within the document that is created based on the template.

Microsoft® Excel® macros can also be stored in a macro worksheet, which means they will be available to any worksheet. This is a good option if you create a general macro which can be used in any spreadsheet.

Testing a macro

Once you have created your macro, you need to test it to ensure it works properly. Simple macros may not need very detailed testing, but you should still consider carefully if there are any situations where your macro might not work properly. Just doing one test of your macro is not sufficient.

If the macro is designed to work with any worksheet (like the *MakeHeader* macro created earlier) you should try it with different worksheets to check that it really does work with any worksheet. For example, you might be temped to just try it on a couple of small spreadsheets. However, since it contains page numbers you need to check it with a multi-page worksheet to test that the numbering still works correctly.

You should also try out some situations that might cause problems, for example:

- what happens if you use the macro on a worksheet which already has a header
- what happens if the spreadsheet is set for landscape printing rather than portrait?

To do the testing properly, you need to create a list of the tests you will do and record the results of the tests along with evidence (such as screen prints or paper printouts). The list of tests is called a test plan. An example test plan for the *MakeHeader* macro is shown in Table 9.1.

Table 9.1: Test plan for the MakeHeader macro.

Test plan			
Macro name: MakeHeader		**Tester:** Alan Jarvis	
Date: 22 March 2010			
Test number	Description	Result	Action needed
1	Test with small worksheet		
2	Test with large multi-page sheet		
4	Test on sheet with header already		
5	Test on sheet set for landscape printing		

You complete the Result column when you actually carry out the test.

- If the test goes as you expected, you can just enter 'OK' in this box or perhaps something more descriptive, such as 'Page numbers printed OK on all pages'.

- If you do not get the result you are expecting, you will need to make an entry in the Action needed column, such as 'Re-record macro to solve this problem'. You don't need to write anything in this column if the test went as expected.

4.2 Shortcuts

Shortcuts are useful because, as the name suggests, they do something the quick way. There are number of different types of shortcut.

Keyboard shortcuts

Keyboard shortcuts allow commands to be selected using the keyboard only. Microsoft® Office® System programs have many built-in shortcuts using the Ctrl (Control) key, such as **Ctrl+S** to save or **Ctrl+B** to make text bold. Also, as we have seen, you can assign a shortcut key combination to a macro you have recorded.

How to... Customise keyboard shortcuts

In Word®, click the **Customize Quick Access Toolbar** button to the right of the Quick Access Toolbar (which is to the right of the Microsoft® Office® button). Choose the **More Commands** option to open the **Word Options** dialog box. At the bottom of the dialog box, click the **Customize** button to display the **Customize Keyboard** dialog box, as shown in Figure 9.32.

Choose a command that is used a lot, such as **FileSave** from the Office menu (see Figure 9.32). The currently assigned shortcut keys are shown in the **Current keys** box. You might decide you want to add your own shortcut key to save a document, for example **Ctrl+q**. You can type that in the **Press new shortcut key** box. If this shortcut is already assigned, this will be shown under the **Current keys** box (as shown).

Note: You should be very careful changing assignments as it could be confusing, especially if you change well-known ones like **Crtl+b**.

You can choose where to save the new shortcut assignment using the **Save changes in** drop-down box. Saving them in the Normal template will affect all documents based on that template. Choosing the current open document will only affect the document you are in. If you really want to make the assignment, click the **Assign** button.

The **Remove** button allows you remove a current shortcut assignment that you have selected in the **Current Keys** box.

The **Reset All** button allows you to remove any assignments you have made and reset everything to the defaults.

Figure 9.32: The Customize Keyboard dialog box.

You can see a list of all the available shortcut keys by searching for 'keyboard shortcuts' in the help feature of any Microsoft® Office® System application. You can also customise the keyboard shortcuts to use your choice of key combinations rather than the default ones.

Hyperlink shortcuts

Hyperlinks provide a quick way to link to a web page. In Microsoft® Office® System applications, if you type a web address that includes the 'www' part, it is recognised as a web address and automatically made into a hyperlink.

How to... Create your own hyperlinks

You can create your own hyperlinks by selecting any text, right-clicking on it and choosing **Hyperlink** (or choosing the **Hyperlink** icon in the **Links** section of the **Insert** tab). This will display the **Hyperlink** dialog box, as shown in Figure 9.33.

Your hyperlink doesn't have to link to a web page. It can link to another document or another place in your current document.

- To link to another document, just select the document in the centre section of the dialog box.

- To link to a web page, either type the web address in the **Address** box at the bottom or click the **Browsed Pages** button and select the address from a list of your recently visited web pages.

Figure 9.33: Hyperlink dialog box.

Drive mapping shortcuts

Drive mapping is another type of shortcut that makes it easy to find network folders on your computer. Local disk drives and USB memory sticks are automatically given a driver letter – C: for your hard disk drive, D: or E: for your CD/DVD drive, etc. But folders you access over the network are not given a driver letter. You can allocate them one to make accessing them easier – this is referred to as 'mapping a drive'.

How to... Map a drive

Before you can map a driver letter to a network folder, you have to find the folder in the Computer window. From the **Start** menu choose **My Computers** then **My Network Places**, then click **View workgroup computers** to display a list of all the computers on your network– see Figure 9.34.

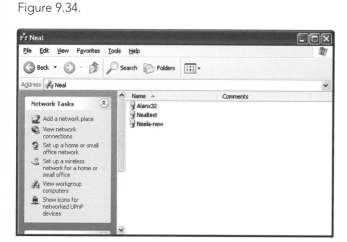

Figure 9.34: Computers on the network.

In this example the folder we want to map a drive to is located on the Nealtest computer, so we double click that computer icon (you may be asked to enter a username and password). You will see a list of the shared folders on that computer, as shown in Figure 9.35.

Figure 9.35: Shared folders.

To map a drive to the shared folder called 'Download server', right click the icon and then choose **Map network**

drive. This will display the **Map Network Drive** dialog box, as shown in Figure 9.36.

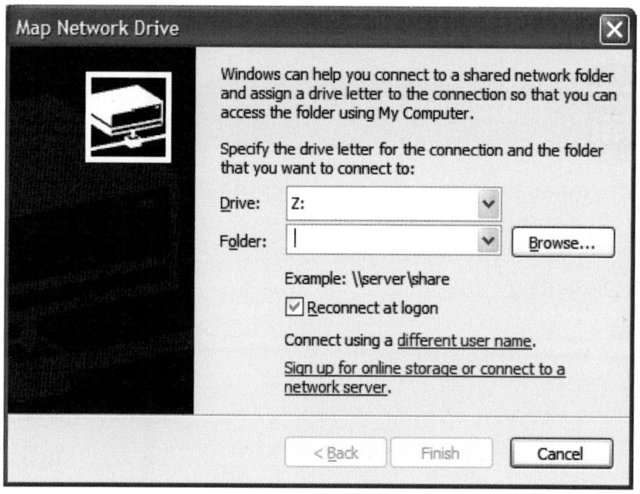

Figure 9.36: Map Network Drive dialog box.

Choose a driver letter from the drop-down box. Leave the **Reconnect at logon** check box ticked, otherwise you will lose the mapping when you log off your computer. Leave the **Connect using different credentials** check box unticked, otherwise you will need to enter a different username and password when you use the folder. Then click **Finish** and the drive will be mapped.

If you now look in the computer window, you will see the mapped drive listed with the other local drives on your computer, as shown in Figure 9.37.

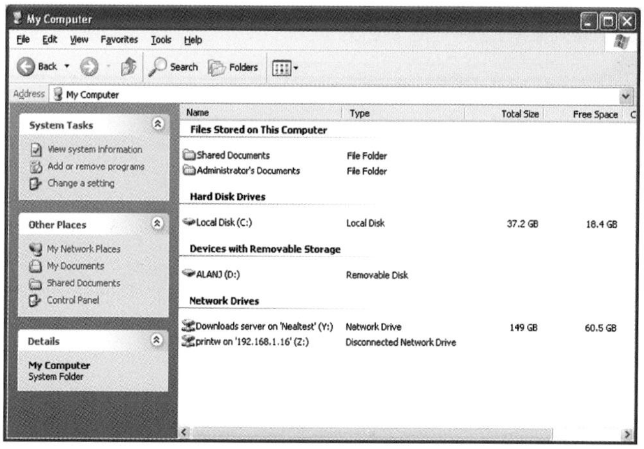

Figure 9.37: Computer window.

PLTS

Explaining the benefits of using a macro will show that you are a **reflective learner**.

Functional skills

Writing the report on the benefits of the macros will provide evidence for your functional **English** skills in writing.

BTEC **Assessment activity 9.3** P5 P6 M2

1. Record two Excel® macros, assigning them to different keystroke combinations.
   - The first should add the following formatting to the current cell (or selected cells): bold text, blue text colour and bottom border.
   - The second should open a new worksheet using the template you created in Assessment activity 9.2. P5
2. Test that the macros work correctly and then assign them to Quick Access toolbar buttons. Demonstrate to your tutor that the different ways of running the macro work. P5 P6
3. Write a report explaining the benefits of using the macros you have created. M2

Grading tip

To work towards a merit you should explain the benefits of using macros. For example, you could explain how the macros you have recorded could save time and make things easier, especially for inexperienced users.

Just checking

1. List the basic steps for recording a macro in Excel®.
2. List two different ways that you can run a macro.
3. You have been asked to write a macro for a novice computer user. What steps should you follow to investigate what the user requires?
4. Explain the steps you should take when creating a new keyboard shortcut in Microsoft® Word®.

Neela Soomary
Training Manager

As a training manager I need to keep track of the results of various exams (functional skills, etc.) that learners do on a month-by-month basis. I use a spreadsheet with an individual worksheet for each month. Each worksheet has the same layout, with number of learners, exams taken and numbers who passed. I found creating each new month's worksheet a bit fiddly. I had to insert a new sheet, copy the contents of the previous month's sheet into the new one, delete the previous month's data and then adjust the column sizes. I had to be careful which worksheet I selected before inserting a new one, otherwise the new sheet would end up in the wrong place. Then a colleague showed me how I could record a macro that did all these tasks. Once the macro was recorded, we created a button on the toolbar to run the macro. Now when I need a worksheet for a new month, I just click on the button and the sheet is created for me. The only thing I need to do is type the name of the month at the top of the sheet.

Think about it!

1. What are the benefits of using a macro to create a new worksheet?

2. Is there a way you could automate the task of inserting the month name at the top of each worksheet?

3. Neela wants to put the spreadsheet on a shared network folder so other staff can look at the learners' results. How can she make it easy for them to find that folder?

4. The other staff also want to use a spreadsheet like the one Neela created, to keep records for their learners. What would be the best way to create a blank version of the spreadsheet which anyone can make a copy of?

Just checking

1. What are the benefits of using macros? What disadvantages have you come across when using them?
2. Think of any businesses you know of (for example, somewhere you went on work placement, a part-time job or places where your friends or family work). What kind of templates do you think these businesses could make use of?
3. Macros and templates aren't the only type of customisation. What other types are there?
4. What is a default setting? Why might you want to change it?
5. What are the main benefits of customising software? (Hint: there are five of them.)
6. What are the disadvantages of customising software? (Hint: there are three of them.)
7. If you want to customise an aspect of the software you use, but are not sure how to do it, where can you go to find out?

edexcel

Assignment tips

- This unit links closely with *Unit 27: Spreadsheet modelling*. For example, any spreadsheet macros you create for this unit will cover part of D2 in Unit 27.

- The creation and testing of a customised application that you complete for this unit could be the project that you plan for *Unit 5: Project planning with IT*.

- If you don't have a copy of Office® 2007 to use on your PC at home, you can download a free 60-day trial at Microsoft® Office Online®. Remember Microsoft® Office Online® has tutorials and videos showing you how to do many of the things covered in this unit including macros and templates. To access Microsoft® Office Online®, please go to Hotlinks and click on this unit, then follow the links to 'Help' and 'How to' on the Microsoft® Office Online® website.

- When attempting the merit and distinction criteria, you may find it helpful to look at the customisations, templates and macros of other learners in your class. This may give you some additional ideas about the benefits and effectiveness of these features.

- When you are evaluating how effectively the templates meet user requirements for M1, try showing the template to someone who is not an IT learner or professional. This will help you get a user perspective on the effectiveness of the template.

Credit value: 10

10 Setting up an IT network

Because networks play an important role in organisations, especially for managing resources, networking skills are particularly valued in the IT industry.

By completing this unit you will develop both theoretical knowledge and practical application skills in networking. You will learn about the role of IT networks in organisations, including their features, services and components. You will learn about different types of networks, the functions of individual hardware and software components within those networks and how they interconnect to create a whole system. You will then apply your knowledge and understanding of hardware devices and software to set up and test a simple local area network for personal or commercial use.

Learning outcomes

After completing this unit you should:

1. know the current use of computer networks
2. know the features and services of local and wide area network technologies
3. understand how network hardware and software components are connected
4. be able to set up a simple local area network.

Assessment and grading criteria

This table shows you what you must do in order to achieve a pass, merit or distinction grade, and where you can find activities in this book to help you.

To achieve a **pass** grade the evidence must show that you are able to:	To achieve a **merit** grade the evidence must show that, in addition to the pass criteria, you are able to:	To achieve a **distinction** grade the evidence must show that, in addition to the pass and merit criteria, you are able to:
P1 describe how the use of computer networks can improve communications for individuals and organisations **See Assessment activity 10.1 on page 184**	**M1** explain how networks improve productivity for individuals and organisations **See Assessment activity 10.1 on page 184**	**D1** evaluate the features and services provided by a local and a wide area network **See Assessment activity 10.2 on page 193**
P2 describe how a network is used by an organisation to manage its resources **See Assessment activity 10.1 on page 184**		
P3 describe potential issues with computer networks **See Assessment activity 10.1 on page 184**	**M2** suggest possible solutions to resolve connectivity problems **See Assessment activity 10.3 on page 199**	
P4 describe the features and services of local and wide area network technologies **See Assessment activity 10.2 on page 193**		
P5 explain how hardware, software and addressing combine to support network communications **See Assessment activity 10.3 on page 199**		
P6 set up and test a simple local area network **See Assessment activity 10.4 on page 206**	**M3** set up and configure security on a local area network **See Assessment activity 10.4 on page 206**	**D2** explain how security issues can be minimised **See Assessment activity 10.4 on page 206**

How you will be assessed

This unit is internally assessed. You will provide a portfolio of evidence to show that you have achieved the learning outcomes. Your portfolio of evidence can be supplied in many formats including electronically as well as paper-based. The grading grid in the specification for this unit lists what you must do to obtain pass, merit and distinction grades. The Assessment activities in this unit will guide you through tasks that will help you to be successful in this unit.

Your tutor will tell you exactly what form your assessments will take, but you could be asked to produce:

- a poster
- a pamphlet or a leaflet
- a presentation
- a practical task with a report.

Andrew MacLeod, a 15-year-old BTEC First student

This unit helped me to understand how important networks are.

I enjoyed looking at how networks are constructed, the hardware and the software elements that are needed, and thinking about the issues of access and security. It was interesting to explore how networks can affect a company's performance. I soon realised that communication is key to success for an organisation and that networks are a fundamental tool in this process.

I thought that studying networks would be mostly theory, so I was relieved to find out there were lots of practical tasks and activities. They helped to make it more relevant for me.

The bit I enjoyed most was setting up my own simple network. I liked investigating current uses of networks and comparing my research results to my friends' results. We looked at LANs and WANs – it was interesting to see how modern technologies have impacted on communication worldwide.

Over to you

- What areas of this unit might you find challenging?
- Which section of the unit are you most looking forward to?
- What preparation can you do to get ready for the unit assessment(s)?

1. Know the current use of computer networks

Facebook

Facebook is a free-access social networking website, providing a way for people to communicate with each other and to share information and photos.

- Are you on Facebook? How many Facebook friends do you have?
- What information do you publish on Facebook? How does Facebook protect the information you don't want to share?
- What other sites offer a similar type of service? In what ways are they similar to Facebook? In what ways are they different?

Key terms

Computer network – a network used to share information and resources.

Network – a system that allows people to share information with each other.

Forum – an online meeting place where people with a common interest exchange information.

Blog (or **web log**) – an online personal journal.

1.1 Communication

A **computer network** might allow communication between just two people or, like the Internet, be accessible to millions.

Computer networks are created by connecting computers to each other. The simplest way is to use a cable to link two computers. However, a **network** can involve millions of connected computers. If the two computers to be connected are in the same room, it's easy to find a cable long enough to link them. If two computers are at opposite ends of a country, or in different countries, that's impossible. Other connections are needed, such as wireless links and broadband connections.

Let's start our investigation into the world of computer networks by looking at some current uses of networks.

Individuals

If you want to communicate right this minute with the person sitting next to you, it's easy: you talk face to face. To talk to someone further away, you might use your mobile phone. To 'talk' to someone on the other side of the world, you might write a letter, but it would take some time to arrive.

Instead, you could use the Internet to communicate instantly with friends and others who share an interest. You might:

- register with a website that offers an Internet **forum** related to a topic of interest, such as sport, music or literature
- set up a **blog** and post your thoughts for others to read and comment on
- set up your own website to keep your friends up to date with what you are doing.

Organisations

For organisations, communication is essential. Without the correct communication channels, organisations would find themselves missing information, holding out-of-date information and losing business opportunities. Organisations use a variety of communication methods:

- **Email** has completely replaced hardcopy communications, such as memos. Unlike a telephone call, email provides a record of the 'conversation' and can be sent to more than one person at a time. The recipient(s) can open the email when it suits, and work flow needn't be interrupted.

- A **wiki** is a website that allows a group of people to collaborate on the information that it includes. They can update the information on each page as ideas occur to them. It provides a shared thinking space. The most well known wiki is Wikipedia, the open source encyclopaedia.

- An **Intranet** offers a solution to organisations which need shared file storage. Access to the Intranet tends to be restricted to those who belong to the organisation. Certain folders or files may also be restricted to particular users within that organisation.

- A **data centre** houses all the IT capability for an organisation. Large organisations may keep responsibility for their IT networks, but small organisations may outsource their IT operations. Electronic communications can be easier, quicker, more reliable, less expensive and less stressful for those involved than phone or snail mail (communications sent through postal service). Electronic communications and networks can also save paper, making this a more environmentally friendly method of communicating.

Key terms

Email – an abbreviation of 'electronic mail'.

Intranet – a type of website that is accessible only within the network in which it has been set up, usually within an organisation.

Twitter – a social networking and **microblogging** service in which users can send and read 'tweets' (messages up to 140 characters in length).

Microblogging – posting regularly to a blog, but only tweet-sized messages.

Collaborative working

Networks allow groups of individuals to work together in informal ways:

- **Social networking** sites, such as Friends Reunited, Facebook and **Twitter**, offer a groups option, so that you can 'talk' to people who went to the same school or like the same pop star or follow the same TV soap as you. Recently, politicians have tapped into social networking sites in an attempt to involve the public in politics.

- **Desktop conferencing** is obtainable via freely downloadable software, such as Skype. This enables voice and video links to colleagues, friends and family in far-flung places. It saves you having to travel and reduces your carbon footprint.

- **File sharing** software, such as Picasa™, lets you share photos with friends, and YouTube allows you to share your video clips.

1.2 Resource management

It is important for all aspects of an organisation's network system to be correctly managed.

A network manager is in charge of:

*   information
*   network hardware and software
*   overall administration of the network
*   security and legal issues.

In large organisations, other people may have specific jobs to help look after the network computer system.

A network administrator might be responsible for monitoring the network and its resources:

*   making sure the network is running smoothly
*   recognising sources of potential problems and fixing any problems that occur
*   ensuring the network is performing to its maximum capability
*   backing up data
*   setting policies, such as an IT security policy, on the use of the network and all its resources
*   providing security for the network and the data held on it.

Let's now look at how data, hardware and software need to be managed.

Data

To avoid loss of data or possible breaches of security, organisations try to hold data as securely as possible. Sometimes, there are legal issues to consider. For example, the Data Protection Act 1998 sets out principles that registered data users are expected to follow. The Data

Controller in each organisation must ensure that data is kept secure and protected from unauthorised access.

Organisations also need to ensure their systems are not overloaded with unnecessary information and documentation. Physical storage space is limited and it costs money. So out-of-date data can be archived if it might be needed again, or deleted, creating more space for current information.

Hardware

The hardware connected to a network is likely to be shared sometimes. It's important to manage hardware, such as printers, storage devices and scanners, to make sure users don't encounter problems.

Shared printers can be controlled using a queuing system. When a user sends a document to the printer, that document may not be first in the queue. It may not print out immediately, even if the printer appears to the user not to be busy. It is important that users know whether any hardware is on a queuing system. Otherwise they might try resending the document and this can result in the same document being printed many times.

Software

When a network system is set up in an organisation, it's important to manage the software.

Software for different jobs

Most organisations need different types of software on the network for different types of job. For example, someone in Accounts might need to use a financial application, but would be unlikely to need desktop publishing. However, someone in Marketing might need to use desktop publishing, but wouldn't have much use for a financial application.

The network can be set up so that, after log on, the person in Accounts and the person in Marketing both have access, but only to the software they need.

Why bother restricting who uses which applications?

- When buying software for a network, you buy a licence for the number of people who will use it. By restricting who has access to an application, the organisation can buy fewer licences (at lower cost).

- Applications that require lots of memory to run can slow down the system. Allowing access only to those people who need to use an application results in fewer problems with the network system.

Illegal software

Another reason why networked software needs to be managed is to make sure there is no illegal software on the system. When the network is set up, only certain people, such as the network administrator, are given permission to install software. This prevents other members of staff from installing software that the organisation may not be licensed to use.

> **i** **Did you know?**
>
> **Wiki gardening** is the term used to describe tidying up a wiki.

1.3 Issues

Networking has its benefits:

- shared software
- shared hardware resources
- shared data
- increased communications and team working
- ease of control of who is using the network and when and for what purpose.

However, there's always a downside. Let's now consider the issues that arise with networks.

Speed

If your centre of learning or workplace had a small **server** to run the network, the people in charge of IT would need to limit the number of people trying to use the system at the same time.

- Inadequate **bandwidth** could result in the server running slowly and users becoming frustrated. Shared USB bandwidth explains why you can't have music and video simultaneously when using Skype, or why a film watched on YouTube lacks continuity and the picture keeps freezing.
- If too many people try to send messages or access the same resource at the same time, **contention** issues could result in a system crash, so that no one could use the system until the problem had been dealt with.

Speed issues can be avoided by having sufficient resources (memory and fast processing speed and appropriate wireless connections) and an operating system that is sophisticated enough to handle the required number of workstations at peak times.

Costs

A networked system is more complex than the same number of standalone computers. The interconnection of the hardware and the network operating system adds to the complexity – and cost – of the system. This problem needs to be addressed by careful design of a **network topology** (see pages 185–189).

Staff skills

Network users need higher skills than people using standalone computers. These skills can be provided through training in:

- how to **log on**
- the importance of **passwords** and keeping them secure
- how to share files
- how to use **work areas**.

Key terms

Server – a networked computer used to manage software and/or hardware resources for all users (clients).

Bandwidth – an information channel's capacity, i.e. how much data it can carry at one time.

Contention – competition for resources where two users or computers attempt to transmit a message across the same wire at the same time.

Topology of a network – how workstations, servers and **peripherals** are connected, and how information travels around the network.

Peripheral – a hardware component that is connected to a computer, e.g. a printer.

Log on/Login – a procedure used to gain access to a computer system (or to a page on a website).

Password – an unspaced sequence of characters which should be known only to the user and to the computer system to which they are trying to gain access.

Work area – space on a computer allocated to one user or a group of users that cannot be accessed by anyone else.

Downtime

At one time, computers were considered more efficient than humans because they never needed tea breaks. However, a network cannot run forever without a period of maintenance. Then access to the network has to be suspended and this is called (planned) downtime. Organisations such as banks schedule downtime at the least busy times for the network, usually in the early hours of the morning.

Networks may also experience problems and crash – this is also downtime as far as users of the network are concerned, but it is unplanned.

Security issues

Imagine if all the people in your class could access your personal record from their workstations. There may be information that you do not wish to share with everyone. For example, you might only want close friends to have your home address and telephone number.

The problem of **unauthorised access** to data is addressed by controlling access rights, but there are other, potentially more dangerous, security issues.

- **Malware** (**mal**icious soft**ware**) includes viruses, worms and Trojans and any other software programs that have been designed to cause an unsuspecting user problems.

- **Viruses** can damage files, but this can be prevented by installing virus protection software and by following procedures such as not opening attachments to emails from unknown sources.

- **Backups** are vital in case disaster strikes. It's essential that adequate backups and a recovery procedure are in place to avoid possible loss of data.

- **Hacking** is the act of breaking into a computer system and is a criminal offence under the Computer Misuse Act (1990). Hacking is best prevented through installation of a **firewall** which creates a software barrier, preventing other network users gaining access to data on your computer.

> **Key term**
>
> **Firewall** – a type of security system, used mainly to protect networks from external threats.

Just checking

1. Explain these terms: forum, blog, Intranet, server, bandwidth, contention, topology and peripheral.
2. What is a wiki? How might it be used?
3. Give three examples of social networking sites. How do they differ?
4. When might a queuing system be used on a network?
5. What is a software licence?
6. What is a firewall?

PLTS

By identifying how a social network can improve productivity and benefits yourself and others, you will show that you are an **effective participator**.

By using the Internet to research potential issues with computer networks, you will show that you are an **independent enquirer**.

Functional skills

By creating an effective poster and leaflet, you will provide evidence of your functional **English** skills in **reading** and writing.

By giving an effective presentation, you will provide evidence of your Functional **English** skills in speaking and listening.

Assessment activity 10.1   P1 P2 P3 M1

You are employed as a junior network technician in a large IT Communications company. The work you do at this early stage of your career is quite varied and besides practical tasks you are often asked to produce informative leaflets and other material which is designed to help other people understand the basics of networking. Quite often you need to look up some of this information yourself which helps with your knowledge and training.

You have been asked to produce some leaflets and slides on the following topics:

1. The Poetry Society has established a presence on Facebook. Describe how using computer networks and, in particular, an Internet social network might improve communication for people who belong to the Poetry Society group on Facebook and for the Poetry Society itself. Produce a leaflet which describes how using computer networks can improve communications for both individuals and organisations. Try to use appropriate diagrams to help in the description. **P1**

2. Networks allow sharing of information, hardware, software and staffing. For an organisation of your choice, create a presentation describing how a network is used to manage its resources. **P2**

3. The Office for National Statistics (ONS) includes questions on electronic business processes in its annual ecommerce surveys. This is to find out whether or not its network is leading to improved productivity. Use the Internet to find examples of individuals and organisations using networks to improve productivity. Create a slideshow to explain how at least one individual and one organisation have improved productivity as a result of using computer networks. **M1**

4. Regulators of sites like Twitter worry about issues such as flawed data security. Use the Internet to research potential issues with computer networks. Present your findings in the form of a leaflet, describing the issues that you discovered. **P3**

Grading tips

- For question 1, check that the leaflet delivers the description clearly.

- Your answer to question 2 could be derived from a case study provided by your tutor or by a structured workplace visit. Alternatively, you might comment on an organisation known to you personally. When you refer to shared data, you should check what aspects of the Data Protection Act (1998) influence how social networks manage data.

- Build on what you discovered in tackling questions 1 and 2 to answer question 3, focusing on the productivity of individuals and organisations.

- Include in your investigation for question 4 issues such as unacceptable response times, risks of security breaches, broken connections, hardware and software failures, and the role of user error in networking problems.

2. Know the features and services of local and wide area network technologies

2.1 Features of network technologies

There are two basic types of computer network that are used today: **LANs** and **WANs**.

Two computers in the same room could be connected to form a LAN, as shown in Figure 10.1.

In both LAN and WAN connections, the workstations are usually connected to a server (see Figure 10.5 page 188) that holds the hardware, software, information and resources that the computers can share.

WANs have to be connected in a different way to LANs because of the problems (or sometimes, impossibility) of connecting workstations using a simple cabling system. The best known WAN is the Internet.

Topologies

There are many different network topologies – the most common are called star, bus and circle (or ring).

Star topology

The star topology consists of a central controlling computer connected to workstations by individual cables (see Figure 10.2). The central computer controls the flow of data between the workstations. Each workstation user can send data to and receive data from the central computer, without having to wait their turn. This makes it a fast network compared to the bus topology.

Key terms

LAN – local area network.

WAN – wide area network.

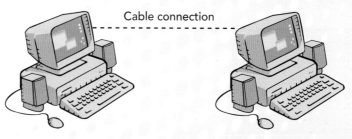

Cable connection

Figure 10.1: A simple LAN connection.

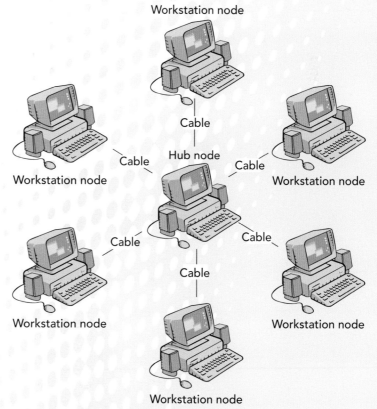

Workstation node

Workstation node

Cable

Cable

Hub node

Cable

Workstation node

Cable

Cable

Cable

Workstation node

Workstation node

Workstation node

Figure 10.2: A star topology.

One of the disadvantages of a star topology is that the entire network is affected if the central computer has a problem or crashes. It's likely that no one will be able to work. However, as each workstation is connected by its own cable, if one individual computer has a problem, then the rest of the network is unaffected.

Bus topology

In the bus topology (see Figure 10.3) all the workstations are connected to a central cable. It works just like a bus following its route on the road. This central cable is not joined up, so the 'bus' travels backwards and forwards along the length of the cable to let data on and off the bus. When data is sent from one workstation, it is carried by the 'bus', visiting each workstation in turn, until it reaches its destination.

With a bus topology, there's no main computer and there's no level of priority between the workstations. All workstations have equal status for transmitting data. So, if the central cable is busy elsewhere, other transmissions have to wait their turn.

The main problem with a bus topology is that only one workstation at a time can send or receive data. So, bus topologies are normally used for small LANs, with few workstations connected to the network. If more workstations are added as an organisation grows, the network topology may need to be changed. Too many workstations connected to a bus topology will make the system very slow and the work rate will fall.

The main advantages of a bus topology are:

- it's easy to set up
- it's a reliable network connection
- because only one main cable is required, it's not as expensive to set up as other topologies.

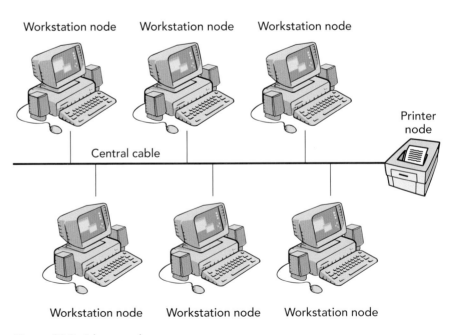

Figure 10.3: A bus topology.

Circle topology

In the circle topology (see Figure 10.4), all the workstations are connected together in a loop. There is no one controlling computer – all workstations have equal status. One computer, the server, holds the files for the network, including the programs and software required.

Data is transmitted in a circle topology using 'tokens'. These tokens travel around the circle and a workstation needs a token before it can send data. The workstation waits for the token to reach it, captures the token and then sends its data with the token. The token passes around the circle, holding the data, until the correct destination is reached. The data is then downloaded, releasing the token so that it can continue around the circle, waiting to be used again.

In a circle topology, if one workstation has a problem this affects the whole network. Also, if workstations need to be added or removed, or new hardware or software put on to the network, then the whole network will be unusable while this is being done.

However, because all workstations have equal status and can use a token as it passes around the ring, no one user should hold up the other users.

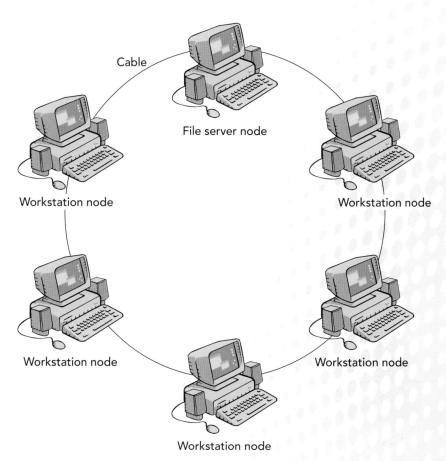

Figure 10.4: A circle topology.

Types of LAN

There are two basic types of local area network: peer-to-peer and **client**–server. Since client–server networks are most common, we'll look at these first.

Client–server network

In a client–server network (see Figure 10.5), one computer holds most of the information, resources and software and is called the server. Other computers that are networked to it can access what they need without having the software or hardware installed on hard disks. These computers are called clients.

How do you access documents and software at your place of learning? Is there a computer in the classroom that you have to log on to? Having logged on, can you access work that you've stored in your own work area on the server's hard disk? You should not be able to access work that someone else has stored in another work area on the server's hard disk.

The computer you're using may have its own hard disk. This can be used to store things temporarily during the session, to install software that is needed only within that classroom, or to process information you are working with. However, when you save something during your lesson, you're not saving it to the computer you're working on but to the server computer.

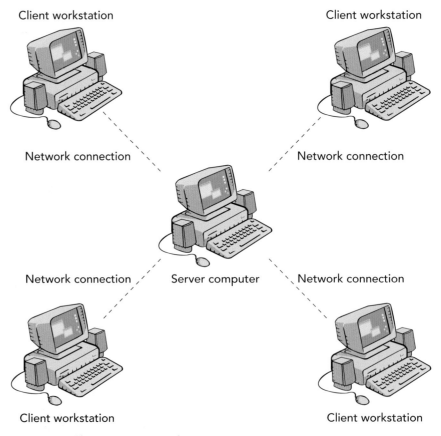

Figure 10.5: Client–server network.

Peer-to-peer network

In smaller organisations, where fewer workstations are to be networked (usually less than 20), a peer-to-peer network (see Figure 10.6) might be set up. Instead of a single server which would upset all the users if it crashed, in a peer-to-peer network every workstation manages its own section of the network and all workstations are equal. The workstations can still share resources, but can also each use printers and store files individually without having to pass the data and/or instructions through a central server.

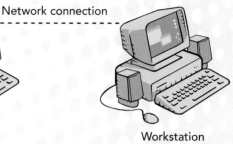

Figure 10.6: Peer-to-peer network.

Peer-to-peer networks do not cost much to set up and run, as only ordinary workstations are needed. Organisations will not need to invest in a powerful server. However, a peer-to-peer network is only suitable for a small number of workstations, as the system can run very slowly if more than one person tries to access the same hard disk at the same time.

Data rates

Data rates are the speed of transmission over the network. Factors that determine data rates include bandwidth and delays. Delays may be caused by a variety of factors:

- The distance that the transmission has to travel – how far away are you from the exchange?

- Errors occurring during transmission and error recovery programs running to deal with these. Is there noise on the line? If so, what has been done to minimise interference?

- The amount of 'traffic' on a network (the congestion factor). For example, what time of day is it? How many other people are trying to access information at the same time as you?

- The processing capabilities of the systems involved in the transmission. Should the host website upgrade the server?

In a network situation, **throughput** takes into account possible delays and then measures system performance, including these delays.

Addressing

If you want to find someone, you need to know their name and where they are – their location or address. The same goes for workstations on a network.

IP address

The **IP address** lets the host computer know 'who' has connected and where to send data if the host or anyone else on the network wants to communicate with that user. In some cases, your IP address stays the same – it's a fixed IP address. Sometimes, though, it is assigned dynamically (i.e. a new number is assigned whenever you connect).

Key terms

Throughput – the amount of work done by a system.

IP address – a number assigned to a device (usually a computer) whenever it connects to a network.
IP = Internet **Protocol.**

Protocol – a set of rules that determines how data is transmitted between computers.

Key terms

MAC (Media Access Control) **address** – a unique identifier assigned to most network adaptors.

NIC (network interface card) – an essential component of a network which is installed in an expansion slot inside the computer and acts as an interface for connection to the network.

An IP address such as 194.176.105.47 comprises four numbers which can each range from 0 to 255. There are only so many combinations of these four numbers.

If the total number of users on your network is low enough, everyone can retain their fixed IP. If there are too many users for fixed IP addresses to be assigned, there must be dynamic assigning of IP addresses. If someone tries to connect and all available IP addresses have already been assigned, that user will have to wait. This is why some sites, especially government sites and banks, log you off automatically if you have been idle for more than, say, 10 minutes. The site needs the IP address assigned to you for someone else.

MAC address

The **MAC address** is a unique identifier, like a serial number, assigned to most network adapters or **NICs** by the manufacturer. It should not change.

Activity: Addresses

An email address is a string of characters that identify a user and enable the user to receive email. For example, hp123@example.com could be the email address of user hp123 who works for a company with the domain example.com.

- What is your email address? Explain each part of the address.
- Go to Hotlinks and click on this unit. You can access a website that helps you to find out your own IP address.
- Connect to the Internet and find out your IP address. Disconnect and reconnect and check your IP address. Is it the same? If not, why not?
- Use the Internet to discover more about IP addressing. What different classes of addressing are used?
- Find out more about MAC addresses. What is MAC spoofing and how does this differ from IP spoofing?

2.2 Services

There are several reasons for setting up a network, including:

- communication
- file transfer
- login
- security
- software deployment.

Communication

A network may be set up to facilitate communication by email. Conferencing is a meeting between two or more people where they can see and talk to each other through a computerised video link. The computer screen is the visual link and speakers are used for the sound link. A video camera attached to each computer sends the images through telephone lines, while a microphone captures the sound. This is a cost-effective way of holding meetings for organisations that have offices and staff located in a number of different places.

File transfer

Resources, such as files, can be shared on a network.

- Setting up a drive to store shared files lets people access the drive from their own workstation and use whatever resources they need. For example, a folder on the shared drive could hold product leaflets or brochures. Staff can then access these to look at or print off information from them.

- Setting up software, such as word processing, on the LAN means it can be shared throughout an organisation. For example, the templates within the word processing package could include outline documents such as sales invoices. Staff can open these from their individual workstations. Once completed, the invoice can be saved into a common folder on the shared drive, creating a record of all the sales invoices.

- Files often need to be transferred between workstations and networks. For example, a chain of shoe shops sends details of takings and stock movements every day to head office. The file transfer has to be secure and as quick as possible and a special protocol called **FTP** can be used for this.

Transferring large files takes time and may slow down a network for other users. To minimise this problem, you can **zip** your files and compress large image files.

Login

A network may be set up to allow many different users to access the same data. For example, criminal records are shared by police forces in the UK. The downside of such networks is the increased risk of security breaches.

Measures can be taken to minimise this risk. When users log into a network system, they enter a user ID and a password; together with the IP address, this identifies who is using which workstation. The **NOS** can then keep track of what hardware and software they are using, which websites they are accessing and any information being downloaded from these websites.

Access rights can be set up individually, attached to the user login, to establish what that person can and cannot do on the system. An audit trail can also be used by the Network Administrator to make sure there is no breach of the IT Security Policy. This also enables an organisation to prevent certain information being altered by anyone who is unauthorised to do so.

Key terms

FTP – file transfer protocol, a set of rules which determine how files will be transferred over the network.

Zip – a file compression format, commonly used before data transfer.

NOS – network operating system, the software used to manage the network.

Security

The greatest risk to data comes from unauthorised access. Physical security barriers are a first line of defence. Then user IDs and passwords are employed to set access rights as discussed in the Login section (see page 191).

Software deployment

Key term

Software deployment – all of the activities that make a software system available for use.

Having set up the hardware and installed an operating system to make a network function efficiently, the next stage is **software deployment** – installing applications software and utilities. Not all users need access to all software, and licences may restrict usage, so the network manager should limit access as necessary and then customise software for those who are entitled to use it.

2.3 Protocols

Protocols have been established to manage data transmission in a standard way. This makes errors during transmission less likely.

Key terms

Handshake – in networking, before any data is sent or can be received the handshake takes place. It signifies that one computer wants to talk to another computer.

Packet – part of an electronic message that includes the destination address of the data within the packet.

TCP/IP – this stands for transmission control protocol/Internet protocol.

- A protocol tells the computers which are trying to communicate when to send and receive data. Communications are opened using a **handshake** procedure which ensures both computers are ready to communicate. They then communicate and, once all the necessary data has been passed between them, they close down the communication channel, freeing it for other communications.

- A protocol also specifies how the data is to be packaged. Just as you might put a letter in an envelope and write the address on the envelope, data can be grouped into **packets** for transmission across the Internet. A large message would be split into a number of packets and each sent separately. Since no two packets take the same route across the Internet, and may arrive within a different time span, one of the things the protocol has to do is to provide identification rules for the packets so they can be put back into the right sequence at the receiving end.

- A protocol also needs to understand addresses – for example, the IP address, the MAC address and the email address – so that the data can be directed to the correct destination.

- A protocol would also determine whether a reply is needed to acknowledge receipt of data, and whether data is to be compressed and/or encrypted.

For example, the **TCP/IP** protocol dictates how networked computers are named and addressed, how different networks can be connected together and how messages are transported across the various networks that form the Internet.

- The IP handles lower level transmissions from one computer to another as a message progresses step-by-step across the Internet.

- TCP operates at a higher level, being more concerned only with the two end systems – where the message originally comes from and where it will eventually be received. (For example, a page request from a web browser sent to a web server.)

TCP has been adopted by many of the Internet's most popular applications: WWW, email, FTP, peer-to-peer file sharing and some streaming media applications.

Activity: Protocols

There are more than 750 protocols in existence. The IP (Internet protocol) family contains a set of related protocols. The higher-level protocols like TCP, UDP, HTTP and FTP all integrate with IP to provide additional capabilities. The lower-level Internet protocols like ARP and ICMP also co-exist with IP.

- Find out what IP, TCP, UDP, HTTP, FTP, ARP and ICMP stand for. Write a brief description of each.

- What is meant by higher-level and lower-level protocols?

- Summarise what protocols are and how they work.

PLTS

By analysing and evaluating the features and services provided by a LAN and WAN, you will show that you are an **independent enquirer**.

Functional skills

By researching and writing an effective report, you will provide evidence of your functional **English** skills in reading and writing.

Assessment activity 10.2

You are in your post as a junior network technician and are continuing to build up your knowledge and skills. Your manager wants you to learn more about the features and services provide by networks, and to produce something written from which others can learn. They will provide you with access to at least one LAN and at least one WAN. Spend time exploring these networks until you are familiar with how they work and what they provide.

1. Write a report describing the features and services of both Local Area Networks and Wide Area Networks. **P4**

2. Extend your report to include evaluations of the things you have described in task 1. **D1**

Grading tip

- For question 1, ensure you include:

  Features: topologies, types, data rates and addressing in your descriptions

  Services: communication, file transfer, login, security and software deployment.

- For question 2, you will need to include notes about good, less good, and what can be done to improve some of the features and services of both a LAN and a WAN.

Just checking

1. What is the difference between a LAN and a WAN?
2. What are the differences between bus, star and circle topologies?
3. In a client–server network, what is a client and what is a server? How does a client–server network differ from a peer-to-peer network?
4. What is throughput? Give four examples of what might result in delays that can affect the throughput of a network.
5. Explain these terms: data rate, NOS and packet.

3. Understand how network hardware and software components are connected

Here is one example of a network card, ready to be installed. Does your network card look like this?

Did you know?

Each Ethernet network card has its own MAC address (see page 190), a unique 48-bit serial number stored within the ROM carried on the card. Each computer on an Ethernet network needs a unique MAC address.

3.1 Hardware

Some hardware components for LANs are needed no matter which type of network is set up on the system. Just as in any type of computer system, the main hardware components required for LANs are the hard disk, monitor and keyboard.

There are then other components and technologies, such as network cards and wireless devices. Let's look at each of these components in turn.

Network cards

To access the network, each workstation requires a network adapter – often called a network card or NIC. This is installed into an expansion slot inside the computer and acts as an interface for connection to the network. The type of network card employed depends on the network topology being used.

- An **Ethernet card** is used when physically connecting a limited number of computers within a small geographical area.
- A **wireless card** is used if you intend to connect to a wireless network. For example, in your home one or more computers might be linked wirelessly to the Internet, using a BT Home Hub or similar device.

Workstations

To access the network, each workstation requires its own NIC.

A workstation may or may not have its own hard disk. In some networks, the workstation is just a monitor and keyboard, and workstations linked to a network can use the hardware and software of the server computer.

Servers

There can be a number of servers on a network:

- A **file server** houses all the software and data.

- Servers often manage and prioritise the use of peripherals that workstations share – these are known as **peripheral servers**. For example, servers that manage printers are known as **printer servers**. Another example is at an airport, where you have lots of screens above the check-in desks and the queue for a flight can be allocated to one or more desks. The **display server** controls which flight information is sent to which screens.

- A **web server** may be set up to handle all requests for Internet web pages from users logged on to the network. The web server delivers these pages to the user and can store frequently used pages to speed up access. The web server software may also keep track of which users accessed, or tried to access, certain pages. Some sites may be blocked, preventing users from accessing them.

The server, whichever its type, 'serves' any other users (i.e. the clients) with any resources needed.

Routers

In networks, such as the World Wide Web, millions of computers can be linked and there may be more than one route from any one computer to another. A **router** will decide which route to establish between networks for file or message transfers.

Switches

A network switch is a device used to connect segments of a network. According to its level of sophistication, it may be referred to as:

- a network bridge, if it processes and routes data at Layer 2 (the data link layer) of the **OSI model**

- a Layer 3 switch or multilayer, if it also processes data at the network layer (Layer 3 and above).

Wireless devices

Nowadays, networks don't have to be physically linked by cables. Networks can use wireless links, using a combination of satellite, microwave or **infra-red communications**.

One problem with wireless technology is that the connection might not be as fast as when using cabling. Also, wireless connections can be adversely affected by interference from other wireless communications.

However, wireless connections are popular – because cables do not need to be laid, the connection is easy to install, and it can therefore be a cheaper alternative. For example, supermarkets use wireless technology for checking stock. Staff members carry portable keypads which have a wireless link to a central computer. The stock checkers count the number of items on the shelf, entering codes and quantities into the keypad. This information is then sent through the wireless LAN to the central computer.

Key terms

Router – a device used to connect networks and direct the traffic across the networks.

OSI (Open System Interconnection) **model** – an abstract model consisting of seven layers of protocols for connecting computers together in a network.

Infra-red communication – uses infra-red waves, which are longer than light waves but shorter than radio waves, to transmit and receive data.

3.2 Communication

Let's now focus on the connectors and cables needed to link all the components of a network.

Network cabling

There are a variety of cabling options:

- **Fibre optics** relies on light signals. The cables consist of glass or plastic fibres (see Figure 10.7). They carry a digital signal and have a very high transmission rate. They are also a secure way of networking – fibre optic cables do not emit electromagnetic radiation so remote sensing equipment cannot detect the signals.

Fibre optic cable

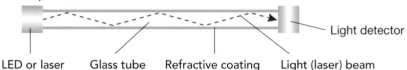

LED or laser   Glass tube   Refractive coating   Light (laser) beam   Light detector

Figure 10.7: Fibre optic cabling.

- Other cabling, such as UTP, STP and coaxial, is made from copper wires (see Figure 10.8).
  - In **UTP** cable, the wires are insulated and twisted together in pairs, held together by a plastic covering.
  - **STP** is similar but has a metal sheath, usually copper braid, inside the outer plastic covering.
  - **Coaxial cable** – as used for connecting television aerials – has a straight copper core surrounded by an insulator and an outer metal sheath, usually copper braid, inside a plastic covering.

Unshielded twisted pair

Coaxial cable

Conductor

Insulator

Figure 10.8: Wire cabling.

Connectors

For a wired network, at the ends of each wire there is a connector, such as the **BNC** connector which is used with coaxial cables.

- The basic BNC connector is male – its centre pin is connected to the centre cable conductor and a metal tube connected to the outer cable shield. Outside this metal tube, a rotating ring locks the cable to any female connector (see Figure 10.9).
- BNC T-connectors are female devices for connecting two cables to a network interface card (NIC).

Key terms

UTP (unshielded twisted pair) – a type of cable in which the wires are insulated and twisted together in pairs and are held together by a plastic covering.

STP (shielded twisted pair) – cabling which is similar to UTP but has a metal sheath, usually copper braid, inside the outer plastic covering.

Coaxial – parts of the cable share the same axis, so when you cut through the cable they appear as a series of rings around the central core.

Key term

BNC – Bayonet Neill Concelman connectors are used with coaxial cables.

Addressing

As mentioned on pages 189–190, each workstation on a network needs an address so that data can be sent to the correct workstation.

- Within an Ethernet network, the unique MAC address identifies the network card within the workstation.
- On the Internet, a workstation can be identified by the IP address it has been allocated.

The allocation of IP addresses can be automatic, and **ISP**s usually use **DHCP** to allow customers to join the Internet with minimum effort.

WAN connectivity

Broadband technologies are capable of using a wider bandwidth than other connection technologies. In telecommunications, broadband describes any signalling method that allows a relatively wide range of frequencies. These are then divided into channels so, while in data communications a digital modem will transmit only 56 kbit/s over a 4 kilohertz wide telephone line (which is considered to be narrowband or voiceband), when that line is converted to broadband, it becomes hundreds of kilohertz wide and can carry several megabits per second.

However, there is no worldwide standard for what level of bandwidth and network speeds actually constitute broadband and providers of lines can only say what speeds you might achieve, rather than what you will actually achieve.

Note also that while dial-up modems may be limited to a bit rate of less than 56 kbit/s and require the full use of a telephone line (which means you cannot have a telephone conversation at the same time), broadband technologies promise more than double this rate and should not disrupt telephone use on the same line.

The most commonly available broadband technologies are ISDN and ADSL.

ISDN

ISDN converts voice to digital and sends data and voice over the standard telephone system with a bandwidth of two megabits per second in both directions. There are no limits on distance or numbers of voice/data links within the bandwidth.

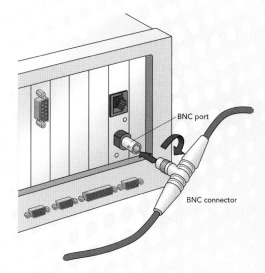

Figure 10.9: A hub showing the BNC port into which a connecting wire can be inserted.

Key terms

ISP – Internet Service Providers are the organisations which charge you for a connection to the Internet; they provide an Internet service.

DHCP – Dynamic Host Configuration Protocol. The DHCP assigns unique IP addresses to devices, then releases and renews these addresses as devices leave and rejoin the network.

ISDN (integrated services digital network) – a type of telephone connection which allows both voice and data transfer simultaneously.

 Did you know?

The term 'broadband' simply means a telecommunications signal of greater bandwidth, in some sense, relative to some other 'narrower' band signal. For example, with radio, a narrowband is all that is needed for Morse code, while a broader band is needed for a spoken message, but an even broader signal would be needed for audio if you want realistic reproduction of music.

Key terms

DSL (digital subscriber line) – another type of communication link offered by telephone companies.

ADSL (asynchronous digital subscriber line) – this communication link simply means higher rates in one direction, i.e. for downloading data.

Did you know?

Internet browsers run on TCP/IP networks and transfer the **HTML** coding, used to create web pages, into a user-friendly front end as text, graphics, animation and videos.

Key term

HTML (hypertext mark-up language) – the code used to create web pages. It allows links (hyperlinks) between one web page and another.

Did you know?

Windows® Internet Explorer® uses an email client called Outlook Express®. Mozilla Firefox® uses an email client called Mozilla Thunderbird®.

DSL/ADSL

DSL/ADSL was primarily developed for home use, allowing data to be sent over the copper telephone cables using unused frequency capacity on the line (separated out electronically in the home). Voice messaging continues to be analogue and limited to one conversation per line.

Much higher data rates are possible than with ISDN – up to 24 megabits per second on ADSL. That's why some businesses now use it, especially for Internet access, using non-ISDN lines. However, subscribers have to be within about two kilometres of the telephone exchange. It is normally offered by telephone companies, although some ISPs can supply an ADSL.

3.3 Software

Let's now look at application-based software, operating systems and utilities.

Application–based software

Application-based software is software written to serve a particular purpose. Three of the most common applications are Internet browser, firewall and email.

Internet browser

This is an application that displays pages that have been created in Web format. Regardless of your make of computer, operating system and network connection, any Internet browser from the range available ought to work on your system. Because there is a standard way of developing websites, they can be fully viewed and accessed whichever browser you are using. However, different browsers offer different functions and features, and this might be relevant when deciding which one to install.

Firewall

A firewall protects a network from attack (see *Security issues* on page 183).

Email

Email is an electronic communication system for sending messages from one user to another through an email client. To use email facilities, you could install an email client software package. But if your computer has a browser loaded, you could already have an email package installed.

Operating system

When you turn on your computer, it is the operating system that kicks into action and controls the interface (i.e. what you see on the screen) and then obeys your commands to load and run software applications.

The network operating system (NOS) is software with special functions that lets you connect computers and other devices to create a LAN. This software also helps you to manage the users that you will allow on your LAN.

Some operating systems (such as UNIX and the Mac OS) have networking functions built in. However, the term NOS is generally used for software that enhances a basic operating system by adding networking features. Novell Open Enterprise Server (OES) and Microsoft® Windows® Server are both examples of an NOS.

Utility

As with a standalone computer, a network needs the standard **utilities**:

- disk checkers and disk defragmenters
- backup utilities
- disk compression and data compression utilities
- archive utilities
- anti-virus utilities.

Most operating systems come with these pre-installed utilities. But network utilities should also analyse the computer's network connectivity, let you reconfigure network settings, and check data transfer or log events.

Any workstation on a network that is connected to the Internet is at risk of Internet-related threats. To protect the network, appropriate **utility software** should be installed to monitor the websites that are visited and to scan for threats to the network.

Key terms

Utility – a single piece of utility software; also called a tool.

Utility software – this focuses on how the computer hardware, the operating system, the application software and the data storage operates. It is designed to help to analyse performance, reconfigure, optimise and maintain the computer system.

PLTS

By communicating what you have learned about network communications to the network users, you will show that you are a **reflective learner**.

Functional skills

By giving an effective presentation, you will provide evidence of your functional **English** skills in speaking and listening.

By creating an effective leaflet, you will provide evidence of your functional **English** skills in reading and writing.

Assessment activity 10.3

BTEC   (P5) (M2)

You have progressed in your training as a junior network technician and your manager thinks you can take on a more active role in the work of the Company. Travelwise, a travel company, have asked for some training and it has been decided that you are capable of doing this work.

1. Travelwise claims to be able to find the cheapest deals for flights, hotels and vehicle hire for their clients. When clients call, the travel consultants use a client–server network linked to the Internet. Your task is to train new travel consultants in the correct use of the network. Prepare a presentation explaining how hardware, software and addressing combine to support network communications. (P5)

2. The new travel consultants will be given a copy of the presentation you produced in your first assignment, but will also need to know about

possible solutions to connectivity problems. Produce a leaflet in which you suggest possible solutions to resolve connectivity problems in networks.

Grading tips

- For question 1, target your presentation to the intended users of the network. Demonstrate how easy it is to connect to the Internet and gain access to online resources. Where possible, avoid technical jargon and use diagrams rather than words.

- For question 2, you only need to suggest how the connectivity problems can be resolved in this leaflet. You do not have to include how they are diagnosed.

Just checking

1. Explain the difference between an Ethernet card and a wireless card.
2. Explain these terms: NIC, router, OSI, UTP, STP, BNC, DHCP, ISDN, ADSL and HTML.
3. Why might a network have more than one server? Give two examples of servers.
4. What is infra-red communication? How does it differ from other communication methods like fibre optics?
5. Describe how UTP cabling is constructed.

4. Be able to set up a simple local area network

4.1 Preparation

As with all activities involving computers, make sure you know what you're planning to do and have everything to hand before you begin. It helps to write notes – a bit like a recipe, showing the ingredients (the components) and each step that you plan to follow during installation of your network.

The components that you will need to collect, ready for setting up your network, are the workstations, the NICs, cabling and all relevant software.

You will need some tools:

- a screwdriver to open the PC casing so that you can install the network card
- a multimeter, in case the network doesn't work and you want to test a cable.

You also need a copy of installation guides and any manuals supplied with the components. Read these carefully before starting.

Activity: Safety first

New plugs come with a handy diagram showing what goes where. Similarly, when setting up a network, it's a good idea to read the manual.

- What risks are there in setting up a network?
- How can you protect yourself from harm?
- What advice can you give others to ensure their safety?

Do you know how to wire a plug? There are three coloured wires to be connected:

- The green and yellow Earth
- The blue Neutral
- The brown Live

To help you remember the positioning of these wires:

- BL = Bottom Left = Blue
- BR = Bottom Right = Brown

The third wire then goes at the top. But what would happen if you wired it incorrectly?

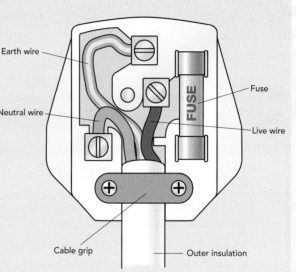

Figure 10.10: Diagram for wiring a plug.

4.2 Setting up

The process of setting up can be broken into two sections:

- physically connecting the hardware
- installing the software.

Ensure security and, at all times, be aware of health and safety considerations for you and those around you.

Hardware

Now you need to connect the hardware that you collected in the preparation stage:

- first install the network card
- then connect the cabling.

Note that the NIC connectors determine the type of cabling to be used on the network and vice versa. However, the network cards are installed first, because the cabling connects to the cards! There are several options for a NIC, as shown in Figure 10.11.

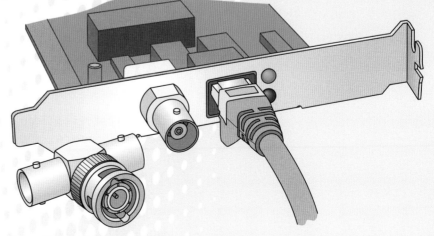

Figure 10.11: NIC options.

Key term

Modem – this word is made up from the names of two processes involved in the conversion of digital to analogue signals and back again – modulate and demodulate.

- You can install a NIC in an open expansion slot on the motherboard and then connect the cabling to the NIC port. Note that the type of NIC card must match the type of slot.
- The PC can be connected through a device, such as a **modem**, attached to a USB port.
- You can use a PC card as a network card for a portable computer, such as a laptop or notepad.

How to... Add/remove a NIC

- Check which slot you are going to use, and that you have the correct NIC board for your PC (see Figure 10.12).
- Check the documentation. Do you need to set a DIP switch or a jumper for the NIC card?
- Handle the card carefully by its non-connecting edges, otherwise you might leave traces of grease or dirt from your fingers.
- Gently place the NIC card into the slot and press it into place.
- To remove a board, release the locking mechanism and then slide the board gently out of its slot.

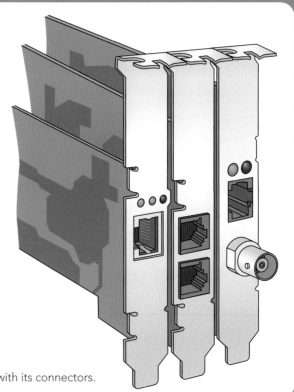

Figure 10.12: A NIC with its connectors.

Key term

Platform – the underlying operating system, e.g. Mac OS or Windows®.

Software

The NOS to be installed will depend on the **platform** you are using.

The choice of platform will limit the options as to which NOS can be supported. Once you have decided on the NOS, installation is straightforward – the vendor will supply the software on CD, and full instructions will be provided. You should follow these exactly!

Before installing software on a workstation, check that you have the necessary licence to do so. The licence gives you the authority to use the software and provides a unique product code as proof of purchase. During software installation you will be prompted to key in this product code. Your use of the software can then be registered online, and the vendor can check that your product code has not already been allocated to another computer.

Security

You will need to set up users and decide what access to allow each individual user to available resources. You may make some resources, such as a printer, available to all users. How to do this will be explained in your software documentation.

Health and safety awareness

Unit 2: Working in the IT industry (see pages 29–47) gives general advice on sensible procedures to follow when handling computers. In particular, to avoid electrocution, you must switch off all electrical equipment before opening the computer case and installing the network card. However, when installing hardware, an additional source of harm to the equipment is **ESD**.

To prevent ESD, make sure that the static charge between you and the hardware you are about to touch is equalised. One way is to wear an anti-static wrist strap (see page 13 in *Unit 7: Installing computer hardware*).

> **Key term**
>
> **ESD** – this stands for electrostatic discharge. It can happen when two things (you and the computer) connect.

4.3 Simple LAN

Refer to page 188 of this unit for a comparison of peer-to-peer and client–server networks.

4.4 Faults

Faults on a network can result in inconvenience for one user or for many users, depending on the topology of the network and the complexity of what's gone wrong.

Commonly occurring faults

Let's consider the most commonly occurring faults:

Address conflict
This can happen when two workstations on a network have been assigned the same IP address. Such a conflict usually prevents either one or both of the workstations from using the network facilities. To resolve the conflict, you might simply have to release one of the IP addresses. But if the fault lies with the operating system's method of assigning IP addresses, you might need to upgrade the operating software.

Network card failure
This could happen if conditions are too dusty or too hot, or there may be a fault in the card itself. Installing cooling equipment and avoiding dust will help in the long term, but replacement of the card will solve the problem in the short term.

Break in a cable
This might happen if the cable is twisted and bent double. The connectivity within a suspect cable can be tested using a multimeter. Replacing a broken cable will solve the problem.

Loss of service

There may also be a **loss of service**, for example:

- A printer might break down or run out of paper or toner. Regular maintenance and keeping enough supplies of consumables should reduce the risk of problems with a printer.
- A file might become corrupted. The file could be recovered if a backup system is in place, but there would be a loss of data of any changes done since the last backup.
- Email access via the Internet could be interrupted if there is some fault on the Internet itself. Users simply have to wait until the fault is fixed.

Activity: Fault recovery

- Find out how to release an IP address.
- Find out how to use a multimeter to test for a break in a cable.
- Find out what backup and recovery procedures apply on your network.

Compare your findings with others in your group.

4.5 Testing

When you install new equipment or software, you should test that the system still works. You need to test both the new functions installed and the functions that the system used to do before the change.

Functionality

Setting up a network will upgrade a number of standalone workstations into a system that should allow communication between the workstations and sharing of hardware and software resources. You should test that this is indeed the case.

Connectivity

A loose cable can result in a workstation not being connected. You should check that everything is properly connected before you check individual workstations.

Addressing

Using DHCP on a network saves you having to configure individually for each client device. This is because devices running DHCP client software automatically retrieve these settings from DHCP servers as needed. However, a DHCP server has to be set up with the appropriate configuration parameters for the network and this includes the pool of available IP addresses.

4.6 Security

Once you have linked a number of standalone computers to form a network, and have installed the NOS, the user interface should recognise this and require each user to log on. You must check that the user interface works as anticipated.

There are other considerations too:

- You will have installed a firewall. How will this be configured?
- You will need to set up file and folder permissions.
- You will need to decide on a policy for access control.
- You will have to determine user rights.

How to achieve the level of security that you want will be fully explained in the software documentation.

4.7 Uses of the network

Let's consider three main uses of a network:

- The main function of the network will be to facilitate communication between users of the network. As the network administrator, you will need to set up email addresses and passwords for users.
- Users might also need to be able to transfer files. For this, you might need to set up FTP facilities for some or all users.
- Finally, part of the process of setting up the software for the network includes allocating user rights and allocating file space to individual users.

4.8 Troubleshooting

When things go wrong on a network, it might not immediately be clear where the fault lies.

- Has a piece of hardware failed?
- Has the link with the Internet fallen down?
- Is there some problem with the software?

Often the on-screen operating system messages will point you in the right direction.

- Is there an address conflict?
- The problem may be due to a breakdown in connectivity (between workstations or with the Internet).

Systematic investigation should lead to a solution. For example, replace suspect components with known working components and carefully check the system settings.

However, if you hit a problem that you cannot solve, the sensible option is to ask for help. Your fellow students might assist you, or you might need to ask your teacher or a technician – this is called **escalation**.

Key term

Escalation – passing on a problem to someone who knows more or has higher authority than you, and should be able to solve the problem.

Just checking

1. What is a multimeter used for?
2. What does a modem do?
3. What is a platform? Give two examples.
4. What is ESD? How can it be avoided?
5. Give three examples of how a network might break down.

PLTS

By referring to all instructions provided to you while setting up your network, you will show that you are an **independent enquirer**.

By using the Internet to evaluate the features and services provided by LANs and WANs, you will show that you are an **independent enquirer**.

Functional skills

By creating an effective leaflet, you will provide evidence of your functional **English** skills in reading and writing.

BTEC Assessment activity 10.4

1. Your initial training as a Junior Network Technician is now complete. Your manager wants to check how competent you are at setting up, using and testing a simple LAN. You may need to work with others for part of this, but you will be assessed entirely on what you can do as an individual. Your manager will tell you exactly what they need to see you do. **P6**

   - First you will collect the appropriate components.

   - Then you will set up your network, referring to all instructions provided to you. Take all necessary precautions to ensure the safety of yourself and others around you and of the equipment you will be handling.

   - Finally you will test your system, troubleshooting any issues as they arise.

2. Having seen you set up the network, your manager now wants to see you set up and configure security on the network. **M3**

3. Your manager needs a training leaflet to be produced for some of the organisations' clients who have problems with security issues. Prepare a leaflet which explains how security issues can be minimised. **D2**

Grading tips

- You will be observed by your manager as you complete tasks 1 and 2, and they will write a detailed statement of what they have seen you do. This will be the main evidence for criteria **P6** and **M3** but you can keep any notes or screenshots which you feel may add to this evidence.

- Alternatively you can be videoed as you complete tasks 1 and 2. A video showing you working and what you are doing will provide sufficient evidence.

- If you are videoed for tasks 1 and 2 then you can provide a commentary or presentation as evidence for criterion **D2** as an alternative to the leaflet.

WorkSpace — Ria View Theatre Club

Cheng, Ling, Ayesha and Phil manage the Ria View Theatre Club and organise theatre trips for its members.

Cheng is responsible for research:

'I've used the Internet to find the websites of local theatres. I subscribe to their newsletters and receive press releases about future productions via email.

'I also organise our management meetings. Before each meeting, I email an agenda to everyone. Between meetings we 'talk' using email, rather than costly phone calls.'

Ling is the programme co-ordinator:

'The theatre websites display dates, times and the cast list for shows. To avoid making mistakes, I copy and paste this information directly into the programme.

'I then email the programme and our newsletter to members, using a distribution list which includes the email addresses of all members. Instead of having to enter every member's email address in the *Bcc:* field, I just enter the group name. All the people on the distribution list then appear in the *Bcc:* field. I update the distribution list by adding new members, deleting members, or amending email addresses if these change.

'For members without email, I do a mailshot. This could be a leaflet, letter or brochure on paper, which is sent in the post. This costs a lot more, as we have to pay for paper, printing and postage. All recipients receive exactly the same message, although it may be personalised with their name. Sometimes I need to target people in a certain age group. To reach customers in this way, I have an up to date membership database.'

Phil is website manager:

'I've launched a website to promote the Ria View Theatre Club. We use it to attract new members, advertise events and provide information, such as our contact number.'

Ayesha looks after bookings:

'I've created a spreadsheet on Google Docs, shared online by myself, Ling and Phil. It's used to record progress with booking shows and sales of tickets to members, so we can all track the financial success (or otherwise) of particular events.'

Think about it!

1. Ayesha manages the membership database. She sends up to date lists to the other committee members at regular intervals. But she'd like the others to update the database themselves and to have access to current information. How could she do this?

2. Phil finds Google Docs clumsy. He wants a shared workspace – something like an Intranet. What options are there for secure online sharing of data?

3. Currently, everyone has a standalone desktop computer or a laptop. How could these be linked into a network that is accessible only by those working for the Ria View Theatre Club?

Just checking

1. Explain these terms: network and desktop conferencing.
2. What is the function of an IP address? How does it differ from a MAC address?
3. What happens when a file is zipped? What is the purpose of zipping a file?
4. Suggest three reasons for setting up a network.
5. What is utility software? Give three examples.
6. What is an address conflict? How can it be resolved?
7. What is escalation?
8. Give three suggestions as to where the fault might be when things go wrong with a network.
9. What is an email distribution list?
10. What is a mailshot? What is it used for?

edexcel

Assignment tips

- The Internet will provide you with all the additional information you might need about networks. Just use Google or another search engine and enter a search term such as 'protocol'. Be careful, though, to check the validity of a site.

- When invited to visit an organisation which uses a network, or when attending a talk about networking, make as many notes as you can. Beforehand, make a list of questions you want to ask or aspects of networking you want to see for yourself.

- Pool information with others in your group. You can learn from them as much as they can learn from you.

- Before tackling something like a poster, study examples of posters that you admire. Ask yourself what it is that makes the poster work so well and try to use the same techniques in your creation. Also look at posters that you think don't work and try to avoid making the same mistakes.

- When watching a presentation given by your teacher or one of your class, notice how they present the information on the slides: how they talk to explain each slide, referring to notes as necessary, and how they hold your attention throughout the talk. Learn from what works well and not so well, so that when you give a presentation you can avoid making any mistakes that you noticed.

- Become aware of how much you rely on networks outside of this course; for example, at home, in other subjects or at work.

Credit value: 10

16 Database systems

Databases are very widely used today by businesses and non-commercial organisations. A retail company will use a database to store information about staff, customers, orders and sales. A college will store information about students, tutors and courses. A charity will store information about donors and fundraising events as well as staff.

It is important that you understand not only what databases can do, but also how they are structured. You will then be in a position to decide whether a database is the most appropriate way in which to store any data that you are working with.

The person who sets up a database is known as a database developer. The person who uses the database is always referred to as the user. So even if you are creating a database for yourself, you will always have to think of yourself as two separate people – the developer and the user.

Learning outcomes

After completing this unit you should be able to achieve the following learning outcomes:

1. understand the principles of database systems
2. be able to create non-relational database systems
3. be able to use database software tools.

Assessment and grading criteria

This table shows you what you must do in order to achieve a pass, merit or distinction grade, and where you can find activities in this book to help you.

To achieve a **pass** grade the evidence must show that you are able to:	To achieve a **merit** grade the evidence must show that, in addition to the pass criteria, you are able to:	To achieve a **distinction** grade the evidence must show that, in addition to the pass and merit criteria, you are able to:
P1 explain the principles of database systems **See Assessment activity 16.1 on page 219**	**M1** explain the importance of maintaining data integrity in a database system **See Assessment activity 16.1 on page 219**	
P2 design a non-relational database system, including different data types **See Assessment activity 16.2 on page 258**	**M2** explain the choice of fields, data types and primary key in a non-relational database system **See Assessment activity 16.2 on page 258**	
P3 create a non-relational database system from a given design **See Assessment activity 16.3 on page 263**	**M3** explain the need to calculate data storage requirements **See Assessment activity 16.2 on page 258**	**D1** test a non-relational database system to meet a given design **See Assessment activity 16.3 on page 263**
P4 import data into a non-relational database system **See Assessment activity 16.3 on page 263**	**M4** sort records in a non-relational database system **See Assessment activity 16.3 on page 263**	
P5 produce queries to extract meaningful data from a non-relational database system **See Assessment activity 16.3 on page 263**	**M5** produce meaningful reports based on database queries **See Assessment activity 16.3 on page 263**	**D2** explain the benefits of using reports **See Assessment activity 16.1 on page 219**
P6 create and use data entry forms **See Assessment activity 16.3 on page 263**		
P7 export data from a non-relational database system **See Assessment activity 16.3 on page 263**		
P8 produce user documentation for a non-relational database system **See Assessment activity 16.4 on page 264**		**D3** justify improvements that could be made to a database system **See Assessment activity 16.4 on page 264**

How you will be assessed

This unit is internally assessed. You will provide a portfolio of evidence to show that you have achieved the learning outcomes. Your portfolio of evidence can be supplied in many formats including electronically as well as paper-based. The grading grid in the specification for this unit lists what you must do to obtain pass, merit and distinction grades. The Assessment activities in this unit will guide you through tasks that will help you to be successful in this unit.

Your teacher will tell you exactly what form your assessments will take, but you could be asked to produce:

- presentations
- supporting documentation, for example printouts, structure diagrams and screen designs
- observation records
- short reports
- screen printouts.

George Clark, a BTEC National learner

Databases are all around us. I expect my details are stored on quite a lot of them, from the student database at my college to the members' database at my football club. Before I studied this unit I thought I knew exactly what information the databases held about me. Now I'm not so sure. It has made me think about what information I give to organisations.

This unit helped me to understand how databases are put together. I have also learned how to create a database of my own. It's not as straightforward as you might think, and you do have to plan ahead to make sure you remember everything. If you leave something out you may have to go right back to the beginning again.

I can now set up a database for someone else to use, so they can see what they need on-screen and print out information. I had to learn how to do queries, which are the hidden bits of magic in a database. Many databases are huge, but queries help you to extract exactly the information you want from them.

Over to you

- Have you created a database in the past?
- Do you know an organisation that could use a database?

1. Understand the principles of database systems

1.1 Database basics

Databases are organised collections of data. They are widely used in organisations to store information and to help them carry out their business. In this unit you will be learning about and creating non-relational databases (see page 216).

Many software packages include simple database features. For example, email software includes an address book where you can store details of people and organisations. The email address book is a simple database, and each entry is a **record**. Data is stored in categories, such as the person's name and their email address – these categories are called **fields**. Other fields might be telephone number, fax number and postal address.

A database management system (DBMS), such as Microsoft® Access® (the software package used throughout this unit), offers a much wider range of facilities than a simple database. In this unit you will be looking at the features that a DBMS offers.

Uses of databases

You will be able to find many examples of databases used in industry. The majority of these are complex databases, with several tables linked together. Here are some examples:

- **Personnel records** — all organisations keep information about their employees, including their name, address, qualifications, training, department and job title. This information is linked into the payroll system, which works out how much each person should be paid each week or month and sends instructions to the bank and payslips to employees.

Key terms

Database – a collection of data. The data is organised so that different kinds of information can be retrieved from it by the users.

Record – the data held in a database about a single item in the real world.

Field – a category used for data in a database. The name of the field is called the fieldname.

- **Telephone directories** — these are very large but simple databases which are available both in print (in telephone books) and online for directory enquiries. They contain the names and addresses of subscribers with their telephone numbers.

- **Stock control** — the database in a shop stores data about all the items that the shop sells. It includes stock codes and descriptions of the items, as well as up-to-date information about how many items are in stock, how many have been sold, and how many should be re-ordered from the supplier.

- **Booking systems** — these databases allow customers to book tickets for entertainment or for holidays either online, by phone or by visiting an agency. Booking systems depend on complex databases that keep a record of all the seats or vacancies and allocate new bookings. It's very important that these databases are constantly updated to avoid double-booking.

Case study: Working as a bank employee

My name is Shari Levi and I work in a bank. Like all banks, we hold accounts for our customers. Every day I help customers who want to put money into their accounts (deposits) or take money out of their accounts (withdrawals). The bank account database holds details of each customer, as well as data about each of the transactions (withdrawals and deposits). Each account in the database has a different account number.

If the customer has set up standing orders or direct debits, these will be recorded in the database as well. Customers can view some of this information at an ATM (cash machine) or when they use online banking.

1. How do you think Shari inputs the information about withdrawals and deposits into the database?

2. How is the information about a customer's account displayed on her screen?

3. What information can Shari print out?

4. How can she search the data?

5. What information about the account can the customer see on a cash machine screen?

Advantages and disadvantages of computerised databases

Computerised databases have for the most part replaced paper filing systems. Here are some advantages of using a computer database:

- the data is organised and easy to use

- the user is able to search all the data for specific information

- the database takes up very little physical space

- the database can be shared between several users at the same time

- the database can be transferred from one system to another.

The disadvantages of using a computer database include the following.

* you cannot access a database if the computer system is malfunctioning
* like all computer data, databases are at risk of unauthorised access, illegal changes and virus attacks.

Database objects

A database consists of data stored in one or more **tables**, together with some **objects** that work with the data. The main objects are forms, reports and queries.

Tables

Databases are usually displayed on-screen as tables. Each row of the table is one record, i.e. information about something in the real world. For example, in a database containing information about people working for an organisation, all the data about a particular employee will be held in one record (see Figure 16.1).

Staff ID Code	First Name	Last Name	Address	Post Code	Phone extension	Sex	Date of birth
BAT386	Christopher	Bathurst	1 Station Road	KM4 2DF	1591	M	06/05/1977
FIT752	Jenny	Fitzgerald	49 George Street	KM4 9YS	1504	F	13/02/1949
KIM980	Jin-Ho	Kim	45 Foxglove Close	KM3 9RT	2315	M	14/09/1967
PAT319	Derek	Paterson	103 Victoria Street	KM7 2GH	2373	M	21/12/1954
PAT504	Meena	Patel	14 Oaktrees Crescei	KM9 4FG	1642	F	13/04/1972
PRY123	Michelle	Pryce	37 Harrison Grove	KM3 5TH	1590	F	01/07/1983

Record: ◄ ◄ 1 of 6 ► ►I ►▣ No Filter Search

Figure 16.1: A table in which each row is a record about one employee.

Key terms

Table – a two-dimensional arrangement of data, usually written in rows and columns.

Objects – in a database the forms, reports and queries are known as objects.

Form – an on-screen user interface designed to view the data in a database.

Forms

Databases allow you to view and browse the data, and to add, delete or amend individual records. As a developer you will be able to view the data in a table. However, the user will normally view the data by means of a **form**, which is a more accessible way of viewing the information. Database forms are meant to be viewed on-screen and are not printed out.

A form can present the data one record at a time (see Figure 16.2). The user can use the form to make changes to the data, add new records or delete records. A form has helpful headings and other information for the user. Buttons can be placed on a form that link to other forms or carry out specific actions.

Figure 16.2: An on-screen form.

In general, the raw data in a table should usually be hidden from the user, and they should always access the data through a form.

Queries

Databases can be searched (or queried or interrogated) for data using a **query**. The query might search for all the records with data that matches some **criterion**. For example, the criterion could be all the employees with the surname Jones. Alternatively, the query could search for data that meets a condition, for example all the records of people born after 1970 (see Figure 16.3).

Figure 16.3: A query has selected all the people born after 1970.

Reports

You can usually print out the data in a database. Any printout from a database is known as a **report**. A report can list all the data in the database or can use a query to select certain records and to present data from only the fields that you want (see Figure 16.4).

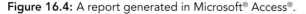

Figure 16.4: A report generated in Microsoft® Access®.

Sort

Most data is sorted before it is presented in a form or a report. There are several methods you can use to sort the data, but as a developer you will probably use a query to do it. The query is then used as the basis for a form or a report.

Key terms

Query – a method for searching and displaying a selection of data in a database.

Criterion – a rule that is used to select data. (The plural of criterion is **criteria**.)

Report – a presentation of some or all of the data in a database in a format that can be printed out.

Data types

In a database, each item of information is of a particular data type. The main data types are:

- **Text** (also known as a 'string') – the user can enter up to 255 characters in a text field. A longer text, with thousands of characters, is sometimes known as a memo.
- **Number** – you usually have a choice of number types.
- **Date or Time** – you can usually specify which format the date should appear in, such as 12/05/05 or 12 May 2005.
- **Logical** (also known as 'Yes/No') – this can simply hold one of two values – 'yes' or 'no'. As alternatives to 'yes' and 'no', the words 'true' and 'false' or 'on' and 'off' may also be used.

There is more information about the different data types used in Access® on page 223.

The data type of a field determines two things:

- the number of bytes of storage allocated to each item of data
- the kinds of functions carried out with the data. For example, you can only carry out calculations with data that has a Number data type.

Size of database

The size of a database is measured in kilobytes (KB). You can check the size of a database that you have created by looking at the filename in a directory or folder. In Windows® you can find this information by right-clicking on the filename.

The size of a database depends on a number of factors, but the most crucial is the number of records that it contains and the size of each record. A method for estimating this is given on page 231, in Section 2.4: Data storage requirements.

1.2 Database structures

As a database developer you will have to decide on the structure of the table that you create.

Table

In this unit you will be creating a **non-relational database**, which consists of a single table. More complex relational databases can also be created, in which two or more tables are linked together.

Fields

Each table consists of rows of data called records. The data in each record is divided into separate categories called fields (see Figure 16.5).

Key term

Non-relational database – a database in which all the data can be stored in a single table.

Staff

Staff ID Code	First Name	Last Name	Address	Post Code	Phone extension	Sex	Date of birth
BAT386	Christopher	Bathurst	1 Station Road	KM4 2DF	1591	M	06/05/19
FIT752	Jenny	Fitzgerald	49 George Street	KM4 9YS	1504	F	13/02/19
KIM980	Jin-Ho	Kim	45 Foxglove Close	KM3 9RT	2315	M	14/09/19
PAT319	Derek	Paterson	103 Victoria Street	KM7 2GH	2373	M	21/12/19
PAT504	Meena	Patel	14 Oaktrees Cresce	KM9 4FG	1642	F	13/04/19
PRY123	Michelle	Pryce	37 Harrison Grove	KM3 5TH	1590	F	01/07/19

Record: 1 of 6 No Filter Search

Figure 16.5: A field highlighted in a table.

The headings at the top of the columns are the fieldnames. The data in a field in a particular record is sometimes called a value. (Note that the term value is not limited to numbers.)

When designing the database, you will give each field a fieldname and a data type. In addition, each field may have some **field properties**. These might include the maximum length of the data in the field and the format required, for example a date.

Records

The records hold the data that is stored in the database. A record consists of several separate data items, each entered in a different field (see Figure 16.6).

Staff

Staff ID Code	First Name	Last Name	Address	Post Code	Phone extension	Sex	Date of birth
BAT386	Christopher	Bathurst	1 Station Road	KM4 2DF	1591	M	06/05/19
FIT752	Jenny	Fitzgerald	49 George Street	KM4 9YS	1504	F	13/02/19
KIM980	Jin-Ho	Kim	45 Foxglove Close	KM3 9RT	2315	M	14/09/19
PAT319	Derek	Paterson	103 Victoria Street	KM7 2GH	2373	M	21/12/19
PAT504	Meena	Patel	14 Oaktrees Cresce	KM9 4FG	1642	F	13/04/19
PRY123	Michelle	Pryce	37 Harrison Grove	KM3 5TH	1590	F	01/07/19

Record: 3 of 6 No Filter Search

Figure 16.6: A record highlighted in a table.

A field in a record can often be left blank if the data is not available. But you may decide that a particular field must contain data in each record. To ensure this, you can set the field properties for that field to force the user to enter data.

Data is normally entered by the user, not by the developer, but the developer will have to enter test data to check that the database works as intended.

Primary key

Often a single-table database will have a **primary key field**. The data stored in this field uniquely identifies each record. Examples of primary key fields are:

- membership number in a database of club members
- account number in a bank's customer account database
- stock code in a database of stock held in a shop.

Key terms

Field property – each field in a table has a number of properties, such as the length and format of the field.

Primary key field – the data stored in the primary key field uniquely identifies each record.

Activity: Primary key fields

In each of examples 1–4 below, determine whether there is a field which could be the primary key field. If not, suggest a new field that could be created for this purpose.

1. A list of the stock held in a warehouse for an online shop, which includes for each item the stock code, a description of the item and the quantity in stock.
2. A list of learners at a college consisting of name, address, course studied and the date a student started.
3. Entries in a telephone book.
4. Mobile phone account details, including name, address and phone number.

Did you know?

Inaccurate data on a database can cause you all sorts of problems. Imagine:

- arriving at an airport to go on holiday and finding that there is no seat on the plane for you
- finding that your new bus pass does not register when you get on a bus
- being unable to get any cash out of your bank account at a cash machine with a new cash card.

Most of these errors are the result of mistakes made by people entering data onto databases.

Key terms

Data integrity – ensuring that the data correctly matches the facts.

Verification – the process of checking whether data has been entered accurately into the computer system by a user.

Did you know?

There are several ways in which data can be validated. These include data type checks, lookup lists, default values, upper limits and lower limits (see pages 225–226).

1.3 Data integrity

It is very important that the data stored in a database is correct. Ensuring that the data correctly matches the facts is known as **data integrity**.

Data can be incorrect for four reasons:

- the original data may have been wrong
- the original data may have been correct but it may have been entered incorrectly into the database
- the facts in the real world may have changed since the data was first entered, but the data may not have been updated accordingly
- the data may have been changed by mistake since it was first entered.

Data accuracy

The original information for a database could have come from a number of sources, such as paper-based lists or old databases – and any of these could have been incorrect. It is important that the user checks the accuracy of the information.

The information for a database is often collected on a paper form and then keyed into a database. The user should always read back the data on-screen to check they have entered it accurately. This kind of accuracy check is referred to as **verification**.

Sometimes a company will collect details over the phone, for example when selling tickets for an event. In this case, the user who is entering the data straight into the database should read the details back to the customer to verify that they have been entered correctly.

Consistency of data

Some data will have to be changed from time to time. For example, when a person moves house, their new address should be entered on any databases that contain their personal details. Other data such as exchange rates, interest rates and tax rates fluctuate, so should be amended whenever necessary.

Keeping data consistent with the real world is an ongoing problem.

Validation

When data is entered into a field, **validation** checks can be carried out by the database software to make sure that the data is as expected for that field. The rules for each field are either set up automatically by the database or are created by the developer. If the user enters data that does not match the rules, then an error message will be displayed.

Validation will not guarantee that the data is accurate, but it will at least exclude some obviously wrong data.

Key term

Validation – a process carried out automatically by a database. It checks that data entered into a field matches rules laid down for that field.

PLTS

By researching the answers to Jones & Smith Ltd's questions, you will show that you are an **independent enquirer**.

Functional skills

By writing your answers to Jones & Smith Ltd's questions, you could provide evidence for your functional **English** skills in writing.

BTEC ## Assessment activity 16.1

The four assessment activities in this unit are based on the following case study:

Jones & Smith Ltd is a new estate agency in your local town. They have hired you to investigate and create a computerised database to hold details of all the properties they will have on their books.

Jones & Smith expect to have about 50 properties (houses and flats) for sale at any one time. But they also want to keep records of old properties that they have sold (together with the asking price and selling price) or which have been withdrawn from sale. They expect to sell or remove about 10 properties a month and to list the same number of new ones.

You can store old and current properties in a single table, but Jones & Smith need some way of generating a report that lists just the properties currently for sale. They also need to generate a report to compare the asking prices and sale prices of all the properties that they have sold in the last three months.

They want to create sheets of information about each property which will include photos. The sheets are then copied to give to customers, and also displayed in the agency window.

You have been asked to design and build a new database system for Jones & Smith Ltd. They would also like you to tell them about the benefits that a database will provide and some of the things to watch out for.

Jones & Smith Ltd have asked you three questions.

1. What will be the advantages and disadvantages for us of using a computer-based database instead of storing all our data on paper? Please explain to us clearly the basic principles of database systems. **P1**

2. We have heard that data integrity is important in a database. Can you please explain why? Try to give us some examples from existing databases. **M1**

3. We would like to have some reports which we can view on-screen or print out. Is that a good idea? If so, please explain the benefits of using reports. **D2**

Grading tips

- For question 1, find out how a business like this might have managed its data before using a computer database system. You need to explain at least two advantages and two disadvantages of using a database system.

- For question 2, make sure you explain why data integrity will be important to Jones & Smith Ltd. Examples from other databases should demonstrate what could go wrong if data integrity is not maintained.

- For question 3, think of all the different kinds of report that would be useful to the business. Some reports will be for the company's use and others will be for customers to use.

1.4 Database design

Whenever you carry out a database software project, there are several steps that you must take:

- identify the problem
- design the database
- build (implement) the database
- provide documentation
- evaluate the database.

The design stage is very important. When you write a document in a word-processing package you can easily edit it by adding and deleting text and by moving paragraphs around. Database management software is different – once you have set up the basic tables, forms, queries and reports, it can be difficult to change them. You should always design a database carefully on paper before creating it in the software.

Right at the beginning you need to design:

- a table
- some queries
- one or more reports, depending on what is required
- at least one form.

Tables 16.1 to 16.4 show the kinds of designs that you should create for a database. We will develop examples of these as you work through the unit.

Table structure

Table 16.1: A table design.

Name of table					
Field	Data type	Description	Field properties	Validation rule	Validation text

Query structure

Table 16.2: A query design.

Name of query	
Table or query	
Selected fields	
Sort field	
Criteria	

Form structure

Table 16.3: A form design.

Name of form			
Table or query			
Screen design	*See sketch*		
Events	Object	Event	Action

Every form design should be accompanied by a sketch of the form, showing the screen design.

Report structure

Table 16.4: A report design.

Name of report	
Table or query	
Layout	

Just checking

1. What data will be kept on a ticket booking system for a football club?
2. In the context of a database system, what is a form and why are forms used?
3. Why is it necessary to define the data type for a field?
4. What is a primary key field?
5. Give three examples to illustrate how data in a database could be incorrect.
6. Why is it important to design a database before you start developing it?

2. Be able to create non-relational database systems

A database management system (DBMS) holds all the data as well as all the forms, queries and reports in a database. It organises the data on the hard disk and controls access to the data by users.

Database users are not really aware of the complexity of the database – the DBMS hides much of it away from them. Users are only aware of the data that they require, which will often appear to them to be a simple single-table database. Different users in the company will want to use different mixes of data within the database, and a DBMS handles all these needs.

Microsoft® Access® is a well known DBMS which is used by professionals to create complex databases. This section and the next contain case studies in the use of Access® 2007 to build databases. You may find some variations if you are using a different version.

Using a wizard

You may use any of the wizards provided by Access®. These include:

- **Form, query and report wizards** — always create a form, query or report using the wizard to begin with. You can then customise them if necessary in Design view.
- **Table wizard** — this is not particularly useful, and it's usually better to create your tables from scratch in Design view.

Constructing a single table database

For Learning Outcomes 2 and 3, you will study how to build databases and provide a user with documentation.

The first database you will create will be called *Resources* and it will have one table in it, called *Books*. This table will contain information about books that you have found useful for your studies. You will be able to view the details of the books on-screen, add notes about them and print out lists for your portfolios.

2.1 Table structure design

To design a table you should:

- list all the fields you will need
- decide on the data types for each field
- identify the primary key field.

Fields

You should start by listing all the fields in the table. You will be creating a database that contains information about books you have found useful in your studies. The list of fields is given in Table 16.5.

Table 16.5: The list of fields in the Books table structure.

Books table
Field
ISBN
Title
Author
Publisher
Year published
Notes
Star rating

Data types in Access®

The data types that can be used in Access® are as follows:

- **Text** — this data type allows the user to enter up to 255 characters in a field. Text can include numerical digits, but the database will not be able to calculate with them as it will treat them just like letters. Each character takes up one byte of memory.

- **Memo** — this is a longer text field that can hold up to 65,536 characters.

- **Number** — you have a choice of number types, including:
  - *Byte* holds an integer (whole number) in the range 0 to 255.
  - *Integer* holds an integer between –32,768 and 32,767. Use this for most integer fields unless the number is likely to be very large.
  - *Long integer* holds an integer in the range –2,147,483,648 to 2,147,483,647.
  - *Single* (also known as 'single precision real' or 'floating-point') holds a number with a decimal point. Use this for most decimal number fields.
  - *Double* (also known as 'double precision real') holds large decimal numbers.
  - *Decimal* holds a positive or negative number with a decimal point. Don't use this unless a high degree of accuracy or extremely large numbers are needed.

- **Date/Time** — you can usually specify the format you want for the date. For example, the date 29th July 2010 can be written 29/07/2010, 29 July 2010 or 29-Jul-10.

- **Yes/No** — this can hold one of just two values – 'yes' or 'no'. The words 'true' and 'false' or 'on' and 'off' can also be entered.

> **(i) Did you know?**
>
> American dates are written in a different order from UK dates, so that 5/10/11 is 10th May 2011 in the USA (i.e. May 10th), but 5th October 2011 in the UK.

In the database table shown in Figure 16.1 on page 220, the first five fields all use the text data type but the 'Phone extension' is a number. When the data is keyed in, the database will not allow the user to enter data that is of the incorrect data type. So if words are entered in the 'Phone extension' field by mistake, the software will display an error message.

The table structure for the *Books* table is repeated in Table 16.6, with the data types defined for each field. A description has also been added to tell the user (you) what each field is for. When a field is selected the description appears in the Status bar at the bottom of the window.

Table 16.6: The Books table structure with data types.

Books table		
Field	**Data type**	**Description**
ISBN	Text	International Standard Book Number
Title	Text	The title of the book
Author	Text	Author, surname first
Publisher	Text	The name of the publishing company
Year published	Number	The year the book was published
Notes	Memo	My notes on the book
Star rating	Number	From 1 (poor) to 5 (very useful)

- You use a Text data type for the ISBN field because the character X is sometimes used in the last position, e.g. 043547152X.
- The Memo data type for the Notes field will allow the user to enter lengthy comments on each book.

Field properties

Once you have defined the data type for each field, you can decide whether to use some additional field properties (see Table 16.7).

Table 16.7: Adding field properties.

Books table			
Field	**Data type**	**Description**	**Field properties**
ISBN	Text	International Standard Book Number	Field size: 13
Title	Text	The title of the book	Field size: 50
Author	Text	Author, surname first	Field size: 50
Publisher	Text	The name of the publishing company	Field size: 50
Year published	Number	The year the book was published	Field size: integer
Notes	Memo	My notes on the book	
Star rating	Number	From 1 (poor) to 5 (very useful)	Field size: byte

Field size (or length)

The field size is the maximum amount of space that is allowed for the field. In Access®, text fields are initially set with a maximum of 50 characters. This can be changed for any particular field to anything from 1 to 255 characters.

You will probably want to leave the field size at 50 for the Title, Author and Publisher fields. But an ISBN consists of either 10 or 13 characters (leaving out any spaces or dashes), so you should set the field size to 13. This will prevent anyone from entering more than 13 characters and will also make the database more efficient.

You cannot change the field size for a memo field, but its maximum size is 65,536 characters, which should be sufficient for all users.

Whatever the field size, a text or memo field only uses one byte of memory for each character that is entered.

The field size of a number field is expressed as a byte, integer, etc., as shown in the list of data types on page 223. The 'Year published' field is best set up as an integer instead of a long integer, as this will save some storage space. The 'Star rating' can be set up as a single byte as the numbers entered will be small.

Format

You can format a number field with a fixed number of decimal points, or as currency, as a percentage or in scientific notation.

There are several options for the formats for date and time fields (see page 216).

Default value

A default value is a value that is automatically used in a field unless you change it. For example, if you run a mailing list for an organisation in the UK, you could set 'United Kingdom' as the default value for the Country in an address. The user can still change the country for an overseas address, but the default value will save them having to key in United Kingdom for most addresses.

Primary key

Every table should have a primary key field (see page 217). The data in a primary key field in one record is known as the primary key (or record key) for that record.

In nearly all organisations, each staff member is given a number which is unique to them and is used for things such as paying their salary. As you can see in Table 16.1 on page 220, the Staff ID Code is the primary key field for the table, and BAT386 is the primary key for Christopher Bathurst.

The ISBN given to each book is unique (see page 222), so it can be used as the primary key field in a database of books.

The primary key field is always underlined in the table structure, as shown in Table 16.5.

Sometimes it is difficult to decide which field should be the primary key field. Often, a new field can be created to do the job. For example, a table may hold a list of people's names and addresses. Some people may have the same name, so the name cannot be used as the primary key field as the data would not be unique for each record. In addition, more than one person could live at the same address, so the address could not be used as the primary key field. A new field will have to be created as the primary key field. This could simply number the records starting from 1.

Validation

There are several ways in which data can be validated, including:

- **Data type checks** — the data is checked to see whether it matches the data type for a field. For example, if you try to enter text in a date field it will report an error.

- **Lookup lists** — the data is checked against a list of acceptable values in a reference table. For example, if you are asked to enter your title (Mr, Mrs, Ms, etc.), you could be given a drop-down list to choose from. This will prevent you from entering an invalid title like *George*.

- **Default values** — some fields may have data already in them. The default value is the data that is used in this field unless the user changes it. For example, if you are asked whether you have any criminal convictions, the default value may be 'no', since most people do not.
- **Upper or lower limits** — the data is checked to make sure that it is less than a value (the upper limit), greater than a value (the lower limit), or between two values. This can be used for numerical fields and also for dates and times. For example, if you are asked to enter your date of birth it could check that the year is after, say, 1900, and warn you if you try to enter an invalid year.

Access® always carries out data type checks automatically. For other validation checks, you must set up validation rules.

In the *Books* table, the number entered for the *Star rating* must be between 1 and 5, so the upper limit is 6. The validation rule is shown as < 6 (see Table 16.8). If a user enters invalid data into this field, we need to give them a helpful error message, which is referred to in Access® as the validation text. In this case the message is 'Error: Please enter a star rating from 1 to 5'.

Table 16.8: The complete design for the Books table.

Books table					
Field	**Data type**	**Description**	**Field properties**	**Validation rule**	**Validation text**
ISBN	Text	International Standard Book Number	Field size: 13		
Title	Text	The title of the book	Field size: 50		
Author	Text	Author, surname first	Field size: 50		
Publisher	Text	The name of the publishing company	Field size: 50		
Year published	Number	The year the book was published	Field size: integer		
Notes	Memo	My notes on the book			
Star rating	Number	From 1 (poor) to 5 (very useful)	Field size: byte	< 6	Error: Please enter a star rating from 1 to 5.

How to... Set up a single-table database

- Launch Microsoft® Access®. Select **Blank Database** (see Figure 16.7).

- On the right of the screen you will be prompted to save your database straightaway (see Figure 16.8).

- All databases created in Access® 2007 are given the file extension **.accdb**. Call the database *Resources*. Click **Create**.

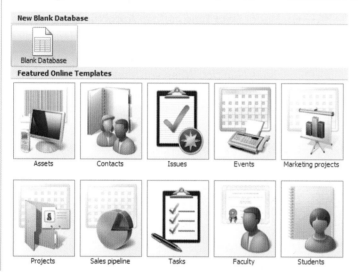

Figure 16.7: Getting started with Access®.

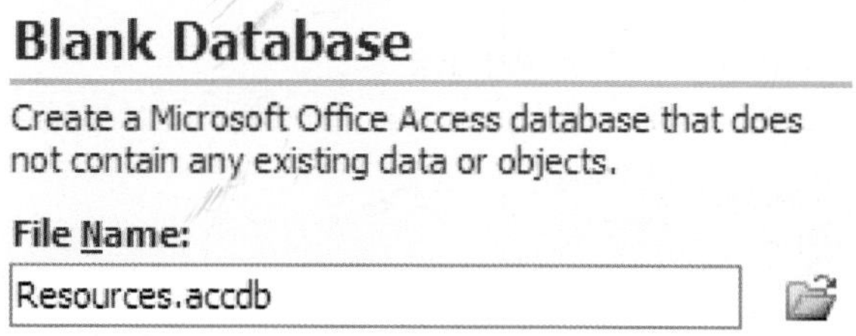

Blank Database

Create a Microsoft Office Access database that does not contain any existing data or objects.

File Name:

Resources.accdb

Figure 16.8: Creating a database.

2.2 Creating tables

We have already developed the table structure for the *Books* table in Table 16.8.

How to... Create a table

When you create a new database, Access® automatically sets up a new table for you, called **Table1**. You are going to create a table to match the design in Table 16.8.

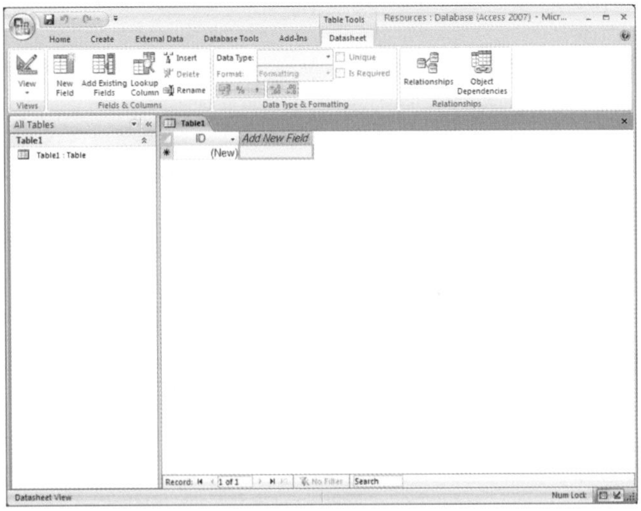

Figure 16.9: The database creates Table1.

Note that you are in the Datasheet tab. Each table can be viewed in two ways: Datasheet View and Design View. You are going to switch to Design View to define your *Books* table.

- Click on the **Design** icon  in the **Views** group at the left end of the ribbon. You will be prompted to save the table. Enter *Books* as the **Table Name**.

- You will now see the Design View of the *Books* table. Note that you are now in the Design tab.

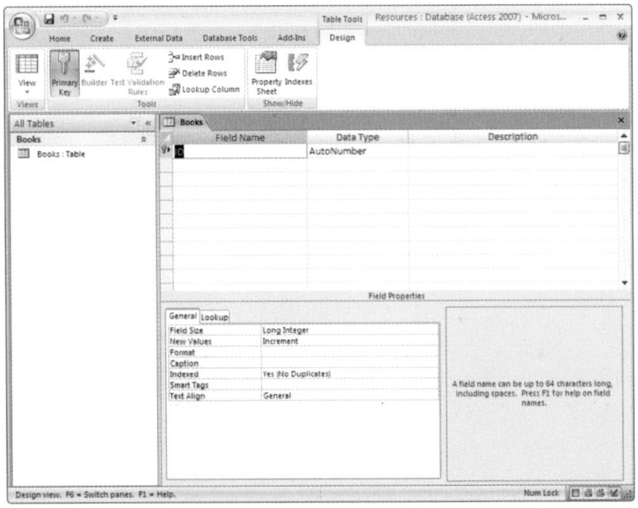

Figure 16.10: The table in Design View.

Access® has already created a field for you called ID. To the left of ID you can see a small key. That is the symbol for the primary key field. Many tables have a primary key field called ID. In our case the primary field is called ISBN, so we will change it.

- Under **Field Name** enter *ISBN* instead of *ID*.

- Under **Data Type** click on **AutoNumber** and select **Text** from the drop-down list.

- Under **Description** enter *International Standard Book Number*. When you later come to enter some data, the description will appear at the bottom of the window to remind you what the field contains.

- At the bottom of the screen you can see the **Field Properties** for the field. The **Field Size** will show the default value of 255. Change the Field Size to *13* (see Figure 16.11).

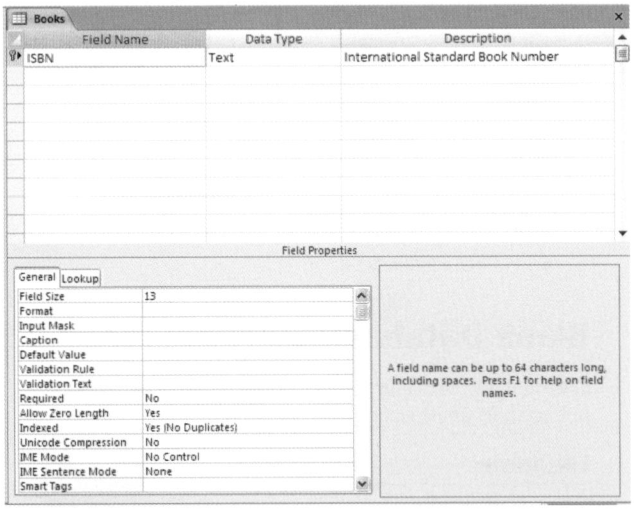

Figure 16.11: The record key field has been defined.

- To define the next field, click on the second row under **Field Name** and enter *Title*. Select **Text** as the **Data Type**. Enter *The title of the book* under **Description**. Change the **Field Size** to *50*.

- Define the Author and Publisher fields as shown in Table 16.8.

- The next field, *Year Published*, has the Number data type, so choose **Number** from the drop-down list. Under the **Field Properties** for this field, click on the **Field Size** and select **Integer** from the drop-down list.

- You can now define the *Notes* field, as in Table 16.8. Set the data type for **Notes** to **Memo**.
- Finally, define the *Star rating* field. Set the **Field Size** for *Star rating* to **Byte**.
- *Star rating* is the only field with a validation rule. Under the **Field Properties** for this field, click on **Validation Rule** and key in *<6*.
- If the user tries to enter a Star rating that does not match this validation rule, Access® will display an error message. You can decide what the error message says. Click on **Validation Text** and enter *Error: Please enter a star rating from 1 to 5.*

Save your changes by clicking on the **Save** icon. If you forget to do this you will be prompted to save the table when you change views or exit the database.

Books

Field Name	Data Type	Description
ISBN	Text	International Standard Book Number
Title	Text	The title of the book
Author	Text	Author, surname first
Publisher	Text	The name of the publishing company
Year Published	Number	The year the book was published
Notes	Memo	My notes on the book
Star rating	Number	From 1 (poor) to 5 (very useful)

Field Properties

General | Lookup

Field Size	Byte
Format	
Decimal Places	Auto
Input Mask	
Caption	
Default Value	
Validation Rule	<6
Validation Text	Error: Please enter a star rating from 1 to 5
Required	No
Indexed	No
Smart Tags	
Text Align	General

A field name can be up to 64 characters long, including spaces. Press F1 for help on field names.

Figure 16.12: All fields have been defined – field properties displayed for the Star rating field.

Entering data

The next task is to enter data for several books that you use.

How to... Enter data into a table

You will enter the data about some books in Datasheet View.

- Click on the **Datasheet** icon in the Views group at the left end of the ribbon.
- Enter your own choice of data for a few books – see Figure 16.13 for an example.
- You can make the window wider if you like. You can also drag the edges of the fields to create more room.

The data is automatically saved as you go along.

Books

ISBN	Title	Author	Publisher	Year	Notes	Star
0198610224	Finding your way through networking	Hill V & Dale T	Lost Books	2005	Very difficult	1
0435454697	Imaginative PC assembly	Lewis A et al	Greatham	2003	Very good espec	4
0707804031	How to be a geek	Entwhistle Y	Almond Harrison	2004	Funny, and I like	3
0735615190	Finding your way through project managem	Rice S & Jam K	Lost Books	2004	Very good but a l	5
076454074X	Finding your way through web design	Selby T & York F	Lost Books	2003	Not very helpful	2
0764541738	Cabling, connections and ports	Stamp H P	Almond Harrison	2003	Didn't understan	2
1904467786	When all else fails: troubleshooting for begi	Bracket K	Jones & Jones	2004	Great book	4
*						

Figure 16.13: The data entered in Datasheet view.

Validation

It's easy for the end user to make a mistake when entering data. Validation checks help to make the database user friendly, as well as increasing the accuracy of the data.

Access® automatically checks that the data you enter is of the correct data type. We've also added a further validation rule and the error message that goes with it. We'll now check that they work properly.

How to... Check the validation

- Enter a new record, but enter a letter instead of a number in the Year field, then press the **Enter** key. You will get an Access® warning (see Figure 16.14).

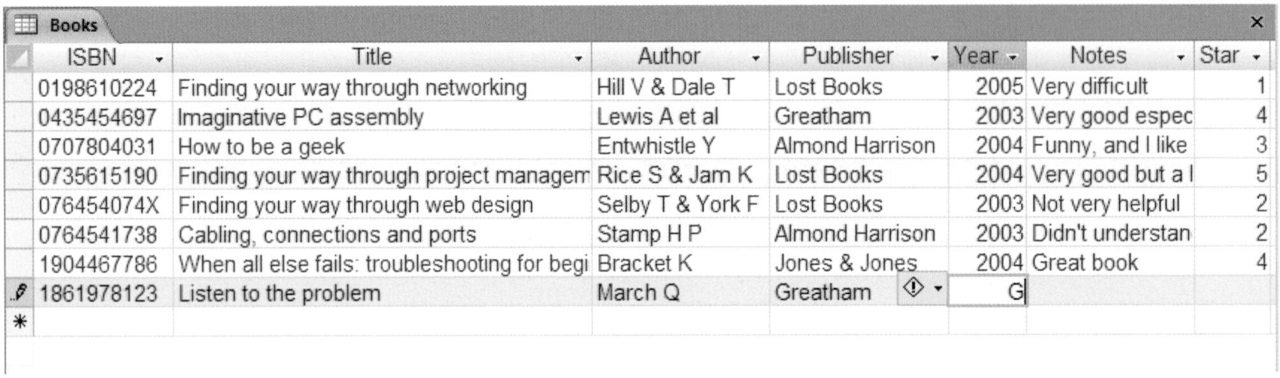

ISBN	Title	Author	Publisher	Year	Notes	Star
0198610224	Finding your way through networking	Hill V & Dale T	Lost Books	2005	Very difficult	1
0435454697	Imaginative PC assembly	Lewis A et al	Greatham	2003	Very good espec	4
0707804031	How to be a geek	Entwhistle Y	Almond Harrison	2004	Funny, and I like	3
0735615190	Finding your way through project managem	Rice S & Jam K	Lost Books	2004	Very good but a l	5
076454074X	Finding your way through web design	Selby T & York F	Lost Books	2003	Not very helpful	2
0764541738	Cabling, connections and ports	Stamp H P	Almond Harrison	2003	Didn't understan	2
1904467786	When all else fails: troubleshooting for begi	Bracket K	Jones & Jones	2004	Great book	4
1861978123	Listen to the problem	March Q	Greatham		G	

Figure 16.14: Warning of data type error.

- Correct the data.
- Now enter an incorrect number in the Star rating field. An error message will pop up, displaying the validation text that you entered for this field (see Figure 16.15).

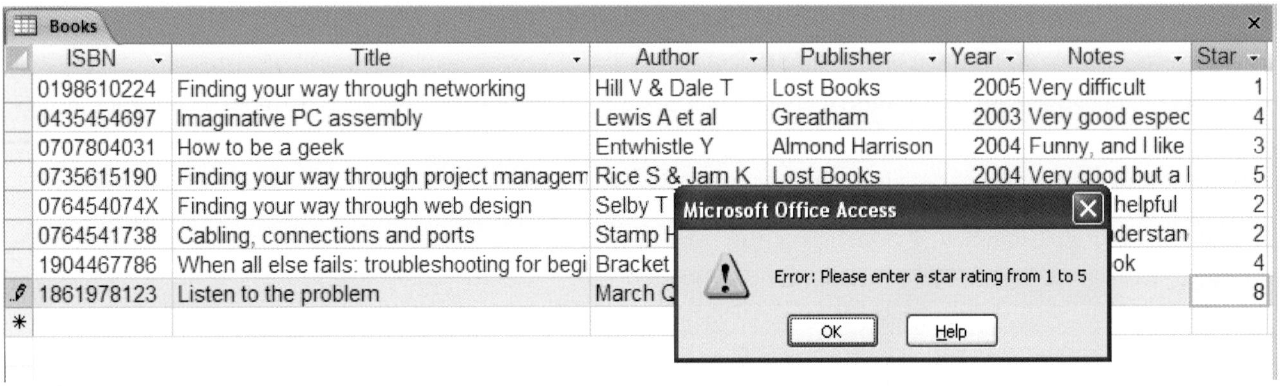

ISBN	Title	Author	Publisher	Year	Notes	Star
0198610224	Finding your way through networking	Hill V & Dale T	Lost Books	2005	Very difficult	1
0435454697	Imaginative PC assembly	Lewis A et al	Greatham	2003	Very good espec	4
0707804031	How to be a geek	Entwhistle Y	Almond Harrison	2004	Funny, and I like	3
0735615190	Finding your way through project managem	Rice S & Jam K	Lost Books	2004	Very good but a l	5
076454074X	Finding your way through web design	Selby T			helpful	2
0764541738	Cabling, connections and ports	Stamp H			derstan	2
1904467786	When all else fails: troubleshooting for begi	Bracket			ok	4
1861978123	Listen to the problem	March Q				8

Microsoft Office Access

Error: Please enter a star rating from 1 to 5

OK   Help

Figure 16.15: Error message for validation rule.

- Correct the error, then click on **Save**.
- You can now close the database by clicking on the **Office** button and selecting **Close Database**.

2.3 Naming objects

The objects that you create in a database should have meaningful names. Tables called *Mytable* or *Project* are not very clear, whereas *Items in stock* or *Contacts* tell you exactly what is in the table.

Objects are often given names without spaces or punctuation. You can use uppercase at the beginning of each word to make the names easier to read, for example *DateOfBirth*. Also, in some conventions, each fieldname may be given a prefix that identifies the data type. For example, the fieldname *txtSurname* might be used. The letters *txt* tell you that it is a text field.

Find out what the naming convention is at your centre of learning and use that. In this unit we've adopted a simple naming convention using one or more words to name each table, form, query, report or field.

2.4 Data storage requirements

Legal requirements

The Data Protection Act (1998) applies whenever information about living persons is stored, but only if it is possible to identify the individual from the data. So if a survey is done but the names of the people who respond are not collected, then this usually does not count as personal data.

The key points for someone who is developing a database containing personal data are:

- data must be relevant – just what is needed and nothing more
- data must be accurate
- data must not be kept longer than necessary
- data must be secure.

Estimating space needed

You can work out how much memory space the data in a database is going to need by a simple calculation.

Look at the field properties for each field in a table. If the field is a number field you can work out how many bytes it needs from the list in Table 16.9.

Table 16.9: Bytes used by each number type.

Number type	Bytes used
Byte	1
Integer	2
Long integer	4
Single	4
Double	8
Decimal	12

Text and memo fields only use as many bytes as the number of characters they hold. So you will have to estimate the average number of characters that will be entered in the field across all the records. You need to add in at least one further byte per field as an 'overhead' – that is, for the system to store information about the field.

- Add up the bytes to find the total for each record. An example is shown in Table 16.10.

Table 16.10: Example calculation for number of bytes per record.

Field	Data type	Field size	Average number of characters	Number of bytes
ISBN	Text	13	12	12
Title	Text	50	25	25
Author	Text	50	15	15
Publisher	Text	50	20	20
Year published	Number	Integer		2
Notes	Memo		100	100
Star rating	Number	Byte		1
Overheads				7
Total number of bytes per record				**182**

- Next, estimate how many records will be entered into the database and multiply that number by the number of bytes per record.
- Number of records (estimate) = 30
- Number of bytes required = 30 x 182 = 5460 bytes
- So the memory storage required for the data is about 5 KB.

In practice, the memory taken by this database, developed in Access®, will be very much larger. The forms, reports and queries will all be added to the data, making a total of several hundred KB.

However, this calculation is particularly important if the database is very large. Imagine a database of books for a library with 100,000 volumes – the amount of memory for the data alone would be:

100,000 x 182 = 18,200,000 bytes, which is around 18 MB.

Testing

You should always check your database as you go along. When you have completed it, you should then set up a test plan and systematically test all aspects of the database. The purpose of testing is to:

- show that the database works as expected
- find any remaining errors.

You will look at test procedures in more detail later in this unit (pages 261–262).

(i) Did you know?

You can import data into a database from a spreadsheet, a text file or from another database. You will find out about importing data later in this unit; see pages 258–260.

Just checking

1. What is a DBMS?
2. Explain the differences between these numerical data types: integer, long integer, decimal.
3. Why is it good practice to define the size of a field?
4. How could the Data Protection Act (1998) apply to a database that you create?
5. Calculate the number of bytes per record that are needed for a database that you have created.

3. Be able to use database software tools

3.1 Sort

For data to be useful, it often needs to be sorted in some way.

Sort order

- Number data can be sorted into numerical order. This could be ascending order (starting with the lowest number) or descending order (starting with the highest number).

- Dates are a special type of number and can be sorted in ascending order (starting with the earliest date) or in descending order (starting with the latest date).

- Text data can be sorted into alphabetical order: ascending order (from A to Z) or descending order (from Z to A).

Sort fields

Access® automatically sorts records into order using the primary key. So in our example, all the books in the *Books* table will be sorted into ISBN order. The ISBN is being used as the **sort field**.

In a table, you can make any field act as the sort field.

Key term

Sort field – the field that is used to sort the data into alphabetical or numerical order (including date order).

💻 How to... Sort records in a table

- If your *Resources* database is closed, open it by clicking on the **Office** button in Access®. You will see a list of recent documents. Click on your database if it is listed. If it is not listed, click on **Open** and browse to find it.

- The area of the screen headed **All Tables** is the Navigation Pane. It shows all the database objects as you create them. So far you have created only one object, the *Books* table.

- Double click on the small **Datasheet** icon beside **Books:Table**. Alternatively, you can right click on

- **Books:Table** and select **Open**. The table opens in Datasheet View.

- You will see small arrows to the right of each fieldname indicating drop-down lists. Click on the drop-down list for *Title*. Select **Sort A to Z** (see Figure 16.17).

- The records will now be sorted in alphabetical order of titles. *Title* is the sort field.

- Try using other fields as sort fields.

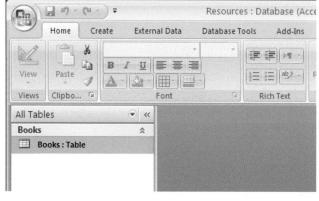

Figure 16.16: Opening the database.

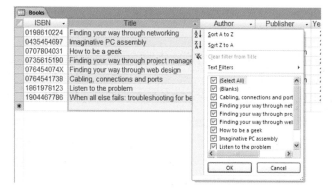

Figure 16.17: Using a field to sort the records.

3.2 Form structure design

When you construct a database, you can view both the Design and Datasheet views of a table. But you are acting as the database developer, and the user does not need to see anything you have worked on so far. Instead, as developer, you should design screen forms that will give the user a simple, non-technical view of the database.

You should always design a form before you try to create it in your database. The form structure design should include a sketch of how you intend the form to look as well as a number of technical details (see Table 16.11).

Table 16.11: Form structure design.

Books **form**			
Table or query	Books table		
Screen design	See sketch		
Events	**Object**	**Event**	**Action**
	Delete record button	On click	Displayed record is deleted
	Report button	On click	Report is displayed

Every form is based on a table or query and this should be listed in the form design. (You will meet queries later on page 244.) One or more **events** are usually associated with a form. An event is an action, such as clicking on a button or entering text in a text box.

A very small program, called a macro, is linked to an event. The macro makes something new happen, such as opening a new window or deleting a record. Access® can automatically write simple macros for you, so you don't need to have any programming skills to create an event.

Our forms will have a number of buttons on them, and these will have events associated with them in the form design. Access® automatically places navigation buttons on forms, so you don't need to list navigation buttons in the form design.

The form design must also include a sketch of how the finished form should look. This should show all the fields, labels and buttons in their correct positions, and indicate the colours and fonts to be used (see Figure 16.18). In our case we have included two button objects. One is labelled "Delete this record". The other is labelled "Print out the full list of books"; when clicked it will display a report which can then be printed.

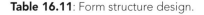

Figure 16.18: Sketched screen design of the form.

Automatic form creation

There are many ways of creating a form in Access®. One of the most useful methods is to use the Form Wizard. This creates a straightforward form on-screen which you can then customise.

How to... Use the Form Wizard

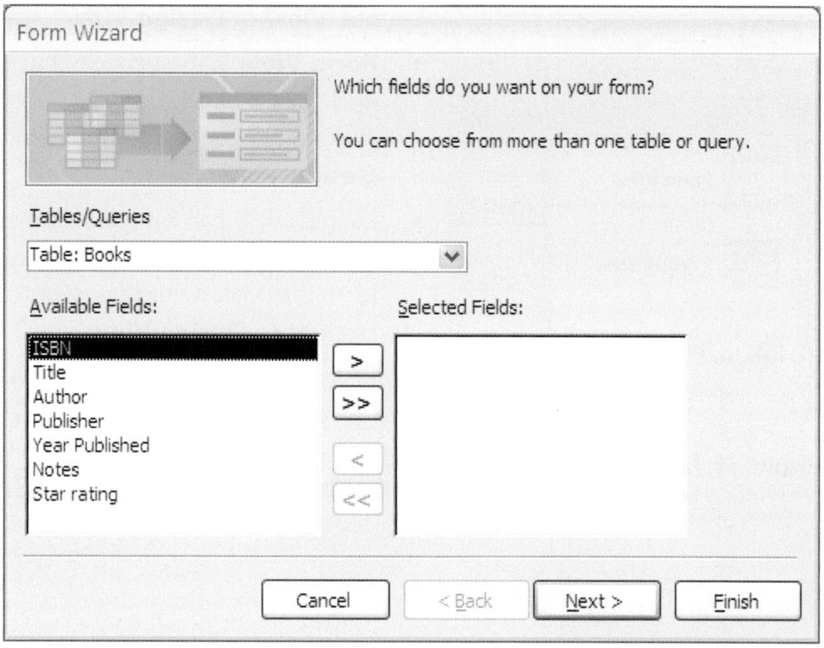

Form Wizard

Which fields do you want on your form?

You can choose from more than one table or query.

Tables/Queries

Table: Books

Available Fields:

ISBN
Title
Author
Publisher
Year Published
Notes
Star rating

> >> < <<

Selected Fields:

Cancel   < Back   Next >   Finish

- Open the *Resources* database if you had closed it.

- Click on the **Create** tab. In the **Forms** group click on **More Forms** and select **Form wizard**.

- On the first page of the wizard, **Table:Books** appears in the top box . The fields in the *Books* table are listed in the *Available Fields* box. Click on the **>>** button to select all the fields. (You could select individual fields by clicking on the **>** button). Click on **Next**. (See Figure 16.19.)

Figure 16.19: The Form Wizard.

- Select **Justifed** layout and click on **Next**. (You can try out other layouts later.)

- Select a style that you like. Click on **Next**.

- Give the form the title *Books Form* then click on **Finish**.

- A form appears with all the fields in it (see Figure 16.20). At the bottom of the screen you can see the navigation buttons which allow the user to click through the records one by one. Find out what each navigation button does.

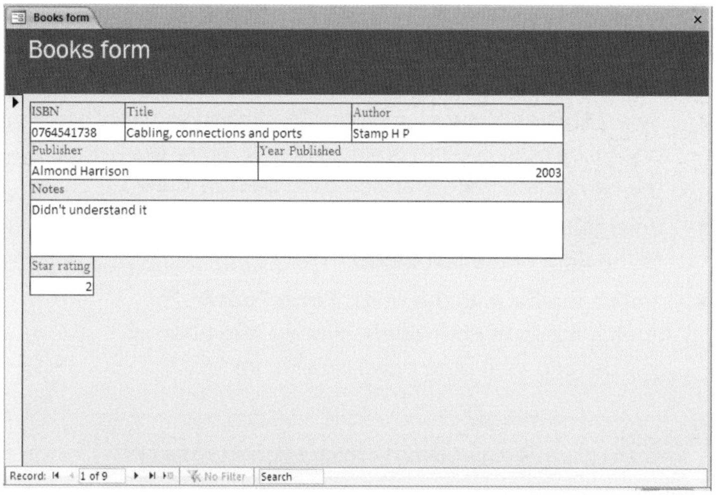

Books form

ISBN	Title	Author
0764541738	Cabling, connections and ports	Stamp H P
Publisher	Year Published	
Almond Harrison		2003
Notes		
Didn't understand it		

Star rating
2

Record: 1 of 9   No Filter   Search

Figure 16.20: A form created by the wizard.

- Change the data in one or two fields of existing records.

- Your user will add new records by using the form instead of the table. The **New Record navigation button** (found on the far right) opens a blank form for a new record.

- Add data in the first field. To move from one field to the next press **Enter** or the **Tab** key on your keyboard.

- Use the form to add some more records. This is how the end user will enter data.

- Close the form.

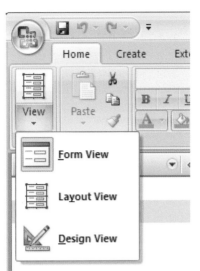

In Access® a table can be displayed in **Datasheet View** or **Design View**. A form can be displayed in **Form View**, **Layout View** or **Design View**.

- **Form View** is the version that the end user will see, but you need to make any changes to the form in **Design View**.

- Layout View can be used to make minor changes to the design of the form, but you would be wise to go straight to **Design View**.

When you have opened a form in either **Design View** or **Form View**, you can switch between them by clicking on **View** in the **Views group** (see Figure 16.21).

Key terms

Label – text on a form that describes the data displayed in a control.

Control – An item on a database form that is used to enter or display data, such as a textbox.

Figure 16.21: Switching between views for a form.

Formatting forms

 How to... Format a form

- Open the *Books* form.
- Select **Design View** as in Figure 16.21. (You can also do this by right clicking on the name of the form in the Navigation Pane then selecting **Design View**.)
- Enlarge the form by dragging the right-hand edge to the right of the text boxes.
- Notice the bar with the words **Form Footer**. To stretch the form downwards, click the top edge of this bar and then drag down (see Figure 16.22).

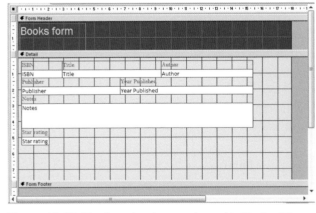

Figure 16.22: The form has been enlarged in Design View.

- Each field on the form has two objects – the **label** and the text box. In this layout the labels are above the text boxes. The text box is known as a **control** because it controls the way the user can access the data. The text box displays the actual data in **Form View**.

- Click on the *Star rating* label, which is linked to the *Star rating* text box. Drag it to a new position on the form. The *Star rating* text box will move with its label.

- Click again on the *Star rating* label and note the small square, called a handle, to the top left of the label. There is another handle to the top left of the text box (see Figure 16.23). If you click on either of these handles you can move the label or the text box independently.

Figure 16.23: Handles on a textbox control and its label.

- You can change the size of any of the labels and text boxes by dragging their edges.

- After you have rearranged the form, save it and close it.

Labels

In Figure 16.22 you can see text boxes, each of which has a label. In **Form View** (which the user will see) the textboxes will be filled with data, but the labels will be displayed exactly as shown in **Design View.**

At first each label contains the fieldname that you used when you designed the table. The header of the form also has a label, which has the name you have given to the form.

- You can alter the words of any of these labels to make them more meaningful for the user.

- You can place any other information you like on the form by adding extra labels. This can help the user decide what to do.

How to... Change the wording on a label

- Open the *Books* form in **Design View**.

- Click inside the label for the *Title* field. The cursor changes to an I-bar. Click again and you can edit the words. Change the label to read *Title of book.*

- Click inside the label in the **Form Header**. You can again change the words to something like *Useful books I have read.*

- You can also change the font and font styles of any label or text box. Highlight the text in the label or text box then use the options in the **Font** group.

- Close the form and open it in **Form View** to see your changes (see Figure 16.24).

| Books | Books form | × |

Useful books I have read

Title of book		Author	
Cabling, connections and ports		Stamp H P	

Publisher	Year Published	ISBN
Almond Harrison	2003	0764541738

Notes	Star rating
Didn't understand it	**2**

Record: ◄ ◄ 1 of 9 ► ►► ►□ No Filter

Figure 16.24: Some improvements to the form.

Data entry order

The data entry order (or tab order) is the order in which the user is guided to enter data on a form. The user presses either the **Enter** key or the **Tab** key to move to the next field. The fields will be visited in the same order as they appear in the original table – in our case ISBN, Title, Author, Publisher, etc.

If you have rearranged the fields in the form, as in the example above, you should change the tab order so that the user is taken from one field to another in a sensible sequence.

How to... Change the data entry order (tab order)

- Open the *Books* form in **Design View**.
- Click on the **Arrange** tab. Select **Tab Order** in the **Control Layout** group. You will see the fieldnames listed in their original order. Drag and drop fieldnames into the new data entry order (see Figure 16.25).

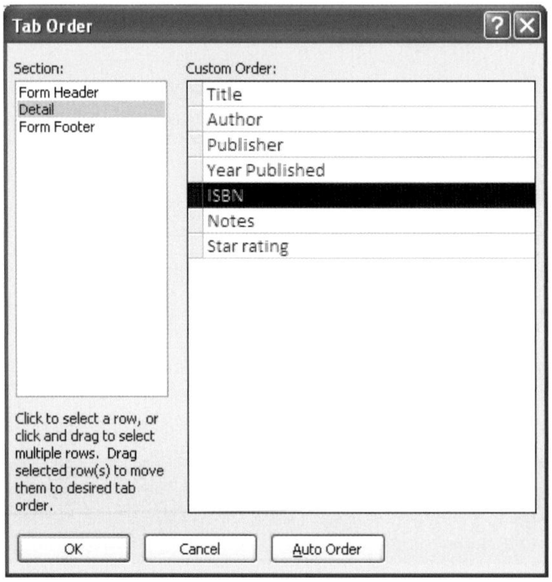

Tab Order ? ✕

Section:

Form Header
Detail
Form Footer

Custom Order:

Title
Author
Publisher
Year Published
ISBN
Notes
Star rating

Click to select a row, or click and drag to select multiple rows. Drag selected row(s) to move them to desired tab order.

OK   Cancel   Auto Order

Figure 16.25: Changing the data entry (tab) order.

Buttons

The user should be able to carry out all their tasks from the form. They can already add a new record and change data in a record. You should now add a button to the form to let them delete a record. A button is a type of shortcut that you can create to help the user work efficiently.

How to... Add a button to delete records

- Open your form in **Design View**.
- You will be in the **Design tab**. Look at the **Controls group**. Pass your mouse over each of the icons to see what they do (see Figure 16.26). Find the **Button** icon.

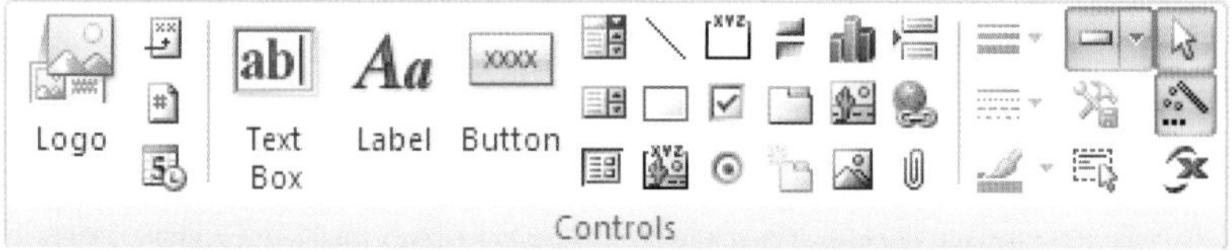

Figure 16.26: The Controls group on the Design tab.

- Make sure that the **Controls Wizard** icon is depressed.
- Click on the **Button** icon then click on the form in the position where you want the button to be placed.
- The button wizard will guide you through the next steps.
- In the **Categories** box, click on **Record Operations**. In the **Actions** box, click on **Delete Record** then click **Next**.
- You can choose whether to have text or an icon on the button. Make your choice then click **Next** then **Finish**.
- Switch to **Form View**. Find a record that you want to delete then check that the button works (see Figure 16.27).
- Close and save the form.

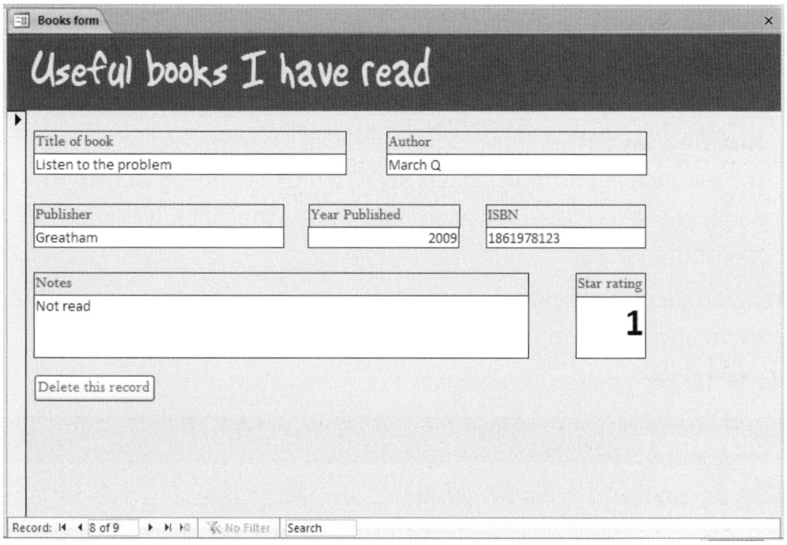

Figure 16.27: The delete button has been added to the form.

3.3 Report structure design

A report is a printed record of data in the database. There are several benefits of presenting information in a report rather than just viewing the data on-screen.

- Reports are very useful if you wish to share some of the information in the database with other people in a printed format.
- Reports can be laid out so they are easy to read and understand.
- Reports can be used to select and present exactly the data that someone needs rather than everything in the database.
- Although reports are intended to be printed as hard copy, they can also be transferred as electronic documents by email.

Like forms, each report is based on a table or query. (You will meet queries later on page 247.)

Layouts

When you use a wizard to create either a form or a report you are asked to choose between various layouts. You can experiment with them all. The three most useful ones are:

- **Columnar layout** — in this, each record is laid out with the fields under each other. The labels are placed to the left of the data. This layout is ideal when there is a lot of data in each record. You can usually print only a few records on each page, and a very long record may spread over more than one page.
- **Tabular layout** — this arranges the data in a table. This layout can be used for forms and reports if the amount of data in each record will fit comfortably on the screen or page.
- **Justified layout** — this displays the data one record at a time. The appearance is a formal boxed style, which fits neatly across the page, with the labels for each field above the data. It makes efficient use of the space.

When you design a report you need to identify the table or query that it is based on and the type of layout you want to use; see Table 16.12.

Table 16.12: Report structure design.

Books report	
Table or query	Books table
Layout	Tabular

Automatic creation of reports

The report wizard, like the form wizard, is a good way to start off a report, which you can then customise.

Access® gives you a number of style options when formatting a report; the simplest is tabular format which is a list of all the data set out in columns.

How to... Create a report

- In the **Create** tab, click on **Report Wizard** in the **Reports** group.
- On the first page of the wizard, *Table:Books* appears in the top box. The fields in the *Books* table are listed in the **Available Fields** box. Select all of the fields, except *Notes*, by clicking on the **>** key for each field. Then click on **Next**.
- Click on **Next** in the following two pages. For the layout select **Tabular** and **Landscape** then click on **Next**.
- Choose the style you want for the report then click on **Next**.
- Give the report the title *Books Report* then click on **Finish**.
- You will then see a preview of your report. Print it out then close the preview.

Books report

ISBN	Title	Author	Publisher	Year Published	Star rating
07645	Cabling, connections and ports	Stamp H P	Almond Harrison	2003	2
9780	Databases for all	Evans G	Jones & Jones	2008	5
01986	Finding your way through netw	Hill V & Dale T	Lost Books	2005	1
07356	Finding your way through proje	Rice S & Jam K	Lost Books	2004	5
07645	Finding your way through web	Selby T & York F	Lost Books	2003	2

Figure 16.28: A report listing all the books.

Editing a report

The report wizard can produce reports in a number of styles. But you may want to make some changes to the appearance and layout of a report. For example, you might want to alter the width of some of the fields in the report, or change the wording of the column headings.

Reports can be viewed in four views – **Report**, **Print Review**, **Layout** and **Design Views** – and you can switch between them in the **Views** group.

Labels and titles

When you use a wizard to design a report, the fieldnames are used as the labels for each field. In fact, you can change these labels in Design View to make them more understandable to the user. As we saw in the section on naming, if you use more advanced database techniques you may have to use fieldnames such as *txtSurname* that will mean very little to your user.

The title that you choose in the report wizard is used for a number of purposes:

- as the filename of the report
- as the name in the tab when you open the report
- as the heading in a report.

Note that you can change the heading in Design View without changing the filename of the report. A report heading can be longer and give more information than the simple name of the report.

How to... Change the design of the report

- Open the *Books* report and switch to **Design View**.

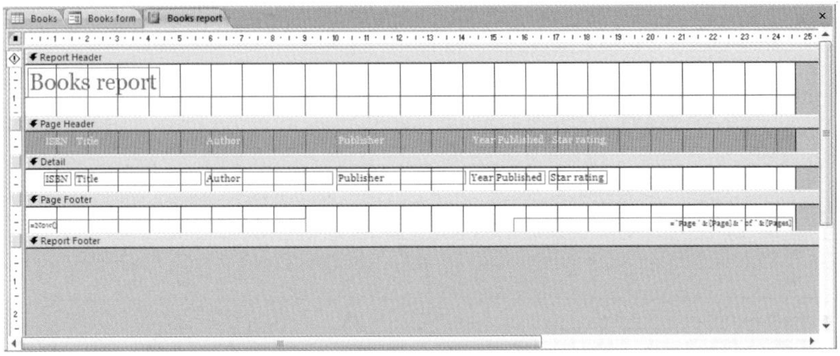

Figure 16.29: The report in Design View.

- The report is divided into five sections:
    1. The **Report Header** appears only on the first page of the report.
    2. The **Page Header** appears on every page, and gives the headings for each of the fields.
    3. The **Detail** section formats all the records that will be displayed in the report.
    4. The **Page Footer** appears on each page and contains the date the report was printed and the number of pages.
    5. The **Report Footer** appears only on the final page of the report. To view it, click on the bottom edge of the Report Footer and drag it down.
- The heading *Books report* in the **Report Header** is a label. Click on this once then make any changes you want to the text. You can use the buttons in the **Font** group to change the font, font size and font colour, etc.
- If you want to add more information to the **Report Header**, you can use the **Label** button in the **Controls** group to create a new label.
- If you decide to make the field columns narrower or wider, do this with care. Make sure that the fieldnames in the **Page Header** line up with the data in the **Detail** section.
- When you have made some changes, switch to **Report View** to check they are correct.

Key term

Expression – a formula or instruction that produces a value.

Special fields

The report wizard places two important special fields in the footer. For each one it uses an **expression**, which is a coded instruction that is recognised by the database system. You have already used one expression, when you set up <6 as the validation rule for the *Star Rating* field. Expressions often begin with **=**.

- **Date/time** — the expression for today's date is **=Now()** (i.e. a pair of brackets with nothing between them). Notice the effect of this in the footer of the report.
- **Page number** — another useful expression displays the page number. Of course, this isn't needed if you only need one page to print out the report, but it becomes very useful with larger databases.

Printing a report

How to... Set the paper size and default printer

- You need to add a button to the form that allows the user to print the report.
- Open the *Books* form in **Design View**. Use the **Button wizard** (see page 239). Select the **Report Operations** category and the **Preview Report** action.
- In the next window select the *Books* report.
- Select text rather than a picture, and use the words *Print out the full list of books*.
- Switch to **Form View** to test how the button operates.

Books | Books form | Books report

Useful books I have read   Print out the full list of books

| Title of book | Author |
| How to be a geek | Entwhistle Y |

| Publisher | Year Published | ISBN |
| Almond Harrison | 2004 | 0707804031 |

Notes
Funny, and I like the way it helps with the technical terms

Star rating
3

Delete this record

Record: 6 of 8 No Filter Search

Figure 16.30: The print button on the form.

Activity: Creating a DVD catalogue database

A friend of yours has an extensive collection of DVDs. They have asked you to create a database that catalogues them all. Before you use Access® you should do these three things:

1. Design a table with a suitable set of fields for recording information about the DVDs, such as film title, leading actors and genre (e.g. adventure, cartoon, romantic comedy). Decide what validation rules you could use.

2. Design the form that will be used to access the information and to add new records.

3. Design the reports that your friend will find useful.

When you go into Access® you should start a new database (since the data in the new database is nothing to do with the Resources database). If a database is already open then close it. Create your own database by following the steps used to create the Resources database (see page 261).

3.4 Queries

So far you have used tables, forms and reports. To really understand the power of a database you need to work with queries. To see how queries work, we'll set up a new database with some additional features.

A database with more advanced features

This next database will contain a membership list for a gym in Kingsmond, called King Gym. The database will be used for a number of purposes, including printing out lists of members. The database will include a *Members* table – the design for this is shown in Table 16.13.

Table 16.13: Table structure for the *Members* table.

Members table					
Field	**Data type**	**Description**	**Field properties**	**Validation rule**	**Validation text**
<u>Membership number</u>	Autonumber	Membership number allocated by the database			
Surname	Text	Surname of member	Field size: 20		
Forename	Text	Forename of member	Field size: 20		
Address	Text	The first line of the member's address	Field size: 50		
Town	Text	The town where the member lives	Field size: 20 Default: Kingsmond		
Postcode	Text	Postcode	Fieldsize:10		
Home phone	Text	Home phone number of member	Fieldsize:15		
Mobile	Text	Mobile phone number of member	Fieldsize:15		
Sex	Text	M or F	Field size: 1	="M" OR ="F"	Please enter either M or F
Junior	Yes/No	Tick the box if this is a Junior member			
Over 60	Yes/No	Tick the box if this member is over 60			
Subscription	Number	The amount of subscription that the member must pay	Field size: Integer Format: Currency	Lookup list	
Date paid	Date/Time	The date when the member paid the subscription	Format: Long date		

Notes

- *Membership number* is the primary key field. Autonumber will automatically allocate a number to each member in sequence.
- Names should usually be divided into surname and forename (or initials). We often sort names by surname, so *Surname* needs its own field and should not just be part of a *Name* field.
- Since most of the members live in Kingsmond, we can save the user a lot of typing by making Kingsmond the default value in the *Town* field. The user can still type in another town if necessary.
- For the *Subscription* field we will be creating a Lookup list (see page 225). This will be a list of the values that are allowed in this field.

You should always provide your user with one or more easy to use forms, so that they can interact with the database without problems. The designs for the form that will be used to access and enter information about gym members are shown in Table 16.14 and Figure 16.31.

Table 16.14: Form design for the members form.

Members form			
Table or query	Members table		
Screen design	See sketch		
Events	**Object**	**Event**	**Action**
	Delete record button	On click	Displayed record is deleted
	Report button	On click	Report is displayed

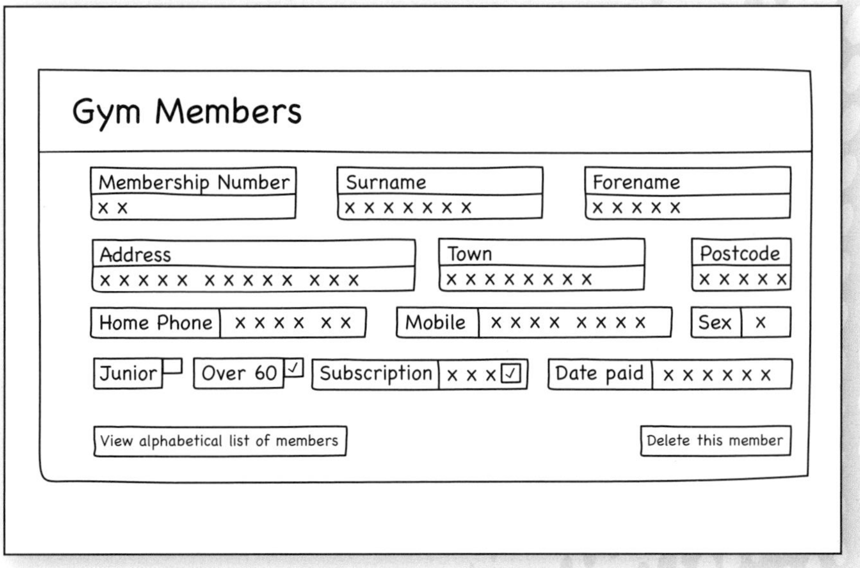

Figure 16.31: Sketched screen design for the Members form.

How to... Create a new database to handle a membership list

- If a database is already open, click on the **Office** button and select **Close Database**. You should always start afresh for a new database.
- Click on **Blank Database**.
- On the right of the screen, name your database *King Gym*. Click **Create**.
- This opens an empty table. Switch to **Design View**. Name the table *Members*.
- Define the table given in Table 16.13.
- In the *Town* field, find the **Default Value** under **Field Properties** and enter *Kingsmond*.
- In the *Junior* and *Over 60* fields, select the **Data Type Yes/No** from the drop-down list.
- In the *Subscription* field, select **Integer** as the **Field Size**. In the **Format** category, select **Currency** from the drop-down list. Now click in the **Data Type** column and select **Lookup Wizard**, which is at the bottom of the list of data types.
- In the first page of the wizard, select **I will type the values that I want**. Click on **Next**.

- For the number of columns, leave this as **1**. Under **Col1**, type in:
  - *300* in the first row – *100* in the second row
  - *0* in the third row (see Figure 16.31).
- Click on **Next** then **Finish**.

Figure 16.32: The Lookup Wizard.

- In the *Date paid* field, select **Date/Time** as the **Data Type**. In the **Field Properties**, click in **Format**, then select the **Long Date** format. The user can enter the date in any format but it will be displayed in the chosen format.
- Save the *Members* table.
- Switch to **Datasheet View** and enter a few records.

- The *Membership Number* is provided automatically, starting from 1, so do not change the value provided.
- Check that the validation rule works correctly for *Sex*.
- Note that the **Yes/No** fields are displayed as tick boxes.
- Click in the *Subscription* field and select from the drop-down lookup list.

Membership Number	Surname	Forename	Address	Town	Postcode	Home Phone	Mobile	Sex	Junior	Over 60	Subscription	Date paid
1	Jones	Sian	27 Station Road	Kingsmond	KM3 4TK	04356567342	07123456789	F	☐	☐	£300.00	23 June 2010
2	Khan	Abdul	1 Elm Road	Kingsmond	KM7 3YJ	04987612345	07987654321	M	☑	☐	£100.00	
3	Herbert	Alan	14 Riverside	Kingsmond	KM2 1FG	04567891234	07654321987	M	☐	☑		
* (New)				Kingsmond					☐	☐	300 / 100 / 0	

Figure 16.33: The lookup list in Datasheet View.

Activity: Use of numbers in databases

Telephone numbers are always given the text data type. Why?

A full phone number in the UK has eleven digits. We should normally store the whole of the number, including the dialling code for a landline number.

Mobile phone numbers all begin with 07 and standard landline numbers all begin with 01 or 02.

Find out what happens if you try to store a number that begins with zero, such as 0123. You can try this out on a calculator to see the result.

How to... Set up the main form

- Create a form based on the *Members* table using the **Form Wizard** (see page 235). **Save** it as *Members form*.

- Rearrange and customise the form in **Design View**.

- Open the form in **Form View** and use it to enter details of at least 12 members. Include males and females, juniors and over-60s, and two or three members who do not live in Kingsmond.

- Note how the **Yes/No** fields and the **Lookup** list appear in **Form View**.

- **Close** the form.

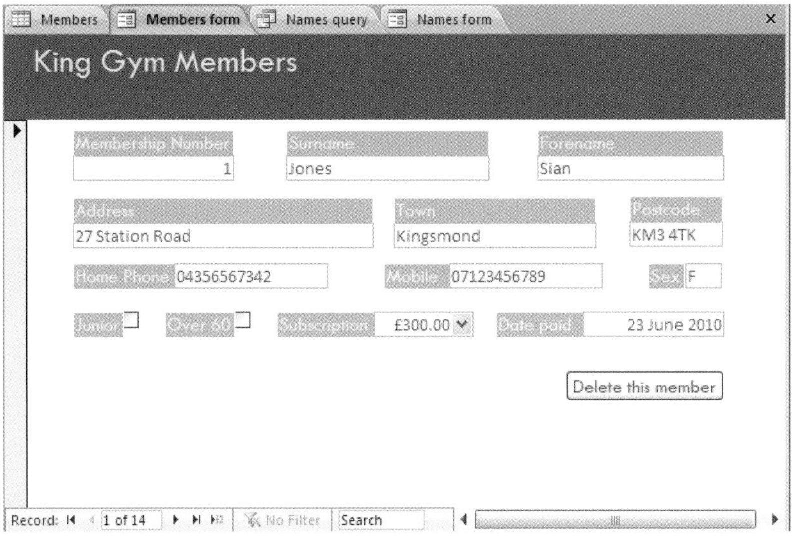

| Members | Members form | Names query | Names form | ✕ |

King Gym Members

Membership Number	Surname	Forename
1	Jones	Sian

Address	Town	Postcode
27 Station Road	Kingsmond	KM3 4TK

Home Phone 04356567342   Mobile 07123456789   Sex F

Junior ☐   Over 60 ☐   Subscription £300.00 ▾   Date paid 23 June 2010

Delete this member

Record: ◄ ◄ 1 of 14 ► ►► ►* 🏷 No Filter | Search ◄ ▬▬▬▬▬▬ ►

Figure 16.34: The Members form.

Query structure design

Users often want to select data from a database. For example, in the King Gym database you may want to see a list of all the members who have paid their subscriptions, or you may want to find all the female junior members. You do this by setting up a query within the database.

Another kind of query is one that displays all the records but gives data only in specified fields. For example, you might want to list just the names and addresses of members.

Meaningful data

Queries help the user to extract meaningful information from a large mass of data. Information is only meaningful, of course, if it is just what the user needs for the purpose they have in mind. For example, it might be possible to use a query to select all the members who have phone numbers ending with 7, but that would not be very useful to anyone. Or a query could be used to find if any members live in a certain postcode area – this may or may not be useful depending on the context. Every time you create a query you are in fact generating a new table that has exactly the data you require.

Creating a query to select fields for display

We will now set up a query that selects all the records in the *Members* table but only displays certain fields. We'll use this to create first a form and then a report which gives a simple list of all members, with their names and membership numbers.

Table 16.15 shows the design for a query that selects data from the *Members* table. It will select only the membership number, surname and forename fields, and will then sort them alphabetically.

Table 16.15: Design for the Names query.

Names query	
Table or query	Members table
Selected fields	Membership number, Surname, Forename
Sort field	Surname (A-Z), Forename (A-Z)
Criteria	

How to... Create a query that selects certain fields only

- Go to the **Create** tab and click on the **Query Wizard**.

- On the first page make sure that **Simple Query Wizard** is selected and click **OK**.

- In the **Available Fields** box click on *Membership number* then click on the **>** button to transfer it to the **Selected Fields** box.

- Repeat with the *Surname* and *Forename* fields then click on **Next**.

- For the title of the query enter *Names Query*. This will also be the name the query is saved under. Click **Finish**.

- The query will run and create a new table, which will be displayed in **Datasheet View**.

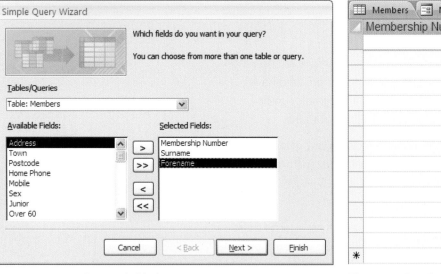

Figure 16.35: Selecting fields for a query.

Figure 16.36: The table created by the query.

Creating forms and reports based on queries

As a database developer you should not allow your user to view the queries directly. Instead, you should design forms or reports that display the data selected by a query. The user will simply choose to see these forms and reports, and will not really be aware of the underlying queries that generated them.

Table 16.16 is the design for a form that is based on the *Names* query shown in Table 16.15. It will only show the data selected by the *Names* query, which will have sorted the data into alphabetical order.

Table 16.16: Design for the Names form.

Names form			
Table or query	Names query		
Screen design	See sketch		
Events	**Object**	**Event**	**Action**
	Print alphabetical list button	On click	Prints *Names* report
	Back to members button	On click	Closes the form

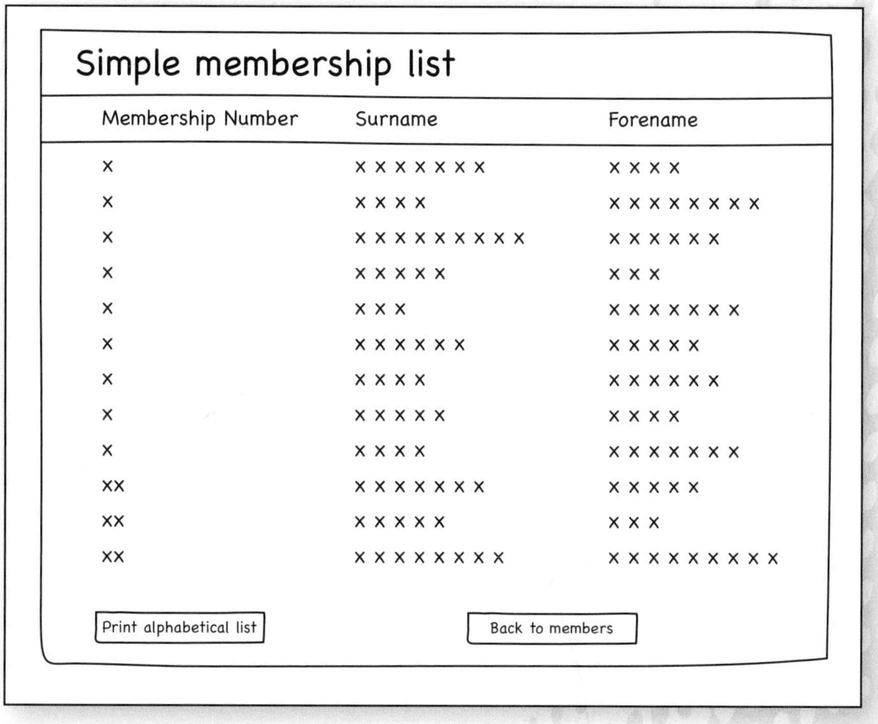

Figure 16.37: Sketched screen design for the Names form.

How to... Use a query to create a form

- Your user should be viewing the output from a query in a form rather than in **Datasheet View**.

- Use the **Form Wizard**. In the first window go to the **Tables/Queries** text box and select the *Names Query*. Select all three fields using the **>>** button.

- We want to present the information as a list on-screen, so in the next window select **Tabular layout** then work through the rest of the wizard. Enter *Names Form* as the title for the form.

- Switch to **Form View** to see what the form looks like.

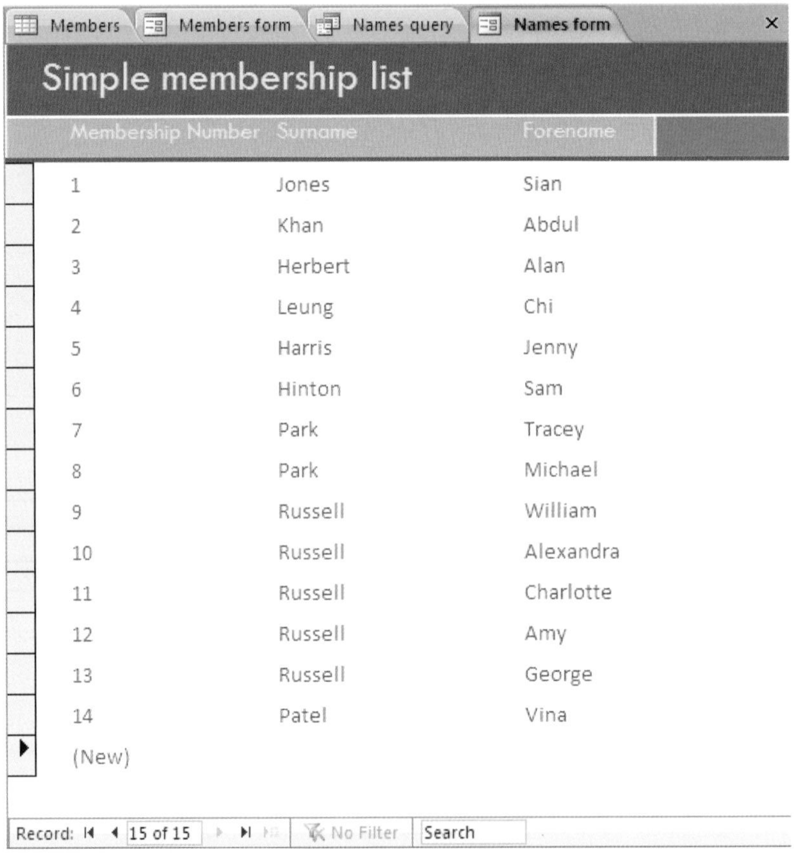

Members	Members form	Names query	**Names form**	

Simple membership list

Membership Number	Surname	Forename	
1	Jones	Sian	
2	Khan	Abdul	
3	Herbert	Alan	
4	Leung	Chi	
5	Harris	Jenny	
6	Hinton	Sam	
7	Park	Tracey	
8	Park	Michael	
9	Russell	William	
10	Russell	Alexandra	
11	Russell	Charlotte	
12	Russell	Amy	
13	Russell	George	
14	Patel	Vina	
(New)			

Record: I◀ ◀ 15 of 15 ▶ ▶I ▶ ☒ No Filter | Search

Figure 16.38: The Names form with tabular layout.

The *Names* query can also be used to generate a report. The report design in Table 16.17 shows that it will have a tabular layout.

Table 16.17: Design for the *Names* report.

Names report	
Table or query	Names query
Layout	Tabular

How to... Use a query to create a report

- The *Names Query* can also be used to print a simple membership list.

- Use the **Report Wizard**. As with the form, in the first window go to the **Tables/Queries** text box and select the *Names Query*. Select all three fields using the **>>** button.

- The next window asks about grouping records. This is only useful for complex reports, so click **Next**.

- The user is not able to choose the sort order for the report so you must do so now. In box 1 select *Surname* and in box 2 select *Forename*. This means that the records will be sorted first by *Surname* and then, if more than one person has the same surname, those records will be sorted by *Forename*. You may need to add some more records later to see the effect of this.

- In the next window select **Tabular**.

- Next choose your style.

- In the final screen, call the report *Names report*.

- Go to **Design View** to make any changes to the layout. You could change the heading of the report to *List of members*.

- In Figure 16.39 note how the Russell family has been sorted.

List of members

Surname	Forename	Membership Number
Harris	Jenny	5
Herbert	Alan	3
Hinton	Sam	6
Jones	Sian	1
Khan	Abdul	2
Leung	Chi	4
Park	Michael	8
Park	Tracey	7
Patel	Vina	14
Russell	Alexandra	10
Russell	Amy	12
Russell	Charlotte	11
Russell	George	13
Russell	William	9

Figure 16.39: The Names report.

Create queries using single criteria

A query can be used to select just some of the records in the database, according to rules known as criteria (see page 215). For example, the query might be used to pick out all the members with the surname Patel. This uses one criterion: **Surname = "Patel"**. Note that you should put double quote marks around the text.

You can also create criteria on number and date fields. For example, the criterion for a query to find all the members who paid their subscription on 1st January 2010 would be: **Date subscription paid = #01/01/10#**. Note that you should place the hash symbols to identify a date.

The equals sign (**=**) is an example of an operator. Criteria can also be used with other operators, such as **<**, **>** or **Not**. Each criterion is applied to just one field. Here are some examples of common operators:

- **Equals** — this will check whether the data is exactly the same as that required. Examples: Surname = "Patel", Subscription = 100, Junior = yes (for a yes/no field).

- **Less than (<)** — this can be used with numbers, e.g. subscription paid < 300. It can also be used with dates (where it means 'before'), e.g. date paid < #01/01/05#. And it can be used with text (where it means 'alphabetically before'), e.g. surname < "Morris".

- **Greater than (>)** — this can also be used with numbers, dates or text.

- **Not equals (Not)** — this can be used to find fields that do not match the data, e.g. town not "Kingsmond".

The design shown in Table 16.18 is for a query that will select all the female members.

Table 16.18: Design for Female members query.

Female members query	
Table or query	Members table
Selected fields	All
Sort field	
Criteria	Sex = "F"

How to... Use a query to select records

- Use the **Query Wizard**. On the first page select **Simple Query Wizard**. Click **Next**.

- Make sure that *Table:Members* is displayed in the **Tables/Queries** box.

- Select all the fields using the **>>** button.

- On the next page select **Detail**.

- On the last screen, name the query *Female Members Query*. Then select **Modify the query**

design (because we have not yet told it to pick out the female members). Click **Finish**.

- The query now opens in **Design View**. The window shows the fields in the *Members* table at the top, and the query design grid below. You can enlarge the top part of the window by dragging down on the line above the query design grid. You can then enlarge the *Members* table to show all the fields.

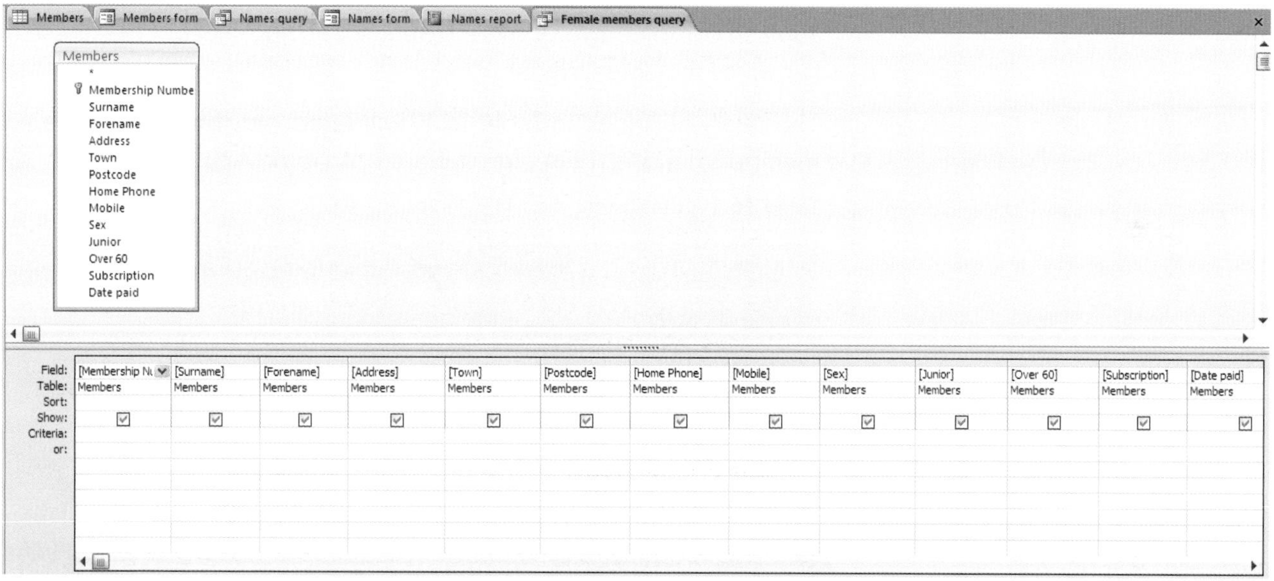

Figure 16.40: The Design View of the query, with the table at the top and the query design grid below.

- You may need to scroll horizontally through the query design grid to find the *Sex* field. Click on the **Criteria** row in the *Sex* column and key in: **="F"**.

- Switch to **Datasheet View** and check that only female members are listed.

- When you close the query make sure you save the amended version.

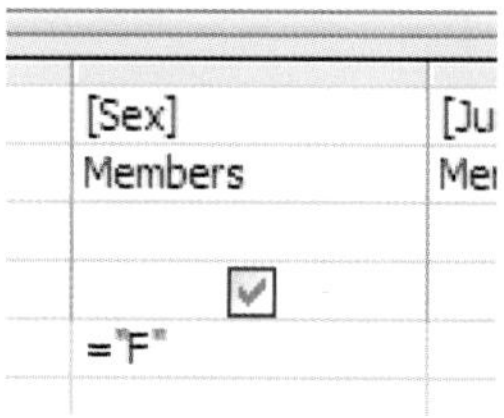

Figure 16.41: Setting up a criterion.

How to... Use other operators in queries

Create a new query for each of the three activities right.

- Close any tables, queries or forms that are open.

- Use the **Query Wizard** as before.

- When the query opens in **Design View**, enter the criterion for the query you are creating.

- Switch to **Datasheet View** and check that the correct records are listed.

1. A query to select the junior members: click on the **Criteria** row in the *Junior* column, and key in: **Yes**.

2. A query to select members who have paid a subscription greater than £100: click on the **Criteria** row in the *Subscription* column and key in: **>100**.

3. A query to select members who paid their subscriptions before 31st March 2010: click on the **Criteria** row in the *Date Paid* column and key in: **<#31/03/10#**.

Activity: Creating queries

Can you create a query to do each of these tasks?

1. Select members who have paid their subscriptions since the beginning of this year.
2. Select members who are not Juniors.
3. Select members with surnames that come after Jones in the alphabet.

Create queries using multiple criteria

You can combine two or more criteria by using AND or OR – these are known as multiple criteria.

The query designed in Table 16.19 will select only the junior male members; i.e. the members who are both male AND junior.

Table 16.19: Design for the *Male Juniors Query*.

Male Juniors Query	
Table or query	Members table
Selected fields	All
Sort field	
Criteria	Junior = Yes AND Sex = "M"

How to... Select records using AND criteria

*   Use the **Query Wizard**.
*   Select all the fields in the *Members* table using the **>>** button.
*   On the last page, name the query *Male Juniors Query* then select **Modify the query design**. Click **Finish**.
*   In **Design View** click on the **Criteria** row in the *Junior* column and key in: **Yes**.
*   Click on the **Criteria** row in the *Sex* column and key in: **="M"**.
*   Switch to **Datasheet View** and check that only male junior members are listed. If you get no results, that is simply because none of your records match the criteria. Try adding some more records that fit the criteria.
*   Create a form based on this query.

	[Sex]	[Junior]	[Over 60]
	Members	Members	Members
✓	✓	✓	
	="M"	Yes	

Figure 16.42: Setting up AND criteria.

Imagine you want to select all the members who pay the subscription at a concessionary rate. The query designed in Table 16.20 will select the members who are either juniors OR over 60.

Table 16.20: Design for the Concessions query.

Concessions query	
Table or query	Members table
Selected fields	All
Sort field	
Criteria	Junior = Yes OR Over 60 = Yes

How to... Select records using OR criteria

- Use the **Query Wizard**.

- Select all the fields in the *Members* table using the **>>** button.

- On the last page, name the query *Concessions Query* then select **Modify the query design**. Click **Finish**.

- In **Design View**, click on the **Criteria** row in the *Junior* column and key in: **Yes**.

- Notice that the row below the **Criteria** row is labelled **OR**. Click on the **OR** row in the *Over 60* column and key in: **Yes**.

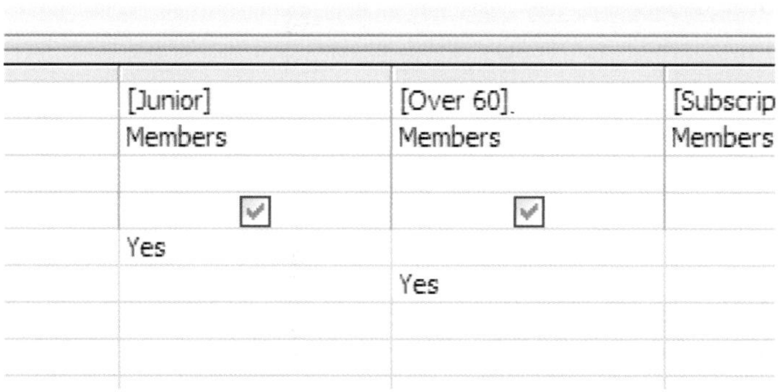

[Junior]	[Over 60].	[Subscrip
Members	Members	Members
☑	☑	
Yes		
	Yes	

Figure 16.43: Setting up OR criteria

- Switch to **Datasheet View** and check that the correct members are listed.

- Create a report based on this query.

As a general rule, AND queries appear on the same row in the query grid, while OR criteria appear on different rows.

You can create forms and reports based on any kind of query, whether they use single or multiple criteria. Make sure that you choose the correct query when using the Form or Report wizards.

Can you work out how to do each of these queries?

1. Select all the members who are female and over 60.
2. Select all the junior members who live in Kingsmond.
3. Select all the members who live either in Kingsmond or in Northwood (or another town name that you have used).

Sorting records in a query

You saw earlier that the default sort field in a table is the primary key (see page 233). You can also specify the sort order for the data selected by a query.

💻 **How to... Set the order in a query**

- **Open** the *Names* form. You will see that the data is sorted by the primary key; i.e. the membership number. **Close** the *Names* form.

- Now open the *Names Query* in **Design View**. This was used to produce the *Names* form.

- In the query design grid click in the **Sort** row under *Surname*. Then select **Ascending**. Next, click on the **Sort** row under *Forename* and select **Ascending**.

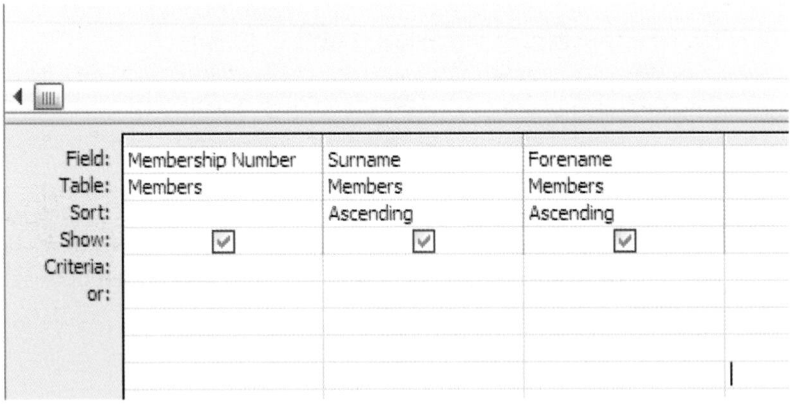

Field:	Membership Number	Surname	Forename	
Table:	Members	Members	Members	
Sort:		Ascending	Ascending	
Show:	☑	☑	☑	
Criteria:				
or:				

Figure 16.44: Sorting data in a query.

- Switch to **Datasheet View** and you will see that the list has been sorted. In our example, the Russell family have been sorted by forename as well. Surname is the first-level sort because it appears first on the query design grid.

- Now save the query and open the *Names* form again. You will find that the data has been sorted in line with the underlying query.

Completing the database

Improving efficiency

The database should be easy for the user to use. Normally you will have one main form with options that link to other forms. In the examples, the *Members* form is the main form.

You can create forms based on any of the queries you have created. You should decide which ones will be useful to the user then add buttons to the main form that link to these. Remember, a button is a type of shortcut that you can create to help the user work efficiently.

Once the user has looked at one of these forms they may want to print out the data, so you can add a button that links to the report.

How to... Add buttons to link to forms and reports

You can add a button to the *Members* form to let the user view the *Names* form.

- Open the *Members* form in **Design View** and use the button wizard. Select the **Form Operations** category and the **Open Form** action.

- In the next window, select *Names Form*.

- Then select **Open the form and show all the records**.

- Select text rather than a picture, and use the words *View alphabetical list of members*.

- Switch to **Form View** to see how the button operates.

- Now add a button to the *Names* form to give the user the option of printing the list.

- Open the *Names* form in **Design View**. We will put the button in the footer of the form. Drag down the lower edge of the form to open up the **Form Footer**.

- Use the button wizard and click in the **Form Footer**. Select the **Report Operations** category and the **Print Report** action.

- In the next window, select *Names report*.

- Select text rather than a picture, and use the words *Print alphabetical list*.

- Switch to **Form View** to see how the button operates.

Finally, you can add a button to the *Names* form so that the user can close the form and go back to the *Members* form.

- Use the button wizard and click in the **Form Footer**. Select the **Form Operations** category and the **Close Form** action.

- In the next window, select *Names report*.

- Select text rather than a picture and use the words *Back to members*.

- Switch to **Form View** to see how the button operates.

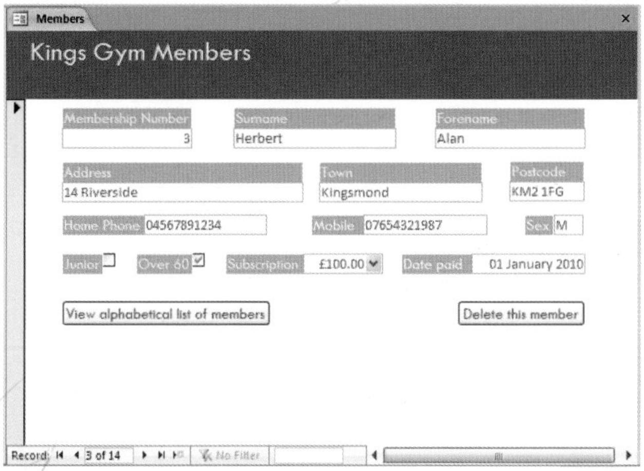

Figure 16.45: Buttons on the Members form.

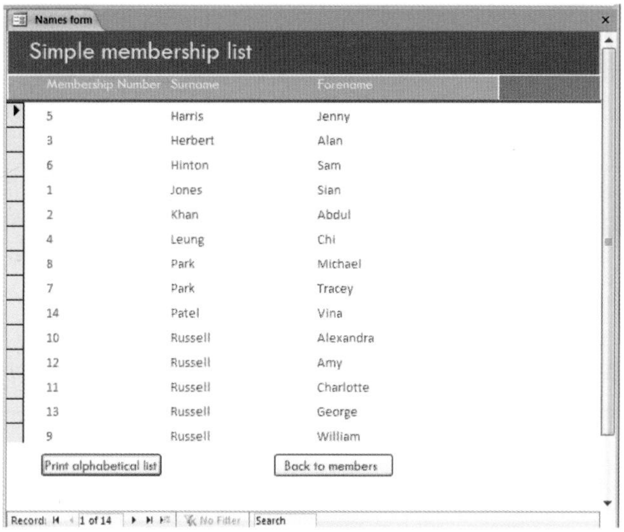

Figure 16.46: Buttons on the Names form.

Read the case study in Assessment activity 16.1 on page 219.

You are now ready to design the database for Jones & Smith Ltd. You should use the design techniques shown on pages 220–222. You will use your design when you create the actual database in Assessment activity 16.3.

1. Design the table structure for the database. You should use at least three different data types in your table. Make sure that you have used a number of validation techniques. **P2**

2. Explain your choice of fields, data types and primary key. **M2**

3. Design the structure of a data entry form for the database. Explain your reasons for your design choices. **P2**

4. Design a query which will be useful for Jones & Smith Ltd. Decide how the data is to be sorted. Explain why you need this query. **P2**

5. Design a report based on the query. Explain why the report will be useful to Jones & Smith Ltd. **P2**

6. Design any further queries, forms and reports that will meet your users' needs. Include at least one button on one of your forms. Explain all your designs. **P2**

7. Explain why it will be necessary to calculate the data storage requirements of the database. **M3**

Grading tips

- When designing the objects in this database (table, forms, queries and reports) use the design structures demonstrated in this unit.

- There is more than one correct solution to this problem, so make sure you give the reasons for all your choices.

PLTS

By answering questions and identifying problems to resolve when designing your database, you will show that you are an **independent enquirer**.

By generating ideas and exploring possibilities for your database design, you will show that you are a **creative thinker**.

Functional skills

By designing your database to meet the specified user need, you could provide evidence of your functional **Mathematics** skills in interpreting.

3.5 Importing data

Sometimes you already have the data you need for your database in another form. For example, you may have created a list in a spreadsheet and you would like to transfer the data to a database. Or you may already have a database that contains some data you need.

The process of transferring data from another software package to a database is known as importing.

It is common to use Microsoft® Excel® to store a list, which is a very simple kind of database (see *Unit 27: Spreadsheet modelling*). However, Excel® does not have the same range of facilities for handling data as Access®, so often users will want to transfer data across into Access®. The important thing to remember is that the headings at the tops of the columns in the spreadsheet should exactly match the fieldnames in the Access® database. They do not have to be in the same order, nor do all the fields have to be present in the spreadsheet, but the fieldnames must match exactly.

How to... Import data from a spreadsheet

Imagine that the names and addresses of the members of King Gym were stored on a spreadsheet before the database was set up. First you need to set up the list in a spreadsheet.

- Launch Excel® and create a spreadsheet as shown in Figure 16.47. Note that the column headings are exactly the same as some of the fieldnames in our *King Gym* database. Not all the fields are present, and the ones that we see are not in the same order as in the database, but this does not matter.

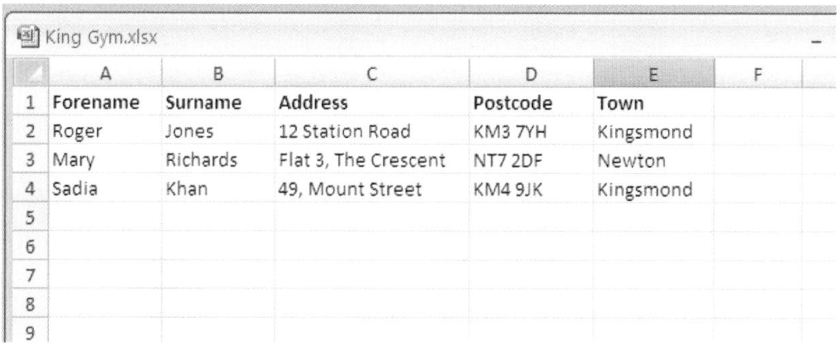

	A	B	C	D	E	F
1	Forename	Surname	Address	Postcode	Town	
2	Roger	Jones	12 Station Road	KM3 7YH	Kingsmond	
3	Mary	Richards	Flat 3, The Crescent	NT7 2DF	Newton	
4	Sadia	Khan	49, Mount Street	KM4 9JK	Kingsmond	
5						
6						
7						
8						
9						

King Gym.xlsx

Figure 16.47: Importing from a spreadsheet.

- Save and close the spreadsheet.
- **Open** the *King Gym* database. Close the *Members* table if it is open.
- Click on the **External Data** tab. In the **Import** group click on **Excel**.
- Under **Filename:** click on **Browse** and find your spreadsheet file.
- Select **Append a copy of the records to a table:** and check that *Members* is displayed. Click on **OK**.

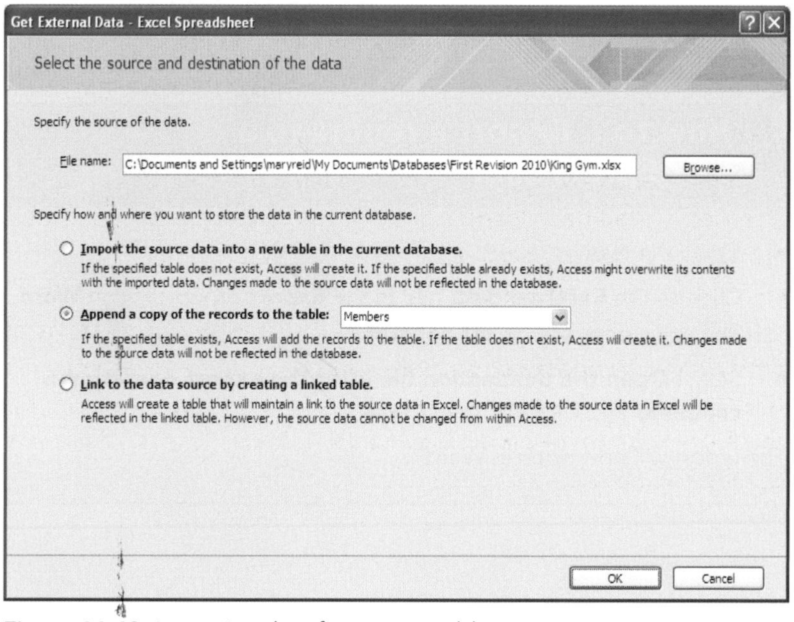

Figure 16.48: Importing data from a spreadsheet.

- On the next two pages click **Next**.
- Click **Finish** then **Close**.
- Open the *Members* table. The data from the spreadsheet should now be shown in the correct fields. Note that Access® has automatically assigned membership numbers to the new records.

Membership Number	Surname	Forename	Address	Town	Postcode	Home Phone	Mobile	S
1	Jones	Sian	27 Station Road	Kingsmond	KM3 4TK	04356567342	07123456789	F
2	Khan	Abdul	1 Elm Road	Kingsmond	KM7 3YJ	04987612345	07987654321	M
3	Herbert	Alan	14 Riverside	Kingsmond	KM2 1FG	04567891234	07654321987	M
4	Leung	Chi	Flat 5, Kelly House, Lat	Kingsmond	KM7 7FD	04111111111	07111111111	F
5	Harris	Jenny	49, High Street	Newton	NT1 6WS	04222222222	07222222222	F
6	Hinton	Sam	32, Carstairs Street	Kingsmond	KM6 2QS	04333333333	07333333333	M
7	Park	Tracey	21, St Peter's Close	Newton	NT6 9HK	04555555555	07555555555	F
8	Park	Michael	21, St Peter's Close	Newton	NT6 9HK	04555555555	07444444444	M
9	Russell	William	19, High Street	Kingsmond	KM1 7TF	04666666666	07666666666	M
10	Russell	Alexandra	19, High Street	Kingsmond	KM1 7TF	04666666666	07666666661	F
11	Russell	Charlotte	19, High Street	Kingsmond	KM1 7TF	04666666666	07666666662	
12	Russell	Amy	19, High Street	Kingsmond	KM1 7TF	04666666666		
13	Russell	George	19, High Street	Kingsmond	KM1 7TF	04666666666		
14	Patel	Vina	2, The Walk	Kingsmond	KM4 6KL	04777777777	07777777777	
16	Jones	Roger	12 Station Road	Kingsmond	KM3 7YH			
17	Richards	Mary	Flat 3, The Crescent	Newton	NT7 2DF			
18	Khan	Sadia	49, Mount Street	Kingsmond	KM4 9JK			
*	(New)			Kingsmond				

Record: 14 4 18 of 18 ▶ ▶I No Filter Search

Figure 16.49: Imported data.

3.6 Exporting data

It is also possible to export data from Access® to a word processor or spreadsheet, or to another database. You might want to export a report into a word processor so you can use some of the facilities, such as mail merge. Alternatively, you might like to capture the results of a query and place the data in a spreadsheet for further analysis (for example, creating a chart using the data).

How to... Export a report to a word processor

- Open the *Names* report.
- Click on the **External data** tab. In the **Export** group click on **Word**. This will create a file in **rtf format**.
- Select **Open the destination file after the export operation is complete** and click **OK** then **Close**.

The report will now open in Word®.

Key term

rtf format – a text format that can be read by all versions of Word® and by most other word-processing software packages as well.

How to... Export a query to a spreadsheet

- In the *Members* database, open one of the queries you have saved.
- Click on the **External data** tab. In the **Export** group click on **Excel**.
- On the first page select **Export data with formatting and layout** and **Open the destination file after the export operation is complete**. Click **OK** then **Close**.
- An Excel® spreadsheet will open with the selected data.

3.11 Testing

A database is not ready for use until you have checked that it works properly.

Even though you have included a number of validation checks, you should still check that any data that you have entered is correct. You should also look carefully at all the forms and reports and try out any buttons.

Test data

There are several ways in which you can check the data in the table.

- **Comparison with the original data** — if the data was copied from a paper document, you should read it through and make sure the data on-screen matches the original. Sometimes it is helpful to have another person carrying out these checks with you – one of you reads the document and the other checks the screen.
- **Spellcheck** — you can check the spelling of any of the data in a table in **Datasheet View**. Highlight the data you want to check then click on the **Spelling option** in the **Records** group. If you want to spell check a whole table, first click on the small triangle at the top left of the table; this selects all the data. Then click on the **Spelling** option.
- **Sorting** — you can often spot data entry mistakes by sorting the records. It is easiest to spot duplications or omissions in **Datasheet View**. For example, by sorting the data on the *Surname* field you will easily be able to spot if you have entered the same record twice, because the two records will appear next to each other.

Check the queries

You should check the processing and output for each query.

- Are the correct records selected?
- Are the correct fields displayed?
- Is the data sorted correctly?

Check layout and output of reports and screens

You should check each form and report to answer these questions:

- are the correct fields displayed
- are the correct records displayed
- can the labels for each field be read easily
- is all the data visible (Sometimes the width of the textbox or column is too narrow and some of the data is hidden.)
- on a form, is the data entry order sensible
- on a form, do the buttons work as expected
- on a report, is there useful information in the header and footer?

Using a test plan

You should formally record all these checks in a test plan. Your test plan could look like the one shown in Table 16.21.

Table 16.21: Example database test plan.

Object tested	Test	Expected result	Actual result	Action
Members form	Check the presence of fields	All fields displayed from *Members* table		
Members form	Is it clear what each textbox and button is for?	All components are suitably labelled		
Members form	Check correct data entry order	Cursor moves across and down the form in a natural sequence		
Members form	Check validation rule for *Sex*	Validation text appears when letter other than M or F is entered		
Female members query	Check that it selects the correct data	All female members selected but no other records		

You should draw up the test plan before you start the testing. The actual results should be entered as each test is completed. At the end of this process you should use the final column to comment on any results that are not as expected and what can be done to address the problem.

BTEC Assessment activity 16.3

P3 P4 P5 P6 P7 M4 M5 D1

Using suitable database software, set up the database that you designed in Assessment activity 16.2. Keep notes on everything you have done and print screenshots whenever possible to show your progress.

1. Set up the table you designed. Create the data entry form that you designed and use it to enter at least 20 records into the database. **P3**

2. On a spreadsheet, create a further 10 records with headings corresponding to the fieldnames in the database. Import the data in the spreadsheet into the table in the database. **P4**

3. Create the queries, reports and further forms that you designed. **P5**, **P6**, **M5**

4. Create screen printouts of your queries and forms. Print at least two reports. Show how the data is sorted. **M4**

5. Test the database and write up the results. Include screen printouts to demonstrate the results. **D1**

6. Export one of your reports to a word-processing file. **P7**

Grading tips

- For questions 1 and 5, make sure that your database matches the design you did for Assessment activity 16.2.

- For question 3 you may create new queries, reports and forms in addition to the ones in the original design. You may also test these as evidence for question 5.

- Make sure that you create at least two reports that are meaningful and based on queries.

3.7 User documentation

Throughout these activities you have been acting as both a database developer and a user. In the workplace, a database will often be created by a professional developer and it will then be used by people who are not database experts.

The office staff at King Gym will use the membership database that you have designed and built. They don't need to know how it works. But they do need to know how to enter new members, delete members who have left, search for members in various categories, print out lists, etc. You could show them how to do this, but they also need a printed user guide that will answer all their questions.

A user guide is normally arranged like this:

- **Introduction** — this describes the purpose of the database – who it is for and what it can do.

- **How to carry out standard tasks** — standard tasks are things like viewing all the members or printing a report. Use headings, such as *How to view all the members*, for each task. The guide should show the user how to do each task in turn, illustrated with screenshots.

- **Troubleshooting** — this section will help users to solve any problems they might have with the database. Use headings that focus on the problems, such as *The report won't print*.

PLTS

By generating ideas and exploring possibilities when creating queries and reports, you will show that you are a **creative thinker.**

By testing your database against the design, you will show that you are a **self-manager**.

Functional skills

By testing your database, you could provide evidence of your functional **Mathematics** skills in analysing.

Assessment activity 16.4 P8 D3

Now write about the database that you created in Assessment activity 16.3.

1. Write user documentation for the database. **P8**

2. Write a report about the improvements that could be made to the database you have designed and created. For example, you could consider extra fields, additional queries and reports or more useful buttons. You don't have to implement these improvements, but you should include new designs. Explain why these changes would improve the database for Jones & Smith Ltd. **D3**

Grading tips

You will be writing for two different audiences.

- The user documentation is for a user who has no knowledge of the technical structure of the database, so you should only describe the parts that are relevant to the user.

- The report on improvements is for yourself and your client, so it can include some technical material.

PLTS

By justifying improvements that could be made to a database, you will show that you are an **effective participator**.

Functional skills

By writing user documentation for your database, you could provide evidence of your functional **English** skills in writing.

Just checking

1. What is a sort field?
2. What are queries used for?
3. What are the differences between a form and a report?
4. What do we mean by multiple criteria for a query?
5. Why might you want to import data from another application?

Olivia Marston
School Administrator

I work with four other administrators in the office at a large secondary school. I am responsible for:

- looking after the records of all the pupils in the pupil database
- morning and afternoon registration
- meeting pupils who are late or need to leave school to go to an appointment
- dealing with applications for places at the school
- recording pupil absences and the reasons why they are not attending.

As a qualified first aider I also look after any pupils who are taken ill during the day.

Typical day

A typical day for me starts quite early, when parents start phoning in to explain that their child is sick and can't attend school. I note this on the pupil's record and make sure that the teachers know. After morning registration, I check whether any pupils are absent without any explanation. If this is the case, I send a message to their parents or carers by text, email or phone.

Later in the morning I check the absences to see if anyone has been away for longer than expected. After that I check the post to see if anyone is applying for places at the school after moving into the area. Once a year we go through a very busy time when pupils apply for places in Year 7 or in Year 12.

The best thing about the job

The best thing about the job is being in contact with young people and helping them with their problems. Some of them need long-term medical care and I am in constant touch with their families to make sure we are meeting their needs. In other cases pupils are unhappy at home and I can ensure that they get the help they need.

I enjoy working on a computer and I like making sure that the data is completely accurate. I can develop the forms and reports that I and other members of staff need. The pupil database enables us to treat each pupil as an individual.

Think about it!

1. What have you learned in this unit that provides you with the background knowledge and skills used by a school administrator?
2. What other skills would you need to do the job?
3. Can you think of other jobs that would require similar skills?

Just checking

1. Give three examples of databases used in the real world.
2. Explain how a field in a table can be used as a sort field.
3. Some databases are very large. Explain how you could reduce the size of records in a database.
4. Verification and validation are two ways in which the data in a database can be checked for accuracy. Explain how each can be carried out.
5. In the context of databases, what do we mean by forms, reports and queries?
6. What are the advantages in using a DBMS like Access® for storing data over keeping records in a word-processed document?
7. Why should you create forms for a user to view the data rather than let them view the data in a table?
8. A query can be used to select particular fields or to select particular records. Give an example of each.
9. Describe a case in which you would want to export data from a database.

edexcel :::

Assignment tips

To work towards a distinction in this unit you will need to achieve all the pass, merit and distinction criteria in the unit and have evidence to show that you have achieved each one.

How do I prepare for the assignment activities?

- Carry out all the activities in this unit yourself. You may already be familiar with databases and with Access®, but you are certain to learn something new as you work through the activities.

- If you are new to Access®, get further practice by creating other databases when you have finished the activities in the unit. Ask your tutor for advice on this.

- Don't be tempted to draw up the design for a database after you have created it. Once you start working on a database it can be very difficult to untangle any errors. You should always think through the problems, and design a solution, before you use Access®.

- Watch out for examples of databases in use in the real world and keep a note of any that you come across. See if you can work out what fields were used in the tables, what queries were set up and how these were used to generate forms and reports.

How do I provide assessment evidence?

- You can present your written findings as a report. Alternatively, you could discuss the topics with your tutor, who can provide observation records.

- You should also provide evidence of the database that you created. This should be a report describing how you created and checked your database. Use screenshots and printouts to illustrate your report. It could possibly be supported by witness statements or observation records.

- All your evidence should be presented in one folder, which should have a front cover and a contents page. You should divide the evidence into four sections corresponding to the four tasks.

17 Website development

In this unit you will explore and analyse a number of existing websites. You will learn to distinguish effective sites from poor ones, and you will discuss the design features that make a site easy to use.

Websites have joined the traditional media of newspapers, radio and television as an important means of communication between individuals and organisations. In the past, the media offered mainly one-way communication, but websites can be used very easily for two-way communication. This meant websites had a clear advantage over the other media when they first appeared in the 1990s.

You will have the opportunity to design and build a website for a client. In the process you will learn a number of skills that could be useful at work. In many small businesses, developing and maintaining the website is just one of several duties carried out by a member of staff.

In order to succeed in this unit you will need to have easy access to the Internet and a good search engine. You should also have the use of one or more web authoring packages.

Learning outcomes

After completing this unit you should:

1. know web architecture and components
2. understand how websites can be used by organisations
3. be able to design website components
4. be able to create website components.

Assessment and grading criteria

This table shows you what you must do in order to achieve a pass, merit or distinction grade, and where you can find activities in this book to help you.

To achieve a **pass** grade the evidence must show that you are able to:	To achieve a **merit** grade the evidence must show that, in addition to the pass criteria, you are able to:	To achieve a **distinction** grade the evidence must show that, in addition to the pass and merit criteria, you are able to:
P1 identify the hardware and software components which enable Internet and Web functionality **See Assessment activity 17.1 on page 278**		
P2 describe the role of web architecture in website communications **See Assessment activity 17.1 on page 278**		
P3 explain the uses of websites in organisations **See Assessment activity 17.1 on page 278**		
P4 design website components, considering client needs **See Assessment activity 17.2 on page 291**	**M1** explain the techniques that can be used on web pages to aid user access to information **See Assessment activity 17.2 on page 291**	**D1** evaluate different design features of a website **See Assessment activity 17.2 on page 291**
P5 use appropriate formatting tools, styles and templates to prepare content for the website **See Assessment activity 17.3 on page 315**	**M2** describe the use of interactive websites and what techniques can be used to provide interactivity **See Assessment activity 17.3 on page 315**	
P6 create website components to meet client needs **See Assessment activity 17.3 on page 315**	**M3** use automated features in web development software **See Assessment activity 17.3 on page 315**	
P7 review website components, suggesting improvements **See Assessment activity 17.4 on page 316**	**M4** refine website components based on user feedback **See Assessment activity 17.4 on page 316**	**D2** explain how a created website meets the defined requirements **See Assessment activity 17.4 on page 316**

How you will be assessed

This unit is internally assessed. You will provide a portfolio of evidence to show that you have achieved the learning outcomes. Your portfolio of evidence can be supplied in many formats including electronically as well as paper-based. The grading grid in the specification for this unit lists what you must do to obtain pass, merit and distinction grades. The Assessment activities in this unit will guide you through tasks that will help you to be successful in this unit.

Your tutor will tell you exactly what form your assessments will take, but you could be asked to produce:

- written reports
- screenshots of website components
- practical work
- a presentation.

Emma Meyrick, a BTEC National learner

I spend a lot of time on the Internet. In fact, I can't remember a time when I didn't use the Web to look up information and get in touch with people. My favourite site is Facebook, but I also like downloading music. In the last year or two I've been doing quite a bit of shopping online as well.

I now have online access to my bank account. This is really useful because I can check my account any time and don't have to wait for the statement to arrive by post.

Websites look very complicated, and I would need to learn a great deal before I could work on a site like Facebook. But you have to start somewhere, and this unit helped me to understand the basic principles. It also got me using Adobe® Dreamweaver® for the first time. Creating a web page isn't as simple as writing a word-processed document, but it wasn't difficult to learn the techniques and it didn't take long before I could produce something quite presentable.

I'm now taking my studies further and hope to go on to study website design on an HND course. There are some really exciting things happening on the Internet and I want to be part of them.

Over to you

- So, what do you think makes a good website?
- Have you created a website yourself? Would you like to develop your skills?

1. Know web architecture and components

How many websites have you visited this week?

Count them up!

- Which websites do you visit regularly?
- Which websites do you find most useful for your studies?
- Which sites do you use to keep in contact with people?
- What sort of things do you do on the Web? Do you play games, download music, shop, chat, upload photos and videos, check out information, follow what is happening in the world, anything else?

It's amazing to think that the Web was only invented in 1991 and that most people were not aware of it for several years after that. How did people manage before the Web came along?

In 1991, Tim Berners-Lee developed the World Wide Web (also known as the Web, or WWW), which very rapidly became the universal standard way of displaying and linking documents on the Internet. Pages on the Web include hyperlinks to other web pages.

Berners-Lee developed three important elements that together make the Web work for users:

- Hypertext MarkUp Language (HTML) – the code used to create all web pages
- HyperText Transfer Protocol (HTTP) – the rules for transferring HTML files from one computer to another
- browsers – software applications that enable the user to view web pages.

The most commonly used browser is Microsoft® Internet Explorer®, but other browsers, such as Mozilla Firefox®, are also used.

1.1 Web hardware and software

You can access the Web from a desktop computer or from a laptop, mobile phone or games console. In each case you need the right hardware and software to be able to download and view web pages. On the other hand, organisations that provide websites also need to have access to servers and other services, all of which use a combination of hardware and software components.

Hardware

Servers

A server is a computer that manages the flow of data through a network. It does this by running special server software. There are several types of servers – file servers and printer servers support local area networks, while **web servers** and mail servers manage the communications with the Internet.

Web server

Each website is stored on a web server, which is connected to the Internet.

Web developers transfer pages and other files from their own computers to the web server. This is known as uploading a file. When you want to look at a website, your browser finds the correct web server and then copies the file or files to your own computer. This is known as downloading a file.

Two different methods are usually used for uploading and downloading files.

- **FTP** is used to upload files to a web server.
- **HTTP** is used to download files from a web server.

Mail server

A mail server is a computer that manages emails. It is connected to the Internet and it both sends and receives emails for its users. Home users will use a mail server provided by an Internet Service Provider (ISP).

Proxy server

A proxy server is another server which acts as a stepping stone between the user's computer and the web server. The proxy server filters some of the data flowing from the Internet to the user's computer. It also speeds things up by caching (storing) some pages and files that are used a lot, avoiding frequent requests to the web server for the same files.

A proxy server also hides the identity of the user's computer from the Internet. Internet Service Providers have many proxy servers. Users' computers log in to the proxy and then the proxy handles all the requests for web pages on their behalf.

Router

A router is a piece of hardware that links two networks together. The ISP provides a network that sends data from its proxy servers to a user's Internet modem. On the user's side there may well be a local network. This could be a full commercial local area network in an office, or it could be a small domestic Wi-Fi network. In either case, a router will take the data from the modem and redirect it to the correct devices in the local network. It also handles the data travelling in the opposite direction.

Key terms

Web server – a computer that stores websites and makes them available on the Internet.

File Transfer Protocol (FTP) – a method for transferring all types of files between computers on a network. It is used on the Internet for a number of purposes, including uploading web pages to a web server.

Hypertext Transfer Protocol (HTTP) – a method for finding and transferring web pages from a web server to an individual computer through the Internet.

Software

Browser

A browser performs a number of tasks.

- It sends a request for a page to the web server where the website is stored. The request identifies the page by its **Uniform Resource Locator (URL)**. The HTML code for that page is then transmitted over the Internet.
- It interprets the HTML code and displays the web page.
- It sends requests to the web server for additional files that are referred to in the HTML code for the page – these could be graphic or sound files.
- When the user clicks on a hyperlink, the browser sends a new page request to the web server.

Browsers have been updated to match the developments in HTML, but not all users have the latest versions. Web pages can appear differently in different browsers and in different versions of the same browser.

Some useful browser features include:

- the ability to store the URLS of your favourite websites
- a history list of all the sites you have visited recently
- the ability to zoom in on a page or to enlarge the text only (this is particularly useful if you have a visual impairment).

Email

There are two main ways of handling emails.

- An email client is a specialist software package, such as Microsoft® Outlook®. This is installed on your own computer, and all the emails that you receive are downloaded and stored on your computer. You must be connected to the Internet in order to send or receive emails.
- Webmail is a system, such as Hotmail®, for managing your emails entirely on the Web. You can log on to your webmail account from any computer that is connected to the Internet.

1.2 Web architecture

The World Wide Web only works across the world because everyone uses the same standards, such as the structure of URLs, the format of HTML, and the use of the HTTP method to transfer files. Together these standards are referred to as web architecture, and they have been agreed by the World Wide Web Consortium, also known as W3C.

Internet Service Providers (ISP)

An Internet Service Provider is a company that provides access to the Internet for individual users and organisations. In the UK, broadband connections are common. In some parts of the world, dial-up modem services are still offered by ISPs.

Popular ISPs in the UK include:

* BT (British Telecommunications plc)
* Talktalk (AOL)
* Virgin Media
* Sky Broadband.

Web hosting services

A website has to be uploaded to a web server in order to appear on the World Wide Web. The web server will be owned by a web hosting company. Many ISPs offer web hosting as part of their services to clients. If you want to put your website on the Web, a web hosting company will be able to provide you with web space on the server. They will, of course, charge you for the service.

The **web host** can also register a domain name for you and make sure that it is linked to your website. Your school or college may already have an arrangement with a web host, so you may be able to upload your website to the Web at no cost to yourself.

It is important that websites are secure, which means that only the right person is able to upload pages or change the website in any way. The web host will assign usernames and passwords to achieve this.

Domain structure

Every single page on the Web has a special web filename, known as a Uniform Resource Locator (URL). For example, http://www.example.com/contact.html is the URL for the contact page on a website.

Sometimes you download other files from the Internet, such as documents or music files. Each of these also has its own URL, such as http://www.example.com/cats.jpg. URLs are sometimes referred to as web addresses.

A URL consists of several parts:

* **http** – this tells the browser to use the HyperText Transfer Protocol, which is the system used to download files from the web server to your computer
* **www.example.com** – this is the domain name for the website.
* **contact.html** – this is the name of the file or page in the website. In this case, the filename ends in .html, so it must be a web page.

Domain names

The **domain name** of a website, such as www.example.com, is the core of its URL. It should be a recognisable name for the organisation or individual who registered it. It has to be registered with one of the official domain name registrars. There is a charge for registering a domain name.

Key terms

Web host – the company that provides space on a web server.

Domain name – the core of a URL. For example, in the URL http://www.example.com, the domain name is www.example.com.

Activity: Domain names

Domain names can end with any of the following suffixes: .com; .org; .net; .co.uk; .org.uk; .me.uk; .info; .au.

1. Find out what each of these endings means.
2. Find out at least five more endings for domain names and write down what they mean.

Nominet UK is the official domain name registrar in the UK. Domain names ending with .uk must be registered through Nominet. In practice, an ISP or web hosting company will usually carry out the domain name registration for a client.

1.3 Web functionality

Web 2.0

Since the early 1990s the Web has become increasingly interactive, with many opportunities for visitors to enter into a dialog on a website. These include online forums and discussions groups, feedback forms, surveys and polls, blogs, chat rooms, games and quizzes. The growth of social networking sites, such as Facebook, has transformed the ways in which people use the Internet and communicate with each other.

In 2004 Tim O'Reilly promoted the term Web 2.0 to indicate that the Web had taken a major step forward with the widespread use of such tools.

Blogs

A blog is a personal website that the owner updates at regular intervals. Blog posts are used by the owner to express their views on any subject that interests them. Usually visitors can leave comments on a blog post, so that a conversation may develop. Bloggers often find they become part of a wide community as they make contact with people with similar interests.

Online applications

The Web offers many online games that can be played solo or between players.

Increasingly, you can now find software applications online that would normally be found on a personal computer. One example is webmail systems (see page 272), but you can also find online applications that allow you to share calendars or documents. It is also possible to find online standard application software, such as spreadsheet and presentation graphics, that do not need to be downloaded to the user's computer.

Just checking

1. What is a web server and how might you use it?
2. What is a browser?
3. Give three examples of real domain names, and describe the type of organisation or individual that registered them.
4. Emails can be managed by webmail or by an email client. Explain the difference between them.
5. What does the term Web 2.0 mean?

2. Understand how websites can be used by organisations

2.1 Uses of websites

Websites created for organisations can do the following:

- **Inform** – all websites provide some information, which is one reason why the Internet became known as the 'Information Superhighway'.
- **Sell** – websites can be used to promote products and services to visitors.
- **Interact** – websites can easily offer interactivity, allowing the visitor to send information and ideas back to the organisation and to engage in dialog.

Many commercial and public service websites are designed for communications with the customers or users of the services. We describe these as customer-facing websites. Other websites are designed for a more limited audience, or specifically for people who work within the organisation.

Customer-facing websites

As the Internet has grown, more and more businesses have emerged that exist only on the Web, including online banks, shops, travel agencies and insurance companies. These companies sell goods and services directly to the customer.

Customers normally pay for products online with a credit or debit card, and they need to be reassured that their payments will be safe. Online payments are usually routed through a secure server, which encrypts all the data.

Goods are sent to the customer either by post or using a distribution company, and successful online businesses generally guarantee delivery within a few days.

Some Internet businesses don't need to deliver goods. For example, online banking has grown very rapidly, and customers can view their balances and make payments at any time of the day. Similarly, travel companies can send documents, such as ticket confirmations, by email and may not need to use the post at all.

Most high street chains now have online **e-commerce** operations as well. Large supermarkets offer a home shopping service, which can be very helpful for people who are housebound, have young children or lead busy lives.

Many commercial websites promote a service or product without actually offering online sales. For example, most rock bands have websites that promote the band and their music, although visitors may not be able to buy albums directly from the site.

Many tourist attractions use the Internet to give people information about their location and opening times, and to encourage people to attend. Similarly, hotels often provide basic information even though you may have to phone to book a room.

Key term

e-commerce – the use of the Internet for selling goods and services to customers.

Activity: e-commerce websites

ASOS, the online fashion store (see Figure 17.1), describe themselves in the following way:

'About ASOS

Established in June 2000, ASOS.com is the UK's largest independent online fashion and beauty retailer. With over 35,000 branded and own label products available and over 1500 new lines added each week, ASOS.com is rapidly becoming the market leader in the UK online fashion world.

Aimed primarily at fashion forward 16–34-year-olds, ASOS.com attracts over 6.9 million unique visitors a month and has 2.9 million registered users.'

(Source: Asos)

• Use your usual search engine to find other e-commerce websites. Can you work out which kinds of business have gone in for e-commerce? Which kinds of business are rarely to be found on the Web?

Figure 17.1: ASOS.com, an e-commerce site.

Internal websites

Intranets

The Internet is essentially a public-access network, so that anyone can visit any site they choose. An organisation may want to maintain a site for internal communications that can be accessed only by employees or members. To do this they can set up an **intranet** (note the spelling).

An intranet is created on the organisation's own network system. It can be used only by users who log on to stations on the network. It will normally include email services and an internal 'website'. (Note that an intranet is not really a 'website' as it does not appear on the World Wide Web.)

An intranet can hold confidential information that should not normally appear outside the organisation, as well as data on day-to-day administrative arrangements. Your place of study will probably have its own intranet.

Activity: Websites for different organisations

Use a search engine to find a wide range of websites developed by organisations. For each site you visit, note down:

- the web address and name of the organisation
- the purpose of the site
- a brief description of the content.

Keep all your research findings – they will be useful when carrying out Assessment activity 17.1 on page 278.

Information repositories

Many organisations hold a large number of documents in a format that is accessible from the Web. They may choose to place these on publicly accessible websites, even though the main users will be members or employees. These stores of information are known as information repositories. One of the best known public repositories is Hansard, which contains the text of everything that is said in the House of Commons during debates.

Some information repositories are only available on intranets in order to maintain confidentiality.

Training facilities

Many organisations use computer-based training systems for their staff. Such training can be loaded onto the network so that any employee can download and access the relevant modules. Alternatively, training can be undertaken online or on an intranet.

Interactive training programs enable the trainee to progress at their own convenience and speed. The systems will record their progress and suggest a route they should take through the modules to meet their training needs.

Key term

Intranet – a type of website that is accessible only within the network in which it has been set up, usually within an organisation.

PLTS

By researching and explaining the different uses of websites, you will show that you are an **independent enquirer**.

Functional skills

Writing a report could provide evidence for your functional **English** skills in writing.

BTEC Assessment activity 17.1 **P1** **P2** **P3**

The Big Blue Web Company has employed you as a junior web developer. Your manager has asked you to review some websites to show that you understand the different ways in which organisations can use them. She also wants you to demonstrate that you understand the basic principles of the Web.

You can present your answers in a report or in a presentation.

1. Identify the key hardware and software components that support the Internet and the Web. **P1**
2. Describe the roles played by ISPs, web hosting companies and domain name registrars in the World Wide Web. **P2**
3. Explain a number of different ways in which websites are used by organisations. Refer to your own research into the different uses of websites. **P3**

Grading tips

- For question 1 you need to remember that many devices are involved in even the simplest process on the Internet.

- For question 2 you can do some research online into well known ISPs and other organisations.

- For question 3 you should include annotated screenshots to illustrate all the points you make.

Just checking

1. What is e-commerce?
2. Give the domain names of two e-commerce websites.
3. What is the difference between the Internet and an intranet?
4. Explain how an organisation can use an intranet for training.

3. Be able to design website components

3.1 Design

Websites should always be designed before they are created. It may be tempting to get started on the creation of a site straightaway, but changes to the fundamental design can result in many hours of extra work. This can be avoided if the design is sorted out first.

If you are creating a website for a client you will need to discuss their requirements with them. For assessment purposes you will be asked to show that you can develop some of the components of a website to meet a particular purpose. You need to set out the requirements of the client (real or imaginary) before you begin. At the end of your project you should review your website by comparing it with the initial requirements.

Activity: Isle of Keiss tourist information website

In this unit we will be designing and creating a website for a fictional Tourist Office. The Isle of Keiss is an imaginary island off the west coast of Scotland. It is well known for its superb beaches and many craft workshops. The Tourist Office is very small and is largely run by volunteers.

We will be designing a website which, in the first instance, will have four pages. More pages may be added later. The initial pages will be:

- the index (or home) page, which will be a graphical welcome page
- a page describing things to see and do on the Isle of Keiss
- a page listing craft workshops on the island
- a page with information about how to contact the tourist office.

Tools

A number of tools are used at the design stage, including storyboards and prototypes.

Storyboards

A storyboard is a series of pictures of what the site will look like. It is usually sketched by hand on paper. The storyboard should indicate:

- the layout of the home page and other pages
- links on the main navigation bar
- use of colour for background and text
- use of images for information and decoration.

The storyboard should be reviewed with the client to make sure that it matches what they need. This discussion will often highlight things that were either forgotten or not clearly described in earlier discussions. At this stage, the client will often be inspired with new ideas for the site and these can also be included. An example storyboard is shown in Figure 17.2.

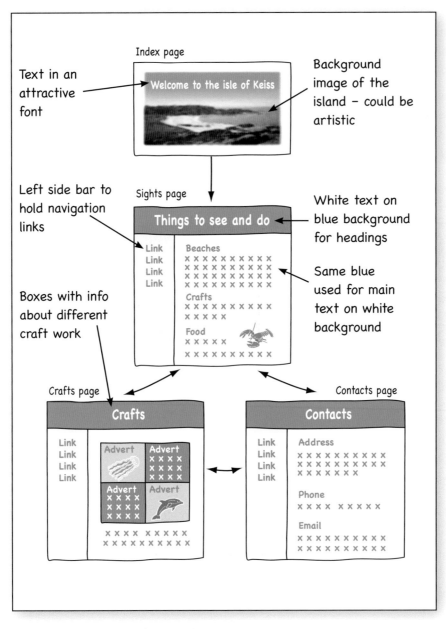

Figure 17.2: A sketched storyboard for the Isle of Keiss website.

Sample pages

A prototype is a set of sample pages from the site which can be used to check whether the design works and the client likes it. The prototype will normally consist of the home page plus a small number of other key pages.

Once the client has agreed on the prototype, the remaining pages can then be created in full.

House style

Most organisations have rules about how their communications should look. They may specify:

- a logo to be used on all letters, leaflets and adverts
- the position and size of the logo
- colours for background, text and highlights
- font styles and font sizes
- where items of text should be placed, for example, in a letter, where the date should appear
- level of language
- designs of signs placed on buildings
- styles used within a shop, such as designs of carrier bags, direction signs and display cards.

All this, taken together, is known as the house style for that organisation.

A house style helps to create an impression of the organisation, known as the corporate image. For example, an organisation may want to appear professional, technical, environmentally friendly, family orientated, international, local, approachable, efficient, etc.

Activity: House styles

Visit the websites of some well known shops. Have they successfully used a house style on the website that matches the one used in the shops?

3.2 Construction features

It is very unusual to find a web page that consists of just text and little else. Most web pages make use of features such as images, hyperlinks, buttons and forms, and you will be learning how to create many of them in Section 4. In this section you will find out how they are used, so that you can decide whether to include them in the design of a website.

Frames

When you have visited websites you may have noticed that sometimes only a section of the page moves when you use the scroll bar. This happens when the page has been divided into two or more frames.

One of the frames may act as a header, and this will remain the same as other pages are downloaded. Alternatively, a side frame may hold the main navigation links, and this too will remain static as pages are selected (see Figure 17.3).

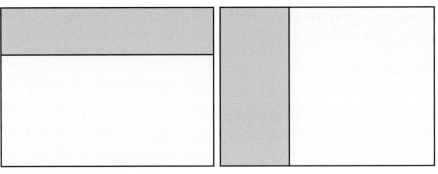

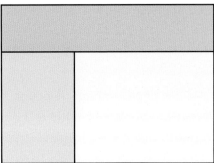

Figure 17.3: Three possible frame layouts.

Templates

A template is a page design that can be used over and over again as the basis for web pages. Many web authoring software packages, such as Adobe® Dreamweaver®, provide a selection of page templates that can be used to set up layouts and colour schemes for web pages.

Action buttons

A button is an image that represents an action. When you click on it with a mouse an action happens. On websites, the action is often to link you to another page.

Buttons can be used for other purposes as well, such as the 'Submit' button on an online form. This action button triggers off a small program, which makes sure that the information entered on the form is sent to the right place.

Hyperlinks

Hyperlinks are essential to any website. Not only do they link the pages of a website together, they also link each website to others, creating a vast interlinked source of information.

Text links

Any section of text can be used as a hyperlink to another web page. Originally text links were all identified by underlining. <u>Blue</u> was the traditional colour for a **link**, with a link that had already been visited changing to <u>purple</u>.

In fact, links don't have to be underlined and can be in any colour, but it should be clear to visitors that they are links. Usually a different colour from the main text is used, or all the links are placed together in a **navigation bar**.

Image links

Images can also be used as hyperlinks. Buttons are image-based links that look like the kind of buttons that you might press in the real world. But any image can be used as a link.

Internal links

Internal links allow the visitor to find their way around the site. Designers have to think about how the pages are related to each other and work out what pages a visitor might want to see next.

A site can use either, or both, of these linking styles:

- **Linking by structure**. A website may have a number of main sections. Links to the first page in each section should be provided in the main navigation bar. This bar should be visible on every page of the site. Each section may then have its own secondary navigation bar. Each page should always have a link back to the home page.

- **Linking by theme**. Not all sites can be as tightly structured as others. The Web allows visitors to browse to any page they like and in any order they like, so it is sometimes helpful to provide links to other pages that cover similar topics.

External links

One of the great advantages of the Web is that it allows websites to provide links to other related sites. External links help to join all the sites on the Web into one vast network.

Hotspots

A large image can be placed on a web page which has within it a number of spots that act as links. An image like this is known as an image map and the spots as hotspots. Hotspots can be used on geographical maps, but they can also be used as graphical navigation bars.

Activity: Hotspots on a map

Go to Google Maps and zoom in on an area near your home or place of study. Move your mouse over the map to find any hotspots and click on them to see additional information. In Google Maps hotspots are referred to as place markers.

Find out how to create your own maps in Google Maps by selecting My Maps. You can add your own place markers and then share your maps with other people.

Download speeds

You will have noticed that it takes much longer for some web pages to download than others. These factors can affect download speeds, in order of significance.

- **The speed of the Internet connection**. While most users in the UK have broadband connections, in some parts of the world very slow dial-up connections are still used. Broadband connections themselves vary considerably in speed from 1 Megabits per second to 24 Megabits per second.
- **The content of the web page**. Images in particular can use a great deal of memory so can take a noticeable time to download.
- **The browser**. Browsers interpret the HTML and other instructions in a web page, and some take slightly longer than others to do this.

Size of images

When we use a computer image we can refer to its size in two senses.

- **The memory needed to store the image**. Most computer graphics use a very large amount of memory. For example, a photograph taken with a digital camera will be 2MB or more.
- **The dimensions of the image measured in pixels**. Images are composed of many tiny spots of colour known as pixels. The width and height of an image are measured in pixels. When you create an image for a web page, you must make it exactly the right size for the space it is going to occupy. This ensures that it has no more pixels than it really needs.

Because of the size problems, images used on websites are stored in one of these compressed formats:

- **jpg** – used mainly for photos and to give photorealistic quality
- **gif** – used for most other images, but limited to 256 different colours
- **png** – a new format, which is gradually replacing gif.

The gif format usually takes up far less memory than the jpg or png formats.

Compression significantly reduces the amount of memory needed to store an image of given dimensions.

You can check the size of an image on a web page by right-clicking on it and selecting Properties. Figure 17.4 shows the properties of an image that has been saved in compressed jpg format. The memory required is 28,406 bytes (around 26KB) and the dimensions are 617 pixels wide by 500 pixels high.

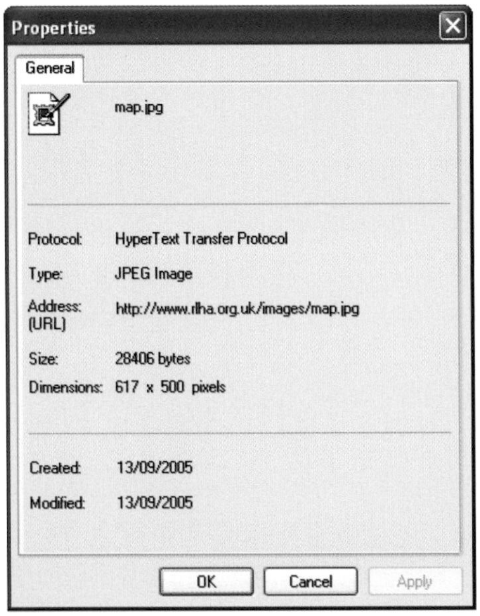

Properties

General

map.jpg

Protocol:	HyperText Transfer Protocol
Type:	JPEG Image
Address: (URL)	http://www.rlha.org.uk/images/map.jpg
Size:	28406 bytes
Dimensions:	617 x 500 pixels
Created:	13/09/2005
Modified:	13/09/2005

OK   Cancel   Apply

Figure 17.4: The properties of an image on a web page.

Interactive features

Email links

An email link enables the visitor to send an email directly to the organisation. When the visitor clicks on it, a New Message window is opened in the visitor's email client software, such as Microsoft® Outlook®.

Registration login

A number of sites ask the visitor to sign in before they can access some pages on the site. On an e-commerce site, the organisation will need the name and address of the visitor if they choose to make a purchase. On other sites, the pages can be personalised to suit the visitor's interests. If a site encourages contributions from visitors in a discussion forum or chat room, then they need to identify the visitor. (Visitors can be barred if they make unsuitable contributions.)

In all cases, personal data should be transmitted securely, which usually means that the data has to be encrypted (i.e. turned into a secret code).

3.3. Interactivity

One of the advantages of websites over many other forms of communication lies in their interactivity. Visitors do not simply look and read, but also respond in some way to the content.

User input

The visitor can interact with a website using the keyboard or the mouse. Interactive actions that visitors can do include:

- select the pages they want to view, using the navigation links or a search tool
- log in to access extra features
- enter information in a form
- select and purchase goods
- send an email
- post a comment to an online forum, social networking site, blog or chat room
- answer a quiz or survey
- play a game
- personalise a web page.

Forms

Many websites encourage visitors to leave information on an online form. Several different types of response boxes can be used on a form:

- text field – this can hold a single line of text
- text area – this can hold longer pieces of text
- radio buttons – the visitor can select one from a number of choices

- check boxes – the visitor can select as many as they like from a number of choices
- select fields – the visitor can select from a drop-down list of options.

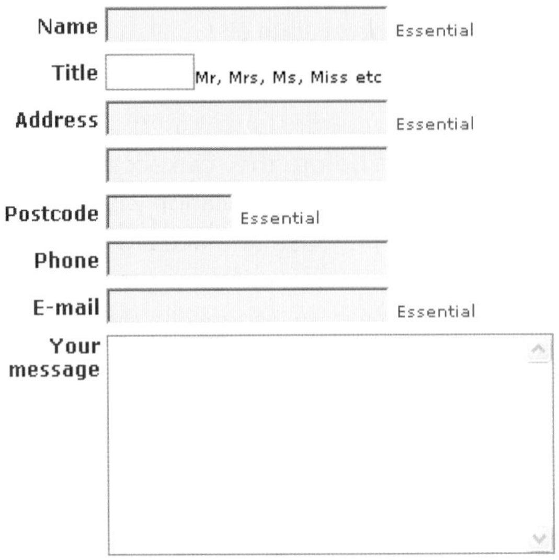

Figure 17.5: A form on a website.

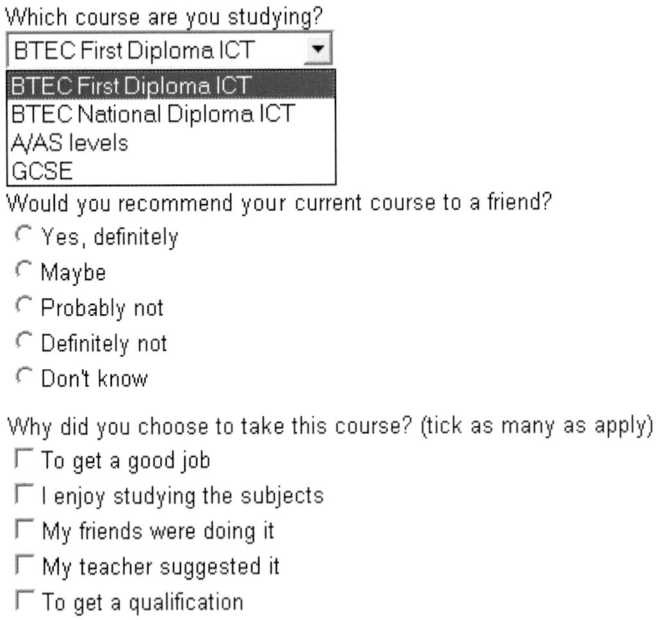

Figure 17.6: Select fields, radio buttons and check boxes on a survey form.

At the end of the form there will be an action button, often labelled 'Submit'. The coding for this button carries out the next action, which may store the data in a database or convert it into an email.

3.4 Client need

Before a web designer begins to design a website for a client, they have to ask a number of questions, in particular:

- What is the purpose of the site? For example, a website for a fan club will be very different from one for a company selling computer supplies.
- Who is the target audience? This is the group of people that the organisation wants to communicate with through the website.

You can ask the same questions about any site you visit. You can judge whether the designer has made sensible decisions about the content and layout of a site. You will then be in a position to form a judgement about the quality of the site and how it could be improved.

Target audience

A web designer needs to know whether the site is aimed at the world in general or at a specific section of the population, such as young people, car owners, parents, football supporters, women, members of a particular religion or residents in a particular town. Most sites are built with a typical visitor in mind.

Here are some questions that you can ask about a website, to help you judge whether it is right for its target audience:

- does the home page give a good idea of what the site contains
- is the home page informative and interesting
- does the site provide the expected information
- is there too much information or too little (The right amount will depend on the purpose of the site.)
- is there basic information about the organisation, what it does and who the key people are
- does the site say how to contact the organisation (This information should always be provided.)
- does the site allow a visitor to contact the organisation directly, for example using an online form or an email address
- is there a privacy policy (This is a statement about how the organisation will handle any information given to them by a visitor. It is necessary to comply with the Data Protection Act (1998) and to give the visitor the confidence to do business with the organisation.)
- is the site kept up to date? (Sites should be maintained as frequently as appropriate; for example, a news site will be updated every day, while a site that gives advice on buying a kitchen freezer needs to be updated only when new freezers come on to the market.)

User need

Visitors to a site will stay on the site only if they find it easy to use. A web designer needs to think carefully about how the pages are designed, how quickly they download and how they are linked together.

Navigation

Navigation refers to the way visitors find their way around a site, using links provided on the pages. Some of the most important links may be positioned together in a navigation bar. Here are some questions to consider.

- Is it easy for a visitor to find their way around the site? The main navigation bar is often along the top of the screen or down the left-hand side.

- Are the methods of navigation consistent? The navigation bar should be in the same position on each page, and the colours and images used should be consistent throughout the site.

- Can visitors find most of the information they want with no more than three mouse clicks? The 'three click rule' should apply to almost all information because visitors leave a site if they cannot find information quickly.

- Does the site offer a search box? A visitor can enter a key word in a search box and a list of possible pages will be displayed.

- Does the site offer a site map? A site map is a diagram that shows how the pages link together.

Activity: Site maps on websites

NHS Direct provides a site map for visitors. This is a separate web page laid out as shown in Figure 17.7.

- Have you seen site maps on other websites? Do they help the visitor?

SiteMap

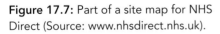

NHS Direct - We're Here Whenever You Need Health Advice & Information

Check your symptoms

Find Your Nearest

Send us a health enquiry

Find your nearest A and E

SiteMap

About NHS Direct

What is NHS Direct?

Core Standards Declaration

History

NHS Direct board

Chair and Chief executive

Executive directors

Non-executive directors

Board meetings

Using the online services

Figure 17.7: Part of a site map for NHS Direct (Source: www.nhsdirect.nhs.uk).

Fast download speeds

Visitors will leave a site if they have to wait too long for a page to download. Although many people now use fast broadband connections, the web designer always has to remember the people using the oldest equipment and dial-up modems. The following questions should be asked with the slowest connection in mind:

- Do pages download quickly? A page should normally download in less than a minute on the slowest communication channel at the busiest time of day.

- Are visitors warned in advance if a page is likely to take some time to download? Visitors may want to view pages with high quality photos, or to download a file in a graphical format like pdf; in these cases they should be warned about the size of the download before requesting it.

Suitability of language

The language used on a website should be clear, simple and straightforward. It is more difficult to read text on-screen than when it is printed out, so, generally speaking, sentences should be short and uncomplicated. But some websites provide links to formal documents, which may contain technical information, legal detail and much longer passages of text. You should ask:

- does the site use language that is appropriate to the subject matter and for the target audience (Business sites tend to use more formal language than sites devoted to leisure interests; the age of expected visitors is also relevant.)

- does the site use technical or specialist terms? (If so, would they be understood by the target audience?)

Choice of images

Images give life to a website, but using them effectively is quite an art. Too many images can confuse the user, so the designer needs to be clear about why they are being used.

- Do images convey additional information? Images, such as photos or drawings, often give information.

- Do images enhance the impact of the site? Some images are used as decoration and to create a mood or style.

- Are the images appropriate for the site? The purpose and audience must not be forgotten.

- Do images have alternative text? Alternative text is the short text description that pops up when you pass the mouse over an image. It should be provided to support users of non-standard browsers and visitors with visual impairment.

- Do Adobe® Flash®, video or other animations add to the quality of the site? For example, lengthy introductions can be irritating.

Appropriate formats

The visual appearance of a site should match the purpose and target audience.

- What impression is the site trying to give to visitors? It could be business-like, friendly, busy, formal or casual.

- Is the text easy to read on-screen? Short paragraphs are easier to read than long ones. Text that spreads across a wide screen can be difficult to read.

- Can the text be downloaded or printed to be read offline?

- Is the text presented in a consistent style? Sites will probably use a number of different text styles, but they should be used consistently.

Layout

The components of a web page, such as blocks of text, images and navigation bars, can be laid out in many different ways. The choice of layout of pages should make the site easy to use.

- Are the most important items on the home page visible without scrolling? Important items should be towards the top of the page.
- Is the page laid out in columns? If not, is it easy to read text?
- Is the page still visible when the window is made smaller? Does the page expand when the window is enlarged?
- Is the layout consistent from page to page?

Colour

Colour should be used carefully – too many contrasting colours can be distracting, but too few can be dull.

- Does the site use an appropriate colour scheme? An organisation might have corporate colours or a set of colours might be chosen to convey an impression.
- Do the colours of the text and background make the text easy to read? Dark text on a light background is best.
- Have the needs of partially sighted users been considered, with good contrast between text and background?
- Is the site readable by someone with colour blindness? This is quite a technical matter, but in general, strong contrast helps. Information should not be conveyed simply by colour – the use of alternative text for images and links is helpful.
- Is the colour scheme used consistently?

Font

A wide range of fonts can be used in website graphics. Fonts that can be used for website text are more limited. Ask yourself:

- Are the fonts used on the site suitable for the target audience?
- Are the fonts suitable for the subject matter?
- Are the fonts readable by partially sighted and dyslexic users?

BTEC Assessment activity 17.2

The Blue Web Company has asked you to design a multiple page website to match the needs of a client. The requirements will either be given to you by your tutor, or alternatively you can discuss with your tutor the needs of a real client.

Task 1:

- Design your website using the tools given in this unit and to match the needs of your client. **P4**

Your employer wants to check that you understand the range of design features available and how they can aid access.

Task 2:

1. Explain how website designers can make it easy for users to access information. You can refer to any techniques that you have used in your own deisgn. **M1**

2. Select a website that uses a number of different design features. This could be a site you have developed or one that you have visited.

    Evaluate the design features used in the website such as frames, action buttons, hyperlinks, hotspots, email links and registration logins. **D1**

Grading tips

- For Task 1, sketch a storyboard and check it with your tutor or your client. Make notes on all the elements of the design, including the page layout, colours, font styles, images, logos, hyperlinks, action buttons.

- For Task 2, question 1, you should consider the needs of users with different types of visual impairment as well as able-bodied users.

- For questions 2 a) and b), you can use the websites that you discussed for Assessment activity 17.1.

- When you evaluate your own design for question 3, you should describe the features you have used, explain why you used them and how they help the user.

PLTS

By generating ideas and exploring possibilities when designing and creating website components to meet client needs, you will show that you are a **creative thinker**.

By asking questions when considering client's needs and adapting ideas as circumstances change you will show that you are a **creative thinker**.

By reaching agreements and managing discussions with clients to achieve results you will show that you are a **team worker**.

By analysing and evaluating different design features on a website, you will show that you are an **independent enquirer**

By explaining the techniques that web designers use to help users access information you will show that you are a **reflective learner.**

Functional skills

Outlining the production of a multi-page website, considering client needs, will provide evidence for your functional **ICT** skills in using ICT.

Just checking

1. List all the factors that affect how long it takes for an image on a website to download.
2. What is a storyboard? Why should you create and use one?
3. What is meant by a target audience?
4. Why do commercial companies want to keep a consistent house style for all their communications, including the website?
5. Give four situations where interactive features on a website can be of benefit to an organisation.

4. Be able to create website components

4.1 Web development software

This section introduces you to the general principles of constructing a website. These principles should be useful whichever software you are using. The case studies in this section provide a short tutorial in the use of Adobe® Dreamweaver®. If you are using a different package then you should check the Help file on your software or visit its associated website. There are also many tutorials available on the Web.

Web pages are created in the computing language HTML (which is short for Hypertext Mark-up Language. But you do not need to learn HTML in order to create a website.

Many websites are created using specialist web authoring software packages (see below). These let you create a web page in much the same way as you would create a document in a word-processing or desktop publishing package. The web authoring software then generates the HTML for you. You can look at the HTML code at any time, and change it or add to it directly.

HTML

> **Key term**
>
> **Source code** – the HTML program that makes up a web page file. A browser interprets the source code and presents it on-screen as a web page.

When you download a web page into a browser, the HTML code is transferred to your computer. This is referred to as the **source code**. HTML code is always stored and transmitted in a simple text (ASCII) file. It usually has a file name with .htm or .html as its file extension; for example, homepage.htm.

In Internet Explorer®, you can view the HTML of a web page by selecting **View** then **Source**. This usually opens up Notepad and displays the code. Notepad is a text editor, and is the simplest means of viewing and creating text files. If you use a different browser you should still be able to view the source code from the **View** menu.

If you scan through an HTML file, you will see references to other files that must be downloaded to complete the page. For example, you may see something like this:

```
<img src="http://www.example.com/cats.jpg" width=100
height=80 border=0 alt="Picture of cats">
```

This tells the browser that it needs to download the picture stored as cats.jpg from the site www.example.com.

You may also spot some links to other files that may be used, such as video or sound, or files that contain program code.

Filenames and file extensions

All web pages are saved with either .htm or .html as the filename extension.

The first page that a visitor to a website will go to is called index.htm or index.html. This is often known as the home page for the site. Sometimes it is best to create other pages before creating the index page.

Specialist software

There are a number of useful web authoring packages available, such as Microsoft® Expression® Web and Adobe® Dreamweaver®.

Web authoring packages will usually allow you to display the page in three views:

- **Design view** – this is the page editor
- **Code view** – this is the HTML editor
- **Live view** – this lets you check what the page will look like in a browser.

You can create web pages in a web authoring package in four different ways:

1. **Using templates.** Most web authoring software provides you with a selection of templates for creating the layout of individual pages. These are very useful. Some software also offers complete page designs, including colours and fonts. These can also be used, but you are advised to change them to make them your own.

2. **Using wizards.** You can use a number of wizards to create web pages. Most of these are useful. However, avoid wizards which create a complete website for you, as you will find them rather limiting. Websites produced in this way are difficult to modify and update, and they look very similar to each other. You may like to look at these wizards for ideas, but you are advised not to use them for your assessment tasks.

3. **Writing HTML code directly.** Professional web developers often work directly in HTML. This is recommended only if you already have considerable experience in web design.

4. **Using the design view.** This is by far the best tool for a beginner to use. You will start with a template and then add text, images and other features in much the same way as you would use presentation or desktop publishing software. As you develop your skills you will be able to read and edit the HTML that the software generates.

Embedded facility in other packages

You can find web templates and wizards in a number of Microsoft® products, such as Word® and Publisher®. You can also convert documents created in Adobe® PageMaker® into web pages. This is useful for creating quick pages, especially for creating sample pages to illustrate your initial ideas. However, you are advised not to use any of these methods for serious web development or for assessment on this course.

Other software used in web design

Some websites make very good use of animation in short movies. Animation can be used:

- as an introductory sequence
- as a short film to educate or demonstrate
- as a decorative feature.

Most website animations are developed in Adobe® Flash® or similar software. These software packages allow you to select images then move them around the screen and apply effects such as fading.

If you use an animation sequence as an introduction to the site, returning visitors may not want to watch it again. They should have the option to skip the sequence.

Activity: Use of animation

Find a website that uses animation. Does it enhance the website or irritate the visitor? Look for good and bad examples of animation.

How to... Set up a website in Adobe® Dreamweaver®

You are going to create a tourist information website for a remote island off the north-west coast of Scotland, called the Isle of Keiss (see the Activity on page 279).

- Launch Dreamweaver®. In the opening screen, under **Create New**, select **Dreamweaver Site**, as shown in Figure 17.8.

You will be asked a number of questions about your site, as shown right. You may be told at your centre what you should enter. If not, then the following would be sensible choices for now:

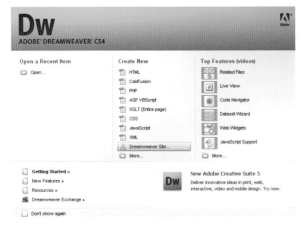

Figure 17.8: The opening screen in Dreamweaver®.

- **What would you like to name your site?** Enter *Keiss* (or your own choice).
- **What is the HTTP address (URL) of your site?** Leave this blank for now. Click **Next**.
- **Do you want to work with a server technology...?** Select **No**. Click **Next**.
- **How do you want to work with your files during development?** Select the first option.
- **Where on your computer do you want to store these files?** Either accept the suggested location or change it to another folder within **My Documents**.
- **How do you want to connect to your remote server?** Take advice from your tutor on this. If you are working on a home computer, select **FTP** and complete the connection details if you know them. Otherwise select **None**. (You can add these later if necessary.) Click **Next**.

When the dialog box closes you will notice the **Files** panel in the bottom left of the window (see Figure 17.9). This displays your site folder.

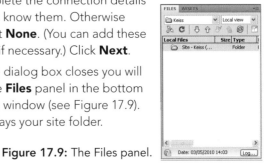

Figure 17.9: The Files panel.

Layout templates

You can choose a standard page layout from the layout templates provided in web authoring software. Some layouts have a header and footer. Some have equal columns or narrower sidebars.
Layouts can also be:

- **Fixed** — this means the page size is a fixed number of pixels in width, however big the browser window is. Fixed layouts are usually centred within the window.

- **Liquid** — in this case, the actual width of the page alters to fit the width of the browser window. This means that the length of the lines of text will vary depending on how wide the window is, so the appearance of a page changes.

How to... Create a page

We are going to develop a website based on the Activity on page 279. The website will have four pages:

- index.html
- sights.html
- crafts.html
- contacts.html.

You will create the index page last.

1. Go to the **File** menu and select **New**.

2. In the **New Document** window, from left to right, select **New Blank Page** then **HTML**. Now choose one of the layout templates. In Figure 17.10, the layout **2 column fixed, left sidebar, header and footer** has been selected. Click **Create**.

3. A new page opens up. You can replace all of the text in the right-hand column with your own. We will use the left sidebar for navigation links.

4. You create the page in **Design** view (see Figure 17.11) then you can check in the **Live** view to see what it will look like when displayed by a browser. At this stage the two views will look very similar, but you will notice the dotted lines that mark out areas in the **Design** view. Other differences will emerge as you use more advanced features. Notice that the text wraps at the end of lines, just as it does in a word processor.

5. The title of a page appears at the top of a browser window. You can enter your choice of title in the text box immediately above the **Design** view.

6. Go to **File** and **Save As** then save your file as *sights.html*.

7. Notice that the name of the web page now appears in the **Files** panel.

8. Notice, too, that a number of useful buttons have appeared in the **Insert** panel.

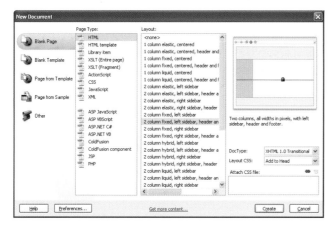

Figure 17.10: Selecting a page template.

Figure 17.11: Entering text in Design view in Dreamweaver®.

How to... Close and open a page

1. If you go to **File** and **Close**, the page you are working on closes. You will then be prompted to **Save** it. You will not exit Dreamweaver® until you select **Exit** from the **File** menu.
2. When you next launch Dreamweaver®, you should see your page listed under **Open a Recent Item**.

4.2 Format and edit web pages

Use of HTML

Web authoring software always includes an HTML code editor. You can switch between the page editor and the code editor at any time.

You can click on the Code button above the page window at any time to look at the HTML code. You are advised not to alter the code unless you are confident that you know what you are doing. Below is an extract from the HTML code for the page shown in Figure 17.11.

<h1> Beaches and more</h1>

<p>The island is well known for its golden beaches. You can spend many happy hours exploring small coves, wide open sands and the rocky shoreline. But there is much more to Keiss than sand and sea.</p>

<h2>Craft workshops </h2>

<p>Many artists and craft workers have been drawn to the simplicity of life on Keiss and its magical light. </p>

<p>Our world famous Keiss woollens are knitted from the fleeces of the sheep that graze across the island.</p>

<p>You can also visit silversmiths, fabric designers, painters and ironworkers. Drop by to look at their crafts – we are sure you will not come away empty-handed.</p>

Key term

Tag – an instruction set between triangular brackets in HTML.

The codes placed between triangular brackets are called **tags**. Tags are mark-up codes – that is, they are instructions to the browser about how the text and images should be displayed.

Tags are not case sensitive, so **<P>** and **<p>** are equivalent. Most tags come in pairs: the start tag and the end tag:

- **<p>** and **</p>** mark the beginning and end of a paragraph

- **<h1>**, **</h1>**, **<h2>** and **</h2>** mark the beginnings and ends of headings.

This is the overall structure of the HTML code on a web page:

```
<html>
<head>
</head>
<body>
</body>
</html>
```

The HTML code is divided into two sections. The head section holds information about the web page; lines placed between the head tags are hidden from the visitor, but contain information used by browsers and search engines. The body section holds the actual contents of the web page.

- **<html>** and **</html>** mark the beginning and end of the page
- **<head>** and **</head>** mark the beginning and end of the head section
- **<body>** and **</body>** mark the beginning and end of the body section.

Changing text styles

When you set up a page using a layout template, Dreamweaver® selects the overall fonts, font sizes and font colours on the page. This information is referred to as a style and is stored in the **<head>** section of the HTML code. You can change the page style without going into the HTML code yourself.

But a word of warning – a visitor's browser will only be able to display a font that is already installed on their computer. You may want to use an attractive but unusual font for a heading, but if the visitor does not have the required font installed, the browser will display the text in the default font for that browser (usually Times New Roman in Microsoft® Windows®). To begin with, you would be wise to stick to Times New Roman, Arial or another widely used font.

How to... Change text styles

- In the **Properties Inspector** panel at the bottom of the window, click on **Page Properties**.
- Under **Category** select **Appearance (CSS)**.
- For **Page font**, select a group of related fonts.
- For text **Size**, you can select both the size and the units. You could choose, for example, **80%**, **16pt** (standard point size) or **medium**.
- For **Text color**, click on the square icon to select from the colour picker.

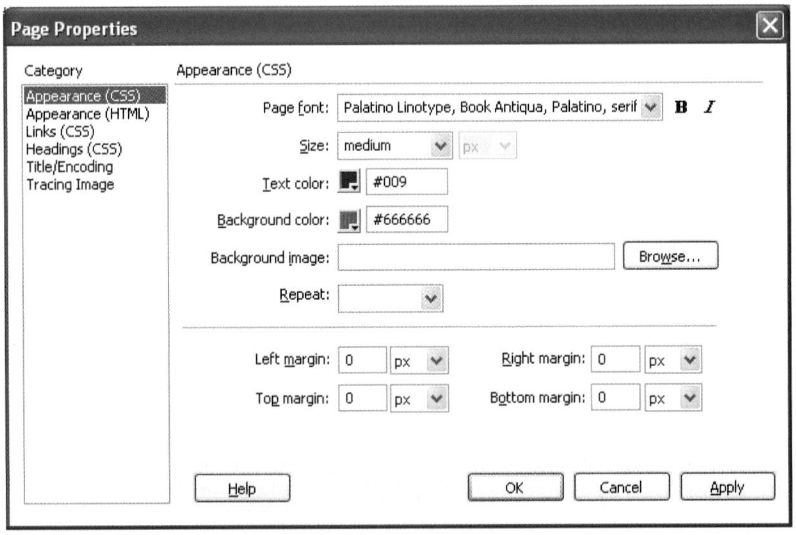

Page Properties

Category	Appearance (CSS)
Appearance (CSS) Appearance (HTML) Links (CSS) Headings (CSS) Title/Encoding Tracing Image	Page font: Palatino Linotype, Book Antiqua, Palatino, serif **B** _I_ Size: medium px Text color: #009 Background color: #666666 Background image: Browse... Repeat: Left margin: 0 px Right margin: 0 px Top margin: 0 px Bottom margin: 0 px Help OK Cancel Apply

Figure 17.12: Changing the font styles in Page Properties.

- To change the heading styles, select the **Headings (CSS)** option. Heading sizes vary from **h1** (largest) down to **h6** (smallest).
- For each heading style select its size and colour. Click **OK**.
- When you key in normal text it will appear in the new text style.
- To apply a heading style, first highlight the text you want to turn into a heading. Go to the **Format** menu and select **Paragraph Format**, then select from **h1** to **h6**.

Formatting small sections of text

You can also format individual paragraphs and lines of text by selecting from the usual options. These leave the overall page styles unchanged but enable you to change the appearance of a few words or sentences.

How to... Use text formatting options

- Highlight the text that you want to format.

- To align text to the left, right or centre, go to the **Format** menu, select **Align** then choose your option.

- To choose a font style, such as bold or italic, go to the **Format** menu, select **Style** then make your choice.

- You can also choose a font colour or alternative groups of fonts in the **Format** menu. Only use this method for small areas of text.

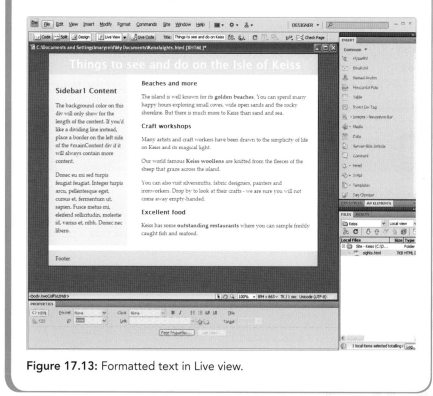

Figure 17.13: Formatted text in Live view.

Below are some extracts from the HTML code for the page shown in Figure 17.13.

```
<h1 align="center">Things to see and do on the Isle of
Keiss</h1>
```

```
<p>Keiss has some <strong>outstanding restaurants</
strong> where you can sample freshly caught fish and
seafood.</p>
```

- **align="center"** is an attribute of the heading, and centres it within its space. Note the American spelling of center.

- **** and **** mark the beginning and end of bold text.

The Live view in Dreamweaver® lets you check how the page will appear eventually. But it is always useful to view it in a browser, to see it as a visitor would see it. To do this, save the page then select **Preview in Browser** from the **File** menu. Select the browser that is installed on your system.

Using graphics

The term graphics covers any kind of image such as photos, drawings or clip art. It also includes lines, borders and backgrounds.

These should all be used with care. It is very easy to be carried away and insert too many graphics. The look and feel of a web page should be thought through carefully at the design stage.

We will look at lines and background colours now, and explore images later.

Lines

You can add a horizontal line to the page, usually using the **Insert** menu on the web authoring package.

How to... Add lines

- In **Design** view, click on the page at the spot where you would like to place a horizontal line.
- In the **Insert** panel on the right, click on **Horizontal rule**. This inserts a narrow dark grey line on the page (see Figure 17.14).

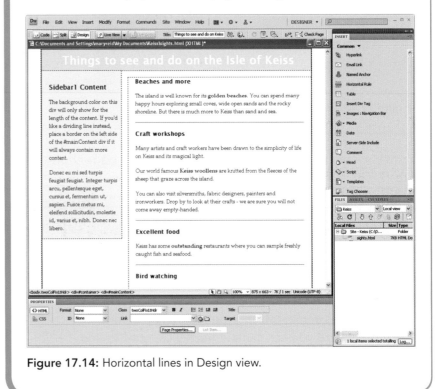

Figure 17.14: Horizontal lines in Design view.

Backgrounds

The whole page has a background colour which can be seen to the sides and below the main text. This may not be visible if you have chosen a liquid page layout.

The colour of the background is part of the style allocated by the layout template, and it can be changed. Most web authoring packages offer a palette of colours.

How to... Change the background colour

- Click on **Page Properties** in the **Properties inspector** panel.
- Under **Appearance (CSS)** you can use the colour picker to change the colour of the background.

You can also change the background colour of specific areas in the layout, such as the header, sidebar or footer.

How to... Change the background colour of an area on a page

You can also change the background colour of the sidebar.

- Move your mouse over the edge of the sidebar area. When the boundary becomes red, click to select it. The boundary will change to blue, as in Figure 17.15.
- In the **Properties inspector** at the bottom of the window, click on **Edit CSS**.

- You should now be able to see the **CSS Styles** panel to the right of the screen. This shows all the styles that apply to the sidebar.
- In the **CSS Styles** panel, double click on **Background-color**. This brings up the **CSS Rule Definition** dialog box. You can now use the colour picker to change the background colour, as shown in Figure 17.16.

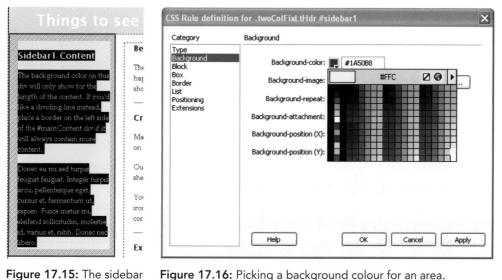

Figure 17.15: The sidebar has been selected.

Figure 17.16: Picking a background colour for an area.

Creating a new page

You will want to use the same styles on all the pages on the website. There are many advanced techniques for doing this, but the simplest method at this stage is to make a copy of your existing page then input the changes you need to create a new page.

How to... Create a new page in the website

You will now set up the *contacts.html* page.

- **Open** the *sights.html* page in **Design view**.
- In the **File** menu, select **Save As**. **Save** the page as *contacts.html*.
- Replace the existing heading with a new one. Add some suitable text. The contacts page should list the name, address and phone number of the tourist office. Once again, do not write in the sidebar yet.
- **Save** the page. You will be using this new page shortly.

Hyperlinks

Hyperlinks can be used to link to:

- another website
- another page on the same website
- another position on the same page.

All web authoring packages allow you to convert text into a hyperlink. Usually the **Insert** or **Format** menu includes a hyperlink item which opens up a dialog box. You can also create links with images.

External links

Links to other sites can be added to any web page. In order to make a link to an external site you need to know the full web address, e.g. http://www.rspb.org.uk/.

How to... Add external hyperlinks

- Open the *sights.html* page by clicking on it in the **Files** panel. You can have more than one page open at the same time. Make sure that you are in **Design** view.
- Highlight the text that you want to turn into a hyperlink.
- In the **Insert** panel click on **Hyperlink**.
- In the dialog box, enter the full web address in the **Link** text box.
- In the **Target text** box, select **_blank** if you want the external site to open in a new browser window, otherwise leave blank.
- Enter the name of the website in the **Title** text box. Click **OK**.
- The text you highlighted will now be underlined to show that it is a link.

Bird watching

With many rare species visiting our island, this is a bird watcher's paradise. You can spot Arctic skuas, puffins and osprey.

The Royal Society for the Protection of Birds has a number of sites on the island with hides and information.

Hyperlink		
Text:	Society for the Protection of Birds	OK
Link:	http://www.rspb.org.uk/	Cancel
Target:		Help
Title:	Society for the Protection of Birds	
Access key:		
Tab index:		

Figure 17.17: Setting up a hyperlink.

Email links

A hyperlink can also be used to send an email (see Figure 17.18). When an email link is clicked, a **New Message** window opens in the visitor's email client software, with the email address in the recipient field.

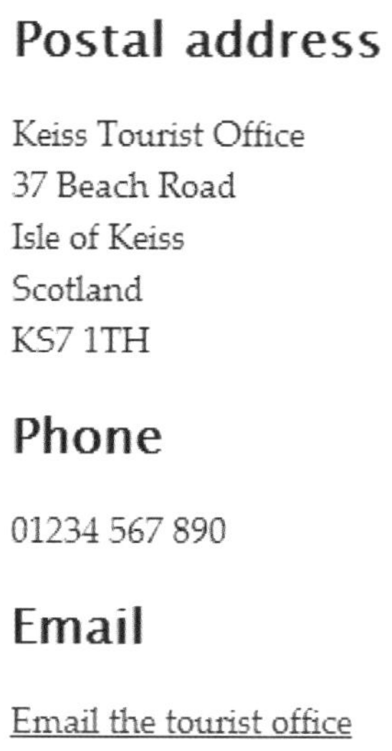

How to... Add an email link

- If the *contacts.html* page is not open, then open the contacts page by clicking on the **Files** panel.
- Enter some suitable text, such as *Email the tourist office*.
- Highlight the text.
- In the **Insert** panel, click on **Email link.**
- In the **Email** text box, enter the email address.

When a visitor clicks on this link a new message window will open up in their email software.

Postal address

Keiss Tourist Office
37 Beach Road
Isle of Keiss
Scotland
KS7 1TH

Phone

01234 567 890

Email

Email the tourist office

Figure 17.18: An email link.

Navigation links

It is important that all the pages are linked together in some way. In a small website this usually means that each page is linked from each of the others. In a larger site you have to adopt one or other of the linking styles that were discussed on page 282–283.

It is not necessary to give the full URL for a page on the same website. If the page is stored in the same folder then it is enough to give the filename, for example *contact.html*.

How to... Add navigation links

- **Open** the *sights.html* page in **Design** view.
- Delete the text in the sidebar and add the names of the two existing pages – *Things to see and do* and *Contact us*.
- You do not need to make a link to the page you are on (*Things to see and do*).
- Highlight *Contact us*.

- In the **Insert** panel, click on **Hyperlink**.
- In the **Hyperlink** dialog box, click on the folder icon to the right of the **Link** text box. Then click on the name of the page you want to link to. Click **OK**. (See Figures 17.19 and 17.20.)
- You should add similar links to the other page.

Figure 17.19: Creating a link to another page on the site.

Figure 17.20: The navigation links viewed in Live view.

Bookmarks

In a browser, a hyperlink can jump to an invisible spot, known as a bookmark, placed elsewhere on a page. Using a page editor, a bookmark can be set anywhere on a web page.

The text that is to become the hyperlink is then highlighted and formatted as a link to the bookmark.

How to... Create links to bookmarks

- On the *sights.html* page, add some more tourist information to the page, with <h2> headings for each topic.

- To insert a bookmark (also known as an anchor), click just to the left of the first heading to be bookmarked, which is *Beaches and more*. In the **Insert** panel, click on **Named Anchor**.

- In the dialog box, enter the name of the anchor – *beaches*. Anchor names should not contain spaces or punctuation.

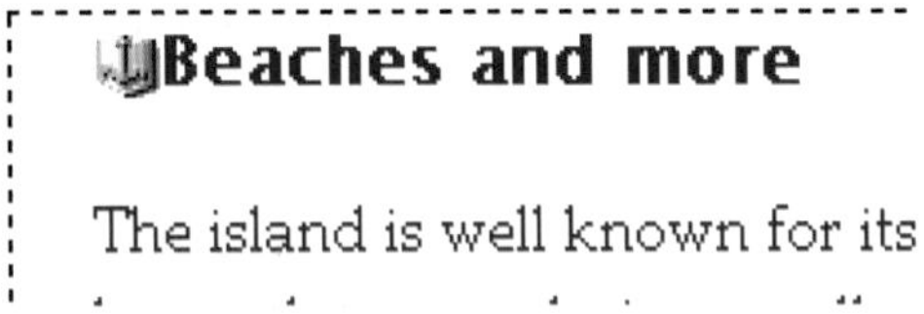

Beaches and more

The island is well known for its

Figure 17.21: An anchor (bookmark) in Design view.

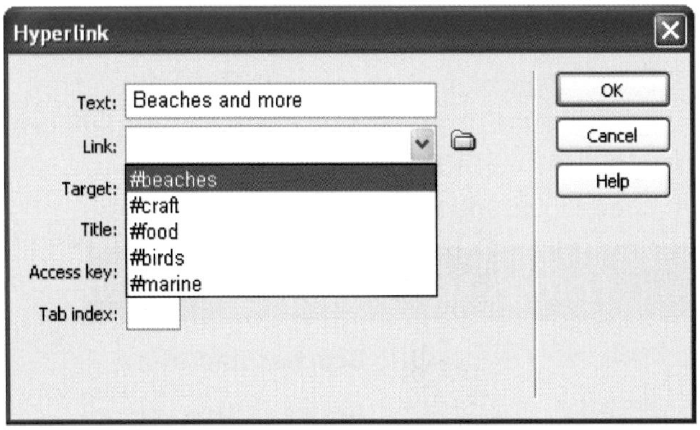

- In **Design** view a small anchor icon will be seen to the left of the heading, although it will be invisible in **Live** view (see Figure 17.21).

- Add bookmarks to each of the remaining headings.

- At the top of the main section of the page, write a new heading (e.g. *Find out more*) then list the topics on the page.

- Highlight the first topic. In the **Insert** panel click on **Hyperlink**.

- In the **Hyperlink** dialog box, click on the down arrow at the right end of the **Link** text box. You will see a drop-down list of all the bookmarks on the page (see Figure 17.22). Select the correct bookmark and click **OK**.

Figure 17.23 shows the bookmark links in **Live** view.

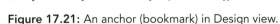

Figure 17.22: Selecting a bookmark.

Figure 17.23: Links to bookmarks in Live view.

Using images

Images on web pages, such as photos or clip art, are stored as independent files alongside the page files. This means that when a page is downloaded into a browser, the browser also has to download each of the image files from the server.

A web authoring package always provides a means of inserting images on a page, often from an **Insert** menu.

Images on a web page should be in jpg, png or gif format (see page 284). You should always create images that are the correct size and in the correct format by using graphics software such as Microsoft® Office® Picture Manager or Adobe® Photoshop®.

The size of images in given in pixels. You need to know the width of a page to understand how images will fit in (see page 284). The fixed layout that we have been using in the examples in this unit is 780 pixels wide. If you use an image that is wider than this then the page layout will be 'broken'. If the page is divided into columns, as ours is, then you should not use images wider than the column it sits in.

How to... Prepare a photo for use on a web page

- You should store photos in the **My Pictures** folder on your computer. You can create folders within the main **My Pictures** folder to keep your photos organised.

- To view all the photos in a folder as thumbnails, click on the **Views** button in the main toolbar and select **Thumbnails**.

- Right click on a photo, select **Open With** and then select **Microsoft Office Picture Manager**, which offers you all the basic photo manipulation tools.

- Click on **Edit Pictures** to view the **Edit Pictures** task pane. Select **Crop**. Cropping handles will appear.

Drag these to remove parts of the photo that you do not want (see Figure 17.24). Click **OK**.

- To change the stored size of the image, select **Resize** from the **Edit Pictures** task pane. Select **Percentage of original width x height**. Reduce the figure from 100%. Note the new size under the **Size Setting Summary** (see Figure 17.25). Click **OK**.

- Select **Save As** from the **File** menu and save the photo in the folder where you have stored your web pages. Use a simple filename, such as *shellfish.jpg*.

Figure 17.24: Using the cropping tool in Microsoft® Office® Picture Manager.

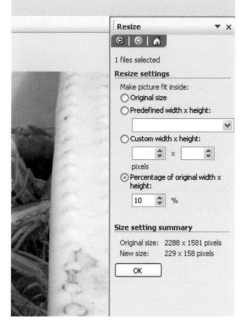

Figure 17.25: Resizing an image in Microsoft® Office® Picture Manager.

When you insert an image on to a web page, you will be asked to provide alternative text. This is displayed as a label when you pass your mouse over an image on a web page. Alternative text is particularly important for visually impaired visitors who use a screen reader. The text will be read out loud, which will give them some idea of what the image represents.

How to... Insert a photograph on a web page

To do this activity you need a photo that is in jpg format, and that has already been reduced to the right size for the page. It should be saved in the same folder as the web pages.

- **Open** the *sights.html* page in **Design** view.
- You should see the image file in the **Folder** panel. Click and drag it to the correct position on the web page.
- The **Image Accessibility** dialog box appears. Under **Alternative text**, type a few words that describe the image. Click **OK**.
- The image should appear in the correct place (see Figure 17.26).

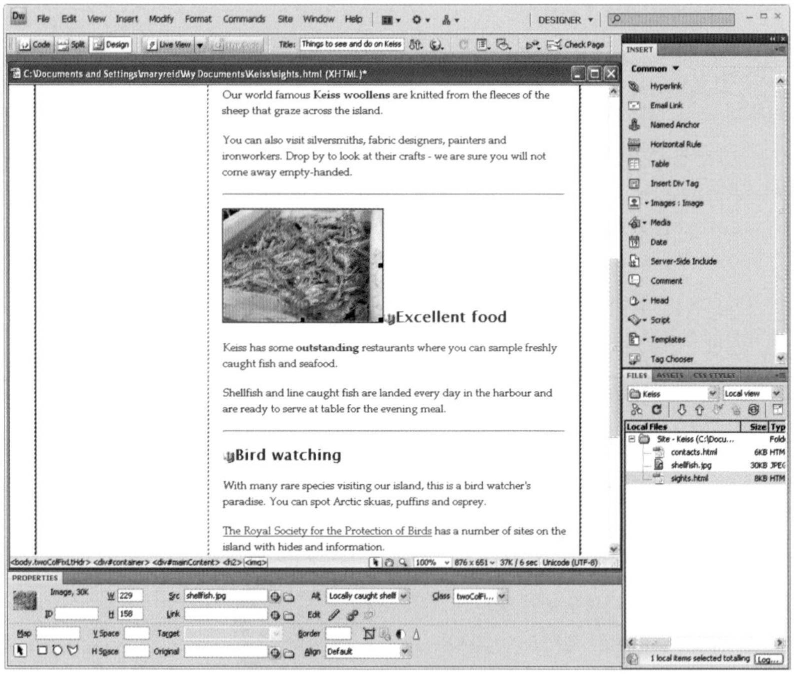

Figure 17.26: Inserting a photo on a web page.

Although most web authoring packages allow you to make an image larger or smaller, you are strongly advised not to manipulate images in this way.

If you make an image smaller in the web authoring software, the actual image file will not be changed. Instead, the browser will reduce the size of the image as it downloads it from the server. That will take extra time and make the download much slower.

If you try to enlarge an image in the web authoring software, it will distort the image and become 'jaggy'. You can, however, change some of the properties of pictures.

Picture properties

Every image on a web page has a number of properties. These include:

- alignment of the image (left or right)
- thickness of the border
- horizontal spacing around the image (to the sides)
- vertical spacing around the image (above and below).

The border and spacing properties are measured in pixels. Most web authoring packages provide a **Picture properties** (or **Image properties**) dialog box which allows you to change these values.

The width and height of the image are also properties. However, do not use the **Picture properties** dialog box to change the width or height properties of the image. This should only be done using graphics software as descirbed on page 309.

How to... Change the picture properties

- In **Design** view, click on the photo. The **Properties Inspector** panel will display the properties of the picture.
- In the **Border** text box, enter **2**.
- In the **Align** text box, select **Right**.
- The border will only be visible when you switch to **Live** view (see Figure 17.27).

ironworkers. Drop by to look at their crafts - we are sure you will not come away empty-handed.

Excellent food

Keiss has some **outstanding** restaurants where you can sample freshly caught fish and seafood.

Shellfish and line caught fish are landed every day in the harbour and are ready to serve at table for the evening meal.

Bird watching

Figure 17.27: The inserted image in Live view.

Tables

You can create tables on a web page, just as you can in a word processor. A table can be used for tabulation (to display data in boxes in the traditional way), but they are more commonly used on web pages as a method of arranging text and images on-screen.

Web authoring packages provide tools and wizards for creating tables, usually from a **Table** menu.

Tables have a number of properties:

- **width** — is the width of the complete table
- **border** — fixes the thickness in pixels of the border around all the cells
- **cellpadding** — fixes the space in pixels between the border and the text
- **cellspacing** — is the space between one cell in the table and the next.

To create an invisible structure for laying out items on a web page, give the border a value of zero – this will make the borders of all the cells disappear.

You can now create the *Craft workshops* page, which will hold information about a number of craft workshops on the island.

How to... Add a new page and update navigation links

- As before, go to **File** menu and select **Save As**. **Save** the page as *crafts.html.*
- Change the main heading to *Craft workshops.*
- In the sidebar, add navigation links to the three pages. **Open** each of the other two pages and add navigation links to the *crafts.html* page. **Save** all the pages.

How to... Create a table to display data

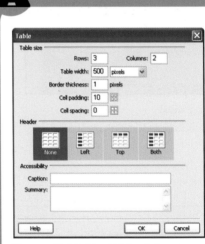

We are going to place information about a number of small crafts workshops in the cells of a table on the *crafts.html* page.

- Click on the page at the position you want to insert a table.
- Select **Table** on the **Insert** panel.
- In the **Table** dialog box, select the number of rows and columns that you require. In our case we want 3 rows and 2 columns (see Figure 17.28).

Figure 17.28: The Table dialog box.

- Choose the table width to fit into the space available. **500 pixels** will sit neatly into the wider column on the page.

- Select a border thickness of **1** or more.

- The cell padding is the space around the text within each cell. **10 pixels** is a sensible choice.

- Cell spacing is the gap between the cells. Enter **0**.

- Finally, you do not want any headers so select **None**. Click **OK**.

- An outline of a table is drawn on the page (see Figure 17.29). Don't worry that it is positioned lower down the page than expected. It will be correctly positioned in **Live** view.

Figure 17.29: An empty table.

- Enter some text in each cell. The cells will change in size to fit the text. You can also insert an image into a cell.

- Each cell has its own properties which will be listed in the **Properties Inspector** panel, in the **Cell** section. For example, you can choose a different background colour for each cell. Text and images can be aligned within each cell.

- Note that your choice of font and font size, etc., will apply to the whole page.

- **Save** the page and view it in **Live** view (see Figure 17.30).

Figure 17.30: A finished table in Live view.

4.3 Combining information

On a website, you can use information derived from a number of different sources.

Using a photo

You can either take a photo with a digital camera or scan in a photo print. Once you have transferred your photos to your PC, you can load them into a photo manipulation package, such as Microsoft® Office® Picture Manager or Adobe® Photoshop, where you can crop and resize them.

After cropping, resizing and enhancing the photo, save it as a jpg and select the level of compression that you want. A more compressed photo will take up less memory but will display less detail. Depending on the software package you are using, if you are asked to choose the quality, select 75%. If you are asked to specify the degree of compression, select 25%. These two choices have exactly the same effect.

Once you have saved a photo in a compressed jpg format, try not to compress it any further, as you are likely to lose some quality.

Other sources of images

There are many ways of finding or creating images to use on a website.

You can also obtain an image from the Web. You should never simply copy images from existing websites, as the images will probably be protected by copyright (see Unit 4, page 115). Fortunately, there are many sources of copyright-free web images online. In many cases the creators do ask you to acknowledge the source of any image you use.

Clip art is freely available on the Web. You will need to check that an image is in one of the web-friendly formats (jpg, gif or png) before you attempt to use it. Some clip art is designed for use in printed documents, not for websites. It is possible to use a graphics package to convert some formats into web formats.

Using an image created in an application package

You can use a simple package such as Microsoft® Paint, or a more sophisticated one such as Adobe® Illustrator®. You will probably be saving your image eventually in 256 colours as a gif, so you should use only the preset colours that are offered to you.

If you want to create a small image, it is sometimes helpful to design a larger image then reduce it in size. Once you have designed your image you should reduce the dimensions (number of pixels) to the exact ones needed on the web page.

How to... Create a small image for a web page in Microsoft® Paint

- Launch Paint.
- Select **Attributes** in the **Image** menu. Set the width and height at 100 pixels by 100 pixels.
- Draw a simple image, like the mobile phone shown in Figure 17.31.
- Select **Stretch** and **Skew** from the **Image** menu. Reduce both height and width to the same percentage, such as 50%.
- **Save** the image. In the **Save as Type** box, select **gif**.
- The image can now be used as a small icon.

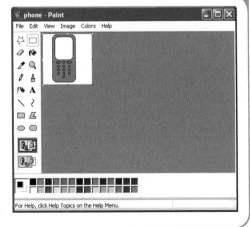

Figure 17.31: An image created in Microsoft® Paint.

Enhancing images

In a graphics package such as Adobe® Photoshop, you can add extra features to an image, for example text, borders, fading and cut-outs. Microsoft® Paint offers some limited features.

Most clip art, and many other images, have a white background, so the image can look very odd on pages with coloured backgrounds.

You can make the background of gif or png images transparent so that the background colour of the page shows through (see Figure 17.32). You can do this in most graphics packages that generate gifs or pngs, although you cannot create transparent backgrounds in Microsoft® Paint.

Animations

You can also create animations from still images using Adobe® Flash® or other flash software. This can be very effective but there are some things you need to consider:

- always add an option to skip a Flash® animation
- visitors must have the correct viewing software to view the animation
- visually impaired visitors will not be able to gain any information from a Flash® animation.

Figure 17.32: An image with and without a transparent background.

How to... Create a graphical index page

We will use a graphical image for the first page of the website.

- First, use a graphics package to create a suitable image. The maximum width of a fixed width page template in Dreamweaver® is 780 pixels. Allowing for a margin either side, your image should be no wider than 740 pixels.

- **Save** the image in **jpg**, **gif** or **png** format in the website folder. In our example, we have used Adobe® Photoshop to apply an artistic effect to a photo and to overlay some text.

- In Dreamweaver®, go to **File** then **New**. Select **Blank Page**, **HTML** and **one column fixed, centered**.

- **Save** the page as *index.html*. The first page of any website is always called index.

- **Delete** the text from the page. Drag your image from the **Files** panel into the page.

- You will be reminded to use alt text for the image to help visually impaired visitors.

- Click on the image.

- In the **Properties** panel, click on the folder icon to the right of the **Link** text box. Then click on *sights.html*. Click **OK**.

- When complete, **Save** the page then view it in **Live** view.

Figure 17.33: A graphical index page.

4.4 Checking your website components

You should always check a website, both before and after publishing it to the Web. Some things can only be checked when the site is online.

Both before and after publishing, check the web pages in a browser, not in the web authoring package that you have been using.

When you check a website you are making sure that it works technically as expected.

Images

- Check that each image takes up the amount of space you intended and is positioned correctly.
- Select the properties of each image to check how much memory each uses. Calculate the total memory used by all the images on each page. Aim to keep the total to under a few hundred KB per page.
- Check how long it takes to download each page, including all the images. If possible, carry out this test on a number of different computers and on both slow and fast broadband connections. This check can be carried out only after publishing.

Colours

- Check that the colours of text and images appear as intended. After publishing, you should check this on a number of different computers.
- Try looking at the site on older monitors as well as new ones, on a small laptop screen as well as a desktop. If possible, check on screens that have been set to different colour depths.

Links

- Check that all of the internal links on each of the pages load the correct pages.
- Check that any email links open a New Message window addressed to the right email address.
- Check that all external links go to the correct websites.

Content

- Check that the text is correctly spelled and is accurate.

Text

- Check that the text is the right size. You should check this on different browsers and on different sizes of screen.
- Check that you have used fonts that are widely available.

Formatting

- Check that the contents are laid out as expected in the browser.
- Drag on the corner of the browser window to change its size and check that the page still looks acceptable.

4.5 Publishing a website

Once you have checked your site, you will then want to publish (upload) it so that others can visit it.

Uploading files

You have two options:

- you could publish your website to the Web, in which case anyone in the world will be able to view it
- you could publish it to an intranet, which would restrict your visitors to those who have access.

When you upload a website you must transfer all the files and folders that you have created – as a minimum, all the pages and all the images.

Publishing to an intranet

Your network administrator will provide you with working space on the intranet, where you will be able to publish your site. You will also be given instructions on how to upload the pages to the site.

Publishing to the Web

In order to make your website available to everyone on the Web, you publish it to a web server. To do this you must have some web space available for your use on a web server. You will also be given a web address (URL) that identifies the web space.

If you are working on a network at your place of study then the network administrator will provide instructions on how to upload your site to the web server.

If you are working from a standalone computer at home, your Internet Service Provider (ISP) should be able to offer you web space on their web server.

Web authoring packages like Dreamweaver® include a publishing tool, which can be found in the File menu. The way this works will depend on the information you entered when you set up the site in the first place, but it will always need:

- domain name
- user name (as registered with the ISP)
- user password.

Maintaining content

Few websites are completely static. Most need to be updated from time to time. Sometimes the contents will have to be amended because the organisation wants to give new information to visitors. Often, new pages will be added and links created.

When a website is first developed, the question of maintenance must be discussed and planned. In some cases the website is maintained by the person who designed the website, but often another person is given the task. That person needs to be trained in the use of the software so they can make any updates as they are needed.

File management

Normally there will always be two copies of your website. One will be the working version on your computer and the other will be on the server where it will be accessible via the Internet or an intranet.

It is important that these two copies are identical. Usually the web authoring software checks for any differences between the two and uploads the latest version of pages. It will notice if files have been deleted or moved and will try to match the server version with the working version.

You can get into a muddle if you try to keep further copies of the site. This could happen if you want to work on your website from home as well as from your place of study.

Filenames and folder structure

You should give all web pages suitable filenames. Windows® allows lengthy file names, but the server may use a different operating system which may not accept longer filenames or names that include spaces or punctuation. Check this with your network administrator. It is good practice to use simple, short filenames without spaces or punctuation, as these will be acceptable on any server.

It is a good idea to use only lower case letters in a filename. Windows® is not case sensitive – in other words, it will recognise the filenames *MyFile.doc* and *myfile.doc* as the same file. But some operating systems on servers are case sensitive.

You can place web pages into folders (directories), and this is a sensible way of organising a large website.

Assessment activity 17.3

BTEC P5 P6 M2 M3

For this task you will create the web pages that you designed in Assessment activity 17.2.

1. Create your web pages using web authoring software. P5 P6 M3

2. Your boss at the Big Blue Web Company is checking that you understand interactivity on a website.

   a) Describe how websites are used.

   b) Describe the techniques that can be used to provide interactivity. M2

Grading tips

- For question 1, work carefully through the design. If you need to change any aspect of the design keep full notes on the reasons for the changes.

- For question 2, you should be able to write about interactivity even if you have not yet learned the techniques.

PLTS

You will show that you are a **creative thinker** by:

- generating ideas and exploring possibilities when designing and creating website components to meet client needs

- asking questions when considering client's needs and adapting ideas as circumstances change.

Functional skills

Creating a website using web development software will provide evidence for your functional **ICT** skills in using ICT (combine and present information in ways that are fit for purpose and audience).

4.6 Reviewing your website

When you have checked your website you should review it. This means that you should go back to the original requirements and check that it meets them. You should also note any features that go beyond the requirements.

You should ask three main questions:

- Is the website appropriate for its purpose and target audience?

- Are there any remaining problems? If your review indicates that there are still some problems, or elements missing, then you should list the problems and try to correct them.

- What improvements can be made to the website?

Finally, if you were working for a real client, you would ask them to review the website and give you some feedback. If you do not have a real client then ask someone to act as a user and give you feedback.

When reviewing a website that you have created, you should go back to the list of client needs and use them to check whether the website meets those needs. You can use the questions on pages 312–313 as a checklist.

PLTS

By supporting conclusions when explaining how a created website meets the defined requirements, you will show that you are an **independent enquirer**.

By identifying improvements when reviewing website components, you will show that you are an **effective participator**.

Functional skills

Reviewing a website that you have created will provide evidence for your functional **ICT** skills in using ICT.

BTEC Assessment activity 17.4 P7 M4 D2

1. Check carefully the web pages you created for Assessment activity 17.3, and give evidence of all the checks you have carried out. Review your web pages by comparing them with the client's needs and your original design. Suggest any improvements that could be made. **P7**

2. Ask your client to provide you with some feedback on the web pages you have created. If you have been working to a scenario, then ask your tutor to provide the feedback. Make some improvements to the website in the light of the feedback. **M4**

3. Explain how your website meets the original requirements. **D2**

Grading tips

- For question 1, you must provide evidence that your website works as intended and show that you have carried out a comprehensive set of checks on it.

- For questions 1 and 3, when you review your web pages you should compare the results with the original brief or the requirements given to you by the client.

- For question 2, make sure you include the evidence of the feedback.

- For question 2, make some improvements to the website so that it suits the client even better. It does not have to be perfect, but you should show that you have tried to match what the client wants.

Just checking

1. What is HTML?
2. List some wizards and templates that you have used when creating web pages.
3. What are bookmarks and how can they be used on a web page? Give an example.
4. List three different types of hyperlink that you can place on a web page.
5. What should you consider when preparing a photo for use on a web page?
6. What should you think about before copying an image from another website?

Charlotte Jones
Web Designer

I started designing websites while I was still at college. At first I just did simple sites for friends, but after a while a friend of my mother asked me to create a website for her dressmaking business. She actually paid me!

It just grew from there, so by the time I left college I was earning quite a bit. I decided to become self-employed as a Web Designer and eventually set up my own company. It was tough in the early days, and I did have to work part time in a shop to make enough money, but I am now designing full time.

Typical day

I have set up a small office in my flat, where I do all my web design work.

If someone contacts me about a new website, I always arrange a face-to-face meeting, which could be anywhere in the country. I like to travel to meet clients by train so I can work on my laptop while travelling. At the meeting I ask them lots of questions about why they want a website, what it should contain and what they want to achieve. We also discuss the look and feel of the website. I like to show them work that I have already done so they can get some ideas. I also sort out any technical issues, such as registering a domain and choosing a web host.

Back home I draw up a storyboard for my client and email it to them for comments. Once we have agreed on the basic structure I then create some prototype pages and upload them to a private web space. We chat about this and I make changes to the pages until they are happy.

All that takes a little time, but once the design has been agreed I can then finish the website.

I usually visit my client again at the end of the process to check that they are happy and to show them how to create and upload new pages to the site.

The best thing about the job

I really enjoy working on websites. New techniques are being introduced all the time, and there is always something to learn. I take pride in finding out what my clients want and creating a fantastic product for them.

I have made quite a bit of money over the last few years, and my expenses are quite low – just the computer system plus my travelling costs.

Think about it!

1. What have you learned in this unit that provides you with the background knowledge and skills used by a Web Designer?
2. What other skills would you need to do the job?

Just checking

1. Describe the main functions of an Internet Service Provider.
2. What do we mean by Web 2.0? Give examples of websites that make good use of Web 2.0 technology.
3. What is a prototype?
4. Why is navigation important on a website?
5. What should you think about when assessing the language used on a website?
6. How can you make a website more accessible for visitors with a visual impairment?
7. On a web page, what is meant by a style?
8. Explain how you can use a table to display text and images on a web page.
9. What checks should you carry out on the images on a web page before publishing it?

edexcel

Assignment tips

To work towards a distinction in this unit you will need to achieve all the pass, merit and distinction criteria in the unit and have evidence to show that you have achieved each one.

How do I prepare for the assignment activities?

• To learn and practise the skills that you will be assessed on, you should carry out all the activities in this unit yourself. You will also be given a chance in class to practise many of the techniques described in Section 17.4.

• You will find it helpful to keep detailed notes of any websites that you visit. Use the questions on pages 312–313 to help you to analyse the sites from the points of view of the organisation and of a visitor to the site.

How do I provide assessment evidence?

• All your evidence should be presented in one folder, which should have a front cover and a contents page. You should divide the evidence into four sections corresponding to the four tasks.

• Evidence can be in the form of a written report, supported by any combination of observation records, checklists, screenshots, photos, presentations and other documents that you have prepared.

23 Computer graphics

Computers can be at their most powerful and exciting when used with graphics. This unit explores how you can create still images using a computer system and change them in many ways to make them perfect for their intended use.

Digital cameras, scanners and other ways of bringing pictures into the computer are covered. You will be using this equipment yourself when studying for this unit, as well as for your assessments.

Computer graphics can be used to create diagrams for many requirements, such as a map of where a business is located or a diagram of how to operate a product. You will gain skills in the software and methods employed by professionals to create and change an image into exactly what's required.

As a future ICT professional, you will need to understand how the user requirements define what's wanted from computer graphics, as well as any limitations or constraints that you need to keep to, such as the exact size of an image. All graphics designers also have to understand and follow the laws and regulations that apply to using images.

But most of all, you should enjoy creating and combining graphics on a computer system to make great pictures. These have value in the business world when they meet the user's needs and are therefore exactly what is required.

Learning outcomes

After completing this unit you should:

1. know the hardware and software required to work with computer graphics
2. be able to create computer graphics to meet a user need
3. be able to use computer graphics to enhance a document.

Assessment and grading criteria

This table shows you what you must do in order to achieve a pass, merit or distinction grade, and where you can find activities in this book to help you.

To achieve a **pass** grade the evidence must show that you are able to:	To achieve a **merit** grade the evidence must show that, in addition to the pass criteria, you are able to:	To achieve a **distinction** grade the evidence must show that, in addition to the pass and merit criteria, you are able to:
P1 identify the hardware and software required to work with computer graphics **See Assessment activity 23.1 on page 338**	**M1** describe the features of different graphical hardware devices **See Assessment activity 23.1 on page 338**	
P2 state the functions of a defined graphics software package **See Assessment activity 23.1 on page 338**	**M2** describe the features of different graphics software packages **See Assessment activity 23.1 on page 338**	**D1** evaluate a graphics software package on its ability to create and edit computer graphics **See Assessment activity 23.1 on page 338**
P3 describe the differences between raster (bitmap) and vector graphics **See Assessment activity 23.2 on page 344**		
P4 use specialist hardware to acquire images for a defined purpose **See Assessment activity 23.4 on pages 355–356**	**M3** use graphics software to edit an image for a given purpose **See Assessment activity 23.4 on pages 355–356**	**D2** explain the impact that file format, compression techniques, image resolution and colour depth have on file size and image quality **See Assessment activity 23.4 on pages 355–356**
P5 create an original graphic for a defined user need using graphics software **See Assessment activity 23.3 on page 350**		
P6 use graphics to enhance a document incorporating acquired images and objects **See Assessment activity 23.4 on pages 355–356**		

How you will be assessed

This unit is internally assessed. You will provide a portfolio of evidence to show that you have achieved the learning outcomes. Your portfolio of evidence can be supplied in many formats including electronically as well as paper-based. The grading grid in the specification for this unit lists what you must do to obtain pass, merit and distinction grades. The Assessment activities in this unit will guide you through tasks that will help you to be successful in this unit.

Your tutor will tell you exactly what form your assessments will take, but you could be asked to produce:

- presentations
- written documents
- hard copies of computer graphics you have created.

Sagaal Abokor, a 16-year-old ICT Professional learner

This was an interesting unit, which introduced me to the world of graphics. In this unit I learned many life skills which will come in handy when I start work. Adobe® Photoshop® is an excellent program, but it was hard to learn and understand. I'm glad we kept at it because it can do so much.

The unit content helped me understand the hardware and software used in computer graphics. I bought a 12-megapixel digital camera, which I chose after we learned about them in class.

I really enjoyed the on-the-spot thinking we needed to put pictures together. It was good to be creative. I was really pleased with how I was able to bring Chris Brown and David Beckham into the same image.

My favourite piece was designing a landscape picture of Bristol. In this we used different views of our city and made them into one view for assessment.

My advice to you would be to get your head down, stay focused, listen and keep on top of your work.

Over to you

1. Sagaal likes Adobe® Photoshop®. Are there any other photo-editing programs you would recommend to her?
2. Sagaal found that knowledge from the unit helped her choose a digital camera. Do you think this unit could help you choose new hardware for yourself? If so, how could it help?
3. What graphics would you like to combine into one image?

1. Know the hardware and software required to work with computer graphics

Start up

Better than the real thing?

Everywhere that advertising is to be found – on billboards and TV, in magazines and newspapers, and at the cinema – you will see that it uses photographs and video to help promote products.

Photographic images used for advertising start with a professional photographer using a digital camera to snap an almost perfect view of the product. Often an attractive model poses with it to help grab your attention.

An ICT professional who specialises in computer graphics will then work on the photograph to make it look even better and more effective, using techniques such as enlarging the pupils in the model's eyes or adding a slight smile to the edges of the mouth and lips.

Can you find any examples of photographs in advertisements where you think techniques have been used to enhance the image?

1.1 Hardware

Let's start by looking at the hardware you will need to work with computer graphics.

You will need a computer system, as well as extra equipment for capturing images, storing them and manipulating them. You will also need a screen to view the images and a printer to produce hard copies.

- **Computer system.** This needs to be powerful enough to easily open large, complex pictures and quickly show any changes you make to these images. So you need to make sure that the computer's internal hardware components are fast and powerful.

- **File storage devices.** Most computer graphic professionals use the hard drive inside their computer or on the network server for saving their graphics. They also use other file storage devices for moving their images to other places, such as pen drives.

- **Input devices.** A range of input devices, including digital cameras, are used to capture images. As an ICT professional you need to have an appreciation of the range of input devices that could be used, including scanners and graphic tablets. You also need an understanding of how the technical specification can affect the quality of the image and therefore the usefulness of the device.

- **Output devices.** You will need output devices such as a screen and a printer, so you can see exactly what the finished graphics will look like.

Internal hardware devices

Internal hardware devices are the components inside a computer system unit, the main part of any computer system. They are very important – if they are not powerful enough, the computer will run slowly. As a result, you won't want to do much with your graphics because you'll be wasting too much of your time waiting for the changes you make to show on-screen. But get them right, and your computer will be a joy to use.

The most relevant internal hardware devices for working with computer graphics are:

- **graphics card** – to create the screen display
- **RAM** – to hold running software and data
- **processor** (CPU) – to run the software
- **hard disk** – as main storage for software and data.

We'll look at each of these in turn.

Graphics cards

Every computer has graphics circuits needed to make the screen display work. Cheaper computers have these graphics circuits built into the **motherboard**. This is called on-board graphics and is usually a bad choice if you want a powerful computer system.

On-board graphics are hardly ever as good as those produced by a graphics card. For this reason almost every powerful computer system has a graphics card and not on-board graphics. The graphics card has a massive effect on the performance of a computer for games and for creating and editing computer graphics.

The type of socket the graphics card plugs into on the motherboard is important, as a faster socket means faster graphics. Older motherboards used AGP (Advanced Graphics Port). Recent motherboards use a faster version of **PCI** sockets, called **PCIe** (express), for the graphics card. PCIe is a newer and better socket than AGP.

Often the specification has a number next to the type of socket, for example PCIe x16. This shows how many times faster the socket is compared to the original version. So a PCIe x16 socket is better than a PCIe x8 socket and runs 16 times faster than the original PCIe socket.

There are two main manufacturers of graphics cards: ATI and NVIDIA. Both these manufacturers produce a wide range of products, so it takes research to find out whether one graphics card is better than another.

The graphics card produces the signal for the screen, so it's important to make sure the output from the graphics card matches the screen **resolution** for the best possible display. The screen resolution is the

(i) Did you know?

Good hardware always helps, but remember – the finest graphics designers are artists who know how to get the best from whatever computer system they are using.

Key terms

RAM (random access memory) – electronic memory inside a computer. As it has no moving parts, it is very fast, working at the speed of electricity. RAM is used to hold programs and data when a computer is running, usually copying them from the hard disk. Anything in RAM is lost when the power goes, so data needs to be saved to hard disk or other storage before the computer is switched off.

Motherboard – the main circuit board inside a computer. Most components, including the processor, RAM and hard disk, plug into the motherboard.

PCI (peripheral component interconnect) – a type of socket found on many motherboards where network cards or similar can be plugged in.

PCIe (peripheral component interconnect express) – a development of the PCI socket found on most modern motherboards. This is where the graphics card can be plugged in.

Resolution – the number of pixels per inch on a screen or other graphical device. High resolution means there are a lot of pixels in every inch and so a lot of detail in the image. Low resolution means that the image quality is poor.

Key terms

Pixel (picture element) – the name given to each dot of colour on a screen used to display images.

Gigabyte (GB) – 1GB is a large number which is roughly 1,000,000,000 (a thousand million) bytes. A byte is a small amount of space in RAM or on a hard drive, large enough to hold a letter such as A or C. Four bytes could be used for the colour in a single pixel.

number of **pixels** (dots) across the display followed by the number of pixels down. A resolution of 1920x1200 uses 1920 pixels across the screen and 1200 down.

Every graphics card uses memory (RAM) to build the picture seen on your display. Lots of memory is good in a graphics card. Most graphics professionals would expect 512MB or more on their graphics card.

The graphics RAM is usually part of the graphics card. A computer also has a different set of RAM plugged into the motherboard for main memory.

RAM

Every computer graphics professional knows that lots of RAM is a good thing. High-quality graphical images, along with several modern applications running at the same time, take up a lot of space in RAM, so the more RAM the better.

You would expect a computer used for graphics to have a minimum of 2 **gigabytes** (2GB) of main memory RAM, and probably a lot more than that – perhaps 4GB or more. Remember, you cannot have too much RAM in a computer!

Processor

The processor or CPU (central processing unit) is the brain of the computer. This is a chip that plugs into the motherboard.

A fast, powerful processor will run the software quickly, as well as being efficient at other tasks, such as changing parts of an image or converting between file formats.

1600 pixels

1200 pixels

Figure 23.1: Images on the screen and printouts are made from pixels.

There are two main manufacturers of processors: AMD and Intel. Both manufacturers produce a wide range of products, so it takes research to find out whether one processor is better than another.

There are two main parts of the specification of a processor that have the most effect on performance.

- **Speed** — the speed is usually measured in **gigahertz** (GHz), although some older processor speeds are measured in **megahertz** (MHz). As 1GHz is a thousand times faster than 1MHz, it is almost certain that a processor specification using MHz will not be as good as one using GHz.

- **Processor design** — the processor design has a large impact on how well it works. Processor design is being improved all the time, so it usually needs research to find out how good a design is.

   Many processors have a single, duo (dual) or quad core, which tells you the number of processor circuits on the chip. A quad core has four, a duo core has two and a single core has one. So a quad core processor is usually better than a duo core, which is usually better than a single core processor.

Hard disk

The hard disk is important because it must have enough space for all your data. The size of a hard disk is measured in gigabytes (GB) or **terabytes** (TB). As 1TB is a thousand times larger than 1GB, it is almost certain that a hard disk specification using GB will not be as big as one using TB.

The speed of a hard disk is also important, as the disk is used a lot to transfer data to and from RAM. This is found in the spin speed, seek time and cache size.

- **Spin speed** — this is how quickly the disk spins around. A larger number here is better, so a hard disk with a spin speed of 10,000 **revolutions per minute** (rpm) should be quicker than one that spins at 7200 rpm.

- **Seek time** — this is how long it takes to find something on the disk. A smaller number is better here, so a hard disk with a seek time of 8.9 **milliseconds** (ms) should be faster than one with a 12 ms seek time.

- **Cache size** — the cache or buffer is memory (RAM) built into the hard disk. The cache works much faster than the drive. If a document is saved to the hard drive it will be copied to the cache, which is very quick, so the rest of the computer can carry on with the next task. The document can then be copied from cache memory to the disk itself by the drive electronics, without involving the computer.

Other internal hardware devices

Many computer graphics professionals like their computer to have a digital camera card slot. Images can then be loaded easily from a camera by taking the card out of the camera and inserting it into the computer. This is usually a faster method of transferring images than plugging a cable into the camera to connect to the computer.

Key terms

Gigahertz (GHz) – a measure of how quickly an electronic device works. 1GHz means that it does 1,000,000,000 (one thousand million) operations every second.

Megahertz (MHz) – a measure of how quickly an electronic device works. 1MHz means that it does 1,000,000 (one million) operations every second.

Terabyte (TB) – 1 TB is a large number which is roughly 1,000,000,000,000 (a million, million) bytes. A byte is a small amount of space in RAM or on a hard drive, large enough to hold a letter such as A or C.

Revolutions per minute (rpm) – how quickly a disk spins around. A disk spinning at 5400 rpm will turn round 5400 times every minute.

Milliseconds (ms) – a measure of time. There are 1000 milliseconds in one second, so 10 milliseconds is one hundredth of a second.

File storage

File storage is used to hold images and other data in a computer system and also to transfer these to different places.

- **Hard drive** — this is the main storage of a computer system. It is a fast, reliable device built into the computer and is usually the first place offered to the user when saving or opening work.

- **CD-ROM and DVD drives** — optical drives such as CD-ROM and DVD are usually included in a computer system. They can be used to load new software and to make copies of data as backups or to take to another system. There are many types of CD-ROM and DVD drives available. They need to be able to write (save) and you need to make sure that you buy the correct optical disks to use with the drive in your computer system.

- **USB storage devices** — these have become very popular as they are small, quick, cheap, reliable, and can hold lots of data. A pen drive is an example of USB storage – you probably use one to take work home from your place of study. USB external hard drives are becoming popular as a way of backing up data.

Activity: Graphics computer

1. Work in a small group to decide on a good specification for a computer system suitable for working with graphics. Consider these aspects:
   - graphics card memory size, e.g. 512MB
   - graphics card slot type, e.g. PCIe x16
   - main memory (RAM) size, e.g. 4GB
   - processor type, e.g. dual core
   - hard disk size, e.g. 1TB
   - hard disk spin speed, e.g. 7200 rpm.

2. Now work for 15 minutes on your own to find a cheap and an expensive computer with the specification agreed by the group.

3. Compare your findings with the rest of your group to identify the cheapest and the most expensive computer the group has found.

4. What are the differences?

5. Which computer would your group recommend to a graphics professional and why?

Input devices

An input device is any hardware used to get data into a computer or to control it. You will already be familiar with using the keyboard and mouse, which are input devices.

ICT professionals who use computers for graphics are also likely to use specialist input devices such as:

- **graphics tablet** – for precise control over editing images
- **digital camera** – for taking their own photographs
- **scanner** – to acquire images from paper or other media.

Graphics tablet

A graphics tablet looks rather like a mouse mat, but is solid and uses an electronic pen (stylus) instead of a mouse. Very few people use both a mouse and a graphics tablet.

The stylus moves a mouse pointer around the screen. Usually there are buttons on the side of the stylus which can act in the same way as the buttons on a mouse.

The tip of the stylus is often pressure sensitive, so pressing harder on the stylus could draw a thicker line in a graphic.

Many computer graphics professionals prefer a graphics tablet to a mouse, because it allows them to be more accurate.

You will be used to getting to the edge of a mouse mat or desk with your mouse, and having to lift it up and move it back onto the mat. This does not happen with a graphics tablet. Touching the same place on the graphics tablet with the stylus will always bring the screen pointer to exactly the same place on the screen.

Some of the more expensive graphics tablets include a display so you can use the stylus directly on an image showing on the display.

Digital camera

There are many high-quality digital cameras available at affordable prices. Digital cameras are also included in lots of other devices, such as mobile phones, so it has never been easier to capture photographs for computer systems.

You usually get what you pay for, so it is sensible to avoid the very cheapest digital cameras and to purchase a camera from a well-respected brand.

Picture quality is important, but can be difficult to predict from the technical specification. This is a strong reason for buying a respected brand, as big companies are more likely to produce digital cameras which take good pictures.

The most important parts of the technical specification of a digital camera are:

- **optical zoom** – how well the camera enlarges the photo subject
- **number of megapixels** – the amount of picture detail.

Optical zoom

Zoom is used to make the picture larger in the camera before taking the picture. Some cameras offer digital zoom, which is not as good as optical zoom.

Have you ever used a graphics tablet with an electronic pen (stylus)?

(i) Did you know?

The first digital camera, developed by Kodak, was as big as a very large toaster and weighed almost 4 kg. The images took 23 seconds to snap and were black and white with 0.1 megapixel resolution. Images were then stored onto digital cassette tapes.

Megapixels are not quite as important as a decent optical zoom lens, as this affects the quality of the image that can be captured by the camera.

- Digital zoom is when the camera electronics make the picture larger, a similar technique to the one used by software on a computer when manipulating an image. The problem with digital zoom is that there can be a loss of quality when the picture is enlarged.
- Optical zoom is a lot better because the optical zoom lens moves, changing the size of the picture that is captured inside the camera, so there is no quality loss.

Megapixels

The number of megapixels in the camera specification is how many million pixels are in the biggest picture the camera can take. So, an 8 megapixel camera can take a picture with 8 million pixels in it.

The more pixels the better, as there will be more detail in the photographs the camera takes. More pixels also means that you can make bigger prints of the photographs you take with the camera. This can be very useful for photographs used for large jobs such as advertisements for roadside billboards.

Why does optical zoom in a digital camera produce better quality close-up photos than digital zoom?

Activity: Digital cameras

Carry out research on your own for 20 minutes to find digital cameras with the following features:
- the largest magnifying optical zoom
- the biggest number of pixels
- the smallest number of pixels
- the smallest digital camera
- the most expensive
- the cheapest
- the cheapest digital camera with wireless connection
- the cheapest digital camera with a docking station.

Now, pair up with someone else in your group and compare notes to see who found the most cameras that met these targets.

Scanner

A scanner is similar to the glass part of a photocopier. You place a picture from a book or paper on the scanner, which then scans the image into the computer. Some of the better scanners also have an adapter, so you can scan projector slides or camera film negatives.

Output devices

An output device is any hardware used to allow information to come out of the computer. Computers used for graphics usually output to the screen as **soft copy** or onto paper or another medium, such as vinyl, as **hard copy**. A **monitor** is an example of a soft copy output device, as it allows you to see what you have created using the computer. Hard copy output devices include:

- **printer** – which outputs to paper
- **plotter** – for large prints
- **vinyl cutter** – for vinyl signs.

Monitor

There are numerous flat screen monitors available for modern computer systems. They come in a variety of screen sizes and resolutions.

The screen size is usually measured in inches diagonally – the distance from bottom left corner to top right, or from bottom right to top left. Typical sizes used by graphics professionals are between 22 and 32 inches.

Graphics professionals like big screens, but they also favour a high-resolution screen. So a large TV plugged into a computer would not be very suitable unless the TV can run at full **HD**.

The accuracy of colour is more important to some graphics professionals, especially if they are involved with producing work for a printing press. They value a screen with the closest match between captured, displayed and printed colours. Such monitors are usually sized around 24 inches.

Printer

A printer is an output device that puts images and words onto paper, card and similar media, such as transparent film.

There are many types of printer technology that are used to make the image on paper. The most interesting and useful types for the graphics professional are:

- **Ink jet printers** — these are cheap to buy, but can be expensive to run. The cost of each page depends on how much ink is used, so a page which is mostly white is very cheap while a page filled with rich colour can be very expensive. Ink jet printers are able to produce superior quality prints and are versatile, being able to print on many materials and at different sizes.
- **Colour laser printers** — these have become a lot cheaper in recent years. Again, the cost per page varies with how much toner is used. They are able to produce high-quality prints at speed.
- **Dye sublimation (dye sub) printers** — these are the only true photo-quality printers. The cost per page is always the same, which can be useful to organisations. However, they are slower than other printer types.

Most printers use A4 paper. Other sizes are available, with some printers able to print as large as A3 or smaller photograph-sized prints.

Some computer graphics systems use a colour photocopier for output using a **RIP**. A system like this will take a little time to prepare the pages, but after that is very quick. It can produce high-quality and cost-effective prints, and is therefore a popular choice when printing flyers, tickets, business cards, and for other medium production runs.

Activity: Printer running costs

Choose one model each from colour laser, ink jet and dye sublimation printers which are currently on sale. Find out the cost of toner, ink or cartridge consumables for each of these products, as well as how many pages each will last for.

Calculate the cost of printing a typical page for each of these printers by dividing the cost of the consumable by the number of pages it can print.

Which is the cheapest to run?

Plotter

Most modern plotters use inkjet technology to print out very big images that can be used for large posters, advertising banners and similar display material. Plotters are expensive to purchase, so they are usually found in large organisations or in specialist print shops that can print out work for the public.

Vinyl cutter

A lot of signs in shop windows and on the sides of vehicles are made by a vinyl cutter. This is similar to a printer, but instead of putting an image onto paper the vinyl cutter cuts shapes from vinyl roll. These shapes can be peeled away from their backing and stuck onto a window, vehicle or sign board.

1.2 Software

Software applications (apps for short) are programs designed to run on a computer system. There are many software products used by computer graphics professionals.

It is important that the computer can run software well, so systems requirements are specified for apps, listing the minimum specification of computer that should be used to run the software.

Broadly speaking, computer graphics are either **vector** or **raster** (**bitmap**). Photos are usually a type of bitmap.

Vector graphics software

Vector graphics take up a lot less space in memory or on storage than bitmaps. This is because vector graphics software creates **objects** using mathematics to show images on-screen or output to a printer. An object might be a line, a circle, a rectangle, text or a bitmap, or anything that can contribute to an image.

Key terms

Vector graphics – these are made up of objects such as lines, rectangles and circles, which have many properties including thickness of the border and fill colour. They are stored in the computer as coordinate points for the corners of the objects, with properties needed to show the objects on-screen and to print. Vector graphics are excellent for scaling to very big or very small images and do not require much disk space.

Raster graphics (also known as **bitmaps**) – these are based on the pixels that make an image, often originating from digital photographs or scanners. They are inadequate for scaling to very big or very small images and require a lot of disk space.

Object – a graphics object is an individual part of an image, such as an oval. Objects have properties which provide several options, for example setting border thickness for the object.

Case study: Vizual Impact

Vizual Impact is a small, busy shop that produces computer graphics for a variety of clients and purposes. The company has a shop on a major road in Bristol so it will attract passing trade. It also has a strong website (to access this site, please go to Hotlinks and click on this unit). Vizual Impact produces signs and other artwork using computer graphics for:

- car graphics
- van signs
- registration plates for vehicles
- shop signs
- sun visors.

Figure 23.2: Vizual Impact use computer graphics to create signs and other commercial artwork. Vizual Impact logo is the Trademark and copyright of Vizual Impact Ltd.

The owner, Martin Oxenham, has heard that you have created some impressive computer graphics and just completed your course. He is interested to find out if you have any fresh ideas on services the shop could offer or new equipment.

The shop already has a fast network with powerful workstations. There is a rolling replacement programme in operation, so the shop will be buying a new computer system during the next few weeks. Martin and the team are too busy with some high-priority jobs to do their research on the new purchase.

1. **Find a choice of large graphics tablets with screens that allow the stylus to draw computer graphics right onto their screens.**

   a. **What are the differences in these tablets?**

   b. **Which would you recommend for the shop?**

   c. **What are your reasons for the recommendation?**

2. **The shop has up to £2000 available to purchase the hardware of a new computer system for the graphics tablet. The new system will need to connect to the shop's gigabit network using cat 6 cabling. Martin would like you to find a choice of systems (including screens, mice and keyboards) within this budget and explain the differences between them.**

3. **A local charity has asked the shop to produce some A4 posters advertising a fundraising day for which tours around the British Aerospace Concord aircraft in Filton can be purchased. The posters are to be placed in shop windows. Martin would like you to create a design for these posters so he can assess the quality of your work.**

4. **Martin would now like you to produce a flyer for a promotional 'Wine and Dine' menu for a new brasserie-style restaurant in the city centre. The flyer is to be A5 and double-sided for posting through letter boxes in the area.**

Key term

Cat 6 cabling – most modern networks use cat 6 (category 6) or cat 5 (category 5) cabling to connect network cards to network switches. Both these types of network cable use RJ45 plugs. Cat 6 cabling is a newer and better standard that can run at 1000 mbps (1 gbps), which is ten times faster than the older cat 5 cabling that runs at 100 mpbs.

Key term

An object is stored in memory, with numbers defining where the corners are, whether the joining lines are straight or curved, the colours and all other **properties**. For example, the properties of a rectangle include:

- a thickness to the border (line around it)
- a colour for the border
- a style for the border, such as solid or dashes
- a fill colour
- width
- height
- position.

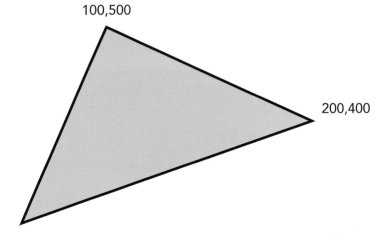

Figure 23.3: Vector images use numbers for their position, colour, size, line thickness and other properties.

Because the software uses mathematics, vector graphics can be made very small or large with no loss of quality. The vector software will calculate the pixels and colours needed for the resolution of the screen or printer that outputs the image.

The objects which make up a vector graphic can be grouped together to produce complex objects. Grouping the objects makes creating and editing images a lot easier – when the objects are grouped, it isn't possible to move part of an image by mistake. For example, a logo might be made up of several objects that are grouped together. The logo can then be used as a single object.

Objects can be placed in front or behind other objects – this is called the order. This is a very powerful and useful technique as you can control how much of an object is seen by placing it behind another object.

Vector graphics software includes:

- **CorelDRAW®** – a general purpose and well respected drawing package that can be used to create most types of vector image.
- **Adobe® Illustrator® CS5** – a well-respected vector drawing package from Adobe® which is part of their CS5 suite of graphics software.

- **Serif DrawPlus** – a very capable and reasonably priced vector drawing package from Serif. It is also available as a free download as the DrawPlus SE cut-down version.

- **Microsoft® Visio®** – a package that specialises in diagrams, such as computer flowcharts, network diagrams, floorplans and similar. An impressive feature of Visio® is that lines can attach to objects, so if a box in a flowchart is moved, the lines connected to it will move as well.

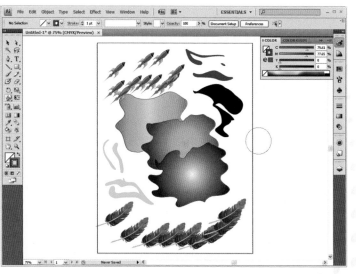

Figure 23.4: Vector software application Adobe® Illustrator® CS5.

Activity: Vector software comparison

Create a table, like Table 23.1 below, to compare some vector graphics software applications.

	Corel Draw	Illustrator CS5	Serif DrawPlus	Visio
Cost				
Typical use				
Screenshot				
System requirements				

Table 23.1: Comparison of vector graphics software.

1. Research these applications to fill in the blank cells in Table 23.1.

2. Which of the applications do you think would be best for each of these situations?

    a) Producing a floorplan design for a trade show.

    b) Producing a brochure for a fast food takeaway.

    c) For use by pupils in a secondary school to produce coursework diagrams.

Dedicated raster graphics (bitmap) software

Raster (bitmap) graphics take up more space in memory or on storage than vector graphics. This is because bitmap graphics remember the colour of every pixel in the image. As most images have several million pixels, the image size can be large.

Raster graphics are sometimes called bitmaps because of the way the image is stored in memory – the colour of each pixel in the image is **mapped** to a number of **bits** in memory (typically 8 bits for 256 colours, 16 bits for 64 thousand colours or 24 bits for 16 million colours). Because the software uses pixels, bitmap images often lose quality when made very small or large, with **blocking**, also known as **pixellation**.

Resizing raster images so they become smaller usually works well, apart from text which often needs to be re-edited after the resize to make it readable. This is because pixels are lost during downwards resizing. This could make a big difference to text, for example if the top few pixels of the letter 'd' are lost it becomes an 'a'.

Bitmap (raster) software is used to create and edit images with tools which are often a lot more basic that those found in vector or photo-editing software.

Bitmap software can usually zoom in to the pixels, so you can edit each one to a colour of your choice.

Dedicated bitmap software includes:

- **GIMP** – excellent open source bitmap software which can be downloaded and used free of charge.
- **Microsoft® Paint®** – the bitmap editor that is bundled in with Windows®, usually found under Accessories. Paint is a popular and useful program for editing bitmap graphics.
- **Corel® PaintShop Photo™ Pro X3** – a popular bitmap software package, originally called Paint Shop. Versions of this program can be found as free trial downloads.
- **Real-DRAW** – a drawing package that combines bitmaps and vectors in one software application.

Key term

Blocking/pixellation – two different words to describe the reduction in picture quality caused by resizing a bitmap graphic image to make it larger. It occurs when the tiny pixels of the original colour have been enlarged so much that they are seen as blocks of colour.

Figure 23.5: Bitmap software application Microsoft® Paint.

Activity: Bitmap software comparison

Create a table, like Table 23.2 below, to compare some bitmap software applications:

	GIMP	Paint	Paintshop Pro	Real Draw
Cost				
Typical use				
Screenshot				
System requirements				

Table 23.2: Comparison of bitmap software.

1. Research these applications to fill in the blank cells in Table 23.2.
2. Which of the applications do think would be best for each of these situations?
   a) Anyone using Windows® who wants to produce simple graphics.
   b) For use on a low-specification computer.
   c) For use in a professional environment on powerful computers.

Dedicated photo manipulation software

This is a type of bitmap editing software with tools to enhance photographs. A typical tool found in photo editing software is the clone tool, which allows you to copy a part of the photograph to another part of the image.

Dedicated photo manipulation software includes:

- **GIMP** — (see above).
- **Adobe® Photoshop® CS5** – industry standard photo manipulation software from the Adobe® CS5 collection. It is used by many computer graphic professionals.
- **Adobe® Photoshop® Elements** – a cheaper photo manipulation software package from Adobe® which is targeted towards anyone who wants to edit photographs.
- **Serif PhotoPlus** – a very capable and reasonably priced photo-editing package from Serif, which is also a free download as the PhotoPlus SE cut-down version.

Other software tools

Many software application packages include graphics facilities. A good example is the Microsoft® Office® collection, where applications such as Word® and Excel® have a drawing toolbar with a good choice of tools to create graphics inside a document. Other software tools include:

- **Image viewers** — these are used to look at files on a hard disk, pen drive or other storage medium. They show a thumbnail or larger image of the file. The viewer gives a good, quick preview of files, to help you choose which one to open. IrfanView is a freeware Windows® graphic viewer with various features, including being able to show animated GIFs.
- **Photo galleries** — these are places where collections of photographs are held, usually online. You may choose to display your photos in a photo gallery or you could use photographs from an online gallery for your own work if they are royalty-free. FreeDigitalPhotos.net is a photo gallery website with many photos that are royalty free and downloadable after registration.

Figure 23.6: Photo software application Adobe® Photoshop®.

Activity: Photo software comparison

Create a table, similar to Table 23.3 below, to compare some dedicated photo manipulation software applications.

	GIMP	Photoshop CS5	Photoshop Elements	Serif PhotoPlus
Cost				
Typical use				
Screenshot				
System requirements				

Table 23.3: Comparison of bitmap software.

1. Research these applications to fill in the blank cells in Table 23.3.
2. GIMP and Serif PhotoPlus SE are both available as free downloads. Which do you think is better and why?
3. What extra features do you get in Serif PhotoPlus compared to Serif PhotoPlus SE? How useful do you think these extra features are?
4. Can you find three features in Adobe® Photoshop® CS5 or Adobe® Photoshop® Elements that you think justify the extra cost of these applications?

BTEC Assessment activity 23.1 (P1) (P2) (M1) (M2) (D1)

The thing you like most is creating computer graphics. Lots of people have told you they like your work, so you have decided to become a freelance graphic designer.

A friend of your family has offered to buy you the kit you need, in return for a small percentage of your fees. First, they need to be convinced you are worth the investment.

Your first task is to assess the hardware and software you will need to create and edit computer graphics.

1. Identify a suitable computer system, including the following:

   - processor
   - RAM
   - graphics card
   - hard disk
   - input devices
   - printer
   - graphics software. **P1**

2. Include the software you would like to use on this system. Name the computer graphics software package you expect to use the most and state the functions it provides. **P1** **P2**

3. Describe the features of some different software packages that can create and edit graphic images. These could be general purpose applications, such as Word®, or specialist bitmap, photo or vector software. You could also include an open source package.

   The features will include:

   - whether they can handle vector or bitmaps
   - the tools they provide
   - the file types they support. **M2**

4. Your sponsor now needs you to describe three hardware devices that work with graphics. You need to look at and compare the advantages and disadvantages of each. You could include reference to:

   - ease of use
   - flexibility of use
   - quality of images
   - control of resolution (dpi or megapixels). **M1**

5. You have almost convinced your sponsor to part with their money. You now need to evaluate the graphics software you would like to use with this system in terms of its ability to create and edit computer graphics. **D1**

Grading tips

- For questions 1 and 2, take care to include both the software and hardware in your system.
- Make sure you state the functions of your software package for question 2.
- For question 3, remember to compare the features of different software packages.
- You could compare a graphics tablet, digital camera and scanner for the three hardware device comparison in question 4.
- For question 5, make sure your evaluation includes how the software can both create and edit graphic images on the computer system.

PLTS

By evaluating hardware and software and the images they produce, you will show that you are an **independent enquirer**.

By evaluating your work you will demonstrate that you are a **reflective learner**.

Functional skills

By producing work for questions 1 and 2 (P1), you will give evidence of your functional **ICT** skills: select, interact with and use ICT systems independently for a complex task to meet a variety of needs.

1.3 File handling

Your graphical work will be kept as files on storage media, such as the hard disk. You will need to use file handling techniques in order to look after your files and folder structure.

Converting files

You may need to convert your graphics files into another format. Reasons for converting a file into another format include:

- **Size** — some file formats, such as BMP, take up a lot of storage space. For this reason they are often converted into another format, such as JPG (also known as jpeg), to save space.
- **Compatibility** — some image editing software cannot open every type of file, so you may need to convert a graphic into a file type that can be used by your editing software.
- **Features** — some types of file have features you need that are not offered by other types. For example, the GIF file format can include animated gifs which might be needed for a web page.

The most common graphics file formats are:

- BMP with no **compression**
- GIF with **lossless** compression
- JPG with **lossy** compression
- PNG with lossless compression
- TIF with no compression.

Table 23.4 provides a summary of graphics file formats and when to use them.

Table 23.4: Summary of how graphics file formats are used.

	Photographic images	Graphics, including logos and line art
Properties	Photos have continuous tones, no text, few lines and edges	Graphics often have solid colours with text or lines and sharp edges
Best quality	PNG or TIF	PNG or TIF
Smallest file size	JPG	GIF or PNG
Maximum compatibility (PC, Mac, Unix)	TIF or JPG	TIF or GIF
Worst choice	256 colour GIF has very limited colour and is a larger file than 24 bit JPG	JPG compression adds artefacts, and smears text, lines and edges

Key terms

Compression – when a file is reduced in size. Compression can be particularly useful for graphics files, which can be very large, taking up a lot of disk space.

Lossless – compression when there is no difference in picture quality when a picture is used again after being compressed.

Lossy – compression whereby some of the picture detail is lost when the picture is shown again.

You can usually convert files into another format by opening the file, using the **Save as** menu option, then choosing the new format. If the file format you need is not available, you may need to find a specialist file conversion program. For example, to open a RAW format photograph in Serif PhotoPlus, you would first need to convert the photo into a compatible format such as PNG using a file conversion program, such as Image Converter Plus.

Converting a file into another format often means that a lot of the benefits of the original are lost. For example, a BMP file might have **layers** which would be merged together if converted into a JPG file.

JPG is a 'lossy' file format, which means that each time a file is saved after editing some quality is lost. If you need to use JPG for a finished computer graphic, it's best to convert to this format only after you've completed all the editing.

File management

It is important to manage your graphics files effectively. This will enable you and others to find the files and recognise what they are easily, without needing to open them.

File management techniques include:

- **Naming files.** Give sensible, professional names to your work. Sometimes young learners give unprofessional names to their documents, such as 'Today's work' or 'Doc1'. A professional name such as 'Digital camera comparison' is much easier to recognise later.

- **Folder structures.** Provide places on your storage space where you can easily find work again.

- **Moving files.** You might need to move files from a folder to a different folder. This is often done by ICT professionals to organise their work. For example, they might have a folder for work in progress and another for completed work. They will move a graphics file to the completed work folder when they've finished it. Files are not often moved from hard disk to pen drive, as it's more appropriate to copy files than to move them. Copying files means that the original is still on the hard drive, and so can act as a backup.

- **Deleting files.** This is an essential part of file management, especially at the end of a project when all the temporary working files, which are not part of the end product, are deleted.

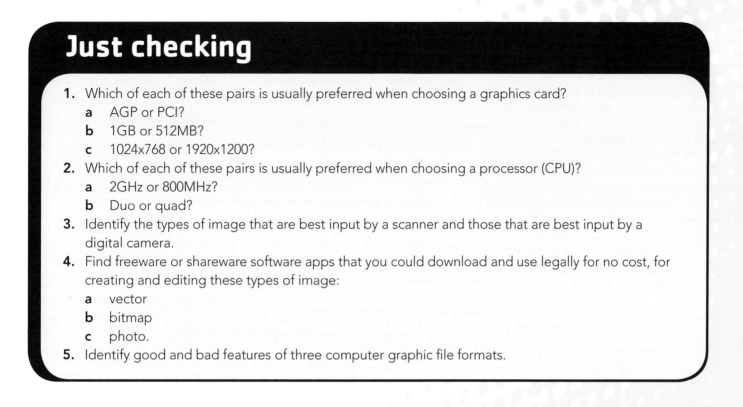

Just checking

1. Which of each of these pairs is usually preferred when choosing a graphics card?
   a AGP or PCI?
   b 1GB or 512MB?
   c 1024x768 or 1920x1200?
2. Which of each of these pairs is usually preferred when choosing a processor (CPU)?
   a 2GHz or 800MHz?
   b Duo or quad?
3. Identify the types of image that are best input by a scanner and those that are best input by a digital camera.
4. Find freeware or shareware software apps that you could download and use legally for no cost, for creating and editing these types of image:
   a vector
   b bitmap
   c photo.
5. Identify good and bad features of three computer graphic file formats.

2. Be able to create computer graphics to meet a user need

Computer graphics professionals create work for clients. They start by identifying the user need and finish by comparing the end product with the original objectives to check it has fulfilled the brief.

2.1 User need

Professional graphics need to meet the user's need. The user need defines exactly what is wanted from the graphic. It also sets out any constraints so the end result is exactly right.

User requirements

The user requirements document for a particular computer graphic job gives details of the purpose of the computer graphic being commissioned. For example, the user requirements for a flyer advertising a new fast food restaurant might be:

- the flyer size is A5
- include the logo of the restaurant
- use the same colours as the shop front
- include a promotional offer
- produce the first proof within a week.

Key term

Font (also known as **typeface**) - shape of lettering for the alphabet, numbers and other characters, such as the Pound (£) currency sign, that can be selected for typing text into a graphic or document. The choice of font has a huge effect on the style of an image or document. Many organisations use one or two fonts as their corporate style to help people recognise them. An example of a font is Arial.

Constraints

Constraints are the rules that need to be followed when producing a piece of work, for example the size of a graphic. The user need often specifies constraints and guidelines that the computer graphics artist must follow when producing images. These may include:

- **House style** — this is where the client already has a standard or style for their artwork and they expect any new artwork to be in a similar style. B&Q is a good example of a company with a strong style – they would probably expect any new artwork, such as a newspaper advertisement, to include their **fonts** and colours.

- **Colours** — these may be defined by the user to fit within a house style or within the limitations of another process, such as printing. Large volume printing usually involves a printing press which uses a plate for each colour in the print. Each plate adds to the cost of production, so an artwork brief might specify just one or two colours to keep the cost of the project within budget.

- **Image size** — the size and resolution of a computer graphic produced for a magazine or book will be specified, so the artist understands exactly what to produce. There may also be size constraints for graphics needed for websites, as large images can take a long time to download and slow web pages down.

Activity: House style

Visit and look at the websites for Comet and Currys. (To access both sites, go to the Hotlinks site and click on this unit.)

Take a screenshot of each of the websites and then annotate them to identify the following aspects of Comet's and Currys' house styles:

- fonts used
- font sizes
- colours
- theme (for example, is the company logo and name always in the same place? Is there a consistent place for the main promotions?)
- sizing of images (for example, are they all the same size? Why?).

2.2 Computer graphics

A graphic on a computer system may be a bitmap or vector graphic type. Bitmaps are usually more photographic and larger than vector graphics.

Bitmaps

Remember that the graphic image has to meet the user needs. If the client needs a graphic containing scanned image(s), it will be a bitmap.

Bitmap graphics are usually sourced from a digital camera or a scanner.

Bitmaps are particularly well suited to photographs, and are excellent for selling products and to catch the eye. You will have opportunity to edit photographs and may transform them into images that are beyond anything real. Such images are often the most eye-catching of all.

A bitmap graphic treats the image as a collection of pixels, remembering the colour of each pixel. So if the image has a resolution of 1024 x 768 then it has 1024 pixels across with 768 pixels down, so there are 786,432 pixels in the picture.

The number of colours that can be in a bitmap graphic is called the colour depth. This is how many colours are available. It is based on the number of bits in memory used to hold the colour of each pixel. The colour depth could be any of those shown in Table 23.5.

Table 23.5: Colour depths for graphics with number of colours available.

Colour depth	Number of colours	Bytes for each pixel
1-bit	2 (black and white)	¼
8-bit	256	1
16-bit	65,536	2
24-bit	16,777,216	3
32-bit	over 4.2 billion	4

1-bit is not very common nowadays. Few graphics are black and white – those that appear black and white will actually have shades of grey, with an 8-bit colour depth for 256 shades of grey.

16-bit is also not very common nowadays as modern computer graphics systems can display and print better-quality images with higher colour depths. Most modern systems will be running 32-bit or possibly 24-bit graphics.

Because bitmaps are based on a collection of pixels, they do not scale into larger or smaller images very well. For example, if a bitmap of 1000 pixels across is re-scaled into 830 pixels across, the computer has a very difficult job to do. This is because the graphics software has to understand what is in the picture and what each pixel shows to make a perfect job of re-scaling the image. Unfortunately, computers and their software do not have such a sophisticated understanding, so will average out the colours to choose the colours for pixels in the new size. Quite often this will be acceptable, but there will be times when it looks wrong. Pixellation occurs when a bitmap image is spoilt by re-scaling (see also page 334).

Bitmap graphics are poor at re-sizing as pixellation can occur.

Vector graphics

The client may request a diagram, floorplan or similar image to be created by the graphics professional. This is likely to be a vector graphic, often used for diagrams. Vector graphics are unlikely to be used for photographs. As explained on page 332, vector graphics use objects to create images. An object might be a line, circle, rectangle, text or even a bitmap, so a vector graphic can be a mixture of graphic types.

Vector graphics are usually created by the artist on a computer. This may be started from clip art or possibly from a graphic software utility program, which converts a bitmap, such as a photo into a vector image.

Vector graphics scale very well into much larger or smaller images.

Comparison between bitmap and vector graphics

Bitmap and vector images are quite different. As a computer graphics professional, you will need to be able to appreciate these differences to help you choose which type is the most appropriate for a particular situation.

Table 23.6: Comparing bitmap and vector graphics.

	Bitmap	Vector
Typical usage	Photograph or scanned picture	Diagram, logo or floorplan
Type of image	BMP, GIF, JPG (JPEG), PNG, TIF	CDR, EPS, PDF
File size	Large	Small
Scaling	Poor	Very good

PLTS

By analysing and evaluating information, and judging its relevance and value, you will show that you are an **independent enquirer**.

Functional skills

By researching information for this assessment activity (P3), you will give evidence of your functional **ICT** skills: access, search for, select and use ICT-based information and evaluate its fitness for purpose.

BTEC Assessment activity 23.2 P3

You have set up as a freelance graphic designer and have your first enquiry for a paid job. The client wants you to prove that you know what you're doing, so they have asked for a description of the differences between vector and raster images. They want your description to include:

- images to show some differences between vector and raster images
- an image showing pixellation
- the advantages and disadvantages of each graphic type
- the best uses for both types of graphics. **P3**

Grading tip

Make sure your examples show the uses of and differences between bitmap and vector graphics.

2.3 Tools and techniques

There is a wide variety of tools that can be used in graphic software applications. You need to be aware of these tools, so you are able to select the most appropriate when creating and editing computer graphics.

Standard software tools

The standard tools listed in Table 23.7 are included in most graphic software applications.

Table 23.7: Standard software tools.

Tool	Use
Freehand draw	Use the mouse or graphics tablet stylus to draw directly into the graphic.
Rotate	Select part of the image and use this tool to turn it around – you specify the angle you want it to rotate.
Flip	This tool creates a mirror image of the selected image.
Resize	The selected part of the image is made into a different size.
Crop	Use this tool to trim unwanted edges off a photograph.
Text	There is usually a text tool so you can type words into the image. Once the text is selected, you will have a choice of fonts and other text properties, such as font size and colour.

Grouping

Grouping is usually a feature of vector packages. It allows the user to make several objects into a single grouped object. This makes it a lot easier to move them around in the image.

*   To group some objects, select them then either right-click and choose **Group** or use a menu or tool in the graphic software.
*   To ungroup the group of objects, select it then either right-click and choose **Ungroup** or use a menu or tool in the graphic software to separate the grouped objects.

Layout grids

Layout grids are usually a feature of vector packages, they help position objects into straight lines or evenly space them apart.

A layout grid looks like rows of evenly spaced dots on the screen. There is usually a menu option or tool to make the grid visible or to hide it. There will also be a control to define the distances (spacings) between the dots in the grid.

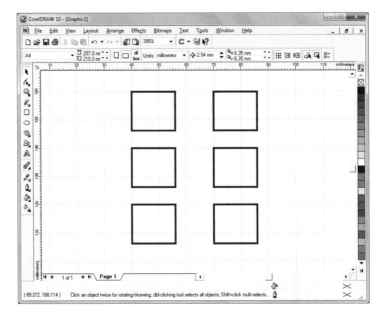

Figure 23.7: In this screenshot their top left corners have snapped to the grid.

When using a grid, it is best to turn on the **snap to grid** function. This means that when you move an object it will snap (jump) to the nearest dot in the grid. This is a great way of getting objects into exactly the position you want them.

Special effects

The following special effects are included in most photo manipulation software applications (see page 336 for examples of these applications). These tools take some skill to apply properly, so it is best to save your work before trying them out.

Sharpen

This is used to make a photograph more sharply defined, with clearer edges to the shapes in the picture. For example, you might want to make animals in a photograph stand out a little more from the background, as shown below.

Sharpen is a photo-editing tool that makes an image crisper. Can you think of other occasions when you might need to use this tool?

Posterise is a photo-editing tool that makes a photograph look like a sketch. How could you put this special effect to good use for a client?

Soften

This is the opposite to sharpen, and is used to smooth out edges in a photograph. For example, to give an old-fashioned 'soft focus' effect to a photograph of a face.

Posterise

This is an effect you can apply to a photograph to make it look like a hand-drawn sketch.

Templates

A computer graphics artist will often need to use graphics within some kind of document, such as a poster or flyer. Some applications, such as CorelDRAW®, have **templates** available when you start a new document, for example a flyer or booklet. Using a template can save a lot of time with documents, for example a booklet or brochure for which there might be several pages on each side of a printed A4 paper. The layout of these pages will be presented on-screen at the right size and it will be clear where you need to insert text and graphics. The template will be designed so that when you print it out, the hard copy can be folded into the booklet or brochure.

Other tools and techniques

There are many other tools and techniques available in graphics software.

Shape libraries

As the name suggests, these are libraries of various shapes found in many graphics applications. They make it very quick and easy to add shapes, such as stars or speech bubbles, to your work.

Key term

Template – many software applications allow you to create templates for documents. A template has the basic settings for a new document and may include any words and graphics that will always be included, such as the organisation's name and logo.

(i) Did you know?

Dress-making templates have been used for centuries to help people mark out and cut the fabric for clothes, such as dresses and shirts. These templates are made from paper or card and pinned to the fabric. They are used to guide the scissors to cut the right shapes for the various parts of the garment, which can then be sewn together.

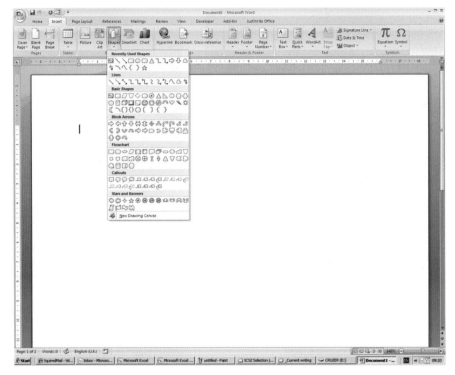

Figure 23.8: Microsoft® Word® has a shape library.

Colour change
This tool allows you to select a colour in an image and change it. For example, a red motorbike in a photograph can be changed to a yellow one.

Colour balance
Computer graphics professionals use this tool to adjust the 'warmth' of the image until it appears correct.

Colour depth
This is the number of colours that can be in an image. For example, a 24-bit colour depth image has a choice of 16.7 million colours. (For more information on colour depth, see Table 23.5 on page 343.)

2.4 Reviewing

You have completed your computer graphic, but this does not mean that your work on the job has finished. All ICT professionals need to check their work against the original requirements to make sure that the finished product meets the needs of the user. As part of this review you will have to:

- check the accuracy of any text included
- review the finished work against the objectives
- make any improvements that are required.

A lot of graphical work needs text. For example, a poster advertising a musical event in a pub will need the date, time, names of the bands, name of the venue and other information, such as any admission charge.

Checking text

First, you will need to check the accuracy of the text. If there is a spell-checker in your graphics software, you should use it to check the spelling of the text in your work. You should then proofread the text carefully yourself, as a spell-checker isn't foolproof – for example, a word may be spelled wrongly in the context of your document, but if it is the correct spelling for another word, the spell-checker won't pick it up (for example, if you accidentally typed 'cause' instead of 'course'). Make sure you use a dictionary to check any words you are unsure of as well as proofreading your work.

As well as spelling and grammar, you need to check the text for accuracy. Dates, times, product details and all other information in the graphics must be accurate.

To be really sure that your text is accurate, ask someone else to proof read your text as well.

Reviewing against objectives

Any completed graphical work needs to be checked or reviewed against the original objectives. This will ensure that the work you have produced has not lost its way and ended up as something different from what was specified in the original brief.

In this review you will need to consider a number of things, including:

- **Size of image** – was the size of the image specified in the brief? If so, does your image meet the size requirements?
- **Download speed** – is the download speed quick enough? This is especially important for graphics on web pages, so you need to check the download speed.
- **Image resolution** – was the pixel size of the image specified? If so, does your image have the correct resolution?

Suggestions for improvements

As well as your own review of your work, the client will also review it and give you feedback. You and/or the client might make some suggestions for improvement. Whether they ask you to act on these improvements will depend upon factors such as budget (i.e. whether there is enough money left in the budget to pay for the improvements) and time (whether the contract allows for extra time to be spent on the graphic).

Functional skills

In your work for this assessment activity (P5), you will give evidence of your functional **ICT** skills: enter, develop and format information independently to suit its meaning and purpose, including text and images.

BTEC Assessment activity 23.3 **P5**

Your first job as a freelance graphic designer is to create a new logo for a band. This logo can be created using any graphics software.

The logo should include the band's name, with other graphics to represent the band and their image.

The user need is for a logo that is instantly recognisable to the public and the fans, giving a good sense of what the band represents. **P5**

Grading tip

Choose a name for the band that will be easy to design a logo for. This will help meet the user need of being instantly recognisable, giving a good sense of what the band represents.

Just checking

1. Why does a computer graphics job need constraints?
2. What is a pixel and in what ways is it important?
3. Identify an image that would be best suited to the following file types:
   a. vector
   b. bitmap.
4. Give examples of situations where the following techniques would be used:
   a. flip
   b. crop
   c. posterise
   d. colour change.
5. What actions are involved in reviewing a graphics job?

3. Be able to use graphics to enhance a document

As a computer graphics professional, you need to be able to use a range of methods for adding images into a document to bring more meaning to the text. Examples of this include enhancing a price list by including photographs of the products, or making an instruction sheet clearer by adding diagrams.

Software using graphics to enhance a document could be a vector graphics application or an office application such as a word processor, spreadsheet, database or presentation.

3.1 Acquired images

Images can be brought in from hardware or from a library of clip art.

Specialist hardware

There are many specialist hardware devices that can be used to acquire images, including:

- **Scanners** — these are used to transfer text and images from a piece of paper on a page in a book or magazine, or even a film slide or negative, into a digital file. (For more on scanners see page 328.)
- **Digital cameras** — these can be used to photograph the exact image(s) you want. You can then transfer the photos onto your computer for manipulation. (For more on digital cameras see page 327.)
- **Mobile phones** — modern mobile phones usually have a camera. This might produce photographs that can be included in a document. The lens quality of a mobile phone camera is often poor, so you would need to use your judgement as to whether any photo taken with a mobile phone camera is good enough to include in a document.

Activity: Scanners and digital cameras

Find three things a scanner does better than a digital camera and three things a digital camera does better than a scanner.

Why is this?

Clip art libraries

Clip art is the name given to pre-drawn images that you can select from and use in graphical documents. A collection of clip art is called a library.

Many computer graphic software applications include a clip art library that you can use. There are many other clip art libraries that can be bought or downloaded.

Web downloads

Web downloads are images found on the web that can be downloaded, usually by right-clicking on the image, selecting **Save picture as**, then choosing a sensible name and place to save it.

When using clip art or images from the web, you should always check that there are no royalty issues and that you have the right to use the artwork.

Editing

Once you have acquired an image, you will probably need to edit it with the following techniques to make it right for its purpose:

- **Cropping.** This removes any edges to the picture that are not wanted. When editing, cropping is used to keep the part of the image that is wanted before saving it to disk.
- **Rotating.** This straightens up an image that has been scanned at an angle or rotates an image to give it more impact.
- **Resizing.** If the image is too large or small when first acquired, then you will need to resize it to meet any constraints in the user requirements.
- **Colour correction.** If, for example, the images used are from different sources (perhaps from different cameras) and look dissimilar, you may need to adjust the colour so that they match each other.

Inserting images into and manipulating images within documents

You can insert an image into a document either from where you have saved it or, often, directly from a scanner. Once you have inserted your graphic within the document, it is likely that you will need to manipulate it in the following ways:

- **Resizing.** Pictures in a document need to be the right size – large enough to see what's in the picture, but not so large that they overwhelm the page. The right size might be down to your judgement or could be specified as a constraint in the user requirements.

- **Cropping.** This is used to remove any parts of the image that are not wanted, or to make the image the right shape to fit the space available in the document. For example, in a document explaining how to use a mixing desk, there might be a photograph of the controls. You could crop the photo to show only the controls described in that section of text, which will make the image more useful for the reader.

- **Text wrapping.** This allows the user to wrap any text around the image and control the distance between the words and the image.

- **Positioning.** This is used to make sure that the image is in the right place in the document.

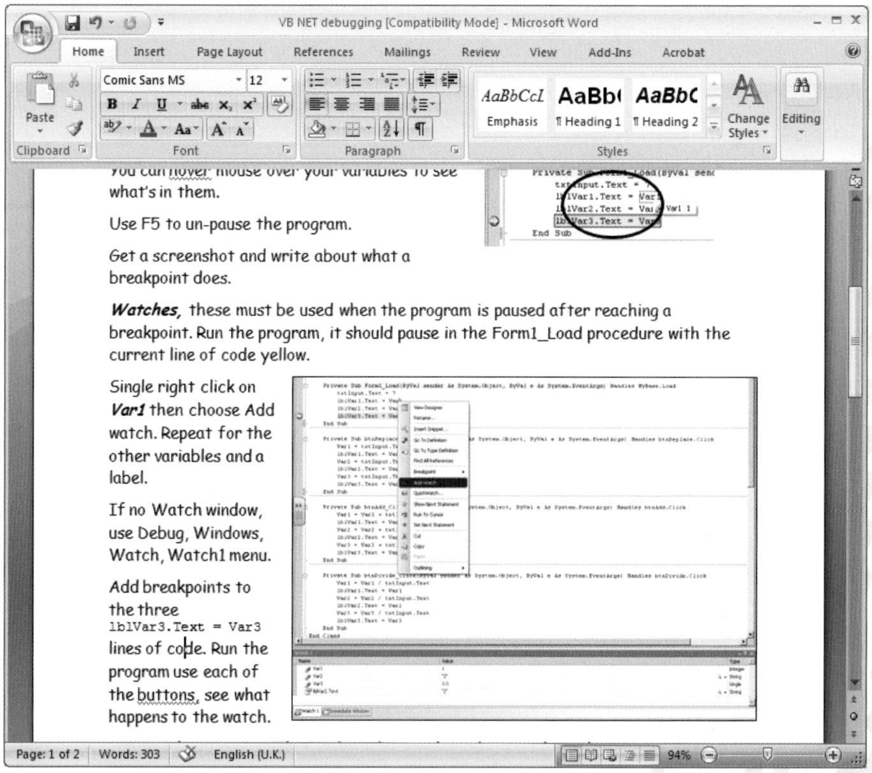

Figure 23.9: Text wrapping around an image in a document.

Relevant laws and guidelines

All computer graphic professionals need to be aware of the relevant laws and guidelines for using images, especially any **copyright** issues when using images that are not yours. For example, it is illegal to download and use certain images from the Internet in your work without seeking permission to do so.

Copyright issues

The most important law about using images is the **UK Copyright Designs and Patents Act (1988)**. This Act states for how many years a work of art has copyright and in what circumstances a piece of artistic work can be used.

When you find a picture you want to use, there will be copyright issues unless it is clearly marked as royalty free. If the photo is on a website, there will be an explanation or link on how to get permission to use it. As you might need to pay a royalty fee for the right to use an image, it's often better to create your own.

Activity: Legal penalties

What could happen to you if you were to break the UK Copyright Designs and Patents Act (1988)?

In what ways could you break this law?

Combining information

Many documents need to combine information, such as words, numbers, graphs, charts or images. You should always try to combine information in the clearest possible way for readers of your document, so that it is easy to follow and understand.

- Graphs and charts are great for enhancing text, as they can show the meaning of lots of numbers in a striking and useful way.
- Images such as photographs, diagrams and maps can help to explain and bring meaning to words and enhance the text.

Always remember that graphics should be there to help explain the words in a document, not just for decoration.

3.2 Objects

An object is almost anything you find in a document or vector image. Objects can be selected and you can usually access and change their properties, such as size or position.

When graphics are made from several objects, such as lines, rectangles and text, it is useful to group them together. This makes it impossible to accidently move part of the graphic. It also makes using the graphic much easier because a single click will select the whole group, which can then be moved or re-sized as a single (grouped) object.

When you use a graphical image to enhance a document, the graphic will be an object which you can position in the correct place and re-size, if needed.

Graphic objects are usually imported, inserted or pasted into the document and might be jpeg, bitmap, clip art or vector graphics.

Modern software applications often offer other graphical objects, such as text (Word Art), shapes and drawings using specialist toolbars in the app.

Assessment activity 23.4

The band like the new logo you have designed. They now want a series of graphics for publicity shots that they can use to make the band look impressive and stand out from the competition. They have come up with the idea of some photos of the band posing in front of different places from around the world.

1. Find three photos of interesting places in the world that can be used as the backgrounds for these publicity graphics.

   Acquire a photo of some people you can use as the band.

   Use a photo-manipulation software application of your choice to combine the band photo with each of the three backgrounds to make three publicity photos. **M3**

2. These graphics must use photographs imported from a digital camera or input from a scanner. **P4**

3. The band also wants you to create a CD sleeve for their new album. The sleeve will have four sides for you to design: outside front and back, and inside front and back.

   The dimensions of the CD sleeve are as follows:

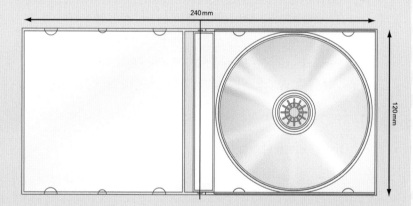

   Make sure you include all the essential elements of a CD sleeve for a music album:

   - band name and publicity photos of band
   - band logo you created
   - track numbers and titles (you can make these up)
   - eye-catching front cover. **P6**

4. The band is interested in adding your artwork to their website. They would like you to explain to them the different factors that will affect the file size of the computer graphics. They are particularly interested in having these issues explained to them:

PLTS

By creating publicity photos for the band, you will show that you are a **creative thinker**.

Functional skills

By creating the publicity photos, you will give evidence of your functional **ICT** skills: select, interact with and use ICT systems independently for a complex task to meet a variety of needs.

By producing the CD cover, you will give evidence of your functional **ICT** skills: present information in ways that are fit for purpose and audience.

BTEC Assessment activity 23.4 (Cont.) P4 P6 M3 D2

- file formats
- lossy and lossless compression techniques
- image resolution
- colour depth
- how resolution and colour depth affect file size and image quality.

Produce a document explaining the above.

Grading tips

- For task 1, you must edit the publicity photos using graphics software.
- For task 2, you will need to provide evidence to demonstrate that you have used specialist hardware to acquire an image. This evidence could be screenshots of the image being transferred from a digital camera or of the scanner being used to scan a photo.
- You will have to give a lot of thought to the layout of the CD sleeve when completing task 3. Do some research by looking at CD sleeves that you have at home. This will help generate some ideas to play with. The rest should be down to your creativity. Put some initial ideas down on paper first, then create the sleeve in *any* software package you like.
- For task 4, you must explain how the file size is affected by types of file, the compression used and the image quality. Giving some examples of file sizes will be useful here.

Just checking

1. What methods are there for acquiring images?
2. What is importing an image?
3. Describe these techniques used in editing images and documents:
   a. rotating
   b. colour correction
   c. text wrapping
   d. positioning.
4. Find three websites giving guidance and advice on the UK Copyright Designs and Patents Act (1988).
5. Find two examples of web pages that combine information. Explain how the images add to the understanding of words on these pages.

WorkSpace Shaun Gregory
Computer graphics professional

I work as a computer graphics professional in the design studio of a large advertising bureau.

We produce promotional displays, posters, packaging and marketing brochures for products and services. We also design distinctive logos for products and businesses, material for Internet web pages, interactive media, multimedia projects and any other graphical work required by clients.

My job is very varied. I am involved in all the stages of our projects, from meeting with clients to planning and development.

We try to find the most effective way to get messages across for clients, whether in print or electronic media, by using colour, type, illustrations, photography, animations and various print and layout techniques.

Our first step in developing a new design is to determine the needs of the client, the message the design should portray, and its appeal to customers or users. We then prepare sketches or layouts – by hand or with the aid of a computer – to illustrate our vision for their design, selecting colours, sound, artwork, photography, animation, style of type, and other visual elements for the design.

Sometimes we need to consult with copywriters on any text that accompanies the design before presenting a completed design to clients for approval.

For some printing jobs we even select the type of paper, so it feels right to the touch, as well as looking perfect.

We mostly use Adobe® CS5 collection software for our graphics projects. Out computer hardware is excellent, with large screens and a really fast network.

My working hours are flexible, but I'm expected to work seven hours a day with an hour for lunch. I usually arrive around 10 a.m. and leave around 6 p.m., although there are times when I need to be in earlier or stay later to meet with clients.

The best part of the job is seeing my work on huge roadside billboards when I drive past, although there's always something I wish I'd done differently or better.

Think about it!

1. What do you think the benefits of preparing sketches and layouts by hand are? What are the benefits of producing these with a computer? Think of a situation for each method where that technique would be best suited.

2. Adobe® CS5 is a well-respected professional package. Identify another similar application at a similar price. How do these compare in terms of the features they offer and the computer specifications needed to run well?

3. Research and write brief descriptions of the following paper types that Shaun might consider for a print job:
   - wove
   - smooth
   - laid
   - linen
   - coated
   - uncoated.

Just checking

1. Which of each of these pairs is usually preferred when choosing a hard disk for working with computer graphics?
   a   500GB or 2TB.
   b   8 ms or 12 ms seek time.
2. Identify two ways you could transfer graphics work from your computer to a client's computer. What are the advantages and disadvantages of each method?
3. In what ways is a graphics tablet different to a mouse?
4. Identify a way in which each of the following types of printer excels:
   a   ink jet
   b   colour laser
   c   dye sublimation
   d   plotter
   e   vinyl cutter.
5. Find an example of a bitmap (raster) graphic and a vector graphic on the Internet. Explain how you identified them as bitmap and vector.
6. What is pixellation?
7. What is clip art? What is it used for?
8. Name four ways you might need to edit an image that is being used to illustrate a document.

edexcel

Assignment tips

- Be careful to read both the assignment tasks and the grading. You should always end up with work which is evidence to show you've achieved the grading, for example M3 needs to include a given purpose.

- Always use good, real examples in your work. This will make your descriptions, explanations, comparisons and evaluations a lot easier for you to write, as well as a lot more likely to meet the grading.

- When you evaluate, you may find it useful to structure your work, in order to describe, then compare and finally conclude with the evaluation to bring it all together.

- Remember, the unit is about computer graphics, so relate the hardware and software in your assessment to graphical work.

- Indicate the targeted grading criteria (such as M2) at the start of the section of your work evidencing it.

- Read grading criteria carefully to ensure your work exactly matches the targeted grades.

26 Developing computer games

The computer games industry has grown phenomenally over the past 30 years and we have now reached the stage where many households have a games console. Games sell in huge numbers, for example *Mario Kart® Wii™* has sold over 21 million copies. These kinds of sales figures mean that the computer games industry is catching up with the film industry in size, and many IT professionals are attracted to work in the industry.

In order to understand the games development process, you must first understand what has happened in the games industry over the last 30 years and learn about the revolution in gaming that has taken place since 2005. You will discover both the benefits of playing games and also the concerns that people have about the playing of computer games.

Games come in many different styles and types; they are categorised into different genres, such as 'action games' or 'strategy games'. All the games within a genre have certain features in common.

This unit provides you with the opportunity to learn about computer game genres, understand how they are developed and even design a game yourself. By the end of the unit you will be able to review games with an understanding of what makes them successful and you will be able to document a computer game in the same way as a professional computer game developer.

Learning outcomes

After completing this unit you should:

1. know the different types of computer game
2. understand the impact of computer games on society and individuals
3. be able to design a computer game
4. be able to test and document a computer game.

Assessment and grading criteria

This table shows you what you must to in order to achieve a pass, merit or distinction grade, and where you can find activities in this book to help you.

To achieve a **pass** grade the evidence must show that you are able to:	To achieve a **merit** grade the evidence must show that, in addition to the pass criteria, you are able to:	To achieve a **distinction** grade the evidence must show that, in addition to the pass and merit criteria, you are able to:
P1 describe the features of different genres of computer games **Assessment activity 26.1 on page 368**	**M1** discuss current game development areas **Assessment activity 26.1 on page 368**	**D1** compare the features of different computer game platforms **Assessment activity 26.1 page 368**
P2 explain the impact of computer games on society and individuals **Assessment activity 26.2 on page 374**		
P3 produce a design specification for a computer game **Assessment activity 26.3 on page 380**	**M2** use appropriate design software tools to create concept art **Assessment activity 26.3 on page 380**	
P4 test a computer game, suggesting possible refinements **Assessment activity 26.4 on page 384**		
P5 produce basic documentation for a working game **Assessment activity 26.5 on page 388**		**D2** present complex documentation for a working game **Assessment activity 26.5 on page 388**

How you will be assessed

This unit is internally assessed. You will provide a portfolio of evidence to show that you have achieved the learning outcomes. Your portfolio of evidence can be supplied in many formats including electronically as well as paper-based. The grading grid in the specification for this unit lists what you must do to obtain pass, merit and distinction grades. The Assessment activities in this unit will guide you through tasks that will help you to be successful in this unit.

Your tutor will tell you exactly what form your assessments will take, but you could be asked to produce:

- class discussions
- short reports
- practical tasks
- design documents.

Beth Kingdom, 16-year-old puzzle enthusiast

Before I did this unit the only games I ever played were puzzle games on my mobile phone. I'd never bought a game and I didn't really take them seriously. To be honest, I didn't even realise how big the computer games industry was.

Once we started looking at all of the different types of games out there I was really impressed with the amount of time spent making a game and all of the different types of people who play games. I am definitely going to start trying different types of games. Some of the ones we saw in class were brilliant.

When we started designing games, I still wanted to stick with my favourite genre – puzzle games. I learned about different types of puzzle games and how to design them using different software tools. We then learned about the programming languages that could make my design into a real game and how a professional developer would document the whole process.

I found the whole unit really exciting – there seems to be a lot going on in the games industry and I'd really like to work in a games-related role in the future. I think I'd like to be a computer games programmer, maybe doing a job where I can figure out how the puzzles are going to work.

Over to you

- What kinds of games do you like playing?
- Have you ever thought about how games are made?
- If you were going to design a game, what kind of game would it be?

1. Know the different types of computer game

What was the gaming revolution?

Twenty-five years ago computer games were made up of simple graphics and came on large cartridges or cassette tapes. Nowadays they are much more complex and a large industry has grown up to create them. There are large communities of users who spend a lot of time and money playing impressive, interactive games.

Today a game can tell a story as gripping as a film or let you have as much fun with your friends as a football match. Games have become technologically advanced in terms of graphics but also in terms of control systems. For example motion controls have become popular in the last five years.

- Compare the games you can play today with games from the 1980s. (Use pictures of the early games.)
- Discuss in groups what you think the gaming revolution was.

In this section, we'll look at the different types of games on the shelves, the elements of a game that have to be developed (such as design and programming) and the different gaming platforms that are available.

1.1 Genres

Games are categorised into **genres**. Similar to music genres or film genres, a game genre is a category of similar games which have common features, styles and objectives. Each genre tends to attract the same types of players. For example, first-person shooter (FPS) games are mostly played by males aged between 12 and 30 years, whereas brain training games tend to be played by females aged between 25 and 60 years.

Some of the most popular games genres are:

- **Action games** – games which require quick thinking and 'button bashing', such as *Sonic the Hedgehog*™ or *Space Invaders*
- **Role-playing games (RPGs)** – games where you develop characters and **level up**, such as *Kingdom Hearts* or *Pokémon*®
- **Adventure games** – games where you follow a story and solve puzzles, such as *Tomb Raider*™ or *Zack & Wiki*™
- **Strategy** – games which require tactical thinking, such as *Age of Empires* or *Fat Princess*
- **Simulations** – games which re-create real life situations, such as *Need for Speed*™ or *Roller Coaster Tycoon*
- **Sports** – games where you play a sport, such as *Championship Manager* or *Duck Hunt*

Key terms

Genre – a category of games which have certain gameplay features and styles in common.

Levelling up – when a character in a game collects enough experience points (XP) to improve their skills.

- **Educational** – games which teach the player something new or improve their skills, such as *My French Coach* or *Maths Trainer*
- **Massively multiplayer online (MMO)** – games which are played across the Internet with thousands of simultaneous players, such as *Star Trek Online* or *Eve® Online*.

Activity: Have a go yourself

You can't complete a unit called *Developing computer games* without playing a few games yourself!

Get together in groups and find out who has access to which computer games platforms and which games they have.

Plan an event, perhaps at each other's houses or in class, where you can all play on different types of games that you haven't played before. After the event, answer these questions:

- Did you get to try any new genres? If so, which ones?
- Did you try any games that you might be interested in playing again?
- If you played more than one game from a particular genre, can you identify any of the common features that the genre contains?

1.2 Games development areas

Creating a software application such as Microsoft® Word® is quite a straightforward procedure. That doesn't mean that it's easy – the application is made of complicated programming code that has to be written by a team of people. But the process only involves a project manager, a systems analyst, a software engineer, programmers and testers.

Creating a game is a completely different process and involves a lot more people. In some ways, creating a game is more like creating a Hollywood film than creating a software application.

Games are made by software development companies that are often referred to as **games studios** or simply **developers**. When they start planning a game they have to think about all of the different aspects that make up a game. We'll be looking at these in this section.

Technology

Computer games have always been driven by technology. For many years it was advances in graphics that changed the way games were designed – the early two-dimensional (2D) games like *Pac Man* were made up of simple sprites, whereas games such as *Heavy Rain* now feature complex three-dimensional (3D) worlds made of realistic graphics that can almost pass for the real world.

Key terms

Games studio – a company where computer games are designed and programmed.

Developer – an individual or company that creates computer games.

Key terms

Items – objects within a game which are collected by the player.

Graphical user interface (GUI) – interface that uses icons, pictures and menus instead of text.

Artificial intelligence (AI) – a set of rules that attempts to make characters appear to be thinking like a human would do.

Non-playable character (NPC) – a character that is controlled by the games platform instead of the player.

2D games

A simple 2D game needs to have an artist who designs the characters, **items** and the layout of the levels. Next it needs programmers who can create them. Programmers create these aspects individually at first before bringing them together with a set of rules that controls how they behave. After this stage a sound designer or an audio engineer finds and adds sound effects and music to the game. At this stage the game is finished, but it still needs to have a **graphical user interface (GUI)** built onto the beginning of it and the game needs to be integrated into the system that it is being run on.

3D games

Things get even more complicated when it comes to creating a 3D game. Specialist 3D designers are needed to design the characters and the environments where the game will take place. Some of these environments are amazingly complicated – it is the ambition of many games studios to create more advanced environments that will eventually be as complex as the real world.

One of the attempts to do this on the Playstation® 2 was a game called *Spiderman 2*. This game was an open-world super hero adventure game where the player had to swing around New York and climb up its buildings. The city in the game was an exact replica of the real city, but scaled down. This involved a huge amount of development work, as well as a very detailed and complicated program. To create the city would have required hundreds of 3D developers, each designing some of the streets and buildings.

Artificial intelligence

The Playstation® 2 was able to run a game like *Spiderman 2* because the processor that it had was powerful enough to cope with the 3D graphics, the sound and the **artificial intelligence (AI)** of the **non-playable characters (NPCs)** within the game. AI is a set of rules and code that control the behaviour of the NPCs – it is often this that determines whether a game is fun or not.

If a character in a computer game doesn't have very sophisticated AI, they will not behave in a way that seems natural or likely. For example, in early games like *Frogger* the NPCs moved along set paths, at the same speed and in the same way every time. In *Frogger* the NPCs were trucks and cars and they moved in perfect unison along the road with the same space between all of them. Have you ever seen a motorway where the cars and trucks behave like this? Probably not.

As computer games technology has improved, so has the AI of the NPCs. In modern computer games, in the sports and fighting games genres, the AI will make the computer-controlled players adapt to what you are doing and make it harder for you. As with most things, as the technology gets better, so does the AI.

Activity: Artifical intelligence (AI)

AI is all about rules. The developer puts in codes of behaviour for all of the important NPCs in a game and sets how they will react to certain things. For example, the ghosts in *Pac Man* move around the maze at a set speed and they have three rules:

1. if you touch Pac Man, eat him
2. if Pac Man has eaten a power-up that makes you change colour, run away from Pac Man
3. if Pac Man has eaten everything but your eyes, fly back to base to regenerate.

Pac Man was made in 1980, over 30 years ago, and computer games technology has come a long way since then.

- **If Pac Man was going to be made today, what kind of behaviour would the ghosts have? Would they have strategies? Would they lay traps?**
- **See what ideas you can come up with.**

Discuss with a friend.

Interaction design

It isn't just the technology that's getting better — it's also the design. Each new game that sells well pushes other games studios and developers to create better games that will out-sell existing ones. As a result, games design is advancing at an impressive rate.

Using graphical user interfaces (GUI)

One of the areas that receives a lot of attention is the design of the GUI. The graphical user interface (GUI) is really important in a game because it includes everything that the user interacts with: all of the opening menu screens, options menu, the pause menu, any in-game menus, such as inventories (where the character's possessions are stored) and the **Heads up display (HUD)**.

The HUD

The HUD is the main game screen. It has information, usually around the edges, that tells you the important things you need to know, such as health or ammunition remaining.

As you can see in Figure 26.1 on page 367, the HUD contains information that is crucial to the player and could mean the success or failure of whatever objective the player is trying to achieve. The design of the HUD is very important – too much information means that the player will need to take their attention off the gameplay, but too little information means they might not know what's going on. A lot of thought is put into the design of the HUD and how to give information to the player without distracting them. Game designers use techniques like sounds and icons instead of text.

Key term

Heads up display (HUD) – small icons and menus that are displayed on-screen throughout gameplay.

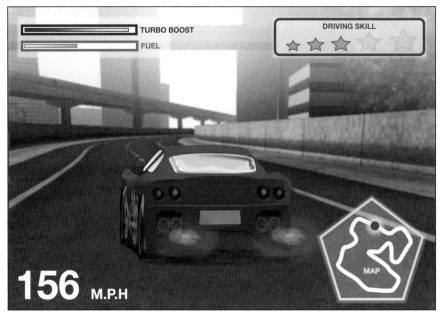

Figure 26.1: An example of a Heads up display (HUD).

Integration

In some computer games, the HUD is integrated into the gameplay itself, so you don't always need to distract the player. This also makes them feel more immersed in the game world.

1.3 Gaming platforms

There are many different **platforms** for playing games. A games platform can be a hardware device or it can be a special type of software that has been designed to play different games. When people first become interested in playing computer games, they tend to play games that are available on a platform that they already have access to. For example, people will play games on their phones or their televisions because they already have these. Platforms such as these tend to have casual games on them which can be played for short periods of time and not taken very seriously. When people want to spend more time (and money) on games, they will usually choose a platform that has been designed specifically for gameplay.

Key term

Platform – the underlying operating system, e.g. Mac OS or Windows®. It might also be the hardware or software system that is used to play games, for example Playstation® 3.

These computer game controllers are for gaming platforms specifically designed for gameplay. How many games platforms can you name?

Table 26.1 shows the different games platforms available, with some examples of the kinds of games that you would play on them.

Table 26.1 Games platforms.

Games platform	Description of games platform
Personal computer (PC)	Most people have a PC in their homes and it is the perfect platform for playing games. PC games can be played using the keyboard and mouse or with specialised controllers. One of the issues people face using a PC to play games is whether their graphics cards can cope with the games' requirements, especially when playing 3D games which need more powerful graphics cards.
Home console	Home consoles are machines that are designed to be primarily used for playing games. While they can often do other things such as browse the Internet or display photos, they are mainly designed to play games that have been developed especially for that make of console. When you buy a game for a certain console you know for sure that it will work on that console. The most popular current consoles available are the Xbox® 360, the Nintendo® Wii™ and the Playstation® 3.
Handheld console	This is a small version of the home console designed to be used outside the house and running off a battery. The handheld console needs to be smaller and lighter, and must have its own screen for displaying the game. Because of this requirement the games are usually simpler than PC or console games, but just as much fun. The first handheld console was the Nintendo® Gameboy. Today people can choose between the popular Nintendo® DSi™ and the Playstation® Portable.
Mobile phone	Nearly everyone has a mobile phone. The first mobile (and car) phones from Nokia came with a game called *Snake* built in. Since then mobile phone games have become very popular. Some phones, such as the iPhone, can run quite complicated games, which are almost as good as games for a handheld console.
Arcade game	Arcade games machines are freestanding units that you can see in arcades, bowling alleys or cinemas. This was how games were played in the 1980s when most people didn't have their own console and PCs weren't sophisticated enough. Arcade classics such as *Space Invaders* and *Pac Man* have been replaced by modern arcade machines such as *Time Crisis* and *Dance Revolution*.
TV (set top box)	As television moved to digital, households started getting set top boxes such as Sky, Freeview or Virgin. These set top boxes contain processors and allow games to be played. The games tend to be quite basic but enjoyable, so this is an ideal platform for casual gamers.
Browser games	A browser game runs inside a web browser on your computer such as Internet Explorer®, Firefox® or Safari. These games tend to be quick-paced, colourful and free. Browser games are a great way for companies to attract people to their websites – they make money through adverts that run alongside the games.
Emulator	An emulator allows people to play games on their PCs that were originally only available on other platforms (such as home consoles). For example, you can run an emulator that allows you to play Sega Megadrive games on your PC. You should be careful to use a legal emulator such as Virtual Console by Nintendo®, as there are a lot of illegal emulators available. (An illegal emulator is one for which the permission of the games' developer was not asked for in the creation of the emulator.).
Network	Network platforms are usually accessed through current home consoles but can also be accessed through a PC. They are special platforms for games that you need to buy and then download. Examples are the Xbox® Live Arcade and the Playstation® Network. Both of these network platforms are very popular and allow the console owners to buy games without having to leave the house. Some people think that this might be the future of how we buy games.

PLTS

By preparing a guide to the different games platforms, you will show that you are a **reflective learner**.

Functional skills

By gathering relevant information on recent advancements in computer games, you will evidence your functional **English** skills in reading.

By contributing to a discussion on the developments in computer games technology, you will evidence your functional **English** skills in speaking and listening.

BTEC Assessment activity 26.1 P1 M1 D1

You have started working as a journalist for a leading games magazine. The first article you have been asked to write is about games genres and platforms.

1. List the different types of games genres and describe the features that are common between the games. **P1**

2. Research the current games market for information on current or interesting advancements in games. Discuss these developments with a friend or in a group. Focus on how these new features or styles of game would affect the development process. **M1**

3. A friend who is new to playing games wants to know what the differences are between the various games platforms. Prepare a guide for your friend that compares the features of the different computer game platforms. **D1**

Grading tip

When looking at what is available in the games market today, the best place to go is an online games shop where new titles are listed and described. You will often find that the developers are eager to show off their games and will list the features that make the new game stand out from the crowd. This would be an excellent basis for your research and discussion for question 2. The same is also true of platforms – games sites will list the features and functionality in an easy-to-understand format.

Just checking

1. What kind of genre does *Sonic the Hedgehog*™ come under?
2. Is *Pac Man* a 2D or a 3D game?
3. What were the NPCs in *Frogger*?
4. What is a HUD?
5. What was the name of the game that old Nokia phones came with?

2. Understand the impact of computer games on society and individuals

2.1 Games in society

Entertainment has taken many different forms over the years. Radio was the most important entertainment system in people's homes until television (TV) became popular in the 1950s. It has taken much longer for video games to become a mainstream form of entertainment. Although they have been around since 1972, home video game consoles were for a long time considered children's toys and PC games as the realm of the nerd!

Expanding markets

In 2004 Nintendo moved away from traditional handheld games and released the Nintendo® DS™, which had an innovative touch-screen interface. The system was designed to encourage new generations of players. Nintendo also had the perfect game for the older player – *Dr Kawashima's Brain Training*™ was the first touch-screen game that claimed to actually make players more intelligent.

Nintendo realised that they couldn't compete with the Xbox® 360 and the Playstation® 3 in terms of graphics, so they turned their attention to family game play. They released the Nintendo® Wii™ in 2006, which used motion controllers in a way that allowed anyone, from a toddler to a granny, to play games.

Better multiplayer

Playing on console games was a solitary experience for a long time. Most consoles had more than one controller, but never very many.

Just your average gamers?

369

Some people are accused of spending too much time alone playing games.

PCs allowed games to be played across a network, but these were very slow until broadband became common. Some of the earlier consoles attempted online connections, but it was the Microsoft® Xbox® that really started the online gaming revolution. The console could be easily connected to the Internet, allowing people to play games against their friends and even talk to them while playing.

Today online gaming is huge. Fast broadband connections mean that people can connect quickly and play online games at the same time as thousands of others. Games such as *Animal Crossing* and *World of Warcraft* attract dedicated players who log on regularly to improve their rankings or beat the next dungeon. All of the current generation of games consoles come with built-in wireless networking, so the ability to connect to the Internet is considered a must.

Concerns

There are various concerns about people playing computer games (see Table 26.2 opposite). These tend to get reported in the media on a regular basis, to the extent that many parents are extremely worried about their children playing computer games.

Benefits

In the past, when considering video games, the focus used to be the concerns various people had about them. Today there is just as much being said about the benefits of computer games.

- **Hand–eye coordination.** Games encourage people to use different combinations of buttons in response to incidents happening very quickly on-screen. It has been proven beyond doubt that this develops hand–eye coordination. Now professionals such as pilots, astronauts and athletes use games to help them improve their hand–eye coordination.

- **Brain training.** Since the first brain training game, *Dr Kawashima's Brain Training*™, every games platform now boasts the ability to develop brain training skills. Numeracy and literacy skills can be improved in a video game using similar techniques to those used in the classroom, but in a more fun way.

- **Thinking and strategy skills.** Many games involve taking on the role of a military commander or creating whole civilisations. These games teach tactics and forward thinking, skills that can come in very handy in the real world.

- **Future impact.** Games could potentially take the place of films as their stories get better and become available on many different platforms.

- **Impact on 'mainstream' application development.** As games interfaces are getting better, other application designers are looking at how to take ideas from them. A good example of this is the way people chat through games; applications such as Skype™ now have text chat built into them in the same way.

Table 26.2: Concerns about playing computer games – and some arguments against these.

Concern	Reasons for concern	Arguments against concern
Excessive playing time	It can't be denied that some people spend too much time playing games. Players of MMORPGs (Massive Multiplayer Online Role Playing Games) can become sleep deprived because they spend so long playing games. People have lost their jobs and have even developed health problems because of their addiction to video games.	There are always extreme examples; it's just that games seem to get reported on more than anything else. People spend as much time watching TV but that doesn't seem to be considered as damaging as playing video games for long periods.
Social isolation	There is concern that people who play too many video games may lose some of their social skills and not be able to make friends as easily. As online gaming has taken off, people now have communities of online 'friends'. These could be people that players have never met in person and parents are often concerned that their children could be at risk.	Multiplayer and family games have gained in popularity over the last five years and have answered this concern. Children may play games with their parents as often as on their own, and these days the console may live permanently in the family room. There are still some game players who sit in front of their PC and play on their own, but there always will be – not everyone is a social animal.
Cost	Video games are expensive. It usually costs £40 for a game and around £200–£300 for a console. People are concerned that younger players spend a fortune on video games and that the price is simply too high.	This is an unfair argument when you consider the cost of similar items. For example, a DVD can cost around £15 and will only provide entertainment for a couple of hours. A video game will usually last for about 10 hours, so if you consider the amount of time that you play compared to how much you spend, it's a bargain!
Separation from reality	There have been many stories in the media about young people who have committed crimes because they were influenced by video games. There are also concerns that people who play too many games won't be able to tell the difference between things that happen in the game world and things that happen in the real world.	The same can be said for books, films and TV programs. The sad truth is that certain individuals in society are extremely susceptible to suggestions from stories. Many crimes have also been committed that were influenced by films or books.
Education	It has been a concern in the past that games will lead to people's intelligence dropping as they are only capable of 'button bashing' and won't be able to understand more complex instructions.	Time has proven that this is no longer a concern. While most games are made for fun, there are a lot of video games designed for educational purposes. In the next section we'll look at games that claim to improve people's educational ability.

Case study: Working in a games shop

Ross works in a local video game shop on Saturdays. Part of his job involves answering questions from customers about new games that have been released. This means that Ross needs to know a lot about the content of the games, but he loves video games so is happy to get the chance to try them all out.

As part of his job, Ross often gets asked questions by the parents of some of his younger customers. A concerned father came into the shop last Saturday and asked for Ross's professional opinion on some of the action-adventure games his 12-year-old daughter wants to buy.

1. **What concerns might parents have about their children playing video games?**

2. **What genres would you recommend to the girl's father that would be suitable for his 12-year-old daughter? Explain your choices.**

3. **How do certain video games claim to improve a person's body or mind?**

4. **As more types of people play games, are they now seen as a major form of entertainment on the same level as TV programmes and films?**

2.2 The impact of games on individuals

How does a game affect you as an individual? To answer this, we need to consider both the psychological and the health factors.

Psychological factors

The reason why games are so popular is that they engage the player's thoughts and feelings at the same time. When you are playing a game, you become completely involved with what is happening on-screen to the extent that you can start to feel like it is really happening. These psychological effects are put in on purpose by the game designers and they are often the reason why we play the game in the first place.

There are different effects that are put in by the designers in order for the game to make us feel certain things. These include the factors listed in Table 26.3 opposite.

Health

There are some genuine health concerns regarding the injuries which could be sustained as a result of playing games for too long or in poor lighting conditions.

- **Repetitive strain injury (RSI).** RSI is the result of performing the same movements over and over again, which is something that happens when playing games. The symptoms of RSI are pain and weakness in the area of the injury – for the games player this will be in their thumbs and fingers. RSI is most likely to occur when someone plays the same game with the same movements for hours at a time and continues to do so for weeks or months.

- **Lack of exercise.** The game player's exercise routine can become disrupted because they are distracted by the games they are playing. In this way they risk becoming overweight and lethargic.

- **Eye strain.** This tends to occur when people are staring at televisions or monitors for long periods without a break. Eye strain is made worse when people play games in poorly lit rooms.

Table 26.3: Different psychological factors and their effects on game players.

Factor	Effects
Use of sound	Fast-paced music and high-pitched noises, such as those in *Super Mario*, make players feel excited. Slow, orchestral music and gloomy noises can make players feel scared, like those in *Luigi's Mansion*™.
High score listings	The first time you play a game you will get a score. The next time you play you will probably want to beat that high score. Keeping a list of all the scores you have ever achieved can make you feel frustrated with yourself and want to play again – only better!
Competitive games	Like sports, competitive games are extremely fun and exciting. What is better than working with a friend to beat another team fair and square?
Peer pressure	When all of your friends are talking about a new game, you will probably want it yourself. This isn't always a positive effect if a person can't afford the game, but it does mean that the good games tend to sell well and the poor games don't. Word of mouth is a powerful marketing tool.
Fun	If a game is fun you will want to play it for longer.
Educational value	Some games will teach you a lot without you even realising it. *Civilisation* is an educational game which teaches you about different historical civilisations and how they prospered. It is also a bestseller.
Expectations	If you have played a lot of games, you might think that you know what's happening next. Surprises are always fun!
Levelling	Levelling is a crucial aspect to many games. Your character will improve the longer you play the game and the better you become. You often also have the ability to customise your character with each new level. For example, a character that levels in a game with magic will usually get more powerful the higher the level.

BTEC Assessment activity 26.2 **P2**

The magazine editors have asked you to write an article about how computer games have affected individuals and society.

1. Choose three very different types of computer games and explain how they could affect either an individual or society as a whole.

2. Select a well-known video game company and explain how it has had an impact on society.

Grading tips

- You will need to consider all of the different concerns and benefits associated with computer games over the years and how different companies and products have addressed these. Think about games that you have played and games that you have heard about in the media.

- Some of the issues that surround computer games make people feel very angry and passionate, so don't be surprised if your research has surprising results. But remember that you are writing a formal document, so you need to keep it free of anything too controversial and consider both sides of the argument.

Just checking

1. Which console is designed for family players?
2. Why is social isolation a concern regarding computer games?
3. Name two benefits of playing computer games.
4. What is the intended effect of high score lists?

3. Be able to design a computer game

As part of this unit you are required to produce a design specification for a computer game. Creating a game is quite a complicated process and you are not expected to do that just yet. But you do need to create a design specification for a game that is similar to the specifications used in the games industry.

3.1 Design

There are many different stages to the design of a new computer game. As with most things, the more complicated the game the more in depth the design needs to be. If you have got any experience with programming or creating websites, you will understand that you must design a program or website before you create it. But don't worry if you haven't created a program or website before, because designing a game will introduce you to some of the concepts that you will be able to use in future. The idea is quite straightforward – if you want something to work well, you need to plan every aspect of it in advance. This is why the design stage is crucial to success. You can always tell when a game hasn't been designed properly because it will have faults or flaws that make it less fun to play.

Deciding on the game elements

The first decisions you need to make are about the different elements of the game. These are:

- **Host platform.** Is the game going to be played on a PC, handheld or home console? The platform will decide how detailed the game can be and what kinds of features and functionality it will contain.

- **Genre.** Will the game be an FPS or an RPG? (See pages 362–363 for game genres.) The genre will decide the gameplay to some extent. It will also help you focus on what kind of game you are designing

- **Graphics.** Will they be simple or detailed? 2D or 3D? **Cel shaded**, cartoon style or **photo-realistic**? If you go for very detailed graphics, the game will take a lot longer to develop and will need a platform that can handle the graphics.

- **Look and feel.** What will the style of the game be? Will it be futuristic with lots of metallic textures and sci-fi sound effects? Will it be set in a fantasy world with castles and ogres?

- **Story.** Is it going to be a casual game where the story doesn't matter? Or will it be an action game where a little bit of story gets everything started? Or an RPG where the story is everything?

- **Control method.** How will the player control the game? With many types of controllers out there, including motion controllers and guitar controllers, this is an important decision.

Tools

Once the designers have decided on the kind of game they are creating, they then start using a variety of tools to create an image of what the game will look like. This sounds simpler than it really is. The image of the game in a design specification isn't just some drawings showing what the game will look like – it is enough information for everyone working on the development of the game to be able to do their job. For example, the level developer or 3D environment artist needs to have detailed maps of what rooms or routes they need to create in a 2D or 3D world. The image of the game might include the aspects listed below.

Storyboards

A storyboard is a set of simple images which show the whole of a game, or the most important stages. Storyboards may not be used in casual games, such as *Pac Man* or *Line Rider*™, where there is only really one

Did you know?

When Nintendo released the Nintendo® Wii™, they surprised everyone by refusing to compete in Sony and Microsoft's best graphics war. Instead they decided that family games and motion control would be more important than graphics – and having sold more consoles than the PS3™ and Xbox® 360, they seem to be right. Sony and Microsoft are now incorporating motion controllers into their systems with the Playstation® Move and Xbox® 360 Kinect add-ons.

Nintendo made a similar choice with the Nintendo® DS™ handheld as well. They decided that the touch screen was more important than better graphics, and time has proven them right again – the PSP™ cannot compete with sales of the DS™ and DSi™.

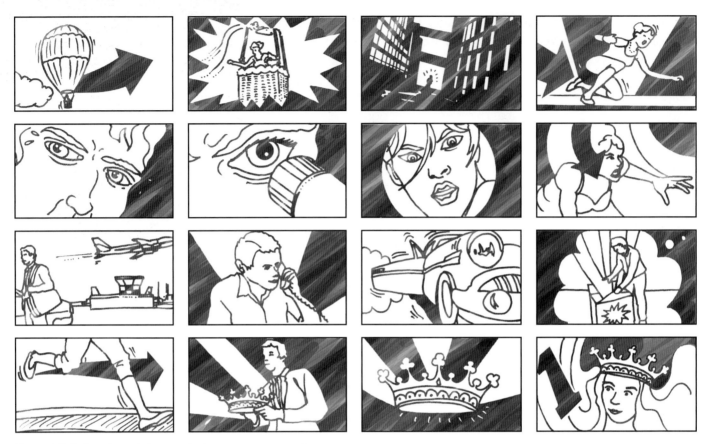

Figure 26.2: Storyboards lay out the important stages of a game.

Key term

Cut scenes – short film clips within a game that tell part of the story.

```
Loop While Hero-Health>1
    If Enemy Attacks Hero
        Hero-Health = -1
    End If
    When Hero-Health <1
        Hero—Lives = -1
    When Hero-Lives <1
        Game Over
    End
```

Figure 26.3: An example of pseudo code. In normal English, this means that the hero can continue playing if they have more than one life. If they don't have any lives the game is over. The hero's health is lowered each time they are attacked by an enemy and when their health reaches zero, they lose a life.

screen. But as soon as multiple levels, different characters and **cut scenes** with storyline are included in a game, storyboards become crucial tools which allow the developer to imagine the whole concept.

Pseudo code

Pseudo code is a design tool used to plan the rules of a game before the actual code is written. Pseudo code lies halfway between normal spoken English and programming languages. You can write pseudo code and then use it to write program code using any programming language.

Pseudo code is informal, which means that there are no set rules. Games designers use pseudo code to set out the rules that the game characters must obey. Figure 26.3 is an example of pseudo code.

Narratives

The narrative includes any information that is given to the player about the story or context of the game. The game designer decides in advance what the narrative will contain. For a story-driven game, script writers are employed to make sure that all of the lines are written out in advance. Most modern games have spoken dialogue and the actors who speak this will all need a script.

Action lists

The designer prepares action lists – detailed action plans telling all team members what they need to do and by what date. This approach is similar to any other project management tool used to organise a large project with different components. Games are made up of various elements created by different people, so the person in charge needs to keep a close watch to make sure that everything gets done.

Graphical tools

Various graphical tools are used to design the game in advance of production. Graphics software such as Adobe® Photoshop or Illustrator® may be used to draw some of the concept art (see opposite) or put together storyboards.

Concept art

Concept art is a collection of drawings and paintings that show what different characters, levels and objects will look like. It is created before the game is made.

The concept art is one of the most important design stages, as it sets up a look and feel for the game. It is passed between all of the different developers to help them understand the kind of game that will be made and its style. Concept art could be detailed paintings or hand-drawn sketches depending on the game that is being created.

Choice of programming language

The programming language to be used will be selected during the design process.
This is something that the programmers may change at a later stage, but it is often a decision forced on them depending on which platform they are developing for. The programming languages used for console or complex PC games tend to be C++ programming languages. These are used to bring together complex graphics and 3D models from a variety of different software sources.

The programmers will use an **integrated development environment** (IDE) to help them write the code and arrange it so that games can be developed quickly and the rules by which the characters must abide put in place. In the next section we will look in more detail at the programming part of the development process.

3.2 Program
Choice of development environment

After the design specification has been created, it can be used by the development team to start creating the game. The developers or programmers will need to decide what kind of development environment they want. This software is used to create the code and will determine the programming language adopted. For example, you might be using a development environment based on language C++, with a simple text editor to write it. Integrated development environments (IDE) are software packages that combine the software and the programming languages, so that the code that is written or generated can be checked as you write. An example of this is Microsoft® Visual Basic®, which allows the developer to draw an interface and then add code behind it.

Concept art tends to be hand-drawn but can be done using graphics software. Which style do you prefer?

Key term

Integrated development environment (IDE) – a piece of software which lets you write code, test it and build it into an application or game.

Key terms

Types of programming languages

Object-oriented – these languages deal with different elements of the game as objects. Each object can have properties that define it and rules that allow it to interact with other objects. A *Pac Man* object would have a 'health' property that sets out how much health it has, and possibly a 'collide' method that tells the game what should happen when it collides with an enemy. Java™ is an example of an object-oriented programming language which is used to make web-based and mobile phone games.

Procedural – this type of language runs the code step by step using different routines to make different things happen. It takes a lot longer to write code like this, but it can produce the most complex games. C++ is a procedural language which is used by both Sony and Microsoft® as their in-house language for creating console games.

Event driven – this isn't truly a type of language, more a way of using a programming language. In a game that is event driven, everything that happens is the result of an event, like a mouse click or a button push. Only the simplest games are event driven – but some of the simplest games can be the most fun. Older adventure games, such as *The Secret of Monkey Island*™, are event driven – everything happens with the click of a mouse or the arrival of a character in a new area.

Scripting languages – simple programming languages that work with other software, such as Adobe® Flash®. Action script is the most popular scripting language used in gaming today. It is code that sits behind a Flash® animation and dictates the rules of the game. This allows interactive Flash® games to be created that can be played on the Internet through a web browser. Flash®-based games tend to be simple games that you can just dip into. *Line Rider*™ is a popular Flash® game where the player draws a route for the game character to sled down. The aim of the game is to beat your own best score by keeping the sled moving for as long as you can.

Choice of language

The language that is chosen is very important. Programming languages are organised into different categories depending on how complex they are.

Different programming languages, and the IDEs that they use, have different features and facilities that will make writing code easier. These may include:

- having different menus and tools to help write or test the code
- saving the files as a project and keeping a set directory structure for ease of access
- having built-in help facilities if the developer gets stuck.

One of the most important jobs an IDE performs is building or compiling the code. This means taking all of the instructions that have been written and changing them into the machine code that is understood by the platform's computer processor.

Good programming practice

The programmer must follow professional practices when writing code because it is often a team effort with multiple people working on the same game. Good practice includes:

- writing comments at the end of a block of code so that people can see what it does
- writing **unitary code blocks** – these do a number of tasks in one place in order to use less memory
- making sure that code is spaced out so that other people can understand which code blocks belong together; this is done by **indenting**
- making sure that any names used clearly describe the thing that is named, for example the amount of coins a character has collected could be called *CarolsCoins*.

These good practices may come from a 'house style' which sets out how the code should be written. This will be unique to the development studio. It will allow all of the other programmers to understand how the game has been developed as soon as they see it. The house style may also include information on how the files should be saved and where they will be stored.

3.3 Coding

The actual programming is often called coding or the coding stage. This is when the developers write the programming code which will form the final game. The code will be different depending on which type of language has been used, but all the programming languages follow certain rules.

Use of program structures

One of the rules of programming is that the code must flow in one of three different ways. These are known as the program structures and they are: sequence, selection and iteration.

- **Sequence.** If the code is written as a sequence, each line of code will run one after the other.
- **Selection.** Sometimes there needs to be options within the code, and this is when selection is used. If there is more than one choice depending on a certain requirement, then the right line of code is selected. The example of pseudo code shown in Figure 26.3 (page 376) had selection in it. Another example is a racing game that only lets you start driving 'if' the chequered flag has been swung.
- **Iteration.** This means that the code is repeated. It might be repeated a few set times or it might be repeated until something specific happens. Iteration is very useful in writing code because it means that you don't have to repeat all of the code you have written – this in turn makes it quicker to run. For example, in the retro classic *Space Invaders* rows and rows of aliens slowly descend towards a ship that the player controls. All the aliens in a row are identical and, instead of writing hundreds of lines for each alien, the code for one alien can be repeated.

Syntax rules for the language

The code must also follow syntax rules. Syntax is different depending on which programming language is used and sets the way in which the code sentences must be put together. For example, in Java™ a semi-colon (;) must be used to finish each line, and braces (or curly brackets – {}) must be used to start and finish a section of code. The programmer working on the game must be a specialist in one or more programming languages and needs to have an in-depth understanding of the syntax – otherwise the game won't work.

Assigning values

One of the aspects that makes games fun is getting different results each time that you play. For example, you might get a higher score or you might find more treasure. These amounts or numbers are referred to as **values** and can be stored in the code. Some languages call these 'variables' and 'properties', or they might have different names in other languages. What is important is that information is stored within the code. This information may only be kept while the game is running or it could be saved onto the system for later games.

Operators

The values can be treated like any kind of numbers or text. Many programming languages use the same operators as in mathematics. Operators are symbols that have an effect on the numbers that they are working on. The main four operators are shown in Figure 26.4.

Programmers also use comparison operators, which look at a value and assess what it is worth. These are shown in Figure 26.5.

Finally, logical operators use combinations of values. The syntax of these differs greatly between languages, so the ones used in Figure 26.6 are intended only to give an example.

Key terms

Unitary code block – a section of code which performs a number of tasks.

Indenting – increasing or decreasing the amount of space between the margin and the beginning of the sentence when writing code, so that it is clear to other people which code blocks belong together.

Values – information that is stored in the game which affects the progress of the game, such as health or score.

```
+ add
- subtract
* multiply
/ divide
```

Figure 26.4: The four main operators.

```
> greater than
< less than
= equal to
!= not equal (or could be <>
   depending on language)
<= less than or equal to
>= greater than or equal to
```

Figure 26.5: Comparison operators.

```
&& and
|| or
! not
```

Figure 26.6: Logical operators.

Input/output statements

Once the main structure of the code is in place, the programmer will plan what information is going to be sent into the code blocks and what will be returned. For example, in a game about marathon running, there is a code block that calculates a score based on miles run and time. The two numbers (miles run and time) are the input; the output is the score. When writing the code, these are called input statements and output statements. It is very important to remember what information is being passed into the code and what happens to it afterwards.

PLTS

By creating your game design, you will show that you are a **creative thinker**.

Functional skills

By creating formal diagrams for the design of the computer game, you will evidence your functional **ICT** skills in using ICT systems.

By using mathematical operators in your pseudo code, you will evidence your functional **Mathematics** skills.

BTEC Assessment activity 26.3

In your role as games journalist you have been researching the process of designing a game. You are now preparing a step-by-step guide for beginners to be published in the magazine. You want to design an original game so that the readers can follow your progress.

1. Create a design specification for a mobile phone game called *Helen's Hamster*. The idea behind the game is that Helen has lost her hamster in a maze of pipes and she has to move the pipes around to get the hamster to a safe place.

   You must include the following:

   - a storyboard showing at least three different mazes and a title screen
   - some pseudo code showing how the health and life of the hamster is dealt with
   - some concept art showing simple, pencil drawings of what the hamster and any enemy characters will look like
   - an action list showing the different tasks that need to be completed to get the game made. **P3**

2. In order to develop your work to achieve a merit, you will need to use software tools to improve your concept art. Use a graphics package such as Adobe® Photoshop, Illustrator® or Microsoft® Paint® to create more detailed concept art that includes the characters and the maze levels. **M2**

Grading tips

- Your design specification should look like a formal document and be presented professionally. Your storyboard doesn't need to be more than one or two pages. Your action list should focus on the different jobs that need to be done, such as level design, programming and designing the box cover.

- For question 2 you will need to create concept art using only software packages. You can still include in your design specification the pencil-drawn concept art that you developed for question 1(P3), but it will not count towards marks awarded for (M2).

Just checking

1. What is the first stage of computer game development?
2. What is pseudo code?
3. What software can be used to create concept art?
4. What does IDE stand for?
5. What does iteration mean?

4. Be able to test and document a computer game

The testing and documentation of a games development project is one of the most important stages. It determines whether or not there will be any problems with the game before it is released to the public and it documents the whole process of creating the game from start to finish.

4.1 Testing

Games that have problems in them don't sell well – it's a fact. If a game is released and it has glitches or bugs, the journalists who review the game and the first people who buy the game will not give it a good review. Games development studios know this, so they take the testing processes very seriously. Indeed, games testing is a full-time job for some people. It might sound like the most fun job that you could get, but you have to be methodical and you may spend days on end playing the same part of the same game in order to ensure that nothing can go wrong. The games tester isn't playing the game to get a high score or save the princess – but to make sure that every movement works and every power-up functions properly, etc.

What could go wrong with a game?

Games have many different elements. When you are making a game you need to make sure that each element is tested thoroughly before all the different elements are brought together and tested as a whole game.

Some of the bugs that games can have include:

- **Crashing** – the screen freezes and the system has to be reset and the game started again.
- **Controls** – problems can occur with characters not moving the way they were intended.
- **Audio** – there are often problems with speech or during cut scenes.
- **Graphics** – certain objects may not appear where they should; textures may not display properly; elements can float weirdly.
- **Camera** – in a 3D third person game, the camera that follows the player is crucial. For example, it would be a problem if it swings inside a wall at a certain angle and blocks your view.

Test strategy

Games testing is similar to the testing used in application software developments, and the nature of the testing will be similar whatever the type of game being tested. The producer of the game will devise a test strategy – an overview of all of the testing for the game and how it will be organised into different test plans (see below). The test strategy is important because it sets out how long the testing will take, how many people will be involved and which areas will be the key focus of the testing.

As described in the 'What could go wrong with a game?' box on page 381, there are many problems that can occur in games. Some areas, such as audio, will require a few quick tests. But other areas, like the camera that follows the player in a 3D game, will need many tests repeated over all levels. The test strategy will break the testing down into unit testing, system testing and end user testing.

Unit testing

The unit tests go through each individual element of the game and test it on its own. For example, a character that has been made in a 3D engine such as Autodesk® Maya® will have its animated movements tested before it is put into the overall game.

System testing

The system test then checks the whole game once it has been put together. The focus of the system test is the interaction between different elements of the game and making sure that they work together.

End user testing

The final test is end user testing. This tends to be done more with PC games, as the games studio can release a beta version of the game before it is available in the shops and get feedback from real-life players. Some of the consoles are now receiving beta versions of games as well.

Test data

The test data is the input which is used to perform the test. For example, if the game requires the player to type in a number, the test data will be an example number which would be accepted. In Figure 26.7 the test data shows the keys that need to be pressed for character movement within the game.

Test plan structure

After the test strategy has been agreed, it is separated into test plans which focus on the different areas of the game. Each test plan is a document that lists all of the different tests that need to be performed and provides an idea of the kind of test data that will be used. Each test is numbered and the date of the test is recorded. Testing can take a long time to complete, so it is important that the manager responsible

Game Title: **Helen's Hamster** Test Type: **System Testing** Test Focus: **Hamster Navigation Through Maze 1**						
Test #	Date	Test Description	Data	Expected Result	Actual Result	Corrective Action
1	18/09/2010	Move Forward	'S' Key Press	Hamster moves forward	Passed	n/a
2	18/09/2010	Move Up	'W' Key Press	Hamster moves up	Passed	Check code
3	18/09/2010	Move Down	'X' Key Press	Hamster moves down	Passed	n/a
4	19/09/2010	Move Backward	'A' Key Press	Hamster moves back	Passed	n/a
5						
6						

Figure 26.7: An example test plan.

for testing is able to track any problems that were found and record how long it took from finding the problem to fixing it. A description of the test is then given in the table to make sure that tests are not repeated or left out. The exact data that was used to perform the test is also added to the table.

All of the tests that are planned have an expected result, which is what the tester expects to happen if the game is running according to its design. The actual result column is not completed until the test is carried out. A problem is highlighted when the expected result does not match the actual result. The final column then contains any corrective action that was taken by the developers to fix the problem that was found.

Error messages

There will be times when an error message in a game is necessary because the game software cannot always rely on everything else working. Most games require 'game saves' to keep you at the point where you last stopped playing. These game saves are stored on the system, often a hard drive or memory card. However, if the storage is full there will be an error message. This is something that the game designers cannot control. But they can make sure that the error message is something the player can understand, and not some computer jargon that may alarm the player and make them think there is a more serious problem. Designing the error messages is an important part of the game design.

Specialist software tools

The testers are helped by some of the more specialist software packages that the developers use. A lot of the unit testing is completed by the programmers when they are writing the code. They may finish a section and then run a unit test. IDEs often have debugging facilities, which will find errors in the code and lead the programmer directly to them.

Assessment activity 26.4 (P4)

The magazine wants to provide a feature on job roles each month, and this month they are focusing on games testers. You don't have much experience in this role so you have decided to test a game using professional practices and then record what you find for your readers.

To complete the feature you will need access to a game that has been finished but not tested. You could ask your tutor to provide you with one, or find examples of games built using IDEs like Game Maker or Adobe® Flash®. You may be able to find games online that could be tested using these IDEs.

1. Write a test plan for a computer game with at least ten different tests that cover various elements of the game, such as movement, enemies, sound, health or power-ups.

2. Execute this test plan, playing the game as many times as necessary. Make a note of whether or not it passes the tests you have designed.

3. After you have finished the testing, make some notes about how you think the game could be refined.

Grading tip

Remember that refinements are not huge changes or improvements – anything too drastic would result in the game having to be redeveloped. You simply need to make sure that you mention some small changes that would make the game better.

4.2 Presentation of documentation

It is vitally important that the documentation for a game is presented in a format that is useful to everyone who reads it. The technical documentation will be kept as a record of the whole process of the games development. It will be used:

- while the game is in development
- during testing

- after release
- when the game is being analysed for potential sequels
- to try and understand why it did or did not sell well.

Document analysis

Documentation analysis means looking at exactly what needs to be documented and how it should be done. This analysis is completed before any documentation is produced. Information can be laid out in lots of different ways and the studio making the game will have its own methods of keeping records and documenting projects. They will analyse these methods and decide whether they are appropriate for the game that needs to be documented. There will be different documentation for the design stage, the implementation stage and the testing stage. All of this will be kept in a professional document that follows certain professional standards.

Design

The documentation that is created during the design stage of the game's development needs to show all of the different design tools that have been created, from the overall synopsis of the game through to the detailed diagrams which show the developers how to proceed with the creation of the game. The design document becomes an important tool throughout the creation of the game, so it is crucial that all of the teams involved in the different development areas have the same design document. This will ensure that when the different aspects of the game are combined, they will work effectively as one.

Implementation

The implementation of the game is documented through the code printouts and testing documents that are completed by the developers. The implementation stage will usually start with different development specialists working independently of each other on their game element, and then finish when each aspect of the game, such as the items, levels and characters, are brought together and tested as one.

Professional standards

The professional standards include:

- following procedures that make the documentation easy to understand by anyone within the organisation
- ensuring that it has elements such as a contents page and different sections marked off for different areas of the development
- using headers and footers that identify the game project and the people working on it
- presenting the documentation properly, for example bound like a book, to make sure that it lasts.

4.3 User documentation

The user documentation for a software product is usually very dull and goes into meticulous detail about the software and how it is used. Games user guides are quite different. They need to be quite short because the player will want to dive right into playing the game. They also need to be fun and entertaining, so they usually follow the same graphical style as the game – with images of the characters and a similar font and colour scheme to the game.

The user guide is designed to give the player an idea of the main purpose of the game, such as 'rescue the princess' or 'become the world's fastest F1 driver'. It also needs to explain how to play the game, but without giving away too much information or storyline.

The user guide will also contain information about the game as a software application. It will explain how to operate the controls of the game and how to navigate the game's menus.

FAQ

The final section of a user guide is often 'Frequently Asked Questions' (FAQ). If it is a new game, the testers will try to guess what problems a player will come across and put the solutions in the FAQ. The FAQ may contain a question like, 'I want to race against my friend next door. How can I do this?' The answer will then explain how the player connects to the Internet and finds their neighbour. Obviously the testers can't guess in advance every question that the player may ask about a game, so games tend to have a website through which players can contact the developers to ask questions.

4.4 Documentation

Two different types of documentation will be created during the development of a game.

- **Basic documentation** — details the gameplay and provides information about any errors or problems that may occur. It is shared throughout the games company and is used by the marketing team to help advertise the game and to provide technical information to games journalists, colleagues within the organisation and hardware companies.
- **Complex documentation** — details every step of the development process. This is kept within the development company and is used to fix any problems with the game. It can also be used to help develop a sequel if the game is successful.

Basic documentation

Basic documentation contains:

- designs for the user interface, with some information about how it is controlled

- a playing guide which explains how the game works and the method by which the player will progress through the game
- instructions for what to do when faced with a fault
- an installation guide for games that will be installed.

Complex documentation

Control measures

If more complex documentation is required, it will go into greater detail regarding the build of the game and how it was put together. The code will be included, with full comments (known as annotations) and notes regarding the different control structures that are used, such as selection and iteration.

Data dictionary

All of the different values that are stored within the game will be listed in a data dictionary. This will include details of the format that the data takes and a brief outline of how it is used.

Algorithm designs

When programming, any complicated instructions or procedures are called **algorithms**, and the designs of these will be included in complex documentation.

Other items that might be included in complex documentation are:

- any diagrams such as **action charts** and **action tables** – these demonstrate the order in which actions need to occur during the development process
- **input–process–output tables** – these show how input and output statements work within the game
- **data flow diagrams** – these give an overview of how information moves through the game
- **class diagrams** – these show the different objects in the game and what properties and algorithms they have. An example of a class diagram is shown in Figure 26.8.

Key term

Algorithm – a set of rules that accomplishes a specific task.

Figure 26.8: Class diagrams can show a lot of information about the objects in a game.

PLTS

By producing documentation for different audiences, you will show that you are a **reflective learner**.

Functional skills

By writing a user guide for a computer game, you will evidence your functional **English** skills in writing – as the spelling, grammar and punctuation of the documentation has to be perfect!

BTEC Assessment activity 26.5

After the success of your 'Guide to Game Design', the magazine wants you to write a guide to creating a game from start to finish. They are happy for you to reuse the same design that you used in the earlier article, but they want you to follow the same processes as a professional games developer would.

1. Produce a user guide for the *Helen's Hamster* game (see page 380). Include details of how to play the game, an introduction to the story and some ideas of how the game is controlled. (You might have to invent some of the details as you haven't made the game in full.) **P5**

2. Using the game that you tested earlier, create complex documentation which includes:

   • a user guide

   • design documents

   • a technical document that describes the programming, any control structures and algorithms and includes a data dictionary

   • testing documentation

   • any diagrams that are appropriate. **D2**

Grading tip

To achieve P5 for this unit, all you need to produce is user documentation. But D2 requires a much more complete document. For D2 you might need to interview the person who created the game (if possible) and find out further details.

Just checking

1. What happens when a game crashes?
2. Why might a bad camera ruin a game?
3. What is test data?
4. What is a data dictionary?

Hazel Fletcher
Games Designer

I work as a games designer for a games development studio that makes Adobe® Flash® games for websites. I specialise in level design and I'm responsible for:

- creating design documents for a game that is just starting to be developed
- drawing maps of each level
- creating the graphics for levels using Adobe® Illustrator® and then putting them together in Flash®
- working with the character developers to make sure that the levels are the right size and scope needed.

My role

I love my job. It's great deciding where these amazing characters are going to be solving their puzzles or fighting their battles. A lot of the people I work with are character designers and get excited about what the hero is going to look like or how ugly the monster will be. I get more excited about designing the worlds which they are going to explore, the rooms and the dungeons. A game can have great gameplay and interesting characters but unless the level is detailed, and players have to be clever to move around it, they will get bored really quickly.

There are many different companies working in the area of making Flash® games for websites and it's become very competitive. This means the games need to be well thought out and really detailed, even though people usually play them for free.

I've been asked to design a game that will be used on an educational website. I need to think about how I can design a game that will affect the players in different psychological ways.

Think about it!

1. How can Hazel encourage people to play the educational game she is designing by including competitive elements?
2. How can Hazel use levelling in her educational game? Suggest an original game idea for a Flash® game and explain how levelling would work.
3. Hazel likes to use concept art and simple maps to design the levels she is working on. What software packages do you think she could use?
4. What sort of testing will Hazel need to plan for her levels?

Just checking

1. What genres do games come under?
2. What are the different development areas in games development?
3. Why is AI important in a game?
4. How has the computer games industry changed in the last ten years?
5. How do games affect individuals?
6. What is concept art?
7. What is an IDE?
8. Why is testing important?

edexcel

Assignment tips

Research tips

- Keep up to date with the computer games industry by watching video podcasts like *Bonus Round* on the GameTrailers website. (To access this site, go to Hotlinks and click on this unit.)

- Read magazines like *Edge* and *Gamer*, which cover both new computer games and job-related articles.

- Visit your local games shop and talk to the people who work there. They are bound to have lots of informed opinions about current games and can let you know what is selling well.

Get playing

- Try playing lots of computer games from different genres, especially genres that you haven't tried before. This will increase your understanding of the games that people buy and why they enjoy them.

- Play a computer game and then its sequel. Try to see how the game has been improved from the first game to the second game. Are there just graphical improvements, or have the control systems changed, or the characters, or something else?

- Try different games platforms to gain an understanding of what capabilities each platform has and how that affects the game.

Designing games

- Try to create some storyboards for a computer game that someone has made and published in order to practise the process of drawing them.

- See if you can find any websites or books that show concept art for popular computer games.

- Write some pseudo code for a computer game that you have played.

Glossary

3G – a fast wireless method of data transmission that uses radio signals and is commonly used for mobile phone networks.

Acronym – a term which is referred to by its initial letters, such as GMT for Greenwich Mean Time or BBC for British Broadcasting Corporation.

ADSL (asynchronous digital subscriber line) – this communication link simply means higher rates in one direction, i.e. for downloading data.

Algorithm – a set of rules that accomplishes a specific task.

Artificial intelligence (AI) – a set of rules that attempts to make characters appear to be thinking like a human would do.

Backup – a copy of software data that is kept in case the original becomes damaged.

Bandwidth – an information channel's capacity, i.e. how much data it can carry at one time.

Blocking/pixellation – two different words to describe the reduction in picture quality caused by resizing a bitmap graphic image to make it larger. It occurs when the tiny pixels of the original colour have been enlarged so much that they are seen as blocks of colour.

Blog – derived from the words **web log**, this is a type of website maintained by a person or group which provides a commentary or diary on general or specific subjects.

Bluetooth – a wireless method of data transmission that uses radio signals to send data between devices over short distances.

BNC – Bayonet Neill Concelman connectors are used with coaxial cables.

Body language – non-verbal communication which includes gestures, facial expressions and body posture. You may not always be conscious that your body language is communicating your feelings, but it is often very easy to see from someone's body language that they are bored, happy or angry etc.

Brand name – the name of a product that identifies it and differentiates it from other products to customers.

Break even point – where total revenue (the amount of money) is equal to total costs.

Budget – an amount of money allocated for a particular purpose.

Bugs – errors or mistakes in the program which prevent it from working properly.

Business plan – a document that shows how a business is going to achieve its objectives.

Capacity – the amount of data that can be stored. Capacity is measured in bytes, kilobytes (KB), megabytes (MB) or gigabytes (GB).

Cat 6 cabling – most modern networks use cat 6 (category 6) or cat 5 (category 5) cabling to connect network cards to network switches. Both these types of network cable use RJ45 plugs. Cat 6 cabling is a newer and better standard that can run at 1000 mbps (1 gbps), which is ten times faster than the older cat 5 cabling that runs at 100 mpbs.

Cel shaded – a graphical style where the images are shaded to look like hand drawings or cartoons.

Client – any workstation connected to a server. It may also be the software that is designed specifically to work with a server application. For example, web browser software is client software as it is designed to work with web servers.

Close – how you finish a letter. In formal letters, you should write 'Yours sincerely' if you know the name of the person to whom you are writing, or 'Yours faithfully' if you do not.

Closed question – a question with a set of answers that respondents must choose from. For example: "Did you have any problems with the spreadsheet? Yes or no?" or "Did you find the spreadsheet (a) easy or (b) difficult to use?"

Coaxial – parts of the cable share the same axis, so when you cut through the cable they appear as a series of rings around the central core.

Components – the parts that make up a computer system. Components can be hardware (e.g. the processor, memory (RAM), video card, etc.) or software (e.g. the operating system).

Compression – when a file is reduced in size. Compression can be particularly useful for graphics files, which can be very large, taking up a lot of disk space.

Computer network – a network used to share information and resources.

Configure – to make changes to a software application to suit a particular user or task.

Consistency – the same style and layout is used on all documents so you can easily recognise that they come from the same organisation.

Constraint – a factor that limits or restricts a decision.

Contention – competition for resources where two users or computers attempt to transmit a message across the same wire at the same time.

Control – an item on a database form that is used to enter or display data, such as a textbox.

Copyright – the exclusive right of authors of original work to produce, publish and sell their work. It protects them from other people copying their work and gives them the right to control how other people use their material. You must expect images from other sources to be copyright protected unless they are clearly identified as copyright free. The permission of the copyright owner is needed if you want to use a graphic image for commercial purposes and you may need to pay a royalty fee. There are exceptions to copyright protection, which include non-commercial research and private study.

Cost-effective – economical in terms of what is gained for the money spent.

Criterion – a rule that is used to select data. (The plural of criterion is **criteria**.)

Ctrl+S – will save a document in most Microsoft® Office® System applications.

Cut scenes – short film clips within a game that tell part of the story.

Cyber bullying – when a person or group try to threaten, tease or embarrass someone using a mobile phone or the Internet.

Data – the general name given to any documents, files and other information stored on a computer system.

Data integrity – ensuring that the data correctly matches the facts.

Database – a collection of data. The data is organized so that different kinds of information can be retrieved from it by the users.

Defaults – the settings that have been set by the application maker. They are the settings that are used, unless the application user changes them.

Developer – an individual or company that creates computer games.

DHCP (Dynamic Host Configuration Protocol) – the DHCP assigns unique IP addresses to devices, then releases and renews these addresses as devices leave and rejoin the network.

Digital divide – the gap that exists between people who have easy access to the Internet and other technology and those who do not.

Domain name – the core of a URL. For example, in the URL http://www.example.com, the domain name is www.example.com.

Drive – another term for a storage device.

DSL (digital subscriber line) – another type of communication link offered by telephone companies.

E-commerce – the use of the Internet for selling goods and services to customers.

Email – an abbreviation of 'electronic mail'.

Emoticon – icons or combinations of characters which express a feeling. For example, writing 'Such a lovely day ☺' shows that you are happy. There are many other emoticons in common use, such as :s, which means confused.

Escalation – passing on a problem to someone who knows more or has higher authority than you, and should be able to solve the problem.

Glossary

ESD – this stands for electrostatic discharge. It can happen when two things (you and the computer) connect.

Evaluation – making a judgement about how successful the solution is, often against criteria such as the original objectives. The evaluation may also involve giving reasons for the choice.

Event – an action, such as clicking a button, which then triggers another action, such as opening a window.

Event driven – this isn't truly a type of language, more a way of using a programming language. In a game that is event driven, everything that happens is the result of an event, like a mouse click or a button push. Only the simplest games are event driven – but some of the simplest games can be the most fun. Older adventure games, such as The Secret of Monkey Island™, are event driven – everything happens with the click of a mouse or the arrival of a character in a new area.

Expression – a formula or instruction that produces a value.

Field – a category used for data in a database. The name of the field is called the fieldname.

Field property – each field in a table has a number of properties, such as the length and format of the field.

File permissions – the rules that are set up by the network administrator for each user, identifying which files they can access or change.

File Transfer Protocol (FTP) – a method for transferring all types of files between computers on a network. It is used on the Internet for a number of purposes, including uploading web pages to a web server.

Firewall – a type of security system, used mainly to protect networks from external threats.

Font (also known as typeface) – the shape of lettering for the alphabet, numbers and other characters, such as the Pound (£) currency sign, that can be selected for typing text into a graphic or document. The choice of font has a huge effect on the style of an image or document. Many organisations use one or two fonts as their corporate style to help people recognise them. An example of a font is Arial.

Footer – text that prints at the bottom of every page. It is often used for things like page numbers.

Form – an on-screen user interface designed to view the data in a database.

Formula – used to carry out calculations in a spreadsheet. A formula must begin with an equals sign and can use either actual values (numbers) or references to cell addresses.

Forum – an online meeting place where people with a common interest exchange information.

FTP – file transfer protocol, a set of rules which determine how files will be transferred over the network.

Games studio – a company where games are designed and programmed.

Genre – a category of games which have certain gameplay features and styles in common.

Gigabyte (GB) – 1GB is a large number which is roughly 1,000,000,000 (a thousand million) bytes. A byte is a small amount of space in RAM or on a hard drive, large enough to hold a letter such as A or C. Four bytes could be used for the colour in a single pixel.

Gigahertz (GHz) – a measure of how quickly an electronic device works. 1GHz means that it does 1,000,000,000 (one thousand million) operations every second.

Graphical user interface (GUI) – interface that uses icons, pictures and menus instead of text.

Handshake – in networking before any data is sent or can be received the handshake takes place. It signifies that one computer wants to talk to another computer.

Hard copy – when a computer outputs to something that can be taken away from the system, for example paper.

HD – High Definition (HD) televisions run at 1920 x1080.

Header – text that prints at the top of every page. It is often used to give the title of the worksheet and maybe the author.

Heads up display (HUD) – small icons and menus that are displayed on-screen throughout gameplay.

HTML (hypertext mark-up language) – the code used to create web pages. It allows links (hyperlinks) between one web page and another.

Hyperlink – the common term for a link on the Internet. Hyperlinks can link to pages that are in different files or directories, and that can be anywhere on the Web.

Hypertext Transfer Protocol (HTTP) – a method for finding and transferring web pages from a web server to an individual computer through the Internet.

Indenting – increasing or decreasing the amount of space between the margin and the beginning of the sentence when writing code, so that it is clear to other people which code blocks belong together.

Infra-red communication – uses infra-red waves, which are longer than light waves but shorter than radio waves, to transmit and receive data.

Inputs – in a simple business plan, the data about resources required to solve a business problem.

Input controls – Windows® features which allow you to input data to an application. Typical examples include text boxes for inputting text and list boxes which allow you to select an input value from a list.

Integrated development environment (IDE) – a piece of software which lets you write code, test it and build it into an application or game.

Intranet – a type of website that is accessible only within the network in which it has been set up, usually within an organisation.

Invoice – a document requesting payment for goods or services.

IP address – a number assigned to a device (usually a computer) whenever it connects to a network. IP = Internet Protocol.

ISDN (integrated services digital network) – a type of telephone connection which allows both voice and data transfer simultaneously.

ISP – Internet Service Providers are the organisations which charge you for a connection to the Internet; they provide an Internet service.

Items – objects within a game that are collected by the player.

Keyboard shortcut – a key combination that runs a certain command. For example, the built-in shortcut **Ctrl+S** will save a document in most Microsoft® Office® System applications.

Label – text on a form that describes the data displayed in a control.

LAN – local area network.

Layers – many graphics applications offer layers to help create and edit images. The user can set up several layers – for example, in a vector application a raster image could be imported into a layer that is locked so it cannot move. This layer could also be set non-printable. Another layer could be used to produce a diagram based upon the raster image using vector tools. Layers can be set to not visible when the graphic designer wants to concentrate on another part of the image.

Levelling up – when a character in a game collects enough experience points (XP) to improve their skills.

Link – a text or graphic on a page. When it is clicked, another page on the same file or directory is loaded. For example, a page in the Help file for an applications package will contain links to other pages in the same file.

Local Area Network – computers and other devices linked together into a network within a building.

Log on/Login – a procedure used to gain access to a computer system (or to a page on a website).

Lossless – compression when there is no difference in picture quality when a picture is used again after being compressed.

Lossy – compression whereby some of the picture detail is lost when the picture is shown again.

MAC (Media Access Control) address – a unique identifier assigned to most network adaptors.

Macro – a method of automating a series of functions within a Microsoft® Office® System application.

Margins – the gaps between the edge of a piece of paper and where the text starts.

Megahertz (MHz) – a measure of how quickly an electronic device works. 1MHz means that it does 1,000,000 (one million) operations every second.